LECTURA
DANTIS
AMERICANA

LECTURA
DANTIS
AMERICANA

Inferno

I

ANTHONY K. CASSELL

Foreword by
ROBERT HOLLANDER

With a new translation of the canto by
Patrick Creagh and Robert Hollander

upp

UNIVERSITY OF PENNSYLVANIA PRESS
PHILADELPHIA

Translation of *Inferno,* Canto I, © 1989 by Patrick Creagh
and Robert Hollander

The Italian text of the *Commedia* reproduced here is that established by
Giorgio Petrocchi and originally published by A. Mondadori, Milano, 1966.
It is reprinted by the kind permission of La Società Dantesca Italiana.

Library of Congress Cataloging-in-Publication Data

Cassell, Anthony K. (Anthony Kimber), 1941–
    Inferno I / Anthony K. Cassell; foreword by Robert Hollander;
with a new translation of the canto by Patrick Creagh and Robert
Hollander.
        p.   cm. — (Lectura Dantis Americana)
    Bibliography: p.
    Includes index.
    ISBN 0-8122-8176-4
    1. Dante Alighieri, 1265–1321. Inferno.   I. Title.   II. Title:
Inferno one.   III. Title: Inferno 1.   IV. Series.
    PQ4445 1st.C35   1989
    851'.1—dc19   89-4751
                                                                 CIP

LECTURA
DANTIS
AMERICANA

a series of readings in Dante's *Commedia*
under the auspices of
the Dante Society of America

CONTENTS

FOREWORD

Ever since the mid-nineteenth century Dante's American presence has been an imposing one. Among the great foreign writers, perhaps only Shakespeare has affected the course of American literary life as deeply as he. And if one restricts the field to those whose work has had to rely on translation to reach its widest audience, it seems clear that Dante is second not even to Homer and Virgil among the ancients, and certainly not to Cervantes and Goethe among the moderns. Perhaps because we, like the French in this, possess no single generally acknowledged national literary figure, we have tended to look beyond our shores for literary stars of the first magnitude. Whatever the cause, the rediscovery of Dante in the nineteenth century has had profound effect on American intellectual life, both within the academy and in the larger world. Longfellow (whose translation, completed in 1867, was to be a major force in the revival of American interest in Dante), Lowell, Norton, and their friends in Cambridge helped to put the *Commedia* into the hands of many professors, students, men and women of letters, and "common readers." The founding of the Dante Society of America in 1881 offered confirming evidence of a widening interest in the great poet. Harvard, Dante's most significant early academic home in America, continued in that role (one thinks of the presence of Santayana and Grandgent at the turn of the century); it was also in New England that Dante's influence had first exercised its power on a major American writer, Hawthorne, extending eventually to Eliot and Pound. It is not my purpose to tell again an already familiar tale.* Suffice it to say that the *Commedia* be-

---

*For a review, with bibliography, of Dante's fortune in America see Tommaso Pisanti, "Stati Uniti d'America," in *Enciclopedia dantesca* 2 (1970): 308–309; also his *Dantismo americano* (Napoli: Loffredo, 1979); also *Dante in America: The First Two Centuries*, ed. A. B. Giamatti (Binghamton, NY: MRTS, 1983); for more recent developments, Dante Della Terza, "L'italianistica negli Stati Uniti," *Bullettino di Italianistica* 1, 2 (1983): 195–204; Fredi Chiappelli, "Dante in America," in *Dante Alighieri 1985: In memoriam Hermann Gmelin,* ed. R. Baum & W. Hirdt (Tübingen: Stauffenburg, 1985), 245–252. For the history of the Dante Society of America see again T. Pisanti, "Dante Society of America," *ED* 4 (1976): 415–417; G. H. Gifford, "A History of the Dante Society," in the *Seventy-*

came a text that almost every American intellectual felt called upon to confront. "Il nostro poeta" the Italians rightly call Dante. He has become ours, too.

The Dante beloved of Americans was, indeed, largely indistinguishable from the towering Italian figure, at least if one inspects his first academic incarnation. American scholarship reflected basic intuitions and critical procedures developed across the water, in Italy as well as in England (where among the greater names were those of Moore and Toynbee). "Dantismo americano," a phrase some Italians currently use to designate a critical approach which seems to some of them new, radical, and controversial, is a recent phenomenon. It traces its origin to the work of Charles S. Singleton, which began to appear shortly after the conclusion of the Second World War. Singleton's essential contribution was to present the procedures of poetic signification in the *Commedia* as deriving from what Dante himself called "the allegory of the theologians." This development was not as utterly revolutionary as Singleton himself apparently believed. He had precursors, distant (e.g., Filippo Villani) and nearer to hand (most significantly, Erich Auerbach). But it remains true that Singleton's focusing of the debate over Dante's mode of meaning became crucial in the self-definition of the next generation of American Dantisti, whether they welcomed or decried the positions taken by Singleton. And there seems to be little reason to believe that the immediate future will witness any significant movement away from a criticism grounded in concerns issuing from this vision of the poem's central mode of signifying.

*   *   *

An enterprise like the Lectura Dantis Americana requires a reason for being. That nothing quite like it exists or has ever existed is not in itself sufficient. It is better to say that we possess commentaries aplenty and that we possess essays—Italian *lecturae* are abundant—on particular cantos by the fives and tens, but that we possess no happy blending of the two. We still have not said why an American series of this kind should exist in the first place. The answer to our question lies in the nature of the changing scholarly approaches to the *Commedia* which have descended from or surged up in reaction to the work completed

---

fourth Annual Report of the Dante Society (1956); and, for an updated version, Anthony J. De Vito, "La 'Dante Society of America,'" *Il Veltro* 25, 6 (1981): 683–693, now available in English as "The First Hundred Years of the Dante Society," *Dante Studies* 100 (1982): 99–132.

and the stances taken by Singleton. What follows is an attempt to describe the more striking aspects of recent and current work in Dante studies being performed in America. It should be immediately apparent to the informed reader that no single Dantista in this country (or abroad) works in such a way as to reflect all these tendencies. On the other hand, the work of many here (and of few elsewhere) does possess many or most of these attributes, not merely one or two. It seems a defensible proposition that most contemporary American students of Dante are concerned with most of the following issues.

*   *   *

There is, to begin with, the *Commedia*'s relation to the exegetical precepts put forward in the *Epistle to Cangrande,* whether these are found in that document or in the text of the poem itself. The techniques of biblical exegesis are treated as highly pertinent analytical tools for the interpretation of the poem, whether or not Dante actually wrote the epistle (although most American Dantisti currently seem to consider it genuine). Since Singleton's own readings of the poem, especially as these are found in his commentary, more often reflect older formulations of Dante's allegory, scholars who accept his basic view of the poem's allegorical procedures have found that there is need to demonstrate the applicability of the general method of biblical exegesis to the form and meaning of the poem as a whole and, perhaps more interestingly, to particular passages in the text.

Following the mode of analysis called for by Singleton, a number of Americans have tended to downplay the importance of traditional literary exegesis, preferring instead to bring to bear the writings of the fathers and doctors of the Church on particular aspects of the poem. These medieval texts are seen as the seedbed of Dante's formulations of his meaning, while the commentary tradition tends to be even intentionally neglected. Where this tradition is invoked, it is seen as being most valuable as it remains closest in time (and therefore, it is claimed, in spirit) to the composition of the poem. As a result, the testimony of commentators who wrote after Benvenuto da Imola (Singleton's own favorite commentator) is often passed over in silence. Indeed, Renaissance readings tend to be considered wrongly based and misleading, while Romantic interpretations are still more vehemently discarded and the recent, rich Italian commentary tradition is adhered to principally for its philological expertise. The main virtue of this position, which privileges theological concerns (often at the cost of formal ones), is that it turns aside from traditional formulations of what the text is taken to mean and of how it reflects more usual philological interests in order to deal with the text as it is perceived to reflect its own intellectual moment. The main weakness of this position, with its historicist emphasis, is that it ignores valuable interpretive contributions and debates as they have been shaped over a 670-year continuum.

It is a similar, if not always related, phenomenon that most American Dantisti prefer to work inductively rather than deductively, from small to large rather than the other way around. In defense of such procedure one senses the presence of a usually unvoiced claim that a great deal of previous scholarship is often based in outmoded categories of perception. Such investigative activity is usually associated with periods of discovery in which there is abroad a sense of revolution or at least of innovation. One can think of only a few books on Dante published in America during the past thirty years that are global in scope. Rather, most have been partial and experimental. The tentative and partial nature of recent and current studies is surely more the result of a shared sense of arrival at a new phase of investigation than it is reflective of the always enormous task of tackling such a great figure, one who is surrounded by so vast a critical overgrowth.

One of the most striking aspects of American work on Dante after the Second World War is its distance from the aestheticizing appreciations of the *Commedia* advanced and championed by such as Croce and Momigliano. Here a central aspect of the issue centers on the appreciation of the great figures of the *Inferno*. In the past thirty-five years major revaluations of the way in which readers should respond to Francesca, Pier de la Vigna, Brunetto Latini, Ulysses, and Ugolino are among the more important American contributions, most of them reflecting the binomial opposition (first put forward on this side of the Atlantic by Leo Spitzer and Singleton) of Dante/poet to Dante/pilgrim.

At least as striking is a perhaps related American *forma mentis,* one that denies the traditional "allegorical" reading of the poem, in which Virgil stands for "Reason," Beatrice for "Revelation," and various incidents recounted in the course of the narrative are interpreted as internalized moral allegory. This position was first stated effectively by Erich Auerbach in his presentation of a figural understanding of the poem, with its insistence on the "historical" nature of all the characters of the *Commedia.* It is here that much current American study of Dante is most crucially at odds with traditional Italian approaches to the poem.

In recent years some American Dantisti, their concerns mirrored by the soon-to-be-available computerized data bank of commentaries on the *Commedia* known as the Dartmouth Dante Project, have been returning to the commentary tradition. And some of these apparently believe that Singleton's own relative neglect of this branch of traditional study of the text constitutes a significant lacuna in his method. Nonetheless, their use of traditional materials is frequently put to the service of the more innovative interpretations that characterize "Dantismo americano."

Some Americans, in this particular going beyond (or at least to the side of) Singleton, have insisted on the *Commedia*'s continuing preoccupation with political imperatives, from its inception to its ending (or at least until *Paradiso* XXX). One of the axioms of a theologically determined poetic would seem to be a simultaneous deflation of so worldly a concern. This formulation, however, holds that Dante presented the empire as having a theological and necessary foundation, that he insisted on politics as being an essential concern of the poem to which both heaven and earth had set their hand.

Recently, several American critics have been advancing the still controversial view that Dante read his classical texts "against the grain," that is, this view insists that he was considering his *auctores*—and to date the principal *auctor* to have been studied in this light has been Virgil—with a probing critical intelligence. This position is currently under scrutiny, some of it hostile. If it gains favor, it will probably be regarded as one of the more significant contributions made by Dante's American students. What it proposes is first of all that the Christian Dante was a far more thoughtful and speculative reader of classical texts than has generally been supposed, that he fully appreciated (and makes his appreciation a subject for presentation in the poem) the distance between his own work and that of his Latin precursors, and that he does not hesitate to question and revise the very sources of so much of his own poetic creativity.

A similar and certainly related approach is that which brings a kindred sensibility to the study of Dante's ordering of his responses to his Provençal and Italian precursors. Here the major focus has been on Cavalcanti. Nonetheless, there is a growing interest in the defining differences which Dante covertly insisted upon and which distance him both from those earlier vernacular poets whom he treats with evident disfavor and from all those from whom he had learned, only to discover that there was much more to learn, if mainly from himself.

Still another controversial and predominantly American vision of Dante (it should be said that this and the previous two positions tend to be conjoined in those who hold any of them) sees another similar phenomenon reflected in the *Commedia*. This involves Dante's palinodic treatment of some of his own previous work. Here the *Convivio* and the *rime petrose* (if rarely the *Vita Nuova*) receive most notice, the *De vulgari Eloquentia* a certain amount, while the *Monarchia* both invites and discourages such attention, primarily because of continuing uncertainty about its date of composition in relation to the already somewhat uncertain dating of the *Commedia* itself.

Some Americans have been urging an awareness of Dante's self-conscious (and, in a few cases, even ironic) treatment of the question of the authority of poetic language. And here two strains may be distinguished. The first, following Auerbach, is primarily interested in the question of the "Christian sublime," the significance of the vernacular and "comedic" nature of Dante's theoretical concerns about poetic language. A second group of readers, reflecting developments in recent literary theory, sees in Dante's self-conscious manipulations of language the signs of the writer's awareness of the impossibility of the very claims for poetic veracity which he has put forward most aggressively. What these two very different positions share is an interest in the linguistic concerns which preceded and accompanied the making of the poem. And in both cases there is an awareness of a writer who is highly self-conscious about his linguistic ends, who shapes his poetic identity with such care that we have been mainly unaware of his making of a literary self.

*　　*　　*

To conclude, I would like to remind the reader that I have not claimed that *all* American Dantisti display *all* these characteristics in their work, that all of these interpretive positions are "correct" or even to be privileged, or that Americans are alone in reflecting various of these concerns. It does, however, seem clear to me that many or most of these dozen characteristics of inquiry are indeed found in a great deal of recent and current American studies of Dante. Further, I would add that those who write on this side of the ocean who do not find certain of these approaches valid find themselves nonetheless constrained to confront them, for they tend to be defining characteristics of the state of discussion in this country at the current moment.

What the future holds is always difficult to prognosticate. I believe that we shall find, for example, more interest in Dante's relation to some of the classical *auctores* other than Virgil (the Statius revival has already begun, Lucan waits in the wings for better treatment, and an American *aetas ovidiana* is probably about to begin); a better appreciation of Dante's "astronomy" (a topic which has been inadequately studied);

and a better understanding of the relation of the *Monarchia* to the *Commedia* (perhaps conjoined to the related problem of Dante's relationship to the work of Cino da Pistoia). As the Lectura Dantis Americana develops, it will undoubtedly reflect such interests as these, as well as many others that this brief prognostication will have blatantly failed to fathom.

Robert Hollander
Bellagio, May 3, 1987

INFERNO

I

and

TRANSLATION

Nel mezzo del cammin di nostra vita
  mi ritrovai per una selva oscura,
  ché la diritta via era smarrita.   *3*
Ahi quanto a dir qual era è cosa dura
  esta selva selvaggia e aspra e forte
  che nel pensier rinova la paura!   *6*
Tant' è amara che poco è più morte;
  ma per trattar del ben ch'i' vi trovai,
  dirò de l'altre cose ch'i' v'ho scorte.   *9*
Io non so ben ridir com' i' v'intrai,
  tant' era pien di sonno a quel punto
  che la verace via abbandonai.   *12*
Ma poi ch'i' fui al piè d'un colle giunto,
  là dove terminava quella valle
  che m'avea di paura il cor compunto,   *15*
guardai in alto e vidi le sue spalle
  vestite già de' raggi del pianeta
  che mena dritto altrui per ogne calle.   *18*
Allor fu la paura un poco queta,
  che nel lago del cor m'era durata
  la notte ch'i' passai con tanta pieta.   *21*
E come quei che con lena affannata,
  uscito fuor del pelago a la riva,
  si volge a l'acqua perigliosa e guata,   *24*
così l'animo mio, ch'ancor fuggiva,
  si volse a retro a rimirar lo passo
  che non lasciò già mai persona viva.   *27*
Poi ch'èi posato un poco il corpo lasso,
  ripresi via per la piaggia diserta,
  sì che 'l piè fermo sempre era 'l più basso.   *30*
Ed ecco, quasi al cominciar de l'erta,
  una lonza leggiera e presta molto,
  che di pel macolato era coverta;   *33*
e non mi si partia dinanzi al volto,
  anzi 'mpediva tanto il mio cammino,
  ch'i' fui per ritornar più volte vòlto.   *36*
Temp' era dal principio del mattino,
  e 'l sol montava 'n sù con quelle stelle
  ch'eran con lui quando l'amor divino   *39*
mosse di prima quelle cose belle;
  sì ch'a bene sperar m'era cagione
  di quella fiera a la gaetta pelle   *42*

At the midpoint in the journey of our life
I found myself astray in a dark wood
For the straight path had vanished.   *3*
A dread thing it is to tell what it was like,
This wild wood, rugged, intractable,
Which, even as I think of it, brings back my fear.   *6*
So bitter it is that scarcely worse is death.
But, to expound the good which there I met with,
I will speak of other things I witnessed there.   *9*
I cannot exactly say how I came to enter,
So full of slumber was I at the moment
When I ceased to follow the true path.   *12*
But then, when I had journeyed to the foot
Of a hill, at the far end of the valley
Which had been tormenting my heart with terror,   *15*
I lifted up my eyes, and beheld its shoulders
Already clad in the radiance of that planet
That leads others straight on all their roads.   *18*
Abated somewhat was the terror
That in the hollow of my heart had lasted
All through the night I had spent so piteously.   *21*
And, as a man who at his last breath has crawled
Out of the high seas, and gains the shore,
Turns and gazes back on the perilous waters,   *24*
So my thoughts, although still bent on flight,
Turned back to look once more upon the pass
No living being ever left behind him.   *27*
Once I had rested my weary bones awhile
I again set off, across the desolate slope,
Keeping the same foot always firm beneath me.   *30*
And, almost at the start of the escarpment,
Lo! a leopard, very lithe and swift,
That was covered with a speckled hide;   *33*
And she did not give ground before my gaze,
But instead she blocked my path in such a way
That more than once I turned to go back down.   *36*
The hour was the beginning of the morning,
And the sun was mounting upward with those stars
Which were with him when celestial love   *39*
First lent motion to those comely things;
Therefore I was encouraged to hope the best
Of that beast with the brightly colored pelt   *42*

l'ora del tempo e la dolce stagione;
　　ma non sì che paura non mi desse
　　la vista che m'apparve d'un leone.　　　　　　45
Questi parea che contra me venisse
　　con la test' alta e con rabbiosa fame,
　　sì che parea che l'aere ne tremesse.　　　　　48
Ed una lupa, che di tutte brame
　　sembiava carca ne la sua magrezza,
　　e molte genti fé già viver grame,　　　　　　51
questa mi porse tanto di gravezza
　　con la paura ch'uscia di sua vista,
　　ch'io perdei la speranza de l'altezza.　　　　54
E qual è quei che volontieri acquista,
　　e giugne 'l tempo che perder lo face,
　　che 'n tutti suoi pensier piange e s'attrista;　57
tal mi fece la bestia sanza pace,
　　che, venendomi 'ncontro, a poco a poco
　　mi ripigneva là dove 'l sol tace.　　　　　　60
Mentre ch'i' rovinava in basso loco,
　　dinanzi a li occhi mi si fu offerto
　　chi per lungo silenzio parea fioco.　　　　　63
Quando vidi costui nel gran diserto,
　　"*Miserere* di me," gridai a lui,
　　"qual che tu sii, od ombra od omo certo!"　66
Rispuosemi: "Non omo, omo già fui,
　　e li parenti miei furon lombardi,
　　mantoani per patrïa ambedui.　　　　　　69
Nacqui *sub Iulio,* ancor che fosse tardi,
　　e vissi a Roma sotto 'l buono Augusto
　　nel tempo de li dèi falsi e bugiardi.　　　　72
Poeta fui, e cantai di quel giusto
　　figliuol d'Anchise che venne di Troia,
　　poi che 'l superbo Ilïón fu combusto.　　　　75
Ma tu perché ritorni a tanta noia?
　　perché non sali il dilettoso monte
　　ch'è principio e cagion di tutta goia?"　　　78
"Or se' tu quel Virgilio e quella fonte
　　che spandi di parlar sì largo fiume?"
　　rispuos' io lui con vergognosa fronte.　　　81
"O de li altri poeti onore e lume,
　　vagliami 'l lungo studio e 'l grande amore
　　che m'ha fatto cercar lo tuo volume.　　　　84

By the time of day and sweetness of the season,
But not so much that I was not dismayed
At the sight of a lion which appeared before me: *45*
This one seemed to be making straight toward me
With head held high and with a rabid hunger,
So that it seemed the air took fright at him.   *48*
And then a she-wolf, who with every craving
Seemed to be laden, in the leanness of her;
Many had she caused to live in misery.   *51*
So heavy was the dread she put on me
With the terror evoked by her appearance
That I lost all hope that I might reach the height.   *54*
And as a man who is glad when he is gaining,
When the time comes round for him to lose
Has never a thought but for lament and grieving,   *57*
So I became, faced with that restless beast
Which, thrusting toward me, drove me back
Step by step, to where the sun is silent.   *60*
While I was plunging down to a place below,
My eyes were greeted by the form of one
Who owing to long silence appeared but faint.   *63*
When I saw him there, in the wide wilderness,
"Have mercy on me," I cried out to him,
"Whatever you are, a shade or a living man!"   *66*
"Not a man, man though once I was,"
He said. "My parents came from Lombardy,
Mantuans by birth, the two of them.   *69*
I was born *sub Iulio,* though late in his time,
And lived in Rome under the good Augustus
In the age of the spurious, lying gods.   *72*
Poet I was, and sang that upright son
Of Anchises, the one who came from Troy
When proud Ilion was burnt. But you?   *75*
Why are you turning back to so much trouble?
Why do you not climb the delectable mountain
Which is the source and cause of all delight?"   *78*
"Oh, are you then that Virgil, and that source"
(I then replied to him, with shamefast brow)
"Which pours forth so broad a river of speech?   *81*
O honor and beacon to all other poets,
May the long labor and great love that made me
Explore your volume stand me in good stead now!   *84*

Tu se' lo mio maestro e 'l mio autore,
    tu se' solo colui da cu' io tolsi
    lo bello stilo che m'ha fatto onore.   *87*
Vedi la bestia per cu' io mi volsi;
    aiutami da lei, famoso saggio,
    ch'ella mi fa tremar le vene e i polsi."   *90*
"A te convien tenere altro vïaggio,"
    rispuose, poi che lagrimar mi vide,
    "se vuo' campar d'esto loco selvaggio;   *93*
ché questa bestia, per la qual tu gride,
    non lascia altrui passar per la sua via,
    ma tanto lo 'mpedisce che l'uccide;   *96*
e ha natura sì malvagia e ria,
    che mai non empie la bramosa voglia,
    e dopo 'l pasto ha più fame che pria.   *99*
Molti son li animali a cui s'ammoglia,
    e più saranno ancora, infin che 'l veltro
    verrà, che la farà morir con doglia.   *102*
Questi non ciberà terra né peltro,
    ma sapïenza, amore e virtute,
    e sua nazion sarà tra Feltro e Feltro.   *105*
Di quella umile Italia fia salute
    per cui morì la vergine Cammilla,
    Eurialo e Turno e Niso di ferute.   *108*
Questi la caccerà per ogne villa,
    fin che l'avrà rimessa ne lo 'nferno,
    là onde 'nvidia prima dipartilla.   *111*
Ond' io per lo tuo me' penso e discerno
    che tu mi segui, e io sarò tua guida,
    e trarrotti di qui per loco etterno;   *114*
ove udirai le disperate strida,
    vedrai li antichi spiriti dolenti,
    ch'a la seconda morte ciascun grida;   *117*
e vederai color che son contenti
    nel foco, perché speran di venire
    quando che sia a le beate genti.   *120*
A le quai poi se tu vorrai salire,
    anima fia a ciò più di me degna:
    con lei ti lascerò nel mio partire;   *123*
ché quello imperador che là sù regna,
    perch' i' fu' ribellante a la sua legge,
    non vuol che 'n sua città per me si vegna.   *126*

You are my master, and you are my author;
You alone are the one from whom I took
The noble style that has brought honor to me.   *87*
Look at the beast which forced me to turn back:
O save me from her, famous sage,
For she makes my veins and pulses tremble."   *90*
"Better for you to take another road,"
He replied to that, because he saw me weeping,
"If you mean to escape this savage place,   *93*
Because this beast, the reason for your wailing,
Never suffers others to cross her path:
No sooner does she stop them than she kills them.   *96*
She is by nature so malign and wicked
That never does she glut her ravenous craving,
But feeds, and is more famished than before.   *99*
Many are the animals she couples with,
And many there will be yet, until the hound
Shall come, who will put her to painful death.   *102*
That one will not feed on lands and lucre
But on wisdom, love, and power,
And his nation shall be between Feltro and Feltro.   *105*
He will redeem that lowly Italy
For which Camilla the virgin, and Euryalus,
Turnus, and Nisus met with wounds and death.   *108*
This hound will hunt her out from town to town
Until he has put her back in hell again—
The place whence primal envy set her loose.   *111*
For your own good I therefore think and judge
That you should follow me; I will be your guide
And take you hence, through an eternal place   *114*
In which you will hear screams of desperation,
And you will see the age-old sorrowing spirits,
Each of whom bewails the second death.   *117*
You will see thereafter those who are contented
In the flames, because they hope to come,
Whenever it may be, to join the blest.   *120*
If you should then desire to rise to these
There will be a soul more fit to help than I am.
Her shall I leave you with at my departure,   *123*
Because that emperor who rules on high,
Since I was rebellious to his law,
Permits me not to come into his city.   *126*

In tutte parti impera e quivi regge;
   quivi è la sua città e l'alto seggio:
   oh felice colui cu' ivi elegge!"   *129*
E io a lui: "Poeta, io ti richeggio
   per quello Dio che tu non conoscesti,
   a ciò ch'io fugga questo male e peggio,   *132*
che tu mi meni là dov' or dicesti,
   sì ch'io veggia la porta di san Pietro
   e color cui tu fai cotanto mesti."
Allor si mosse, e io li tenni dietro.   *136*

Everywhere he holds sway, but there he reigns,
There is his own city, his lofty throne:
Happy the one whom he elects to enter!"   *129*
And I to him: "Poet, I beg of you,
In the name of the God you never knew,
In order to escape this plight, or worse,   *132*
Lead me to the places which you speak of,
That I may see the doorway of St. Peter
And those you tell me are so full of sorrow."
Then he set out, and I kept close behind him.   *136*

(translated by Patrick Creagh and Robert Hollander)

PREFACE

When we read or recite the first *terzina* of the *Commedia*,

> Nel mezzo del cammin di nostra vita
>   mi ritrovai per una selva oscura,
>   ché la diritta via era smarrita[1]

the lines ring so familiarly that we almost fail to hear them, so fixed are they in rhythm and received interpretation that, like well-versed concert-goers at the first bars of an encore, we gain our pleasure and inwardly applaud more in secret self-congratulation over our own recognition of the work than from any meaning it might hold. Through overintimacy some portion of the sense is dulled, and we regret that we cannot read or hear those verses as we first read them, with fresh eyes and ears.

Thus, before setting about the daunting task of tracing the history of the criticism on *Inferno* I, my initial challenge was to attempt to approach the work with the intensity of a first reading. I then made a concentrated effort to test and re-evaluate with new evidence the interpretations with which I had, through the years, become so comfortable. My aim was not to give revisionist explications but rather to follow the logic of the poem in its unfolding.

Subsequent re-readings resulted in the rediscovery of a few basic truths. The first, of course, was that Dante expects his reader to work very hard; he is one of the most manipulative of authors, compelling his audience to complete his meaning, inviting (literally), even forcing us to interpretation. I began to realize that an appreciation of the poet's polysemousness[2] implied not just an intellectual game of recognizing the multiplicity of meanings in the text, but that the act of choosing among the many purposefully encoded messages in the narrative was an active exercise in the theological doctrine of free will: the poet applies the Christian interpretive imperative in forcing us to choose and in challenging us later to choose again. Dante never allows his reader merely to read and dream; with subtlety and design he constantly disrupts his narrative line to lead us into the contemplation of the poem's ethical allegory. He was fully persuaded that the pleasure and usefulness of poetry was intensified by the recognition of the rigor of its creation and by the experience of the arduousness of its interpretation.[3]

The second fact concerned the cruxes: although these seemed to fall into many categories—philological, textual, linguistic, and so on, I felt that I was here concerned with two main types: first, those caused by the reader's loss or neglect of the cultural discourse and context in which they were to be understood (for example, the problem of the *lonza*) and, second, those that constituted real riddles set into the text by the poet himself. Of the latter type I felt that there were again two kinds: those possible of solution (such as the "piè fermo" or "chi per lungo silenzio") through the application of the right intellectual key, metaphorical code, or body of lore (those specialized codes of theology, poetry, philosophy, and so forth), and those that were intentionally without resolution (such as, perhaps, the identity of the *veltro*).

A third fact, corollary to the first two, was that the poet elicited certain immediate reactions, knowing that the reader would be likely, without much reflection, to apply his ready, "received" categories of interpretation piecemeal to parts of the text as he progressed serially along the narrative. Let me hasten to interject here, however, that I did not believe that these obedient consecutive interpretations were "wrong" reactions in the sense that Dante had not fully foreseen and actively encoded them, but only that they were meant to be revised as the poet altered the bases of the didactic, hermeneutical exercise as the poem progressed. I began to recognize afresh that just as a word, image, or episode conveyed several significances when examined synchronically, those same features of the text changed or gained additional significance diachronically as new contexts were reached.[4] My study attempts to show that the text itself leads the reader through different stages and changes of interpretation in its process of teaching a practical, moral lesson.[5] For example, the shining mountain of the prologue definitely evokes ideas of virtue, contemplation, and metaphysical enlightenment, but this interpretation must undergo a radical reversal imposed not only by the many intertextual resonances and implications but more especially by the fabric of interlocking metaphors that make up the poem's narrative totality. The glittering mountain in the northern widowed clime of the prologue can only be seen as some sort of delusion once Purgatory is sighted and scaled. Interpretation that is limited to the single component can be at the antipodes of the truth imparted by the poem as a whole.

This last I saw only too well as one of the inherent dangers of the *lectura* tradition where one canto is explicated at a time. I hope I have overcome some of the limitations of the genre by explicating the detail while trying, as much as possible, to remain mindful of the entire work, interpreting it not only in its cultural context but in the way Giambattista Giuliani described in his *Metodo di commentare la Commedia di Dante Alighieri* of 1861 as the surest and most convincing: to interpret Dante with Dante.

All biblical quotations are from the Vulgate and Douay-Rheims versions. Where the numbering differs in the King James version (AV) and Revised Standard Version (RSV), I have so noted it.

A. K. C.

ne dilunga (cioè quella che va nell'altra parte), e molte altre quale meno allungandosi e quale meno appressandosi, così ne la vita umana sono diversi cammini, de li quali uno è veracissimo e un altro è fallacissimo, e certi meno fallaci e certi meno veraci.

For the author and his time, the idea was almost beyond reflection; the concept had nearly lost its status as a metaphor.

Two literary topoi of classical origin also play a part in the introductory verse. First, like Virgil in the *Aeneid*, but unlike some ancient epic writers, Dante does not devote his first line to an invocation; he delays his appeal for divine poetic aid until later (*Aeneid* I, 8; *Inferno* II, 7). Secondly, Dante obviously seeks to apply to his *Commedia* Horace's advice in the *Ars poetica* that writers of an epic begin "in medias res." But he does so in a particularly Christian manner.[4] The "res," his story of conversion, must be, of itself, a decisively new beginning; it cannot properly be a "midst." The "midst" of his poem, therefore, starts chronologically in the mid-point of the path of our life, then to become narrowed, in exemplar, in the second line, to that of the protagonist.

For the most part, traditional critical glosses on the first verse have insisted on its chronological and biographical implications.[5] "Nel mezzo del cammin di nostra vita" refers to the central point in the years allotted to man according to Psalm 89 [90] 9–10: "dies annorum nostrorum . . . septuaginta anni . . ." [The days of our years . . . are threescore and ten years . . . (Douay)], a tradition Dante reflected in the *Convivio* IV, xxiii, 9: "Là dove sia lo punto sommo di questo arco, per quella disaguaglianza che detta è di sopra, è forte da sapere; ma ne li più io credo . . . che ne li perfettamente naturati esso ne sia nel trentacinquesimo anno." Since, as Boccaccio informs us, quoting an eyewitness at the poet's deathbed, Dante was born in 1265,[6] most commentators agree that the poetic journey is to begin during the wayfarer's thirty-fifth year, thus making the date 1300.[7]

This interpretation of the line has much about it that is attractive: the significance of thirty-five as the conventional "midpoint" fits archetypically with Dante's poetic fascination with numerical and structural centers, reflected so often in the numerology of the *Commedia*.[8] Pietro di Dante, in particular, is emphatic that the allusion is chronological: "Tamen dic, ut praemisi, quod ad tempus humane vitae se refert, cuius medium est trigesimus quintus annus" [Say, however, as I stated above, that it refers to the length of human life whose middle is the thirty-fifth

ACKNOWLEDGMENTS

As the long toil of research and writing comes to an end, there remains the enjoyable task of thanking those who have patiently helped me to finish this study. My first and most especial thanks go to the members of the Editorial Board of the Dante Society, Joan Ferrante, Robert Hollander, Anthony Pellegrini, and Aldo Scaglione, who all in various degrees have generously shared their expertise with me. To David Larmour, my research assistant and now a colleague, I am grateful for much invaluable help in amassing the bibliography and for the friendly intellectual exchange as the work progressed. To the John Simon Guggenheim Foundation I express my gratitude for its generous support of my research both here and in Italy in 1984–85. To the Research Board of the University of Illinois goes my heartiest appreciation for additional help in completing the project; publication of the volume was aided by a generous grant from the Dante Society of America.

Most of all, my debt is to Janet, my wife, who read, edited, then re-read and re-edited the manuscript in all of its stages and buoyed me for five years with her unstinting advice, encouragement, and love.

A. K. C.
Champaign, 1989

CHAPTER I

The First *Terzina*

"Nel mezzo del cammin"

"In isto primo cantu autor prohemizat ad totam universaliter et genera-
liter Comediam."[1] Guido da Pisa's assessment (com 1327–1328) typifies
those of most of the early commentators. The canto, indeed, more than
fulfills the expected proemial function by introducing two of the *Commedia*'s main characters, giving the ambience of the opening sequence,
arcanely alluding to the chronology of events, and foretelling the gran-
diose scope of the adventure to take place in the three realms of the
world beyond. Precisely how the canto's narrative governs and is gov-
erned by our reading of the rest of the *Commedia*, however, has been a
question of much controversy and will be the major concern of this
lectura.[2]

Let us begin, logically, with the first verse, "Nel mezzo del cammin
di nostra vita," and examine its cultural context and how it is structurally proleptic of the poem's theological and poetic themes. The concept of life as a path and journey inherited from classical antiquity was
readily associated with allegorizations of the Exodus as the path to salvation in Christian thought.[3] As the titles of some of the age's famous
treatises bear witness—*De gradibus humilitatis, Itinerarium mentis in
Deum*—life was an upward and inward pilgrimage to God. Dante himself gave the idea an extended gloss in *Convivio* IV, xii, 14–19:

> E sì come peregrino che va per una via per la quale mai non
> fue, che ogni casa che da lungi vede crede che sia l'albergo. . . .
> Veramente così questo cammino si perde per errore come le
> strade de la terra. Che sì come d'una cittade a un'altra di neces-
> sitade è una ottima e dirittissima via, e un'altra che sempre se

year].[9] The protagonist's age is a sign of the mythical quality of the text; it resonates with the traditions concerning the length and divisions of human life and mid-life conversion.[10]

S. Battaglia (*Esemplarità* I, pp. 59–68), has pointed to the Pythagorean and Platonic, magico-symbolic significance of man's life being the number seventy, a seven-times ten: ten, the number of perfection multiplied by the "full" number of seven with its manifold meanings for the stages of man's life and the full development of reason at its center—a tradition well known to Dante from Plato's *Timaeus* I, 34a and Macrobius's *Commentary on the Dream of Cicero*, book I, chapter 6. N. Mineo (1968) notes that the first verse echoes the conventions of biblical prophecies in which the specification of time and date was seldom omitted.[11] The wealth of significance encapsulated and evoked in the brief phrase thus transcends any biographical referentiality to take on a moral and exemplary value; it signifies an experience in the midst of the life of *all* men, as emphasized by the *Commedia*'s first adjective: "Nel mezzo del cammin di *nostra* vita." It marks a symbolic milestone of crisis, of conversion, in a universal human biography.

But this interpretation of the first line has not been immune from the exegetical controversy that besets so many verses of the first canto. Through the centuries there have been a few who tried to interpret the line in a mode sharply different from that of the mainstream. Guido da Pisa (com 1327–1328) labeled the poem an oracle, a prophetic vision and a dream,[12] and in 1333, the Ottimo[13] suggested, as an alternative to his own main chronological explanation, that the line signified the state of sleep, that which, according to Aristotle's *De generatione animalium* V, 1, 778, lay between life and death, and, which, as the philosopher said in the *Nicomachean Ethics* I, xiii, 1102b, took up one-half of the course of our lives: "Medium namque vite humane secundum Aristotelem somnus est."

In their wake, the "falso Boccaccio," Benvenuto da Imola, and Giovanni da Serravalle, while holding to a chronological interpretation of the line, were also led to classify the poem as a traditional *visio per somnium*, or dream-vision, a generic identification that would cause some discomfort to some ancient and modern Dantisti.[14] The line "tant'era pien di sonno" probably occasioned the misapprehension, and the idea resisted such sound objections as those offered in the *Chiose marciane*.[15]

Those who interpreted the poem as a dream did not take into sufficient consideration, as Boccaccio did,[16] the traditional metaphor of the "sleep of sin" that appears, perhaps, in its clearest statement in Romans 13:10—13:

> knowing the *season*, . . . it is now *the hour for us to rise from sleep*. For now our salvation is nearer than when we believed. *The night is passed* and the day is at hand. Let us therefore *cast off the works of darkness* and put on the armour of light. *Let us walk* honestly, as in the day.

The thematic parallels with the first lines of *Inferno* I—"l'ora del tempo e la dolce stagione," "Temp'era dal principio del mattino," "la notte ch'i' passai," "la selva oscura," "il cammin di nostra vita," "il mio cammino"— prove the case for interpreting the wayfarer's sleep metaphorically. Further, if minor, corroboration lies in the fact the word "sonno" occurs in verse 11: in numerological tradition eleven was the number of all sin.[17]

The metaphor of sleep as a symbol of habitual sin is a patristic commonplace. St. Augustine's *Confessions* (VIII, 5) was an influential expression of the concept; he complains of the torpor of his sinful cares:

> The burden of the world was a kind of pleasant weight upon me, as happens in sleep, and the thoughts in which I meditated on You were like the efforts of someone who tries to get up but is so overcome with drowsiness that he sinks back again into sleep. . . . For the law of sin is the strong force of habit, which drags the mind along and controls it even against its will.

St. Bernard also identifies the twelfth and last step of pride as "habitual sinning" in the same way in chapter 21 of the *De gradibus humilitatis* (*The Steps of Humility*); that this step for him is also metaphorically the *midpoint* at which either damnation or conversion must be reached is also helpful for interpreting the wayfarer's plight:

> Concupiscence revives as *reason is lulled to sleep [sopitur ratio] and habit becomes binding*. The wretch sinks into the evil depths . . . the wicked man who has dropped down to the bottom is ruled by evil habit and unchecked by fear, hastens boldly toward death. . . . *It is those in mid-course who grow weary* and are distressed, *now tormented by fear of hell, now held back by old habits as they strive to go up or down*.[18]

A. Pagliaro (*Ulisse*, p. 2) noted perceptively that the poet-narrator makes no effort to treat of the circumstances of a dream, as is normal in the *somnium* tradition, and that he begins instead as if his work were a medieval travelogue or allegorical adventure. It seems most likely that some commentators' reading of the poem as a vision was based on a simple desire to categorize the *Commedia* within a familiar and comfortable literary genre rather than to deal with its uniqueness and with the totally non-oneiric structure of the poem's narrative after the first sixty-one lines of the first canto.

The majority of critics who accept the more convincing chronological interpretation adduce two major events: first, as we have noted, the biological age of the wayfarer-poet, born in 1265, and, secondly, the coincidence of the otherworldly journey with the Jubilee Year of 1300, proclaimed by Dante's archenemy, Pope Boniface VIII, on December 25, 1299.[19] The historical circumstances of the celebration are of major interest in the genesis of the poem.

Toward the Jubilee Year Dante held mixed and conflicting attitudes. The year 1300 had, for him, been marked by considerable political success. On May 7 he had been sent as ambassador to San Gimignano by the Florentine Republic, and, for the period of June 15 to August 14, he had been elected for a two-month term to the priorate, from which, he was later to lament (as reported by Leonardo Bruni from a lost letter[20]), "all his troubles and hardships derived." Other government tasks were required of him, but his participation in the White Party's embassy to Rome to plead with the pope to change his policies began the exile from which he was never to return. The coincidence of the date of the poem with the centenary year and the fortuitous correspondence with the midpoint of his own age clearly made the events more momentous. As a Christian who necessarily divorced respect for office from the unworthiness of the incumbent, the poet overlooked the character of the jubilee's proclaimer and recognized the event as one of spiritual renewal for Christendom. Perhaps also, as S. Battaglia (*Esemplarità* I, p. 58) has suggested, through a secret and haughty desire to vie with his hated oppressor, he seized the opportunity to commemorate the year as a rebirth of faith and justice in a way that was to be remembered long after Boniface's proclamation had been forgotten in the popular mind. The result was doubly ironic: as he engraved that malodorous record from which the pope's reputation has never recovered, he also memorialized the man responsible for his lifetime banishment.

*　　*　　*

The initial three lines of the *Commedia* vibrate with further resonances: let us look closely again at the text's diction and some of its other theological senses:

> Nel mezzo del cammin di nostra vita
>   mi ritrovai per una selva oscura,
>   ché la diritta via era smarrita.[21]

As Boccaccio noted, along with most commentators after him, the lines contain a metaphorical allusion to the Gospel of John 14:6: "ego sum via et veritas et vita" [I am the way and the truth and the life].[22] Two of the lexical elements, "cammin" and "vita," are present in Dante's first line; the reference of the first is reinforced and made more precise by the use of "via" in the third verse. While the allusion has become a commonplace gloss among editors, there is, I believe, an additional significance implied by the text. For when the reader examines Jesus' words in John's Gospel account of the Easter story, they provide an ironic gloss on the events of the first sixty-one lines of the poem. At the Last Supper on the night before the Crucifixion, Thomas asks "Domine nescimus quo vadis et quomodo possumus viam scire?" (John 14:5) [Lord, we know not whither thou goest. And how can we know the way?]. And Christ replies: "Nemo venit ad Patrem nisi per me" (14:6) [No man cometh to the Father, but by me].

Even in the first verse, therefore, the poem sets forth, intertextually, the reason for the wayfarer's failure to attain his goal later in the canto, the cause of his ruining down at line 62, and his need for "another journey." The biblical subtext reveals that the wayfarer fails in the first sixty-one lines of *Inferno* I because he is not following the way of Christ. Rather, in self-deception, he seeks to gain his vision of beatitude totally under his own powers; he does not realize that, by himself, he cannot even discern his true goal, let alone reach it, without the prevenient grace of the Redeemer. Only later is the allusion to John 14 made explicit, in *Paradiso* VII, 35–39, where Beatrice couches the sin of the Fall in the same terms:

> questa natura al suo fattore unita,
>   qual fu creata, fu sincera e buona;
> ma per sé stessa poi fu ella sbandita
>   di paradiso, però che *si torse*
>   *da via di verità e da sua vita.*

The Easter connotations of the first lines become clearer when we encounter the second major time reference of the poem in *Inferno* XXI,
112–114, where we learn that the journey begins on Good Friday. There,
a devil lies in telling about the wholeness of a broken path that he hopes
will block the wayfarer.[23] Mixing truth with falsehood in the manner
literally typical of his kind, the demon describes events surrounding
the earthquake at Christ's death and its effects on the rocks of hell:

> presso è un altro scoglio che via face.
> Ier, più oltre cinqu'ore che quest'otta,
>   mille dugento con sessanta sei
> anni compié che qui la via fu rotta.   (*Inferno* XXI, 111–114)

There in *Malebolge* the wayfarer is again deceived about the way (although it may be, perhaps, a measure of his progress that it results this
time not from his own ignorance but from that of his guide). The path
is impassable, and Virgil must rescue the wayfarer once more. Beyond
specifying in retrospect the date of the opening lines of the poem, the
demon's lie in the *bolgia* of the barrators and hypocrites also ironically
underlines the paschal messages of the first chronological reference by
making us reflect upon a major term present in Jesus's words at the Last
Supper but absent in the first line of the poem: *Truth*, "ego sum veritas." The devil speaks of the central truth of Christianity, the Redemption of the Crucifixion that comes in the midst of Christian time.

Further direct biblical echoes also shed light on the meaning of the
verses. When we look back from *Inferno* III and the wayfarer's entrance
into hell, we realize that the first lines are calqued also on Isaiah 38:10:
"I said: In the midst of my days I shall go to the gates of hell."[24] For
Giovanni Getto (*Lect. Scaligera*, 1960, p. 5), the recollections of the
book of Isaiah "evoke a solemn atmosphere in which the discourse ac-
quires liturgical dignity" and give it "the breath of prophecy." Getto's
aesthetic appreciation is exact, but the effects of the echoes are even
more far-reaching, for the text and context of these biblical passages
confer also a rich semantic value when intercalated into our reading.[25]

Isaiah's words are the beginning of the thanksgiving song of King
Hezekiah (Ezechias). Having been ill and warned that he should die,
the king had prayed for the prolongation of his life; God turned the sun
back and added fifteen years to Hezekiah's span. As that Old Testament
song of thanksgiving expressed gratitude for the restoration of life after
a physical illness, so Dante's poem will be a song of thanksgiving for

benefits bestowed by God, a *eucharistia* for deliverance from a spiritual sickness, that is, for "il ben" that the wayfarer discovers in the dark wood.[26] The two major biblical echoes, therefore, reveal some of the the the fundamental purposes of the *Commedia*: the story will deal with the manner in which the way, the truth, and the life came to the wayfarer (and also, in a Christian sense, the manner in which it was granted to him to come to them); we are filled with expection that the tale will narrate the process of cure, renewal, and salvation.

We can also observe that the first verse reveals that the journey is made *in imitatione Christi*, for the age of the protagonist reflects as closely as possible the age of Christ himself at the Redemption as Dante calculated it. Departing from current theological views that the Savior had been put to death in his thirty-third year, Dante preferred to keep closer to the biblical and Aristotelian traditions of the allotment of man's years and his physical and mental growth and decline, generation, and corruption.[27] Reading Psalm 15:10 in its traditional sense as a prediction of Christ's death ("Nec dabis sanctum tuum videre corruptionem" [Nor wilt thou give thy holy one to see corruption]), Dante's *Convivio* IV, 23 applies it theologically to Christ's resurrection as recounted in Acts 2:27 and 31, 13:35 and 37 and dates the Redeemer's death before human decline, that is, in his thirty-fourth year: "E muovemi questa ragione: che ottimamente naturato fue lo nostro salvatore Cristo, lo quale volle morire nel trentaquattresimo anno de la sua etade; ché non era convenevole la divinitade stare cos[ì] in discresc[ione]." Thus, as Christ died and harrowed hell at the zenith of his powers, so the poem's wayfarer performs his *katabasis* at the midpoint of his years. With such a parallel, the poem suggests a hopeful note, to be borne out in the coming of the first stage of divine grace later in the canto (v. 63) and eventually culminating in the Light of Glory, grace's perfection, the *lieto fine* of the *Commedia*.

However, the optimism aroused by the *Commedia*'s first line is immediately clouded with pessimism by the second: "mi ritrovai per una selva oscura." This reversal begins the ambiguous negativity of the next sixty lines necessary to prepare both wayfarer and reader for the pilgrimage to follow.

"Mi ritrovai"

The "selva oscura" provokes dread in the wayfarer and evokes an eerie sense of familiarity in the reader. The voice of the narrator penitently records his sinful history: at mid-life he found himself yet again in a state of sin where the straight way was lost;[28] mournfully he affirms and confesses recidivism or backsliding. There is nothing positive in the letter of the verse "mi ritrovai per una selva oscura"—"I found myself again within a dark wood" when we first come upon it in the poem; it signifies a return to sin and sadness, a fact essential to the theology and narrative structure of the *Commedia*.

Some of the early commentators dealt with the metaphoric nature of the lines. In the first redaction of his *Commentarium*, Pietro Alighieri (p. 29) interprets them thus: "Et metaphorice procedendo fingit se ipsum reperisse in quadam sylva obscura, hoc est in statu vitioso" [And going on metaphorically, he describes himself as having found himself [again] in a dark wood]; and Jacopo della Lana wrote similarly: "Dice che si ritrovò in una selva oscura. Selva, s'intende in vita viziosa."[29] Among twentieth-century critics, Giovanni Getto (1965) eloquently set forth the semantic and poetic value:

> il ritrovarsi di Dante in un luogo, fuori strada, in una selva, in una direzione falsa, segna uno spazio che è fisico e metafisico insieme, un luogo che è del corpo e dell'anima, e stabilisce l'iniziale profilarsi di un ordine spaziale che, abbracciando la terra e il cielo, si dilaterà su visioni di cosmica vastità.   (pp. 406–407)

Giovanni Battista Bronzini (1978) recognized the note of grief and shame in his gloss: "A un punto indeterminato del camminare, che è il vivere umano, mi ritrovai (il *ritrovai* ne esprime anche il sentimento di doglianza) errante per una selva oscura al punto in cui (=che) la 'diritta via era smarrita'"(p. 175).

Surprisingly, however, current critical and editorial opinion disagrees with the straightforward understanding of these early commentators and modern critics.[30] Other scholars prefer a different interpretation, convinced, perhaps, by an early interpolation—and an omission,[31] as we shall see—of Dante's other son, Jacopo Alighieri, who earlier re-wrote and glossed the line as "*s'avide* ch'egli era in una oscura selva, dove la dritta via era smarrita. Per la quale, figuratamente, si considera la molta gente che nella oscurità dell'ignoranza permane." Buoyed by presumptions of the Renaissance and Enlightenment concerning the power of human reason, many modern commentators, among them Scartazzini, Passerini, Vandelli, Sapegno, and Montanari, pass over the literal, physical, and spatial senses of the verb "ritrovarsi" and substitute other verbs more cerebral and less poetic that stress the wayfarer's waking or awareness: they repeat, in the wake of their Renaissance predecessors, Landino and Vellutello: "*si accorse* di esser dentro un'orrida e fitta selva."[32] They thus ignore the indispensability of the verb itself in evoking of the unknown and frightening whereabouts of the sinner—the subject of John Freccero's fine essay of 1966 (rprt. 1986 pp. 1–15), "Dante's Prologue Scene: The Region of Unlikeness."[33] The poem defines the place of the wayfarer's fall as an earthly one, yet it is a place, as Singleton reminds us, that we cannot mark on any map. By effacing the force of the verb, translators and commentators have ignored both the important theological tradition and the textual concerns of spatiality and bewildering non-spatiality that sin involves—the "no-whereness" that is the shadowy locus of temptation and succumbing. I believe that Singleton's and Freccero's citing of St. Augustine's *Confessions* is central here: "It is in no space-occupying place that we slip down to the depths."[34] The exegetical or editorial leap of other scholars away from the literal and directly to the inward and spiritual senses omits an important part of the poetry and the rich subtext of traditional Christian metaphors.

Some commentators have even ignored the essential distinction, now commonplace,[35] between "Dante viator" and "Dante poet"; they forget that the original verb is a preterit spoken not by the lost, wayfaring protagonist but by the persona of the converted scribe. They not only foresake the text as written but substitute a verb of awakening and awareness in the present tense, such as: "*si accorge* di andar errando per una selva oscura."[36] Many English translators, beguiled by conventional commentaries, have similarly ignored the text and translated the gloss instead: the Carlyle-Wicksteed (com 1932) and Sinclair (com 1939) versions rendered the verb as, "I came to myself"; Lawrence Binyon (com 1933–1943) strayed far from the original, "I was made aware that I had strayed."

If we examine the line in the context of theological language, the hermeneutic consequences reveal the unnecessary difficulties caused by such substitutions. One recent critic, Fernando Figurelli (1977), changes the sense of "mi ritrovai" into a spiritual awakening and an awareness so full and self-sufficient that he can describe the wayfarer in these very first lines as "having redeemed *himself*" ("redentosi," "essersene redento"): "Il pellegrino *ormai redento* cominciò l'ascesa del colle."[37] Such modern Pelagian or semi-Pelagian interpretations of the first three, and, indeed, of the first sixty-one lines of the poem do not fit the context of grace and redemption of this poem that absorbs and presupposes so much from such writers as St. Augustine and St. Thomas Aquinas.[38]

The theological and exegetical failure of "s'avvide" and "s'accorge" to render the poem's meaning can perhaps best be revealed by reflecting that the awareness of sin, the knowledge of good and evil, was a product not of virtuous enquiry but of the Fall. In Christianity, knowledge of sin is never sufficient: as St. Paul expresses in anguished dilemma in Romans 7:14–15: "For we know that the law is spiritual. But I am carnal, sold under sin. For that which I work, I understand not. For I do not that which I will: but the evil which I hate, that I do." Indeed, upon this point turn all of St. Augustine's arguments in *The Spirit and the Letter*, where, echoing St. Paul in interpreting the Jewish Law as the "letter," he taught that the Decalogue, full as it was of good and holy commands, brought only the knowledge of sin but no means of justification. The power to do righteousness was lacking without the granting of grace.[39]

It is not facetious to remark that if the wayfarer could secure his own salvation under his own powers, Virgil's arrival at verses 62–63—and indeed, perhaps, the rest of the poem—would be superfluous. As I noted in the first part of this chapter, when the poet introduces the *Commedia* with an allusion to Jesus' words at the Last Supper ("I am the way. . . ." John 14:6), our readers' memories subjoin the rest, "No man cometh to the Father but by me." Simply put, the implications and evocations of the first line of the *Commedia* are anti-Pelagian; only with the descent or condescension of the chain of grace, through its last link in Virgil, can the wayfarer begin to achieve success in his journey to God.

In cases where editors and translators attempt to preserve the meaning of the root verb "trovare," there is still an element of "mi ritrovai" missing. Vittorio Rossi (Rossi-Frascino, com 1923–1948) reads Dante's lines as "Nel folto d'una selva, dove, smarrita la via buona, [Dante] *s'è trovato*" (vol. 1, p. 41). Siro Chimenz (com 1962) interprets them: "Dante *si trova* smarrito . . . nella selva." Cary (com ca. 1806–1814) renders it "*I found me.*" Charles Eliot Norton (com 1891–1892) and Allen Mandelbaum (com 1980) give "*I found myself.*" Antonino Pagliaro (*Ulisse*, 1961a; 1967, p. 3) compromises with "Dante all'improvviso ha coscienza di trovarsi smarrito in una selva oscura."[40] Dorothy Sayers (com 1949) and Mark Musa (com 1971), similarly, double the verb: "*I awoke to find myself.*" Hermann Gmelin translates the phrase: "Grad in der Mitte unsrer Lebensreise / *Befand ich mich* in einem dunklen Walde."

We observe that not one of these versions pays attention to the "ri-"

prefix, since commentators and translators have assumed, often tacitly, that the "ri-" is merely an intensive (such as in "riguardare" or "rimanere"). But let us grant, at least, the possibility that it has semantic value, for the first canto of the *Commedia* is dense with an unusual number of verbs of repetition. In the first sixty-one lines, there are five verbs or verb-clusters in the preterit or imperfect that tell of the wayfarer's ill-aimed persistence and his failure to escape from sin:

— *mi ritrovai* per una selva oscura
— l'animo mio / . . . *si volse* . . . *a rimirar* lo passo
— *ripresi* via per la piaggia diserta
— *fui per ritornar* più volte vòlto
— la bestia . . . *mi ripigneva* là dove'l sol tace.

And two such verbs in the present tense reiterate the emotion of the experience and its re-telling from the book of memory by the poet: "rinova la paura," v. 6; "non so ben ridir," v. 10. The abundance of verbs of repetition supports the interpretation of a studied selection in the repetitive prefix in the first verb of the poem. Because the poem reflects such care in lexical choice throughout and because the text is so prolific in its number of verbs with prefixes (even challenging the reader with neologisms to convey significance where normal verbs would be inadequate—compare "trasumanar," "ingigliarsi all'emme," "inluiare," "incinquarsi," "inmiare," and so on), it seems reasonable that the *Commedia* not only deserves but demands that we accept and respect a like precision in the selection of its first verb. It can be no accident that the *Inferno* is framed by verbs with an "ri-" prefix: the final verb echoes the first as Dante and Virgil issue forth from hell to see the stars again: "E quindi uscimmo a *riveder* le stelle" (*Inferno* XXXIV, 139).

Before citing theological traditions or specific infratexts to shed light on the interpretation of this initial "ri-" as a true repetition, let us examine the occurrence of the verb "ritrovarsi" in the poem, for it is, in fact, found *in only one other instance* in the *Commedia*: in *Inferno* XXVII, 43–45, as the wayfarer tells Guido da Montefeltro that the city of Forlì, which had withstood a long siege in 1281–1282 and had won out against the French and the Guelphs sent by Pope Martin IV, now *"finds itself again"* under the "green claws" of the Ordelaffi:

La terra che fé già la lunga prova
 e di Franceschi sanguignoso mucchio,
 sotto le branche verdi *si ritrova*. [41]

Should we be unconvinced by this major clue to the literal sense of the verb, let us consider the major patterns of the wayfarer's return to sin, or his recidivism, as it develops in the narrative. In *Inferno* XV, as the wayfarer converses with Brunetto Latini, he recounts, in terms that echo the first verses of the poem, *an earlier time* in which he first fell into the wooded valley of error:

> Là sù di sopra, in la vita serena,
> . . . *mi smarri' in una valle,*
> avanti *che l'età mia fosse piena.*
> Pur ier mattina le volsi le spalle:
> questi m'apparve, tornand'io in quella,
> e reducemi a ca per questo calle. (vv. 49–54)

He had gone astray in a valley *before* his age was at its full; but only "yesterday," the day of Virgil's coming, had he turned in the opposite direction. As we saw earlier in this chapter, in the *Convivio* IV, xxiii, 6, 9, Dante had compared human life to an arc whose central and fullest point was thirty-five years—the fictional age of the wayfarer as the poem opens. Thus, if we look at the time sequence revealed in the Brunetto episode, we learn that this second textual reference to going astray "*avanti* che l'età mia fosse piena" occurs *before* the fullness of years of mid-life, "nel mezzo del cammin di nostra vita."[42]

The echo, therefore, affirms an actual repetition. The *Vita Nuova*, whose narrative is presupposed by the *Commedia*, records in its very title the beatific effects that Beatrice had had upon him: in theological language, "new life" itself means conversion.[43] Beatrice's great and unexpected diatribe in *Purgatorio* XXX, in which she excoriates the pilgrim for following the way of error, is the culmination of the revelation of his backsliding; he had turned from the truth and grace that he had seen revealed through his beloved and fell to following false images:

> questi fu tal ne la sua vita nova
> virtüalmente, ch'ogne abito destro
> fatto averebbe in lui mirabil prova.
>
> . . . .
> meco il menava in dritta parte vòlto.
> Sì tosto come in su la soglia fui
> di mia seconda etade e mutai vita,
> questi si tolse a me, e diessi altrui.
>
> . . . .

e volse i passi suoi per via non vera,
  imagini di ben seguendo false,
  che nulla promession rendono intera.   (vv. 115–132)

We can understand in retrospect that this turning away from the grace
of a conversion earlier gained is the message of the first verb and second
verse of the *Divina Commedia*: "mi ritrovai per una selva oscura." The
wayfarer found himself *again* in a state of sin.

That the path to conversion involves repeated failures is a Christian
axiom.[44] St. Augustine, for example, relates in his *Confessions* VII, 4, his
uncounted failures to grasp the truths of the faith: "And so, though I
tried to raise the eyes of my mind from the pit, I fell back into it again,
and as often as I tried, so often did I fall back." Theologically, the notion of a daily falling into sin is a tenet of belief. No one is without sin;
the only historical exception was Christ himself. In the sixth and seventh petition of the daily recitation of the Oratio Dominica, every
Christian begs the Deity that he be led not into temptation and delivered
from evil; yet that dread will never end on earth. As St. Augustine elsewhere affirms: "There is no ground for hope that this can be brought
about in our present life, for it cannot come to pass as long as we are
carrying about us the mortality to which we have been brought by the
enticement of the serpent."[45] St. Gregory returns often to the question
of repeated sin in his famous commentary on the trials of Job in the
Moralia: "The mind is also consumed by sin through long habit so that
though willing to rise, it is quite unable to do so because of the weight
of evil habit that presses on it from above."[46] Once in a state of sin, man
is easily stimulated to sin again and cannot escape except by the outside
operation of prevenient grace; in short, without grace, sin is repeated.
The canto's reiteration of verbs prefixed with "ri-" represents rhetorically the *habitus* of sin, a state of helplessness that the suffering subject
cannot control without outside aid.

"Per una selva oscura"

At first reading, the economy of detail, or rather the reduction of detail
to spiritual emblem, intensifies the sense of mystery and the certain, imminent malignity of the "selva oscura."[47] The text evokes a waking
nightmare in all its psychological effects of insubstantiality, chimera,
hallucination, delusion, dread, despair, and helplessness; the magisterial
opening draws the reader into sharing the frustration and bewilderment
of the protagonist.[48]

The symbolic and non-mimetic nature of the dark wood has been recognized throughout the history of criticism on the *Commedia*. Jacopo Alighieri, the *Chiose marciane*, the Ottimo,[49] Benvenuto, the Anonimo Fiorentino, and Filippo Villani see it as this present life; indeed, a majority view continues to hold that it signifies life in its mere physical aspects, dominated by the instincts, that is, the life of ignorance and sin, or sin itself.[50] Theodore Silverstein (1932, pp. 81–82) noted that Bernardus Silvestris had already glimpsed the same meaning behind the symbolic "silva" in verses 179–189 of *Aeneid* VI:

> *In silvam* [in the woods], in the totality of the things of this world. *Umbrosam* [shadowy] and *immensam* [immense], because the shadows are everywhere. *Antiquam* [ancient], born in the beginning of time. . . . Philosophy calls those who are immoderate, pigs; the fraudulent, foxes; the garrulous, dogs; the truculent, lions; the irascible, boars; the rapacious, wolves; the torpid, asses. All of them dwell amidst the things of this world [*temporalia bona*].[51]

Other critics point to St. Augustine's metaphors of a "bitter forest" for the *saeculum* in his *Homily on John XVI* (*In Joannis Evangelium* XVI, 6: "Amara silva mundus hic fuit"), and in the *Confessions* X, 35: "tam immensa silva plena insidiarum et periculorum" [such an immense wood filled with ambushes and perils]. E. Curtius, E. Auerbach, and F. Mazzoni point to the frequency of the forest setting as a topos for beginning a poetic narrative of adventure in medieval literature.[52] Vellutello (com 1544) seems to have been the first to note Dante's use of the image in the *Convivio* IV, xxiv, 12: "L'adolescente, che entra ne la selva erronea di questa vita, non saprebbe tenere lo buono cammino, se da li suoi maggiori non li fosse mostrato."[53]

With Cristoforo Landino (com 1481) came a decidedly Platonist interpretation that reflected more closely the thought current in his age than that of Dante's poem: the wood is the body:

> Né è senza cagione che lui ponessi la selva pel corpo, et consequentemente pel vitio perché Platone et molti altri philosophi chiamano la materia corporea in greco hyle et in latino selva [sic], et chome l'animo ha ogni excellentia et felicità per la natura sua indivisibile incorporea et incorruptibile, chosi per l'opposito ha ogni calamità et ogni vitio per selva cioè pel corpo el qual è corruptibile.[54]

That the body per se is corruptible rather than suffering the (for Dante, historical) effects of the Fall is an assumption outside the purview of the *Commedia*, for it neglects the original creation of man who, though made of the slime of the earth, was created in God's image (Gen. 1:27; 2:7). The text actually implies that the *selva* does not represent the body itself, but rather that it is a threat to both the body and the soul; further, the senses' aberrant apprehension of that threat pertains more to the mental than to the corporeal. A minor medieval numerological argument, to judge from its reappearance in an emphatic anadiplosis in the fifth line of the poem, would seem, perhaps, to identify the *selva* with the conventional number of the *saeculum* (the world and the worldly), and of the senses, the number five.[55]

Most convincing is Pagliaro's interpretation of the forest as man's self-debasement by which he renounces all reason in moral choice and surrenders dominion to the lower faculties of the soul, to the animal, and here, to the vegetative (*selva*).[56] The wood is the "bitter" life[57] of the appetite without the light of judgment; Dante's *Convivio* IV, vii, 11, offers an earlier statement on the subject:

> Per ciò che vivere è per molti modi (sì come ne le piante vege-
> tare, ne li animali vegetare, sentire, muovere e ragionare, o vero
> intelligere), e le cose si deono denominare da la più nobile
> parte, manifesto è che vivere ne l'uomo e ragione usare. Dun-
> que, se 'l vivere è l'essere [dei viventi e vivere ne l'uomo è
> ragionare usare, ragione usare è l'essere] de l'uomo, e così da
> quell'uso partire è partire da essere, e così è essere morto. E
> non si parte da l'uso del ragionare chi non ragiona lo fine de la
> sua vita? e non si parte da l'uso de la ragione chi non ragiona il
> cammino che fare dee?

The sudden textual discontinuity between the literal (material forest) and the abstract, symbolic senses (bitterness, death) in verse 7, "Tant'è amara che poco è più morte," points up the message: for man, not to use reason is death itself.[58] Most critics, such as Pagliaro (*Ulisse*, pp. 10–17), Pietrobono (com 1946, p. 5), T. Spoerri (1946; Ital. trans. 1966, p. 42), Chimenz (com 1962, p. 5), and others, have followed the "canonical" reading in interpreting the *selva* as a moral opposite to the luminous mountain. I believe, however, that upon second reading this dichotomy will prove to be illusory and that the poet's strategy in using the light-darkness theme is more sophisticated than it appears at first. Our suspicions should be aroused by any whiff of Manichaeanism, as if good and evil existed in things rather than in the human will. Although the objects of fear, the forest and the path, seem to give way to a mirage of aspiration in the glittering mountaintop, we must keep in mind that this is only the point of view of the lost protagonist. We should be suspicious of allowing ourselves to be so empathetically caught up in the narrative adventure of the climb recounted in this textual segment that we lose all other perspectives. Dante's Cato will rightly censure that kind of reading in the second canto of the second canticle.[59]

In fact, the wayfarer can make no progress along the path. He cannot find the "diritta via" that he has lost, precisely because he, as a faulty "reader" of his circumstances, has also falsely interpreted the mountain as a good to be pursued and the forest an evil to flee. The wayfarer's error and his moral bewilderment should compel us to recognize that the message here is not the stereotypical metaphor that we first assumed it to be: the emotions of the protagonist do not square with the values expressed in the whole tissue of theological metaphor used to describe his experiences and perceptions. There is a blending of different types of language here, but there is also jarring contradiction. We have obviously been trying to unlock the text with the wrong key. Dante's Christian orthodoxy could provide the cultural substructure. Perhaps St. Augustine best represents the traditional view:

> [God] dwelleth on high, yet is near to the low . . . the proud He seeth afar off; He is all the less near to them the higher they conceit themselves to be. Then didst thou seek a mountain? Come down, that thou mayest reach Him. But dost thou wish to ascend? Ascend, yet seek not a mountain. . . . A valley implies lowliness. Therefore do thou all within.[60]

Perhaps what we had been led to assume as the convention to follow (that is, the philosophical ascent in contemplation viewed as a positive striving) may turn out to be its very violation. Perhaps the wayfarer's assumptions are perverse: the hill and, consequently, the direction he is taking on the path are lesser goods equally to be rejected. Guided by theology and its expression in certain specific texts, we, as readers, should legitimately expect that in some mysterious way the wooded valley will transvaluate.

And the reading imposed by the total structure of the *Commedia*'s narrative makes that transvaluation an inevitability. In the first sixty-one lines of the poem, the way through the forest ("non so ben ridir com'io v'entrai") and the path up the hill are one and lead in one direction, a direction diametrically opposite, both geographically and morally, to the way the protagonist will have to take with Virgil's guidance.[61]

If the illuminated hill signifies contemplation, then we must see, logically, that the striving for contemplation itself, together with the direction taken for that striving, is somehow wrong in the grander narrative scheme that will provide a cure. We begin to understand that the text has manipulated the reader into accepting the clouded point of view of the wandering sinner. Critics who interpret the mountain and the wood as ultimately antithetical are forced to fall themselves into the *non sequitur* of stating that the wayfarer cannot escape from the darkened forest because he has lost the true, straight path, only then to have him temporarily "escape" from the wood by persisting in the same, wrongful direction.[62] On the contrary, the exalted position allotted to contemplation in the earlier *Convivio* is here recanted. The way up the mountain is the "falsa via," the very direction that leads the wayfarer to ruin down where light, in fact, is absent, "là dove il sol tace." The wayfarer must take a different direction: "A te convien tenere *altro viaggio*."[63]

Yet in a further ironic twist, the text reveals that the wayfarer has been, all the time, on the very path he seeks, only that he has been facing the wrong way; the path was, in fact, "smarrita"—not lost, mislaid— only in his own mental aberration and mistaken choice of direction. As the reoriented wayfarer (I use the adjective with care) embarks on the way that will eventually lead to the sight of God, he must first re-enter the very wood he had tried to flee from in a journey that descends to humility: "intrai per lo cammino alto e silvestro" (*Inferno* II, 142). As his direction on the path is reversed, so is the value of the *selva*, the locus no longer of sin but the beginning of salvation.

CHAPTER II

"Al piè d'un colle"

"Guardai in alto"

A few critics and commentators have read the words "guardai in alto" as a glance toward the sun.[1] They have thus interpreted the gesture as a symbol of *conversion* (literally, of course, a "turning toward"), instead of *aversion* from the Deity, who (as all readers agree) is here symbolized in the *pianeta* of verse 17.[2] The letter of the text, however, states that the wayfarer raises his eyes not to the sun but to the shoulders of a shining mountain bathed in the sun's rays; he sees only reflected light:

> Guardai in alto e *vidi le sue spalle*
>   vestite già de' raggi del pianeta
>   che mena dritto altrui per ogni calle.   (vv. 16–18)[3]

The prologue scene (*Inferno* I, 1–61), unlike the journey of the rest of the *Commedia* beyond the first two cantos, takes place in an allegorically and symbolically earthly setting, where, in Christian tradition, the way of truth is not to be found by the unaided seeker. Such a site and such a quest have a long tradition in patristics. Lactantius, for example, writing his *Divine Institutes* ca. A.D. 304–311, urges the Christian wayfarer always to keep the sun as a guide (IV, 8); he even uses the traditional image of the seafarer that will find a repetition in *Inferno* I, 22–27:

> *Whoever strives to hold the right course of life ought not to look at the earth, but at heaven* . . . not to refer all things to the body but to the soul, not to give his attention to this life but to eternal life. So, *if you always raise your eyes toward heaven and watch*

the sun, how it rises, and *keep it the guide of your life as though of a ship, your feet will of their own accord be directed onto the road*. (my italics)[4]

Elsewhere the Christian apologist specifies that such a journey without the direct light of the sun represents the pagan notion of an ascent in contemplation; the way is an uncharted sea[5] where philosophical mariners lose their way: he warns that Satan uses philosophy not to enlighten but to keep man from clarity of vision: "He [the enemy, Satan] casts philosophy into the eyes of those who seek wisdom so that he may blind them with the *likeness of light*, lest anyone comprehend and hold the truth" (my italics).[6] Seekers of wisdom are adrift; without guidance they cannot find the true way:

> This is the way which the philosophers seek, but they do not find it for this reason, that *they seek rather upon the earth where it is not possible for it to appear. They wander*, therefore, *as if on a vast sea*, nor do they know where they are being borne, since *they neither discern any way nor follow any leader . . . unless these watch some light of heaven*, they wander in uncertain courses. (my italics)[7]

The poem tells us that the wayfarer does not heed such traditional caution as Lactantius recommends. The protagonist glances upward to see only an earthly mountain clothed in the rays of the sun, not the sun itself. The *Commedia* presents all of the elements of Lactantius's admonitions. Clearly, in both texts, the "pianeta," or the sun, is symbolic of the spiritual "sol iustitiae," the Sun of Justice.[8] This is why the voice of the narrator in the *Commedia*, writing "in retrospect," notes that the "planet" leads "altrui," *others*,[9] aright, and not his earlier self who followed not the source of light but the mirrored, deceptive light about which the early Fathers gave warning.

If the wayfarer were facing the rising sun still low on the horizon with the hill before him, the hill would loom as a dark silhouette. Logically, for him to see the hill cloaked (literally, "dressed") in radiance as he mounts upward, facing its lower peaks, he must have the sun at his back (or, let us grant, at least, to one side). Later allusions to the sun's light in the *Commedia* would appear to confirm that this is so. Since the hour is near dawn ("temp'era dal principio del mattino," v. 37), the wayfarer must be walking westward, not eastward toward the sites of the Incarnation and Redemption. What seems a minor detail is, in fact, a point made much of in theology. Again, on this let us consider Lactantius as he discusses the path of life in the context of reward and punishment:

> *That one road, the better one, is turned toward the rising sun; the other, the worse, toward its setting,* since he who follows truth and justice will secure possession of the accepted reward of immortality, perennial light; but he who has preferred vice to virtue, falsehood to truth, ensnared by that evil guide, must be *borne to the west and to eternal darkness.* (my italics) [10]

The wayfarer's wrong direction in the prologue scene is internally glossed by its parallel in the Ulysses canto,[11] where, in that ill-conceived sea voyage to learn of the "vizi" and "valori" of men, the Greek hero turns his stern, not his prow, to the morning sun to sail westward: "e volta nostra poppa nel mattino" (*Inferno* XXVI, 124).[12]

The wayfarer's position in *Inferno* I, 1–61, parallels that described by St. Augustine in the *Confessions*. In book 4, chapter 16, he confessed his need, as he strove for the truth, for a light different from that of philosophy in order for his soul to be truly illumined. He too aimed to reach divine truth; yet at the same time "was being forced back from God so that [he] might taste death." Augustine had also failed in his early efforts and recognized: "I had my back to the light and my face to the things on which the light shone; so that the eyes of my face saw things in the light, but on my face itself, no light fell." Put into biblical and theological perspective, the wayfarer's failure to glance to the sun indicates perversity beyond that of mere ignorance; his situation could be seen, in fact, as a figure or fulfillment of that in Job 24 : 13: "They have been rebellious to the light; they have not known His ways; neither have they returned by His paths." The church fathers teach that God often patiently permits proud apostates to persist long in their sins; left to themselves they may by their free will damn themselves. As St. Gregory glosses the passage in Job, refusal to see the light actually signifies the blindness resulting from pride:

> Wicked people . . . know the right things . . . yet neglect to follow what they know; and so they are "rebellious against the light," in that following their desires, they contemn the good they know. They, then, that *do wrong not from ignorance, but pride,* present the shield of their exaltation against the darts of truth, that they may not be stricken in heart to their good. By

this same pride of theirs it is brought to pass, that whereas they will not do things that they know, neither do they know the good they should do, but that *their own blindness should utterly exclude them from the light of truth*. (my italics) [13]

We can therefore begin to see emerging a clearer sense of the true circumstances of the wayfarer in the first sixty-one verses of the poem. Having found himself again in a state of sin, he proudly tries to find escape in self-reliance, following not the Light of the World, but its mere reflection in human philosophy. This point in the narrative marks the first use of a certain leitmotif of consonance that will be observed between the wayfarer and his guide who is "ribellante" to the laws of God (v. 125). Further, the tradition of the blindness of pride, once recognized as a cohesive theological and poetic theme, effectively helps to gloss the catachresis of verse 60 where the wayfarer is driven back by the wolf: "mi ripigneva là dove il *sol tace*."

The wayfarer's climbing of a hill in *Inferno* I immediately catches the reader in a tangle of conflicting responses. [14] The positive Mosaic tradition of the Decalogue on Mount Sinai, the waters of Mount Horeb, the holiness of Mount Sion, the Mount of Olives, and the hill of Golgotha are surely meant to come to mind. [15] However, along with this *in bono* tradition of "climbing the mountain of the Lord," there is also evoked another tradition *in malo* that I believe has been almost entirely neglected by commentators. Indeed, to gaze in longing at a mountain and then to climb to its peak can resonate with human sinfulness not only in the context of Christian attitudes toward pagan philosophy but even more in the context of the genesis of sin and the cure of faith and conversion. We think immediately of Satan's boastful song in Isaiah 14:12–15, [16] where, in a figure of all sin to follow, the proud morning climb of a mountain in the northern hemisphere led to a fall to the depths:

How art thou fallen from heaven, O Lucifer, who didst rise in the morning? How art thou fallen to the earth, that didst wound all nations? And thou saidst in thy heart:

"I will ascend into heaven. I will exalt my throne above the stars of God. I will sit in the mountain of the covenant, in the sides of the north. I will ascend above the height of the clouds. I will be like the most High."

But yet thou shalt be brought down to hell, into the depth of the pit.

In theological perspective, a mountain, like anything in God's universe, can be confused for a primary, rather than a secondary good; its value depends on the individual's responsibility to choose and use it rightly.

The image of a climb in pride was linked also to other ideas of impiety. In the Old Testament the prophets railed against the idolatry of those Hebrews who forsook the temple in Jerusalem to worship Baal on wooded hilltops.[17] The textual parallel of the first verse of our canto with the first verse of the song of King Hezekiah ("In the midst of my days I shall go to the gates of hell" [Isaiah 38:10]) discussed in Chapter 1, might earlier have seemed simply incidental; it is, however, a subtext of some importance for our understanding. Hezekiah was traditionally considered to be the author of the Book of Kings, and he also enjoyed especial honor because he had destroyed the cults of mountaintop apostasy in pursuance of the Deuteronimic program of banishing idolatry from the Kingdom of Judah and centralizing worship at the temple in Jerusalem: "He destroyed the *high places* [Hebrew "bamoth"; Vulgate "excelsa"] and broke the statues in pieces, and cut down the groves" (IV Kings 18:4; AV/RSV II Kings 18:4). Later in the *Commedia*, Hezekiah appears not only as the model of contrition and thanksgiving but as the exemplar of the just monarch within the very eye of the Eagle in the Heaven of Jove (*Paradiso* XXI, 37–54).[18] Perhaps we are to see that the righteous acts and prayer of Hezekiah are in some way a measure against which Dante, the "poet of rectitude," would have us judge his song of justice and the actions of its narrative.

Unlike the books of the Old Testament that abound in negative mountain imagery, the New Testament does not present or assume the same, consistent doctrine concerning either the privilege of mountains or the danger of their misuse. There are, however, two major examples: first, Satan's temptation of Christ in Matthew 4:8–10 and Luke 4:5–8 that identifies mountain peaks as signifying vain, worldly pride, power, and idolatry, and, second, Christ's saying to the Samaritan woman in John 4:21, "Neither on this mountain, nor in Jerusalem adore the Father," which Augustine glosses uncompromisingly, "seek not a mountain."[19] The Fathers and Doctors of the Church cling closely to these passages and to the Old Testament tradition, amply treating the threat that the "abuse" of mountain-worship can pose. The raising of the eyes to mountains and the ascent of mountains become for them a sign of the impious pride and elation of the Christian backslider and of the error of pagan philosophers, particularly the Stoics. St. Augustine has much to say on the topic; consider, for example, the passage that Petrarch chose from the *Confessions* (X, viii, 15) as the climax of his famous letter on the "Ascent of Mont Ventoux": "And men go abroad to admire the peaks of mountains and forsake themselves." While commenting on Psalm 121 (Vulg. 120), "Levavi oculos meos in montes unde veniet auxilium mihi?" [I shall lift up mine eyes unto the hills whence cometh my help?]—so often misinterpreted[20]—Augustine roundly dismisses the notion that aid is, indeed, forthcoming from mountains, for, even if they are clothed with the light of the sun, he says, they have no light of their own:

> "I have lifted up mine eyes to the mountains, from whence help shall come to me." *Do not suppose, however, that the mountains themselves will afford you hope*: whatever they give, they receive; they do not give of themselves. And if you stay on the mountains, your hope will not be unshakeable: your hope and confidence must rather be in Him Who sheds light upon the mountains. . . . *Do the mountains give you help? Not at all.* Listen to what follows: "My help is from the Lord, who made heaven and earth." (my italics)[21]

He continues, giving a dire warning against the deceptiveness of other metaphorical mountains:

> Other mountains there have been . . . were any man to steer his course by them, he would end in shipwreck. Heresiarchs have raised themselves up and become mountains. . . . Many men, setting eyes on these mountains and desiring land, longing as they did to be free from the waves, have been driven against the rocks and shipwrecked on the strand.[22]

Another of Augustine's accounts of the disaster of such a philosophical sea voyage and mountain climb is a passage of the *De beata vita*, I, 3 (*PL* 32, cols. 960–961; first noted by Freccero in 1966; rprt. 1986, p. 22). The pursuit of philosophy is there revealed as vainglory embodied in a deceptive mountain clothed with light;[23] those who climb it fall through its insubstantial surface to their destruction:

> All those carried thus to the region of the happy life, find an immense mountain directly in front of the port. Since this may cause great difficulty to the incoming sailors, it is to be feared and very cautiously to be avoided. It has great glamor and is clothed with an enticing light. Thus it not only offers the ones

that sail in and the ones already in a domicile with the promise of stilling their desires for the happy life, but it also extends generally invitations to those people within the port. Then it retains those who, enchanted by the very height, take pleasure in looking down upon their fellow men. They frequently admonish people just arriving, not to be deceived by hidden rocks nor to believe they can easily climb up to them. With a great kindness they inform these newcomers how they can enter without danger, because of the nearness of the land. To those who are envious of vainglory, they point out the place of security.

For those who are striving toward philosophy or who have already entered into it, what mountain does reason wish them to dread more than the proud study of vain glory, so empty and groundless inwardly that it submerges and absorbs the conceited through the fragile ground upon which they presently walk? Thus it throws them back into the darkness and snatches away the home, so much desired and almost in sight. (my italics)[24]

The climb in pride without God can only be, in Augustine's words (*Confessions* IV, 12), a climb not to God, but a climb against him: "But how can you rise if you are in high places and your clamor reaches heaven? Come down from those heights, for then you may climb, and, this time, climb to God. *To climb against Him was your fall*" (my italics).

With these warnings in mind, the cautious reader should approach the mountain in "the widowed northern clime" of *Inferno* I with the full awareness that the wayfarer there is in the same predicament as Lactantius's and Augustine's voyagers. In the language of the Fathers, philosophy cannot do what the ancients claimed it could. Along with lust (*Purgatorio* XXVII), it is pride to which Dante's projected persona confesses as a besetting sin in *Purgatorio* XII, 1–9. He has his wayfarer walk apace with Omberto Aldobrandesco with head bowed as "oxen go in a yoke," thereby anticipating his own future purgation. Virgil, little comprehending this expression of his charge's Christian humility, bids him to hasten on, but the pilgrim's thoughts remain "bent down and shrunk," and in the following canto he confesses his dread of pride's scourge:

Troppa è più la paura ond'è sospesa
    l'anima mia del tormento di sotto,
    che già lo'ncarco di là giù mi pesa.

(*Purgatorio* XIII, 136–138)

David Thompson (1967; 1974) and R. Hollander (1980, pp. 99–102), among others, following Masseron (1922) and Bruno Nardi (1949; 1966), have pointed to Dante's biography and have observed a consuming devotion to philosophy at the expense of theology in the works that the poet wrote between the *Vita Nuova* and the *Commedia*.[25] Indeed, within the text of the poem it is a sin of the intellect and not merely of the flesh for which Beatrice reproaches the wayfarer later in *Purgatorio* XXX.

Her first words ironically rebuke Dante for indulging in the presumption and vainglory of philosophers: not of his own merit did he come, but through her agency in the chain of grace was he made worthy to climb the mountain of Purgatory: "Come degnasti d'accedere al monte? / non sapei tu che qui è l'uom felice?" (vv. 74–75). Her central concern is man's true, ultimate and eternal happiness, the goal from which the wayfarer had strayed when he abandoned her, the spiritual guide, who was to lead him to it: "Questi si tolse a me, e diessi altrui." He had followed instead another woman whom he had allegorized as a Boethian "donna gentile" of philosophy. Beatrice continues in lines that clearly refer this truancy to the events of the prologue scene, to the wayfarer's "diritta via smarrita," to his ruining down to the depths, to the descent of grace, and to the necessity of the journey through hell:

> e volse i passi suoi per via non vera,
>
> . . . .
>
> Tanto giù cadde, che tutti argomenti
> a la salute sua eran già corti,
> fuor che mostrarli le perdute genti.   (vv. 130–138)

Beatrice insists on the pilgrim's personal error, for error, in Christian theology, is not the same as ignorance inherited by all men from the Fall as one of the wounds of original sin, nor is it, as in pagan philosophy, a necessary part of groping after truth. Rather it is defined as an active rejection of truth already received and is characterized by recidivism, unfaithfulness, or unbelief.[26] Its disobedience causes blindness and, as in the apostasy of Israel, leads to idolatry (Amos 2:4; Isaiah 44:20; Wisdom 12:24). In the Bible such apostasy is figured by the literal wandering that is often its punishment, as in the wandering of Cain (Genesis 4:12), the bestial exile of Nebuchadnezzar (Daniel 4:29–30),[27] or the wandering of Israel (Hosea 9:17) like sheep without a shepherd to return them to the fold (Isaiah 13:14; 53:6; Ezechiel 34:16; Luke 15:4–7; I Peter 2:25).

The wayfarer in the prologue scene can be viewed, then, not only as a figure of the proud philosopher who attempts to mount up through contemplation but also as one who, although a baptized Christian, pursues his own blind course, forgetful of the Christian facts of history—the Fall and Redemption.[28] He is the backsliding sinner who would mount up to what he identifies as the light of truth without admitting or confessing that he needs the grace of God both to recognize the real goal and to succeed in its attainment. Later in *Purgatorio* XXXIII, Beatrice makes her charges clearer:

> "Perché conoschi," disse, "quella scuola
>   c'hai seguitata, e veggi sua dottrina
>   come può seguitar la mia parola;
> e veggi vostra via da la divina
>   distar cotanto, quanto si discorda
>   da terra il ciel che più alto festina."   (vv. 85–90)

At that point, having drunk of Lethe's waters of oblivion, the wayfarer recalls nothing. Yet his forgetfulness is proof of his sin; for as Beatrice points out, since only sins and not good deeds are thus blotted out, had it not been a sin to have left her to follow this "school," he would have recalled all. In preparation for this cleansing, he had to descend to witness the condign punishments of those in perdition—and first among them, the pagan poets and philosophers comprising the *scuola* into whose number the wayfarer had proudly seen himself received "sesto fra cotanto senno" (*Inferno* IV, 102). In *Purgatorio* XXI, 31–33, Virgil employs the same term as he confesses his own pagan limitations and those of his companions in Limbo.

> . . . io fui tratto fuor de l'ampia gola
> d'inferno per mostrarli, e mosterolli
> oltre, quanto'l potrà menar *mia scola*.

For Beatrice, the term "scuola" describes those who persist in the mistaken belief that man's ultimate happiness can be reached without the true wisdom of God's grace. In contrast to the wayfarer, the poet-persona, writing with the total experience of the journey to justice and of the very sight of God, refuses to recount the substance of the conversation among the six: Dante has him humbly decline, for now "il tacere è bello."[29]

The references to a pagan "scuola" of which the wayfarer is made part lead us to understand, in retrospect, that the wayfarer's wandering, failure, and fall in *Inferno* I result not merely from the weaknesses of concupiscence and ignorance of all men who bear the mark of Adam, but from the private, intellectual failing of the pilgrim himself: a personal sin of pride. Contemplation and knowledge, without belief, without humility, or the grace of God, gain not heaven but hell, as the presence of the ancient sages in hell's Limbo bear witness. In Augustinian terms devotion to anything at the exclusion of the Deity means idolatry. Dante portrays his wayfarer as unwittingly following a sinful paradigm: the wayfarer fails to look to the sun for guidance; he chooses the wrong mountain to ascend, allowing it to absorb all his attention.

The theme of the sun's light, material and spiritual, and the wayfarer's approach to it is a major, expanding matrix of the poem, and, thus, the gestures of glancing to the sun (to God, to the light of truth) become evermore explicit as the *Commedia* progresses. In Canto III of *Purgatorio*, the as-yet unpurged pilgrim finds himself in the same physical attitude before he begins his climb of the mountain of true beatitude as he found himself before the deceptive mountain of delight in *Inferno* I; the second purgatorial gesture of turning his back to the sun recapitulates and begins the exorcism of the first:

> e diedi'l viso mio incontr' al poggio
> che'nverso 'l ciel più alto si dislaga.
> Lo sol, che *dietro* fiammeggiava roggio,
> rotto m'era dinanzi, a la figura,
> ch'avëa in me de' suoi raggi l'appoggio.   (vv. 14–18)

There the pilgrim's gesture symbolizes his need for purgation; the sun's blocked rays behind forming a shadow before him create a clear message about that sinful "something of Adam" which he has brought with him; in the second realm his journey upward is marked by ever-increasing references to the sight of the guiding sun and its effects. The image is made literal in the very action of the *Purgatorio* where, as Sordello makes clear in the cornice of sloth (*Purgatorio* VII, 44–60), the souls can make no progress upward after sunset. But in the daylight the wayfarer will now be led as other men: here the sun, "lo bel pianeta," is guide on an easier journey, as Cato explains in *Purgatorio* I: "'lo sol vi mosterrà, che surge omai, / prendere il monte a più lieve salita'" (vv. 107–108). The sun and Dante's strength are one, and he prays as the "planet" sets: "O virtù mia, perchè sì ti dilegue?" (*Purgatorio* XVII, 73). Finally, in *Purgatorio* XXVII, 133, as the second part of the journey draws to its close at the mountain's topmost step, Virgil "crowns and mitres" the pilgrim over himself to signify his attainment of control over his will and bids him face the sun directly as its rays are reflected now upon his brow: "Vedi lo sol che'n fronte ti riluce."

The gesture and its metaphorical meaning become evermore united, even indistinguishable, in the course of the poem. Furthermore, just as the metaphor of facing the light is reiterated as the journey unfolds, so too is its antithesis—turning one's back to the truth—also intermittently repeated.[30] The actions again make literal the central moral themes of the poem: aversion and conversion. In *Paradiso* VIII, the Angevin Charles Martel promises to impart a truth concerning human heredity with the words:

> . . . S'io posso
> mostrarti un vero, a quel che tu dimandi
> *terrai lo viso come tien lo dosso*.   (vv. 94–96)

The soul then closes his disquisition with an insistent repetition: "Or quel che t'era dietro t'è davanti" (v. 136). Charles then turns again to the Sun, that is, to God:

> E già la vita di quel lume santo
> rivolta s'era al Sol che la rïempie
> come quel ben ch'a ogne cosa è tanto.   (*Paradiso* IX, 7–9)

Later in the same canto (*Paradiso* IX, 127–128), the universal significance of turning one's back is finally revealed; the gesture, like that of the ascent of the mountain, symbolizes the archetype of all sin when Folco describes Satan turning from his creator as "colui . . . / che pria volse le spalle al suo fattore." The echo of "vidi le sue spalle" in "volse le spalle" unites the two actions verbally.[31]

The glance aloft to an earthly mountain in the lower, sinful, northern hemisphere[32] in the first canto of the *Commedia* is corrected in the last canto: in *Paradiso* XXXIII, 49–50, St. Bernard signs for the wayfarer to look upward: "Bernardo m'accennava, e sorridea, / perch'io guardassi suso." The wording echoes the opening of the *Commedia* as the pilgrim's gaze finally fixes on the real terminus, the center of the universe, the real Sun, the sight of God himself: "e più e più intrava per lo raggio / de l'alta luce che da sé è vera" (vv. 53–54). In words recalling his bewildered state in the prologue, the pilgrim dares not avert his eyes:

> Io credo . . .
> . . . ch'i' sarei smarrito,
> se li occhi miei da lui fossero aversi.   (vv. 76–78)

In the context of the narrative as a whole, it becomes clear that the concepts of sight and knowledge in the *Commedia* are based on I Corinthians 13 : 12. In *Inferno* I, the lost wayfarer sees only a reflection, as in a glass darkly and, surely, in an enigma.[33] Only later does he glance to the sun itself, and, later still, in *Paradiso* XXXIII, see all that it figures, face to face.

"La paura un poco queta"

> Allor fu la paura un poco queta,
>   che nel lago del cor m'era durata
>   la notte ch'i' passai con tanta pieta.   (vv. 19–21)

At verse 19 the wayfarer's fear, which had lasted through the night spent in such "pietà" ("pieta"), is somewhat quieted. Since the word "paura" occurs five times in the first canto and the words "paventare," "tema," "temere," and their adjectival variants some eighteen times in the first four cantos, twelve times in the first two alone, it seems wise to explore the uses in the poem of the historically ambiguous theological concepts of fear. Fear is, in fact, so central to the canto's vocabulary, thought, and structure that one critic has entitled it "Il canto della paura."[34]

Generally, critics have taken Virgil's negative view of fear (*Inferno* II, 45–51) as if it were intended to be the expressed philosophical opinion of Dante as the historical author and, therefore, as the only view of fear necessary for interpreting the action of the *Commedia*'s first cantos; it is, on the contrary, a philosophical view expressed by the persona of Virgil that helps to characterize him as a pagan with only a limited understanding of Christianity. Citing St. Thomas, scholars correctly declare fear a physiological passion and assert that it prevents bodily progress.[35] The physical fear of harm and corporal death does, indeed, impede the wayfarer's progress in the first sixty-one lines of the poem, but we must keep in mind that the first, failed journey is a wandering on the "via non vera," one that leads not toward the true source of light but down to where the "sun is silent," a journey not *in via* but *in invio*. We could, then, logically conclude that those things that prevent movement in a wrongful direction might ultimately be considered beneficial.

The terms "paura" and "tema" surely mean something *beyond* physical fear; the literal significance points to a spiritual sense, and, indeed, the verse, "l'animo mio ch'ancor fuggiva," reflects St. Augustine's definition that "timor animi fuga est" [fear is the flight of the spirit].[36]

We might remark, moreover, that when the *Commedia* first mentions fear (v. 6), it is in the mind and expressed in the voice of the poet-narrator who is, within the fiction of the poem, in a post-conversion state of grace, fresh from glimpsing the Deity face to face in Paradise. He describes his fear as renewed: "nel pensier rinova la paura." This re-experiencing by the narrator, for whom salvation has been foretold and by whom it has been foretasted, immediately signals to the reader that there is a maturer value of "paura" in the poem's first canto that acts at once as a foil and complement to the baser sort experienced by the wayfarer.[37]

The whole theological background underlying the poem includes, of course, many biblical and theological dicussions that treat of the benefits of fear. Judeo-Christian teaching traditionally extolled it in believers as, for example, in the litany of the whole first chapter of Ecclesiasticus [Sirach]. While base, worldly fear is a vice, the gift of fear, on the other hand, is the state of mind most apt for the reception of divine instruction and truth: it is the beginning of wisdom: "For he that is without fear, cannot be justified: for the wrath of his high spirits is his ruin."[38] Theology holds that fear comes first as a cowardly, servile dread of punishment and hell, but it leads eventually to filial fear and the love of God. Although the sinner does not at first actively desire the good, his dread and avoidance of evil set him on the path toward righteousness. St. Augustine explains:

> There are men who fear God lest they be cast into Hell, lest it happen that they burn with the devil in everlasting fire. This is the fear which introduces charity: but it comes that it may go out. For if you as yet fear God because of punishments, you do not yet desire good things but you are afraid of evil things. Yet in that you are afraid of evil things, you correct yourself and begin to desire the good.[39]

St. Gregory offers further elucidation as he describes the progress from necessary fear to fortitude:

> The more that we ourselves learn what we should have occasion to fear, the more we have infused in us from God by interior grace what we may call for love, so that both our contempt little by little may pass away into charity. . . . And thus, as it were, the foot of the mind first by fear we set below, and afterwards by charity we lift it to the heights of love, that from that by which a man is puffed up, he may be checked, so that by

fear, and from that which he dreads, he may be lifted up, that he may have boldness.[40]

In the opening lines of the *Commedia*, we learn that the valley had filled the wayfarer's heart with both dread and compunction, but by verse 19, his fear has been somewhat quieted. The abatement of fear initiates a series of obvious and traditional negative gestures: backward glances, a stop for rest, and then persistence on a wrongful path on one firm, yet infirm, foot. The leopard bars the way, but we note that that very hindrance turns, oddly, into a cause "for good hope." Dread returns again at the sight of the she-wolf. The *lupa* drives him to despair of the mountain heights he has chosen and pushes him back again "là dove il sol tace," to ruining down to the lower depths. At verse 61, the wayfarer seems to have failed his trials so completely that we are made to feel that all may be lost.

As discussed earlier in this chapter, the wayfarer's climb is in itself a sin of pride, most particularly in its aspect of self-assurance and self-sufficiency or "presumption," defined by St. Thomas as "an inordinate conversion to God": "As to hope whereby a man relies on his own power, there is presumption if he tends to good as though it were possible to him, whereas it surpasses his powers, according to Judith 6:15: 'Thou humblest them that presume of themselves.'"[41] Fear could have aided the wayfarer, for in Christian theology, as St. Gregory affirms, fear is corrective of pride.[42] St. Thomas explains: "Inducement of fear suffices to exclude presumption."[43] Ironically, then, fear marks a spiritual advance toward conversion from which the wayfarer retreats as he continues his climb up the mountain: instead of preparing himself for the assaults of temptation, he negligently rests, ignoring biblical injunctions and the warnings of such Christian fathers as St. Gregory:

> Truly conversion produces security: but security is the common parent of negligence. To keep security from generating negligence, it is written, "My son, in coming to the service of God, stand in justice and fear, and prepare thy soul for temptation" [Ecclus. 2:1]. For he says, not "for rest," but "for temptation," because our enemy is the more eager to conquer us as long as we are in this life, the more he discerns that we are rebelling against him.[44]

Although the wayfarer's most human fear of harm and death returns intermittently and waveringly in the prologue scene, it only returns in its full theological sense as servile fear, a cowering dread of hell, after the arrival of Virgil, the bearer of *gratia gratis data*, grace freely given,[45] and his proposal of the journey to salvation.

We must temper the currently held critical position, then, for we can only conclude that the abatement or denial of fear, not fear itself, is among the many errors preventing the wayfarer from taking the real path—the as-yet-unrevealed "altro viaggio"—to the truth; he has lost the salubrious dread that he had felt the night before the poem opens.

United in Christian doctrine with the theology of the gift of fear is that of *pietà* (*pietas*, "piety" or "pity"). Theological treatises, such as that which Dante recommends to Can Grande, St. Bernard's *De diligendo Deo* (*On Loving God* XIV, 38), make clear that fear and *pietas* are inseparable in the Christian conscience:

> *Piety mixed with fear does not destroy fear; it chastens it. . . .*
> When one reads: "Perfect charity drives out fear" [I John 4 : 18], this must be understood of the fear of punishment which is inseparable from servile fear; it is a figure of speech in which the cause is given for the effect. (p. 130)[46]

Most important, fear and piety form the first two consecutive steps in post-conversion progress to God enumerated as the seven Gifts of the Holy Spirit (according to the order given in St. Augustine's *De doctrina christiana* II, 7, 9–11, reversing that in Isaiah 11 : 2–3, these are fear and *pietas*, followed by knowledge, fortitude, the gift of counsel, purity of heart, and, lastly, wisdom). The use of these two terms in the prologue signifies that, before sliding back into sin, the wayfarer had made two strides in his progress toward the light of truth; in other words, he had gained fear and, before the poem began, had attained even to *pietas*, a state of bewailing his sin: "la notte che passai con tanta pieta."[47] However, while the valley of shadows had earlier inspired the wayfarer with fear and compunction, when we meet him at the start of the poem, he no longer feels these effects of spiritual discipline in their necessary and essential fullness.[48] The fact that not only his fear but also his *pietà* has not endured into the dawn symbolizes both his rejection of grace and of the true and dangerous extent of his backsliding.

First Intimations of Virgil's Fallibility

Virgil, although sent as a messenger of divine grace, will often prove less than perfect in his comprehension of Christian theology,[49] and perhaps an early example of this fallibility comes in regard to fear: he cannot comprehend its benefit. Attending only to the physical, human and worldly aspects, he interprets the wayfarer's misgivings about descending into hell in *Inferno* II as "viltà" and makes every effort to free him from his terror ("tema," *Inferno* II, 51):

> "Qui si conviene lasciare ogne sospetto;
> ogne viltà convien che qui sia morta."

Earlier, as Virgil recounts Beatrice's descent and her charge to him, he expresses puzzlement at her lack of fear of hell. As one of the blessed, she is justly untouched by any dread of the pains of damnation; and although fearfully hastening in pious intercession for the living, she is untouched by pity for the sufferings of those in perdition: "la vostra miseria non mi tange" (v. 92). Without a Christian awareness of beatitude, however, Virgil can only mistake her transcendent unconcern for the underworld as some form of philosophical intrepidity; just as he interprets her, in Boethian terms, as Lady Philosophy (the "donna di virtù, sola per cui / l'umana spezie eccede ogne contento / di quel ciel c'ha minor li cerchi sui" *Inferno* II, 76–78),[50] likewise, he can only construe her blessed state in accordance with his own Roman Stoicism.

The *Commedia* juxtaposes the pagan and Christian evaluation of fear with surprising results. That the wayfarer now fears hell and its punishments, faced as he is with the imminent prospect of its horrors, is theologically, as well as psychologically, reasonable and orthodox. But this new-found dread must be overcome for the journey to begin. Solution is reached in paradox: Virgil's strict martial and pagan understanding of worldly fear as merely the opposite of fortitude (and though Virgil may not know it, such servile fear in Christianity is also so defined) must now serve the divine command to lead the wayfarer's extraordinary visit to the realms of the dead; however, the wayfarer is convinced not by Virgil's censure but by the pity of Beatrice and the courtesy and speech through which Virgil relays her divine message (*Inferno* II, 133–138). For some mysterious reason, the journey requires the special aid of this guide rebellious to monotheism. There is use both for his rhetoric and his ignorance.

"Il piè fermo"

Verse 30, "sì che il piè fermo sempre era'l più basso," remained a crux for centuries because critics and commentators failed to consider the line in the context of the traditional metaphoric use of the word foot ("piè," "piedi," or "pes, pedes") in philosophy and patristics.[51] The *Commedia's* polysemousness here involves three major strains of theological metaphor: first, the image of the "feet of the soul," that is, the "foot" of earthly desire and the "foot" of the intellect; second, the image of the "wounding of nature," the wound of original sin seen as the bite of the serpent in the lower, left foot of the soul, which hinders man's progress toward the good; and third, the metaphorical punishment upon the presumptuous taken from the Psalter, the "foot of pride" sent to those who trust too much in themselves rather than in the Lord.

Among the earliest and most influential Christian instances of the metaphor of the "feet of the soul" was St. Augustine's use of it in his exegesis on Psalm 9, verse 16:

> *The foot typifies the soul's affection*, which when depraved is termed cupidity or lust, but when upright, love or charity. . . . Cupidity is followed by an enjoyment which brings ruin, love by one which brings profit. Hence cupidity is called a root, the root being like the foot to a tree.[52]

Approximately seven hundred years later, and some one hundred years before Dante's birth, Richard of St. Victor described the inner state of post-lapsarian man in similar fashion in his homonymous treatise, *De statu interioris hominis post lapsum*, based upon the verse from Isaiah 1:5–6: "omne caput languidum, omne cor merens, a planta pedis usque ad verticem non est in eo sanitas" [The whole head is sick, and the whole heart is sad. From the sole of the foot unto the top of the head, there is no soundness therein]. Richard identified the head as free will, the heart as counsel, and the foot, since it was the lowest member, as the desires of the flesh: "Pes in imo jacet, et carnale desiderium per appetitum infimus inheret" [The foot lies below, and carnal desire, through its appetite, keeps to the lowest place].[53] Later, in chapter 5 of his work "De infirmitate carnalis desiderii,"[54] Richard uses vocabulary of the same tradition from which Dante was to draw: note especially Richard's Latin pun on "infirmus" [infirm] and "infimus-inferus" [lower], so similar to Dante's vocabulary ("fermo," "più basso," and "basso loco"):

> But, just as nothing is more useful than prudent counsel, so nothing is lower [*nichil inferius*], nothing is more infirm [*nichil infirmius*] than carnal desire, for this reason, that, by virtue of its similarity to the foot, it holds the lowest place [*infimum*

locum] and, through its delight in the fleshly, keeps to earthly things.[55]

Thus, we can recognize the validity of the assertion of Dante's son, Pietro Alighieri (one also made by Benvenuto, the Anonimo Fiorentino, and F. Villani) that the "firm foot" ("piè fermo," "pes firmus") of verse 30 signifies the "lower" foot ("infimior") of the soul, and thus, the "affectus." Citing the Bible, and especially St. Augustine's exegesis on Psalm 9, Pietro goes on to say that the "bent" foot signifies "cupiditas" as man chooses the lesser good; since, in his view, the two feet of the soul go in different directions, the upper foot to the good, the lower foot to earthly things, the wayfarer, therefore, must be proceeding with a *limping* gait towards the summit: "et sicut claudus ibat."[56]

Later, Benvenuto da Imola, in his *Commentarium* (1373–1380, p. 33), saw both a literal and a moral meaning in the line: Dante describes his manner of climbing. At the same time, the commentator continues: "moraliter loquendo, pes inferior erat amor, qui trahebat ipsum ad inferiora terrena . . . per pedes figurantur affectiones" [morally speaking, the lower foot was love, which was dragging him towards lower, earthly things; desires are figured by the feet], but he mentions nothing specifically about limping.

Pietro's words "et sicut claudus ibat" seem to have gone unheeded until 1959, when, in a magisterial article (rprt. 1986, pp. 29–54), John Freccero, marshalling a number of classical and patristic texts, demonstrated that Dante was referring specifically to his left foot, the "firm" or more staid foot, the foot that indeed represented the affective part of the soul, while the right foot, traditionally considered swifter and stronger (*fortior*), symbolized the intellect.

Freccero also convincingly showed the link between the "feet of the soul" and the second major group of metaphors relating to the results of the Fall. The "piè fermo" was that part of the soul wounded by concupiscence through original sin; man limps because, metaphorically, he bears in his left heel the "vulneratio naturae," the wound inflicted by the serpent upon man in Eden that changed human nature from that of a perfectly ordered creature to one whose intellect could not rule his senses and appetites.

A third traditional metaphoric basis for verse 30 comes from Psalm 35:12: "Let not the foot of pride come to me." On this St. Augustine gave, perhaps, the most eloquent exegesis and one that was to supply a nexus of metaphors concerning the foot to be repeated throughout the Middle Ages. He included several themes in his gloss on *superbia* as the beginning of all sin, the fall of Satan from his angelic state to the depths (based on the song from Isaiah 14:12–15 cited earlier in this chapter), original sin and the wound of nature, the "foot" of the passions, and the fall of the proud to the depths. Pride, he said, is especially dangerous to those who have earlier experienced conversion, lest they glory in their own excellence, lapse and fall to the nether regions. His formulation is worth citing at length:

> *"Let not the foot of pride come to me."* . . . When anyone begins to be very plenteously refreshed from this wellspring, he must beware of growing proud. From this danger Adam, the first man, was not immune; on the contrary the foot of pride came to him, and the hand of the sinner, in other words, the proud hand of the devil, moved him. For even as he who seduced him said of himself: 'I will set my throne towards the north' [Isaiah 15:13], so, likewise, he persuaded Adam, saying: 'Taste, and you shall be as gods' [Genesis 3:5]. Through pride, then, we have fallen so as to arrive at this perishable state of mortality. And since it was pride that had wounded us, it is humility that heals us. God came in humility, to heal man of pride's grievous wound. . . . But why so terrified of pride? It seems as if the response [v. 13], 'There all the workers of iniquity are fallen,' were given to show that they have come to that deep [abyssum] of which it has been said: 'Thy judgments are a great deep'; they have sunk to that abyss to which haughty sinners are fallen. 'Are fallen': what first caused their fall? The foot of pride. Listen; note the 'foot of pride': 'When they knew God, they have not glorified Him as God.' The foot of pride, then, touched them, and thereupon they sank to the abyss [in profundum]. . . . Why has he called it the foot? Because pride has led man to forsake and depart from God. His foot denotes his passions. . . . The serpent is watching when the foot of pride approaches you, so that when you falter he may throw you headlong. But do you keep an eye on his head: 'pride is the beginning of all sin.' 'There the workers of iniquity are fallen: they are cast out and could not stand.' First of all, he who did not stand firm in the truth, and afterwards, through his agency, those whom God banished from Paradise.[57]

St. Bernard, too, whom Dante chooses as the wayfarer's ultimate guide in the *Commedia*, had, historically, contributed a major treatise on the theme of ascent to the truth with his *De gradibus superbiae et humilitatis*, or *The Steps of Pride and Humility*. In a vein similar to that of Augustine, Bernard depicted himself also as a *viator* with shortcomings identical to those Augustine had warned of. Bernard's journey toward the light, indeed, bears many further points of similarity with that begun in *Inferno* I: it occurs in an almost identical setting, at the same time of year, Eastertide; as wayfarer he delays, takes rest, and suffers from a sluggish limp. In chapter 9 he prays for the success of his conversion by the special aid of grace freely given; most important, he prays lest the "foot of pride" prevent him from standing in the truth (just as St. Augustine had warned lest the foot of pride come to the convert as it came to Adam and Eve):

> You have numbered my steps, O Lord, but I am a slow climber, a weary traveller, and I need a resting place. Woe is me if the darkness should overtake me, or if my flight should be in winter or on the Sabbath, seeing that now, in an acceptable time, on the day of salvation, I can hardly grope my way to the light. Why am I so slow? O, if any is to me a son, a brother in the Lord, a comrade, one who shares my journey, let him pray for me! Let him pray the Almighty that he may strengthen the weary foot and *not let the foot of pride come nigh to me*. The weary foot is a poor help in climbing to the truth, but the other cannot even stand on the place it has gained: "They are cast out, they cannot stand." This is said about any of the proud. (Conway trans. pp. 53–54; my italics) [58]

Then, echoing the "felix culpa" theme, Bernard desires not to rejoice in his own progress but to humble himself in his own infirmity, the mark of Adam's sin, for through it is God's grace necessitated:

> How glad I too should be, Lord Jesus, to glory, if I could, in my infirmity, in the shrinking of my sinew, that your virtue, your humility, might be made perfect in me. Your grace is sufficient for me when my own virtue fails. With the foot of grace firmly planted on the ladder of humility, *painfully dragging the foot of my own weakness behind me*, I should safely mount upward, until, holding fast to the truth, I attained the broad plain of charity. There I shall sing my song of thanksgiving: "Thou hast set my feet in a spacious place" [Statuisti in loco spatioso pedes meos]. Thus I warily enter on the narrow way, step by

step safely ascend the steep ladder, and by a kind of miracle climb to the truth, behind the time, perhaps, and *limping*, but still with confidence [*ad veritatem licet pigrius tamen firmius claudicando acceditur*]. (Conway trans., pp. 54–55)[59]

St. Bernard's special interest in the image of Satan's proud ascent as an assumption of autonomy leading to his fall and that of all mankind seems, like St. Augustine's, particularly relevant to our discussion. His *Sermo super Cantica Canticorum* 85:5 might stand as a corrective to the opinion of those critics and commentators who have cited Psalm 24:3 [Douay 23:3], "Who shall ascend into the mountain of the Lord?" as the basis of their unalloyed, positive interpretation of the wayfarer's progress. The idea of climbing or mounting up, like nearly any concept in figurative theological language, has a dual significance and typifies the medieval pleasure in paradox. To mount in pride is to fall to perdition; to descend in humility is to rise to God. St. Bernard emphatically explains that the metaphorical climb of the Lord's mountain is only for the righteous who humbly mount with grace as guide; the foot of pride he identifies as the punishment of self-sufficiency:

'Who shall ascend into the hill of the Lord?' Whosoever shall take upon him to ascend to the top of that mountain, that is to say, to attain the perfection of virtue, must consider how arduous is that ascent, and how easy to fall without the assistance of the Word. . . . How can all things fail to be possible to a man who depends in his endeavors upon Him who can do all things? . . . Thus it is that the soul, *if it does not presume upon its own powers, but is strengthened by the Word, will be able so to rule over itself that no unrighteousness shall have dominion over it. . . . Would you have no fear of violence from without? Then let not the foot of pride find place within you*; so the hand of the violent shall not cast you down. '*There are the workers of iniquity fallen*' (Psalm 35:13). It *was thus that the devil and his angels fell.* They were impelled to evil by no force from without; nevertheless, they were not able to stand, but were driven forth from Heaven. He did not stand fast in the truth, who did not rely upon the Word, but trusted in his own strength [Bernard refers to Lucifer's song from Isaiah]. . . . *Therefore let the soul that stands, if it does not desire to fall, not trust in its own strength, but lean upon the Word. The Word Himself warns us: 'Without me ye can do nothing'* (John 15:5). That is most truly the case; without the Word we can nei-

ther stand firm in the good to which we have attained, nor rise
up towards any fresh good. (my italics)[60]

The sermon helps us comprehend how widespread were the concepts
and particularly how commonplace was the idea of a climb as a sin of
presumption.[61] Dante's combination of the images of a wearied pilgrim
struggling for conversion yet held back by one foot echoes a metaphor
of the struggle for virtue central in Christian literature. The poet has the
wayfarer in *Inferno* I reflect all the circumstances found in tradition: the
wayfarer cannot mount up with his "firm foot" and ill holds his ground.
Like the proud he is cast down, *nec potuit stare*, nor can he stand (Psalm
35:13). He is *homo claudus* bearing the wound of nature. Like all men he
has a "pes piger," an infirm foot inflicted upon Adam and his progeny
by an envious Satan.

There is, however, something in addition to his general plight and
weakness as "everyman": the wayfarer suffers not only from the concupiscence of his lower soul and the original wound of pride common
to all mankind, but he suffers also from the sin of his own commission
of which his disordinate seeking of the heights is, in fact, the proof: the
personal sin of his own pride expressed in ambition, presumption, and
curiositas. As St. Augustine asks rhetorically, "Quid est autem superbia
nisi perversae celsitudinis appetitus?" [Moreover, what is pride but a
craving for perverse elevation?] (*DCD* XIV: 13).[63] In the metaphors of
the Church, the "foot of pride" has come to the wayfarer and he falls.

* * *

A more complete understanding of the symbolic and allegorical significances that the term "piè" held for Dante develops as we read the rest of
the poem and consider the prologue scene in the context of the whole.[64]
The term "foot" appears in the text in one or another of its forms each
time his wayfarer meets a guide or a figure representing the descent of
grace or the imparting of grace. The word *piede* becomes charged with
ever more meaning as the poem progresses; its symbolic implications
punctuate and measure the journey.

When, in *Purgatorio* XXX, after the wayfarer has been purged, the
"P's" representing "peccati" removed from his forehead and the rational
governance of his own soul restored through personal justice,[64] he aptly
receives Beatrice's scolding standing on his two feet in the Earthly Paradise where Adam lost original justice, the right order of the soul, and
burdened man with the "wound of nature." The allusion to the feet reflects the pilgrim's progress. At verse 84 the poet notes that the angels
are singing Psalm 30 (Vulgate) but cease at the words "pedes meos."

> . . . e li angeli cantaro
> di sùbito "*In te, Domine, speravi*";
> ma oltre "*pedes meos*" non passaro.   (vv. 82–84)

The two fragments of the psalm quoted evoke the missing part, "*in loco spatioso* statuisti pedes meos" [Thou hast set my feet *in a spacious place*].[65] The psalm might also provide the reader with a numerological clue: foot imagery (*il piè fermo*) first occurs at verse 30 of *Inferno* I, and the consonance of canto line and psalm number in the Vulgate may well point up a consonance of meaning. Indeed, St. Augustine in his exegesis of the psalm's verse had interpreted the "spacious place" as the place of justice--the right order of the soul—and had contrasted the two feet of the just with the limping foot of the unredeemed. "What is the meaning, then of 'Thou hast set my feet in a spacious place'? In plain speech, thou hast made the works of justice which once I found difficult easy for me."[66]

The Bishop of Hippo begins his second discourse on Psalm 30 according to its title as a song of rapture and ecstasy; quoting St. Paul in II Corinthians 5:13–14, he addresses the reader in the guise of a humble guide leading the lame:

> How could you, so faltering of foot, follow us to those more sublime and secret regions, did not the charity of Christ . . . "taking the form of a servant" again compel us to realize that we ourselves are servants?[67]

St. Augustine goes on to explain the psalm itself as an affirmation of halting man's dependence upon God's grace to enable him to descend to humility so that he might by charity rise to justice and bliss. Augustine considered lameness the opposite of justice and allied the two concepts in his imagery of conversion, just, as we recall, St. Bernard was to do some seven hundred years later in chapter 9 of the *De gradibus*. Dante had ample basis for conjoining the concepts in his poem and ample reason for assuming that his readers' familiarity with the exegesis on the psalm would support his meaning.

In *Purgatorio* XXI, 7–11, when Statius appears as a "semi-guide" to accompany the wayfarer beyond Virgil's tutelage through the end of Purgatory, the pilgrim's feet again draw our attention:

> Ed ecco . . .
> ci apparve un'ombra, e dietro noi venìa,
> dal *piè* guardando la turba che giace. . . .

Another locus in *Inferno* I follows the pattern in a more complicated fashion. Virgil, at his first appearance in the poem, gives his own "vita Virgilii,"[68] yet, as if in a brusk display of modesty, he suddenly breaks off to question the wayfarer:

> "Poeta fui, e cantai di quel giusto
> figliuol d'Anchise che venne di Troia,
> Poi che'l superbo Ilïón fu combusto.
> Ma tu perchè ritorni a tanta noia?
> perché non sali il dilettoso monte
> ch'è principio e cagion di tutta gioia?"   (vv. 73–78)

The disjuncture between verses 75 and 76 leads us to believe, if only for a fleeting moment, that "tanta noia," rhyming with "Troia," refers to the *wayfarer's* wrongful desire to remain amidst a destruction caused by pride in the suffering of a razed city. The effect is strengthened by our recollection of Aeneas's long confession to Dido in the *Aeneid* that he himself had been tempted to remain behind in Troy to die a hero's death in battle. The reader begins to sense that the joining of the pagan protagonist with the wayfarer is no accident, but, at first reading, dismisses it as his own personal confusion or *lapsus* in understanding and reverts to the belief that Virgil's real meaning is clear as the sage goes on to refer to the climbing of a "mountain of delight" (v. 77).[69]

The strategy of ambiguity continues, however, for the text does not give Aeneas's name, but presents him only in a Virgilian circumlocution, "figliuol d'Anchise." Why does the poem emphasize Anchises and give retrograde attention to "proud Troy" and not to Aeneas's quest for Italy?[70] Wrong direction, lameness, and pride are again thematic motifs lying just below the surface. Not only was Aeneas's temptation wrong but Anchises was lame, crippled for having pridefully boasted that his son had been born of Venus. The old man's infirmity had forced Aeneas to bear him on his shoulders from the flames of proud Ilium. Anchises, bearing a wound of pride, cannot escape without the aid of his son any more than the wayfarer, hampered by the foot of pride, can make progress until Virgil, introducing himself with these images, comes through a chain of grace to aid him on his journey.

Lastly, in *Paradiso* XXXII, 4–6, when the final guide, St. Bernard, begins to tutor the pilgrim, he points to Eve sitting at the feet of the Blessed Virgin. His speech repeats a theme that the historical Bernard had treated so often in his works—the *vulneratio* of the Fall:

La piaga che Maria richiuse e unse,
    quella ch'è tanto bella da' suoi piedi
    è colei che l'aperse e che la punse.

Here Dante skillfully exploits and renews the Ave-Eva topos: fittingly, Eve, cause of the Fall, sits humbly at Mary's feet; for through her came man's foot of pride, as through the Virgin came its cure. Significantly, this marks the last use of the term "piè"/"piedi" in the *Commedia*; the image of the "foot" has come full circle: redeemed from a *piè fermo* of pride, it becomes, in the feet of the Blessed Virgin, an icon of humility.

The pattern is fulfilled. At the appearance of all the guides party to this descent of grace, the poet in some way refers to the foot, lameness and pride. As the guides signify the working of divine grace, so the foot signifies the helplessness of man left to himself. The symbolism is consistent and underlines the necessity of these guides to aid the pilgrim; it also throws into sharp relief the absence of dependence upon such divinely sent aid in the early part of the prologue scene.

The final use of the term *piedi* invites a contemplation of that "piè fermo" in *Inferno* I where the journey begins. The wayfarer, standing with his weight on his "firm" foot, cannot there hold his ground; like the proud sinner that St. Bernard described, he cannot stand for long, leaning with his weight on only one foot:

> "Let not the foot of pride come to me" (Psalm 35:12). For pride has only one foot, the love of its own excellence. And so the proud cannot stand for long, like one who leans on only one foot. For who can stand on that foot, on which have fallen those who worked iniquity as an Angel in heaven, and a man in paradise?[71]

In the prologue there on the *via non vera*, where progress toward God was not possible, we note that the word was singular: "piè fermo." In *Purgatorio* XXX, 84, on the path of justice it is plural, *pedes meos*. Dante's use of the singular and plural reflects the same theological pattern used by St. Bernard: pride has one foot; humility has two:

> Therefore that you may stand firm [*secure*], stand in humility; *stand not on the one foot of pride, but on the feet of humility*, that your footsteps be not shaken. *For humility has two feet*, the consideration of Divine Power, and of its own weakness. O beautiful feet and firm [*et firmi*], neither wrapped in the darkness of

ignorance, nor stained with the slippery soil of luxury! Do *you,* then, *who are placed on high, refrain from high thoughts, but fear;* and humble yourself under the powerful Hand of Him, who will bow down in His strength the necks of the proud and lofty. (my italics) [72]

The tradition absorbed from St. Bernard acts as a theological and structural matrix: the term *piè* is singular until the cure of concupiscence and ignorance is attained in the place of humility and justice; thereafter the term is plural: *Inferno* I, *piè*; Statius, *piè*; Beatrice, *pedes*; St. Bernard of the poem, *piedi.*

CHAPTER III

Three Beasts

Historical Interpretations

The wayfarer is, on all counts, unequal to his philosophical climb, but it is the encounter with the three beasts that ultimately terrifies him, drives him back repeatedly and, at last, sends him hurtling down to where the sun is silent.

The "tre fiere" have singly and collectively occasioned considerable critical speculation. We can divide the numerous identifications roughly into four basic groupings: the first holds that the creatures represent the major lusts, desires, or temptations of all men as identified in I John 2: 16–17; the second that they symbolize corrupt and corrupting political entities of the society and times in which Dante lived; the third that they represent the sins most besetting the Florence of the time, pride, envy and lust, according to the the censures of Brunetto Latini and Ciacco in *Inferno* VI, 74, and XV, 68; and the fourth that they represent internal besetting sins common to the wayfarer and all men, sins related to the dispositions or gradations of man's fall into sin, chiastically ordered to the three divisions of hell.

The first and earliest interpretation is based on the three sins listed in the First Epistle of St. John 2:16–17: "For all that is in the world is the concupiscence of the flesh and the concupiscence of the eyes and the pride of life, which is not of the Father but is of the world." For most early commentators the beasts represented, in order of appearance, the vices of lust, pride, and avarice. Boccaccio's formulation has often been cited to encapsulate the tradition:

> Le quali, quantunque a molti e diversi vizi adattare si potes-
> sono, nondimeno qui, secondo la sentenzia di tutti, par che si

debbano intendere per questi, cioè per la lonza il vizio della
lussuria e per lo leone il vizio della superbia e per la lupa il vizio
dell'avarizia.   (*Esposizioni*, p. 73)

Almost all the earliest commentators[1] held to this view except the
maverick Jacopo della Lana, who saw the *lupa* as avarice, the *leone* as
pride, and the *lonza* as *vanagloria* (pp. 109–110), a somewhat tauto-
logical interpretation since, theologically, *vanagloria* was considered a
form of pride, and often the two terms of pride and vainglory were used
interchangeably.[2] Such commentators and critics as G. M. Cornoldi
(com 1887), G. Busnelli (1909, esp. p. 31), T. Casini (1913, p. 23), F. Torraca
(com 1905), G. Mazzoni (*Lect. romana*, 1918), Porena (com 1951, pp. 16–
17), N. Sapegno (com 1955; rprt. 1957), F. Mazzoni (com 1967, p. 100),
R. Giglio (1973, p. 140), A. Mandelbaum (com 1980, vol. 1, p. 323), and
G. Holmes (1980, p. 49) have clung to Boccaccio's interpretation.

Although the consensus of the early commentators is impressive
and their agreement has been used as a strong argument for the validity of their point of view, other critics have rightly pointed out that
the consistency in their interpretation does not derive from a number
of independent views but that it represents, rather, a case of routine
borrowing following the medieval and early Renaissance tradition of
encyclopedism.[3]

In the second category of interpretation are those critics who have
held that the three beasts have an external, political significance allied,
or unallied, to spiritual meanings internal to the wayfarer. The *lonza,
leone*, and *lupa* represented political bodies destructive of justice in contemporary Europe, and, thus, forces destructive of Dante's own political and social career responsible for driving him into perpetual exile.

As the drive that culminated in the Risorgimento gathered strength
in the early nineteenth century, criticism of the *Commedia* reflected the
intellectual climate by giving political identifications to the beasts and
associating specific states and governments with each. For Giovanni
Marchetti, in 1819, Gabriele Rossetti (com 1826–1827), Foscolo (*Discorso*
[com 1842–1843], vol. 1, pp. 385–395), C. Balbo (com 1853, pp. 275,
403–405) and N. Tommaseo (com 1837), the *lonza*, with its black and
white spots, was factionalized Florence; the lion, the royal house of
France; and the wolf, the Roman Curia.[4]

Allied to this interpretation is the third grouping, those commentators and critics such as P. Fraticelli (com 1852), G. Poletto (1892, vol. 8,
p. 75), F. Cipolla (1895), Buscaino Campo (1894), G. Galvani (1894),
D'Ovidio (1901, pp. 318–325), I. Sanesi (1902, esp. pp. 70–71), who, in

the wake of the Renaissance commentary of Castelvetro (com ca. 1570) saw the *lonza* as symbolic of envy; they urged that the situation of *Inferno* I be interpreted as narrowly reflecting Dante's experiences in Florence at the fictional date of the *Commedia*. Citing Ciacco's labeling of Florence as a city "piena / d'invidia sì che già trabocca il sacco" (*Inferno* VI, 49–50), they viewed the beasts as "le tre faville che hanno i cuori accesi" (*Inferno* VI, 75), that is, in the order in which they appear, envy, pride and avarice. To corroborate their opinion they pointed also to Brunetto Latini's words in *Inferno* XV, 68, where the notary labels the Florentine people "avara, invidiosa e superba."

While F. Flamini went too far (1904) in totally rejecting the political interpretation, seeing the *tre fiere* as only the internal "abiti viziosi" of Dante (he commented wryly, "È concetto tutto moderno quello del così detto 'ambiente' sugli uomini," p. 118), later in the twentieth century, the political and historical interpretation received its own stricter modification. Bruno Nardi, the major exponent of a narrowly political interpretation of the beasts, denied the three beasts any interior, moral value and saw them not as the personal vices of the wayfarer as an individual (these he saw represented by the *selva oscura*), but as the vices of historical persons and institutions surrounding Dante in the factional strife of Florence and in the machinations of the papacy. The *lonza* signified the lusts of the world against which Dante had girded himself; the lion symbolized the violent pride with which Florentine parties struggled against each other; the wolf was avarice, personified historically by Boniface VIII.[5]

Nardi was not alone, of course, in seeing the necessity of a political interpretation; most scholars, however, both before and after him,[6] in spite of considerable differences in their basic interpretations, have generally, and less arbitrarily, viewed the political significances as an adjunct to a moral, internal meaning.

Indeed, the "*querelle*" between an exclusive interior, moral and spiritual meaning and another purely exterior and political interpretation begins with a false premise. In Chalcidius's translation of Plato's *Timaeus*,[7] Dante read that human morality was based upon cosmic order, and from St. Thomas's *Commentary* on Aristotle's *Nicomachean Ethics* V, 11, 2; 1138b (lecture XVII, 1106), he adopted the axiom that the internal relation between the parts of a man (that is, between his rational and lower soul) was metaphorically identical with that between ruler and subject.[8]

The concept of man as microcosm had again returned to favor in theology some one hundred years before Dante, especially among the

Victorines, with whose writings he was especially familiar. That man was *in minore mundo*, a miniature world in himself, was an idea that had been preserved from antiquity. It had first passed into Pythagoreanism and then, through Philo's *De opificio mundi*, found its way into such patristic treatises as St. Ambrose's *Hexaemeron*, St. Augustine's *Exposition on the Epistle to the Romans*, and St. Gregory the Great's *Homilies on the Gospel.*[9]

The term "microcosm" itself had originated, in all likelihood, with Isidore of Seville (570–638), spreading via Scotus Erigenus (ca. 810–ca. 877) to such twelfth-century works as Bernardus Silvestris's *De mundi universitate libri duo sive megacosmus et microcosmus*, cited by Boccaccio in his *Esposizioni* II, ii (p. 134).[10]

In Richard and Geoffrey of St. Victor, the concept meant that the interior order of the soul reflected the order of the universe.[11] Especially for Richard in the *De statu interioris hominis post lapsum*, the converse was equally true: the disorder of man was reflected also in the universe. Since there was a strict correlation of cause and effect between what occurred inside man and what occurred about him, man was morally responsible for the society in which he lived. Just as nations confronted nations, families fought with families and man struggled with other men, so, within man, vices struggled with virtues in the soul.[12] As a consequence of the Fall, the interior disorder of man was the cause of world disorder. Before sin, all creation had obeyed man as he, in turn, had obeyed God; man's rebellion against God caused the revolt of the world against man. The comparison of microcosm and macrocosm was, therefore, more than an analogy: it was moral reality.

The polarities of "external" versus "internal," "political" versus "spiritual," thus simply did not exist for Dante in the realm of social morality; politics was a subdivision of ethics. Justice meant right order whether in the soul or in the state. As he had written in *Monarchia* III, 4: "Devices such as governments are remedies for the infirmity of sin" (LLA trans., p. 59). Regarding the relation of justice to concupiscence or *cupiditas*, he could follow the Bible, Aristotle, and St. Augustine in seeing the sin both as the "root of all evil" and as "the extreme opposite of justice" (*Monarchia* I, 11). The cause of Italy's woes, along with those of all the empire, lay in grasping rulers incapable of curing or controlling the base passions of mankind. There is, consequently, no question of an either/or political identification of the beasts.

Thus, in whatever manner we otherwise interpret the trio of *Inferno* I, we may understand that they cannot be seen to involve only the soul of the individual, be it that of Dante Alighieri or "whichever man," nor can they be viewed as exclusively signifying exterior politics; rather, they inextricably involve both at the same time. The beasts do not represent specific political entities in themselves but forces preying on the dispositions to corruption within bodies politic, just as they prey upon dispositions to sin within the individual.

The fourth and most influential group of critics attempted to square the interpretation of the beasts with the penal system of Dante's *Inferno*. Many nineteenth- and twentieth-century critics, beginning with Vincenzo Barelli in 1864, and, more influentially, with Giacinto Casella in 1865 (1884, pp. 384–385),[13] identified the *lonza, leone*, and *lupa* with the "tre disposizioni che il ciel non vuole"; that is, the beasts corresponded, roughly, with the "Aristotelian" categories outlined by Virgil (*Inferno* XI, 81): "malizia," "forza" or "matta bestialitade," and "incontinenza," or fraud, violence, and incontinence. They thus heralded and signified the three major areas of hell itself.

This view, followed by I. Del Lungo (1901, p. 14; 1925, pp. 18–19) and by C. Grabher (com 1934–1936, p. 6), received, and continues to receive, wide acceptance. It did not, however, go without amendment: in 1898, G. Pascoli (1898, p. 144; 1912, p. 114), followed by L. M. Capelli (1898, pp. 353–375), L. Pietrobono (1925; rprt. 1959), Charles Williams (1943; rprt. 1961, pp. 109–110), and Dorothy Sayers (com 1949, vol. 1, p. 75), reversed the roles of the *lonza* and *lupa*, seeing the "beast with the gay skin" rather as incontinence and the wolf as fraud; since they considered fraud to be the most serious, they thus left this last sin as the obstacle that eventually impedes the wayfarer and brings about his fall to the depths.[14] As other critics have noted, however, this reversal in the identification of the first and last of the beasts is nowhere supported by Dante's text.[15]

Casella's original thesis, that the *lonza* was fraud, the *leone* violence (*matta bestialitade*), and the *lupa* incontinence, has had the largest critical following among British and American scholars and translators. Among others, J. S. Carroll (1903, pp. 15–17), Helen Flanders Dunbar (1929, p. 164), Charles Hall Grandgent (com 1909–1913; rprt. 1933, p. 11),[16] John Ciardi (com 1954), and M. Musa (com 1971–1984, vol. 1, pp. 6–7) saw the beasts as adumbrating the three major divisions of hell and, thus, as a foreshadowing of the journey itself. In Italy the thesis found a firm and eloquent defender in Francesco Flamini (1904), who expressed his view as follows:

A nostro avviso, non si tratta già di tre categorie di peccati; ché già s'è notato quanto sforzo occorra a trovare l'immagine di più e diversi vizi in un simbolo solo: e neppure si tratta di peccati veri e proprî (nel senso che suole communemente attribuirsi a questa parola); *bensì di disposizioni al peccare*, di mali abiti generici, donde i vizî speciali scaturiscono. Ogni abito si crea, com'è noto, *ex multiplicatis actibus*, ed alla sua volta è principio e cagione di nuovi atti. (pp. 127–128)

Two years later in 1906, the argument received another clear and persuasive—yet critically neglected—defense from Gregorio Lajolo:

> . . . si capisce perchè nell'inferno dantesco viene colpita l'umanità colpevole, secondo un triplice ordine di peccatori uno degli *incontinenti*, uno dei *maliziosi violenti*, ed uno dei *maliziosi frodolenti*; ed evidentemente, quando Minosse "giudica e manda," si basa non sulla natura del peccato, ma sulla colpa, cioè "esamina le colpe," i diversi gradi di colpevolezza; e manda *l'avaro*, o meglio chi è cupido di possedere fra gli *incontinenti* per il mal uso che ha fatto del denaro; e lo manda fra i *violenti* contro natura, se la cupidigia lo ha spinto agli eccessi dell'usura. (p. 46)

The theory thus gained a logical corollary: since the distribution of punishment in the *Inferno* was apparently not made according to the principle of sin, defined by St. Thomas as both "blame" and "punishment," "colpa" and "pena," but solely according to the various gradations of the first, "colpa" (that is, "blame, guilt, sinfulness, or human responsibility"[17]), the three beasts, she-wolf, lion, and leopard represented the three major areas of hell insofar as they signified man's descent into evil, not of kind but degree: incontinence, violence, and fraud.

Although Dante's plan for the punishments of hell has often been described as roughly Aristotelian, it is actually quite eclectic; and its relationship to Aristotle is problematic: sinners such as the heresiarchs, along with other categories such as the neutrals, the unbaptized, and the proud giants, are simply impossible to fit into a strictly Aristotelian scheme.[18] Most significantly, Aristotle makes no decision whether fraud is more serious than violence; and St. Thomas, as Dante seems to have been aware, finds violence more serious than fraud in *ST* II–II, qu. 116, art. 2, ad. 1,[19] but reverses himself when tracing the interrelation of sins in the "daughters of avarice" tradition (*ST* II–II, qu. 118, art. 8) that we outline below. For the ordering of his two lower divisions, Dante preferred to follow Cicero's *De Officiis* I, xiii, 41, where the orator lists the two ways of sinning against justice, "either by fraud or by force." As Cicero continued, "Both are most alien to man, but fraud is more hateful."[20] But Dante, while accepting the greater odiousness of fraud, had suffered the deceit of the papacy and of his fellow Florentines; he knew from bitter experience that fraud was hardly alien to man: it derived from the misuse of human reason, and was "dell'uom proprio male" (*Inferno* XI, 25).

Critics have seen that the "bestie illustri" clearly bear some correspondence to the three parts of the soul left wounded after the Fall: the intellect and will suffering the wound of ignorance; the concupiscible soul, the wound of concupiscence (or cupidity); and the irascible soul, the wound of impotence (that is, the defect of the control of power, fortitude, the cause of violence).[21] Casella and Flamini's scheme of viewing the beasts as associated in some way with the three "disposizioni" is still persuasive, but I disagree that the beasts, as *impedimenta* (cf. *Inferno* II, 62 "impedito"; 95 "impedimento"), are themselves simply "la triplice infermità"[22] within the soul, since that infirmity is symbolized by the wayfarer's "firm" foot. If we can rely on the correspondence between the literal and symbolic-allegorical senses and if we keep in mind that the beasts challenge the wayfarer from without, it would appear most logical to view the beasts as representing external *temptations* (viewed both as distractions of the *saeculum* as well as trials sent by God through Satan) that can affect the internal dealings of the state just as they affect the interior of man. In the literal sense, the beasts come from the *selva* or the *colle* in the prologue scene and the *lupa* claims a specifically Satanic origin in Virgil's prophecy of the *veltro*. Thus, a consistent reading would hold that the beasts are symbolic of external lures or threats appealing to or preying upon internal human weaknesses.

Although this pattern—incontinence, violence and fraudulence—which fits more easily into the system of hell and other related imagery, may at first seem to contradict the scheme proposed by the early commentators, it does not, in fact, do so. It is obvious that avarice, like lust and pride, can be indulged in through incontinence, through violence, or even through fraudulence. We recall from the First Epistle of John 2:16 that "concupiscence of the eyes," "concupiscence of the flesh," and "pride of life" are all that is in the world; thus, in the *città terrena* that is hell, we would not expect these sins to be absent in some areas and present merely in a few others. Indeed, these specific *modes* of sin, avarice, lust, and pride, as Lajolo (1906, p. 45) and Busnelli (1909, p. 57) have seen, are found in *all three* of the divisions of hell—from the Vestibule to the Gate of Dis, from Dis to Geryon (the "sozza imagine di froda"), and from Geryon to the hulk of Satan. Without resorting to a tediously exhaustive listing, we can simply note that avarice, for example, is punished not only among the incontinent in *Inferno* VI, but also among the violent with the tyrants, murderers, and highwaymen in *Inferno* XII ("Oh, cieca cupidigia e ira folle, / che sì ci sproni nella vita corta, / e ne l'etterna poi sì mal c'immolle," vv. 49–51), among the usurers in *Inferno* XVI–XVII, and among the fraudulent with the simonists, barrators, and thieves in *basso inferno*. Pride is punished not only in the incontinent and wrathful Filippo Argenti, "persona orgogliosa" (*Inferno* VIII, 46), but in Capaneus (*Inferno* XIV, 64: "in ciò che non s'ammorza / la tua superbia, se' tu più punito") among the violent against God, with the Giants (*Inferno* XXXI, 91: Ephialtes, "questo superbo") and with Lucifer in the area of fraudulence and treachery. Lust receives its due not only with the incontinent Cleopatra, Dido, and Francesca but among the sodomites violent against nature and with the incestuous, dissembling Myrrha who fraudulently lay with Cinyras ("che divenne / al padre *fuor del diritto amore* amica," *Inferno* XXX, 38–39).

We can see, then, that the beasts, as fraudulence (*lonza*), violence (*leone*), and incontinence (*lupa*), each present themselves as temptations of a certain seriousness while clearly suggesting one or more of the specific sins contained within those degrees. While this scheme seems the most workable, one must accept the cautions of those critics who have warned of the dangers of trying to make Dante's original poetic scheme accord too closely with that of some supposed predecessor or, we could add, the folly of making all of Dante's myriad tripartite patterns square more than numerically with one another.

Excursus: The Interrelation of Sins

Although this *Lectura* on a single canto, obviously, has not the larger task of accounting for the "ordinamento penale" of hell, a number of short observations are appropriate here. Most discussions of that subject have, with few exceptions,[23] ignored the interrelation and interpenetration of sins. Critics have tended to consider a sin once punished in an earlier circle of hell as being unrepeated or having no connection to sins in a later circle. Such a discrete view of particular sins is contradicted by theology. The widespread doctrine of the "filiae superbiae" and the "filiae cupiditatis," that is, the "daughters of pride" and "the daughters of covetousness" or "avarice," is based on the assumption that graver sins grow on and out of those that have been committed before. St. Gregory outlined the concept most influentially in the *Moralia* XXXI, 87, where he declares that pride, the "beginning of all sin," is forebear to the "root of all evil," avarice:

> Pride is the root of evil, of which it is said, as Scripture bears witness: "Pride is the beginning of all sin." But seven principal vices, as its first progeny, spring doubtless from this poison root, namely vainglory, envy, anger, melancholy, avarice, gluttony, lust.

Each of the seven mortal sins in turn "produce from themselves so great a multitude of vices . . . they bring, as it were, bands of an army after them." In particular, under the sin of avarice, the following dramatic catalogue can be found: "From avarice there spring treachery, fraud, deceit, perjury, restlessness, violence, and hardness of heart against compassion" (*Moralia* XXXI, 88; *Morals*, vol. III, pt. 2, p. 490). Some six hundred years later, St. Thomas Aquinas illustrated the list more fully, but in reverse order, in the *ST* II–II, qu. 118, art. 8, where we observe an ever-increasing guilt, or culpability similar to that presented in the *Inferno*, as the sins progess through *cupiditas* and violence, to deceit, fraud, and treachery:

> The daughters of covetousness are the vices which arise therefrom, especially in respect of the desire of an end. Now since covetousness is excessive love of possessing riches, it exceeds in two things. For in the first place it exceeds in retaining, and in this respect covetousness gives rise to *insensibility to mercy*, because, to wit, a man's heart is not softened by mercy to assist others with his riches. In the second place, it belongs to covetousness to exceed in receiving, and in this respect, covetousness may be considered in two ways. [1] First as in thought (*affectu*). In this way it gives rise to *restlessness*, by hindering man with excessive anxiety and care, for "a covetous man shall not be satisfied with money" (Ecclesiastes 5:9). [2] Secondly, it may be considered in the execution (*effectu*). In this way, the covetous man in acquiring other people's goods, sometimes by *force, which pertains to violence*, sometimes deceit, and then if he has recourse to words, it is *falsehood*, if it be mere words, *perjury* if he confirm his statement by oath; if he has recourse to deeds, and the deceit affects things, we have *fraud*; if persons,

then we have *treachery*, as in the case of Judas, who betrayed Christ through covetousness.

Mortal sin is vice that has increased in culpability through habitual commission and is characterized by unrepentance; obviously, more serious sins do not cancel out, but bear with them, the effect and quality of those sins that have gone before.

While the process by which souls can damn themselves may be codified in a general pattern, I must sound two warnings against oversimplification.

First, we must not confuse the relation of sins with modern scientific biological nomenclature, taxonomy, or generation, for it will hamper our thinking. St. Thomas himself distinguished between the *species of vice* and the *interrelation of vices*: vice is a moral and metaphorical metamorphosis: species and filiation need not correspond (*ST* II–II, 118, art. 8, reply to obj. 1):

> There is no need for the daughters of a capital sin to belong to that same kind of vice: because a sin of one kind allows of sins even of a different kind being directed to its end; seeing that it is one thing for a sin to have daughters, and another for it to have species.

Secondly, individual damnation need not, of course, involve *all* the sins in the hierarchy, for some are skipped over in the sinner's plunge into evil; nor does damnation necessarily involve only the worst of sins: lack of faith can damn the soul without further wickedness; unrepentant incontinence, we know, condemns Francesca. Clearly, moreover, the death of the sinner, physically or spiritually, can cut short the moral descent to those sins that are most heinous.[24]

Once souls embark upon a life of sin, they follow—with or without their own awareness—an inevitable paradigm. If unrepentant, they persist to their ultimate doom through paths of different lengths and directions within that hierarchy, much as if they were following the various branchings of the illustrations of the traditional *arbor mala*.[25] While Dante's concept is bewilderingly complex and derives from no single predecessor, his use of the broad outlines of the traditional theological scheme is obvious in the familiar pattern of the careers of the sinners.[26]

Obviously, the *degrees* of culpability are interrelated: those guilty of violence are far from blameless of incontinence, and those guilty of fraud are not blameless of violence. The damned are sent to a specific circle not merely on the basis of their most serious crime but for a life-time's accretion of habitual, unrepented sin.[77]

Similarly, the beasts of the first canto, in their role as symbols of temptations, prefigure chiastically the three areas of hell, and each re-flects several interrelated categories of sin. Later in this chapter, I will examine the beasts in further detail to clarify that they are to be consid-ered as temptations in the full meaning that this term bears in theology: that is, not only do they signify promptings or outward stimuli to sin, but the three encounters also represent trials that the wayfarer under-goes. Concerning the latter sense, we will examine how temptation to sin is both God's punishment upon mankind's pride and apostasy and His method of correction.

"And he was with beasts": The Beasts as Temptation

The metaphor of wild beasts as temptation and punishment occurs in many places in the Bible. In Hosea 13:4–7, for example, God rails at the people of Israel for their sins and predicts punishments in the form of a leopard and a lioness before promising final deliverance:

> But I am the Lord thy God from the land of Egypt: and thou shalt know no God but me, and there is no saviour beside me. I knew thee in the desert, in the land of the wilderness. According to their pastures they were filled and were made full: and they lifted up their heart and have forgotten me. And I will be to them as a lioness, as a leopard in the way of the Assyrians. . . . Their help is only in me. . . . I will deliver them out of the hand of death. I will redeem them from death.
>
> (Hosea 13:4–7, 9, and 14)

A comparison of the themes and circumstances of these verses—the reference to an exodus through the wilderness, the falling away from God, the punishment of the unfaithful by wild beasts—with those of the *Commedia*'s prologue reveals that the poetic message is expressed in paradigms believed, theologically, to be at once historical and ordained by God. The experience of the canto, though at first opaque to the way-farer's eyes—and to ours—also implies ultimate deliverance after chas-tisement and salvation after wandering and error.

This interpretation is supported by another biblical passage long recognized by critics as a major source of *Inferno* I.[28] The episode occurs in the fifth chapter of Jeremiah, a book of the Bible that seems to have appealed especially to Dante's censorious spirit; he turned to it, for example, in other urgent times of crisis to mourn the death of Beatrice in the *Vita Nuova*, and again in the proem of his scathing *Epistola* XI (VIII), to chastise the Italian cardinals in 1314. In the passage he chose as his calque for the beasts of *Inferno* I, Jeremiah 5:6, three predators— a lion, a wolf, and a leopard—are foretold as scourges of the disobedient and rebellious:

> "idcirco percussit eos leo de silva lupus ad vesperam vastavit eos pardus vigilans super civitates eorum."   (Jeremiah 5:6)

> [Therefore a lion from the forest hath slain them, a wolf in the evening shall despoil them. A leopard watcheth for their cities.]

The poem presents the beasts not in their biblical sequence but in a new poetic order of "malignancy and terror."[29] Surprisingly, few attempts have been made to explore the full context of the verse in Jeremiah or to examine, through its patristic exegesis, the intertextual implications for the hermeneutics of the *Commedia*'s prologue.[30] The sense of this major subtext can shed light on the true nature of the wayfarer's predicament: this biblical verse, like so many that form the background to Canto I, deals with the punishment of apostasy. The rest of the poem will reveal that the beasts serve a didactic function like those of Jeremiah, divinely sent to chasten in the interests of an ultimate salvation. Specifically, in Jeremiah's prophecy, the beasts are a scourge of the Jews' recidivism recounted in his preceding chapters and verses—that is, for their hill-top adoration of gods other than the Lord in Jerusalem— that is, the same apostasy that was discussed above in Chapter 2.

To God's command, "Convertimini filii revertentes et sanabo aversiones vestras" (Jeremiah 3:22) [Return, you rebellious children and I will heal your rebellions], reply is given, "Ecce nos venimus ad te enim es Dominus noster *vere mendaces erant colles* multitudo montium, vere in Domino Deo nostro salus Israhel" (Jeremiah 3:23) [Behold, we come to thee; for thou art the Lord our God. *Truly the hills are a delusion*, the multitudes (or "orgies," RSV) on the mountains: truly in the Lord our God is the salvation of Israel]. The traditional patristic exegesis of these chapters of Jeremiah confirmed the lesson of the text as an invitation to turn to God and extended it also as a prefiguration of the conversion of the gentiles, that is, of all men. A major commentary by Rabanus Maurus glossed the passage, explaining once again that the scaling of mountains signified not only the repetition of apostasy but its core, pride; the prayer of conversion should be that of any who are penitent:

> Dicat hoc poenitens, et omnem superbiam derelinquens, et multitudinem sive altitudinem montium et collium, per quam superbiat contra Deum, et humilitate prostratus loquatur: "Vere in Domino Deo nostro salus est [Hieremias 3:23]."
>
> (*PL* III, col. 832)

> [Let the penitent say this, and putting aside all pride, and the multitude, or altitude of the mountains and hills by which he rises in pride against God, and prostrate in humility, let him say: "Truly in our Lord God is our salvation" (Jeremiah 3:23).]

The context of Jeremiah 5:6 provides an even more striking model for Dante's beasts since it foretells that to those who disobey and go forth from Jerusalem, that is, from true, orthodox worship, shall come the disasters figured in the lion, wolf, and leopard; especially to the great among the city's populace and to those who have known the way of the Lord, that is, to the rebellious, shall come the greatest punishment for their obduracy:

> Go about through the streets of Jerusalem, and see and consider, and seek in the broad places thereof, if you can find a man that executeth judgment and seeketh faith: and I will be merciful unto it. . . . I will go therefore to the great men [*optimates*] and will speak to them: for they have known the way of the Lord, the judgment of their God. And behold these have altogether broken the yoke more and have burst the bonds. Wherefore a lion of the wood hath slain them, a wolf in the evening hath despoiled them; a leopard watcheth for their cities; everyone that shall go out thence shall be taken, because their transgressions are multiplied, their rebellions are strengthened. (Jeremiah 5:1–6)

Traditional exegeses of the passage further represented the beasts as temptations and even interpreted their role as envoys of the devil himself (as in Hugh of St. Victor: "Mystically the lion is the devil").[31] Thus, in the literal meaning of the poem's prologue, the beasts are exterior to the wayfarer just as Jeremiah's are external threats to the straying citizens in the Bible. Likewise, symbolically, they signify exterior temptations by which the Prince of this World attracts the submission of the individual parts of the soul of all men; that is, they are those temptations by which God allows Satan to test the proud sinner, the Deity aiming not to damn him but to bring him to humility. By such trials, as St. Gregory teaches, man is tried and proven, not for his destruction but for his instruction.[32] As we know, in the *Commedia*, the near fall to the "basso loco," through God's will, turns ultimately into a salutary experience, humbling the wayfarer ("*Miserere* di me!") and preparing him for the reception of divine grace.

Each beast takes a part in chastening the pilgrim. The *lonza* and the *leone* present only temporary impediments, although they halt and force him to turn back many times. From the first he has good hope of escape; from the second a renewal of his dread. Although they both have the effect of a serious lesson, he does not surrender to them. He meets near-damnation only with the *lupa*, signifying that his weakness is incontinence; but while the narrator later will reveal this as taking the form of intemperate lust, he does not portray his former self as guilty of having capitulated habitually to the more serious temptations of violence and fraudulence. He confesses vulnerability to the least and most insidious degree of sin; yet he also represents himself as a wayfarer being, like all men, tempted by sins in the more serious realms of *matta bestialitade* (incipient force and violence) and of *malitia* (incipient fraud) and as suffering from such degrees of sins committed by others against him.

The wayfarer's plight before the beasts has a more hopeful New Testament subtext as well; his experience as "whichever man" is made to reflect the triple temptations of Christ[33] before the beginning of his ministry, particularly as related in the Gospel of Mark:

> et erat in deserto quadraginta diebus et quadraginta noctibus et temptabatur a Satana. *Eratque cum bestiis* et angeli ministra-
> bant illi.   (Mark 1:13)

> [And he was in the desert forty days and forty nights, and was tempted by Satan. And *he was with beasts* and the angels ministered to him.]

The narrative of the first two cantos of the *Commedia* parallels the biblical account in action, desert setting, beasts, temptation, and ministration of heaven-sent messengers. This New Testament subtext emphasizes that the wayfarer's experience is *in imitatione Christi*,[34] a submission to temptation before a call to the higher prophetic duty to be fulfilled in the act of writing and in the message of the poem itself.

The allusive intercalation of the temptation of Christ, who "was with beasts" and who was "tempted even as we are, yet without sin," provides a further clue that the beasts signify temptations rather than interior dispositions to sin or actual, committed sins. The subtext, bringing into interpretive play the gift of redemption through Christ, prepares the reader at this most frightening and dramatic moment for the next occurrence. Though, unlike Christ, the wayfarer fails in the face of temptation and, at verse 61, he is actually plunging down "in basso loco," the effects of salvation in Christ come immediately to his aid in verse 62 with Virgil's arrival.

"Una lonza"

> una lonza leggiera e presta molto,
> che di pel macolato era coverta;   (vv. 32–33)

In regard to the *lonza*, critics have tried to solve two basic problems: first, the species of the beast and, secondly, the way in which that literal identification suggests or imposes an allegorical significance.

For positivistic criticism, the major crux was the animal's zoological taxonomy, a question arising from the differing and confusing views of the fourteenth-century commentators. Jacopo della Lana (com ca. 1324–1328) had merely paraphrased the *Commedia* and compared the beast's dappled hide to that of a leopard: the *lonza* is "molto leggiero e di pelo maculato a modo di leopardo" (I, p. 109). The Ottimo (com 1333, I, p. 6) saw it as a "panthera." Pietro di Dante opted for a more strictly literary derivation and gave the unlikely identification of the *lonza* as a lynx, "id est lupe cerverie" (com p. 39, Ottobonian version), recalling the Virgilian hemistich, "maculosae tegmine lyncis" [a dappled lynx's hide] of *Aeneid* I, 323.[35]

Benvenuto da Imola (com 1373–1380) gave three possibilities: "Tria sunt animalia praecipue habentia pellem variis maculis distinctam, scilicet lynx, sive lynceus, qui vulgariter dicitur lupus cerverius, pardus, et panthera" [There are three animals in particular that have a coat marked with various colors—that is, the lynx, or the *lynceus*, which is commonly called the bobcat, the pard, and the panther] (p. 34). He chose the *pardus*, stating that it exceeded the lion in fraud, and cited Boccaccio as an eyewitness that such a beast actually existed in Florence:

> Credo tamen quod autor potius intelligat hic de pardo, quam
> aliis . . . istud vocabulum florentinum *lonza* videtur magis im-

portare pardum, quam aliam feram. Unde, dum semel por-
taretur quidam pardus per Florentiam, pueri concurrentes
clamabant: vide lonciam! ut mihi narrabat suavissimus Boc-
catius de Certaldo.   (p. 35)

[I believe, however, that here the author is thinking rather
about the pard than of the others . . . that Florentine word
lonza seems to mean the pard more than any other wild animal.
Wherefore, when, at one time, a pard was carried through
Florence, boys running alongside would shout, "See the *loncia!*"—as that kindly man, Boccaccio da Certaldo, used to
tell me.]

While Benvenuto's gloss has the ring of immediacy and truth,
highly puzzling was a sentence in Francesco da Buti's *Commento* (com
1385–1395) that "questa lonza è uno animale di quattro piedi, *poco maggiore che la lepre*" [an animal with four feet *slightly larger than a hare*]
(p. 31). It was probably not he but another who confused the term "lepre" with "lievora" (attested in the Magliabechian MS; "levriere" =
"cane da lepre," or "greyhound"), a word applied at the time, in translations, to the Middle Eastern hunting leopard or cheetah.[36] A few lines
later, probably with a copy of Benvenuto at his elbow, he added: "è la
femmina di quello animale che si chiama pardo" (p. 33). The Anonimo
Fiorentino (com ca. 1400; p. 14) also identified the creature with a
"liopardo," and Giovanni da Serravalle (com 1416–1417) echoed Benvenuto, stating that the "leontia est femella in specie leopardi" [the
lonza is the female of the leopard species]. Guiniforto delli Bargigi (com
ca. 1440), however, returned to inverisimilitude and, possibly translating Pietro Alighieri's interpretation into the vernacular, contended
again for the female lynx: "questa lionza è la femmina del lupo cerviere"
(p. 12).

Although in most aspects the taxonomic guessing-game, which has
continued from the fourteenth century until our own time, provides us
with little more than amusement, some information that it garnered
does prove useful for a comprehension of the passage, especially concerning the lexical choice of a term that is, ultimately, not arcane, but
one familiar in the language of contemporary Florence.

Although many critics believe that the word "lonza" itself derives
ultimately from the Latin "lynx," perhaps through French "lonce"
("l'once," hence, English "ounce"), Enrico Proto (1907, pp. 1–16) con-
trived, though without much success, an etymology from the feminine

Graeco-Latin adjective "leontia" and claimed that his thesis was bolstered by the fact that the medieval Latin "lcuncia" was attested. Some manuscripts of the *Commedia* show, indeed, alternate forms such as "leonça," "liunça," and other variants.[37] Supporters of the more likely first theory, on the other hand, saw "leonza" as a popular deformation of *lonza*, similar to such forms as "leofante" and "liocorno," and interpreted the vulgar Latin term as a re-formation on the pattern of the vernacular. Regardless of the word's etymology, however, some critics realized that common sense rejected the idea that the *lonza* was a lynx: the narrative required, obviously, a swift, spotted beast large enough to be threatening to a man. The leopard and the hunting leopard seemed to be the obvious candidates.[38]

Most useful for the solution in a variety of ways was the evidence that a *lonza*, or, rather, a series of them, had actually been kept as mascots in Florence. We have cited Benvenuto's information from Boccaccio concerning its presence, and we can point also to the *Consulte della Repubblica fiorentina* that preserve the proposal of one Raniero del Sasso, made on June 29, 1285, "de curiis faciendis iuxta Palatium Potestatis, in loco in quo morabatur leuncia" [concerning the administrative details to be carried out next to the Palace of the Podestà (the Bargello) in the place where the *leuncia* was kept].[39] The documents establish that Dante and his fellow citizens could have seen the beast daily in its cage either there or at the site of the present Loggia del Bigallo facing the Battistero, where, from 1260, lions, and in 1290 and 1291, a leopard in its "domuncula" are also recorded.[40] We not only know of the beast's existence but also that it was a popular curiosity in Florence and a token of its civic vanity.[41] The choice of the Florentine word "lonza" instead of "pardo," was not an indulgence in hermeticism but instead the choice of a term readily intelligible. The satiric effect of choosing a Florentine mascot as a symbol of temptation to sin must guide our interpretation of the political significances of the canto.[42]

However, the historical documents do not, unfortunately, provide a description of the animal and, therefore, they do not help identify the creature by a modern Italian or English name, nor do they grant any hint of its mythical meaning. For answers to these questions, critics have turned for the most part to the uncertainties of the bestiaries and of the encyclopedias of natural history. Immediately a major problem was encountered, for although the term *lonza* appeared in vernacular texts, no Latin bestiary treated it.[43]

Among the many animals that scholars have suggested, four especially have been considered as serious candidates: the lynx, as we have noted, the leopard, the pard (considered to be a different animal), and the panther.[44] Enrico Proto disqualified the lynx (or "lupo cerviero") not because of size, but on literary grounds: classical sources character-ized it as pusillanimous, and St. Albertus Magnus (*De animalibus* 22 : 13) testified that the beast was harmless to man, "innocuum est homini."[45]

Neither the lynx nor the leopard appear by name in the bestiaries of the mainstreams of the medieval *Physiologus* tradition.[46] Bestiaries, such as those of the pseudo-Hugh of St. Victor and Albertus Magnus (*De animalibus* 22 : 131, and 109)[47] written in the wake of Pliny (III, 2) and Isidore (*Etymologiae* XII, 2, 10–11), do treat of the pard and leopard, the former being a "genus varium ac velocissimum et praeceps ad san-guinem" [a mixed and very swift species, and one that rushes headlong for blood] that kills at one pounce, "saltu enim ad mortem ruit" (*Ety-mologiae* XII, 2, 10). The "leopardus" they generally label as a mongrel or hybrid of the lion and pard, as its etymology suggests.[48] If Dante was not directly familiar with Thomas of Cantimpré's *Liber de natura rerum* IV, 55, he could have found the material collected there in many other bestiaries and works on natural history. Thomas repeats the view that the leopard is a hybrid and adds that the female is fiercer than the male: "Leopardus . . . animal est generatum ex leone et pardo. Horum femine sunt audaciores et fortiores maribus" (IV, 55) [The leopard . . . is an ani-mal generated from a lion and a pard. Of these the females are bolder and stronger than the males].[49] However, under a separate listing, "De pardis," later in his text, Thomas misinterprets Isidore (*Etymologiae* XII, 2, 10), but, all the same, classifies that animal correctly as of the same order as the panther, although he adds the curiosity that panthers are known by the particoloration of their spots: "secundum genus a pantheris, que notate sunt varietate macularum." Isidore had written simply "pardus secundus post pantherem est," the pard is second after the panther. Thomas goes on to speak of the pard itself as a hybrid, although, again, scribal error cannot be ruled out: "In Affricam propter inopiam aque diverse fere congregantur ad amnes, *ubi leone miscent se variis bestiis vel vi vel voluptate; et inde pardi procreari dicuntur*" [In Africa, because of the shortage of water, many wild animals gather at the streams where lionesses cohabit with various beasts either by force or desire, and thence pards are said to be produced].[50] Thomas's work, one of the most respected of the medieval catalogues of beasts, is also a typi-cal, amusing example of the repetitions, distortions, and conflations en-demic to the genre.

Most critics believe that Dante was acquainted with the material found in the vernacular *Bestiario toscano*,[51] although it exists only in copies postdating the *Commedia*. That work says nothing of the hybrid nature of the "leopardo" but attributes to it two prime characteristics (para. 73): the "bellissima bestia" is one of the most "ingengnose animali che sia"; and it possesses "leggereçça grandissima." In the next entry (73) a "loncia," on the other hand, is described in ways reminiscent of the "leopardus" in Thomas; it is an "animale crudele e fiera e nasce de coniungimento carnale de leone con lonça o vero con leopardo con leonissa, e cussì nasce lo leopardo. La lonça sempre sta in calura d'amore et in desiderio carnale, launde sua fereçça è molto grandissima."[52]

Despite the bestiaries' confusion, textual and zoological, a glimmer of useful information still shines through: that the term "pardus" meant the "leopardo," or "leopard" in the modern usage of Italian and English, and that "leopardus" denoted, instead, a real or imagined hybrid.

The association of the *lonza* with the panther is somewhat problematic, but ultimately it only comforts the identification with the modern leopard. Even if we disregard the fact that in modern nomenclature the panther is the black form of the leopard, we have Pliny's testimony (VIII, 16–17) that the male panther was called a "pardus" in Roman times; even medieval bestiaries continued to identify the panther as the same species as the *pardus*. Most important, writers as widely separated in time as Isidore (*Etymologiae* XII, 2, 8, 9) and the Tuscan bestiarist described the panther, too, as having a spotted hide: "La pantera si è una bestia molto bella et è negra e biancha macchiata."[53]

The confusions rife among the "lonza," "pardus," "leopardus" and "panthera" in the bestiaries seem best resolved, perhaps by Brunetto Latini's choice of the French term "lonce" ("longe") to render the word "pardus" from Isidore in his own *Trésor* I, 190:3 (ed. Carmody, p. 167). The facts seem to square with the contention of Benvenuto and the Anonimo Fiorentino that the *lonza* is itself a "pardus," and the view of Buti and Serravalle that Dante's first beast is simply the female of that species. E. Proto (1907) and K. McKenzie (1910) championed this interpretation at the beginning of the century, and most modern commentators accept it as convincing.

Beyond the arguments in favor of the "pard" based on the bestiary tradition, critics, such as P. Chistoni (1903, p. 838) and G. Busnelli (1909, pp. 37–45), have seen a surer ground for its identification with the *pardus* in the Vulgate Bible and the traditional exegesis on those passages advanced as Dante's sources for the image of the three beasts. Such intertextual considerations now allow us to turn to the *lonza*'s possible allegorical significances.

In addition to the text of Jeremiah 5:6, examined earlier, which names the wolf, lion, and leopard as the scourges of Jerusalem, the reader recalls the vision of the leopard "et ecce alia quasi pardus" (compare "Ed ecco . . . una lonza") among the four apocalyptic beasts in Daniel 7:6. In Richard of St. Victor's important exegesis on this verse in the *De eruditione interioris hominis* III, xi, we find not only a metaphoric identification of the leopard with fraud, but also the paradigm of the generation of *fraudulentia*. Richard describes the swiftness and cunning of the beast, and he sees it as figuring human "malitia" that leads, in turn, to fraud and then to fraudulence:

> Quid enim aliud est fraudulentia, quam astuta malitia, ad omnem fraudem tam prona quam prompta? Recte hypocritarum fraudulentia in pardo figuratur qui per totum corpus maculis quibusdam respergitur. Nam hypocritae quidem sanctitatem opere praetendunt, sed perversum est quod diligunt.

> [For what else is fraudulence but cunning malice, as *prone to as it is prompt* to every fraud? Rightly is the fraudulence of dissemblers symbolized by the *pard which is speckled with spots over its whole body*. For dissemblers indeed make a show of holiness by their work, but what they love is perverse.] [54]

The parallels to the description of the *lonza* in *Inferno* I ("leggiera e presta molto," "di pel macolato era coverta"), to Virgil's description of the ordering of lower hell in *Inferno* XI, 82, and to the appearance of Geryon in *Inferno* XVII, 10, 15, are striking enough, perhaps, to be more than mere coincidence. Richard's instant leap from the outward appearance to the symbolic parallels the oscillations between the *sensus litteralis* and the *sensus spiritualis* attending the *lonza* in the prologue of the *Commedia*. In Richard's text as in the poem, the generic disposition of malice through a sinner's consenting to temptation becomes active fraud (*fraus*); thereafter, by constant repetition, fraud develops into the habit of the sin that he terms "*fraudulentia*":

> Tunc procul dubio *fraus in fraudulentiam excrescit*, quando *ex multa jam malitia menti* accidit, ut libenter omnino decipere velit cum possit, et *post multum usum*, et exercitium, nihilominus per multam jam astutiam suppetit, ut decipere facile possit cum velit.

> [Then there is no doubt: *fraud grows into fraudulence*, when *from an already great malice of mind* it happens that one wishes

freely to deceive in every way when one can; and, *after much practice and exercise*, it happens inevitably that through much adroitness one can now easily deceive at will.][55]

It appears obvious that the *lonza* of the *Commedia* alludes to the biblical pard and that it symbolizes the temptation of *malizia*. The identification accords with some scholars' criticisms of Casella and Flamini's equating the *lonza* too specifically with fraud, and it answers the intelligent protest that Geryon and the *lonza* cannot both symbolize the same thing.[56] If we take the view that the first beast of *Inferno* I preys upon man's potential for sinfulness and that it signifies not the committed sin of fraud, but rather the test of man's potential for malice, then the monster Geryon (joined to the beast by verses 106–108 in *Inferno* XVI: "Io avea una corda intorno cinta, / e con essa pensai alcuna volta / prender la lonza a la pelle dipinta") is left to symbolize the consequences of submission to the *lonza*'s allure. This monster from the pit (*Inferno* XVII, 7) is malice's offspring, "quella sozza imagine di froda," the result, through temptation, of the capitulation to a disposition reviled by heaven.

"Un leone"

Through a conventional, almost heraldic, symbolism the poem presents the lion not only as pride but also as force that leads to violence:

> ma non sì che paura non mi desse
> la vista che m'apparve d'un leone.
> Questi parea che contra me venisse
> con la test'alta e con rabbiosa fame,
> sì che parea che l'aere ne tremesse.[57]   (vv. 45–48)

The artifice of a litotes in verse 45 emphasizes that this beast's ferociousness lies beyond mimesis—why would the narrator even call into question any doubt about the wayfarer's fear except to point more clearly to the code in which the reader must interpret the events? The poetic lexicon here is primarily that of bestiaries and of the Bible. "The proud lion, ferocious by nature," and "the lion, proud in its own strength" are commonplaces of the medieval catalogues. Bestiaries concur in the lion's irascible nature, especially when hungry. Consider Albertus Magnus: "Leo . . . quando est famelicus, est valde malus et asper et iracundus."[58] That this lion's raging hunger is so fearful that it seems to make the very air tremble adds a touch of conventional hyperbole designed more to evoke than to describe. Its posture, "con la test'alta," echoes biblical language concerning the proud who "walk with outstretched necks."[59] Within the poem's narrative, the beast prefigures the proud, unbending Farinata in *Inferno* X ("nè mosse collo nè piegò sua costa," v. 75) and the proud of *Purgatorio* XI–XII whose necks are bent in humility beneath rocks as they are purged. The purgatorial punishment, which literalizes the convention of the metaphor, provokes the poet's sarcastic rebuke to Christendom:

> Or superbite, e via col viso altero,
>   figliuoli d'Eva, e non chinate il volto
>   sì che veggiate il vostro mal sentiero!
>
> (*Purgatorio* XII, 70–72)

Again here for the lion, the primary calque is the "leo de silva"[60] of Jeremiah 5:6 and its traditional exegesis, but the allusion is complemented by classical tradition. Critics (such as Casella, vol. 2, p. 385) point to Ovid's "insani leonis vim"; and since the order of the sins of violence and fraud in the *Inferno* follows Cicero, the canto's predator may also mirror the orator's image in a key passage of the *De Officiis* I:13, "vis leonis videtur."

Since the time of the anonymous glossator of the Codice Cassinese, many critics and commentators have hesitated between pride and *ira* for the significance of this second beast, but such a choice is unnecessary. Theologically, pride not only pertains to the irascible (as St. Thomas Aquinas classifies: "Pride must needs pertain in some way to the irascible faculty"[61]), but (again according to St. Thomas) in the downward progress of the evil hierarchy of sins, wrath is also the result of pride.[62] The characteristics of the *leone* signify general temptations corruptive of the irascible soul.

"Ed una lupa"

As for the other beasts, the major source for the wolf is Jeremiah 5:6, "lupus ad vesperam vastavit eos," and the subtext is again embellished and intertwined with other rich strands of negative symbolism drawn from a number of writings and traditions that used the wolf as an emblem of insatiable rapacity—among them, again, the bestiaries, classical literature, the Bible, and early Christian euhemeristic writings.

Many glosses on the *lupa* from the beginning of this century to the present note that much of the creature's literal detail and spiritual sense is based upon the fantastic and pseudo-scientific traditions of the "books of beasts." Particularly useful are the contributions of R. T. Holbrook (1902), A. Pézard (1950 and 1957), R. E. Kaske (1961) and A. Scolari (1982).[63] Scolari concentrated especially on the canto's vocabulary, noting, for example, that even the word "natura" (v. 97: "e ha natura sì malvagia e ria") was a technical term employed in both Latin and vernacular bestiaries to express an animal's traits and habits; bestiary entries regularly begin with a variation on a formula such as "della natura del lupo."

The major characteristic of the *lupa*, its "brame" or voracious rapacity, is an aspect of wolves attested in the *Etymologiae* of Isidore of Seville and in the many bestiary entries deriving from it:

> The name *lupus* is of Greek origin transferred into our [Latin] language: they call the wolf *lykos*. It is named *lykos* in Greek on account of its nature since, because of its raging rapacity, it kills whatsoever it finds. (*Etymologiae* XII, 2, 23)[64]

Thomas of Cantimpré, Vincent of Beauvais, and Albertus Magnus noted the wolf's perpetual leanness, "magrezza," and cited the reason in their bestiaries: the wolf never fattens because it gulps its food without chewing, "comedit sine masticatione." Thus, popular tradition believed that it *literally* could not fulfill its "bramosa voglia," and that it was hungrier after eating than before (*Inferno* I, 98–99).[65]

Another reflection of bestiary tradition concerning wolves (employed again in the poem in regard to Cerberus) accounts partially—at least in the literal sense—for Virgil's odd assertion that the *veltro*, in contrast to the *lupa*, will *not* feed on earth ("non ciberà terra," v. 103). The legend of the wolf's ingestion of dirt, yet another manifestation of its voracious appetite, finds a place in scientific and pseudo-scientific treatises from Pliny through Albertus Magnus, Thomas of Cantimpré, Bartholomaeus Anglicus, and Brunetto Latini.[66]

A. Pézard (1957) and R. E. Kaske (1961) noted that bestiaries also provide an explanation for the curious physical effect that the wolf has on the wayfarer:

> questa mi porse tanto di gravezza
> con la paura ch'uscia di sua vista,
> ch'io perdei la speranza de l'altezza. (vv. 52–54)

The popular tradition that the sight of a wolf cuts off the human voice, noted in classical writers and repeated in many medieval works of a religious, scientific, and encyclopedic nature, led to a corollary attested in the *Bestiario toscano*, that the sight of the wolf—or more correctly, its *active stare*—can deprive a man of his strength: "[il lupo] tolle lo vigore all'omo, se ello vede l'omo 'nansi che l'omo vegga lui."[67]

Bestiary lore not only puts many details of the text of the first canto into a cultural perspective, but also improves our understanding of the larger thematic implications of the beast whenever it reappears as an image of ever-increasing poetic and moral weight in the poem.

We earlier observed that preconceived categories of sin, too narrow to accommodate the multifaceted roles of each of the beasts in the imagery of the poem, have generally vitiated critical attempts to appreciate their significance; identification of the animals with specific, single sins ignores the polysemous, "both-and" quality of the poem's symbolism, in which one significance of an image complements rather than displaces another. Perhaps, as D. W. Robertson has suggested, our tendency to think in oppositions and polarities is a modern vice not shared by the fourteenth century.[68] In the case of the wolf, exclusionary assumptions and interpretations hold that if the beast signifies lust, it cannot therefore signify avarice. On the contrary, the text of *Inferno* I implies that the *lupa* signifies a lure to both these sinful dispositions and more.

Just as we have seen that the *lonza* and *leone* suggest temptations beyond those of isolated fraud and pride, so also the text presenting the *lupa* suggests something including, yet more encompassing than, the fully realized sin of *avaritia* or *cupiditas*[69] in its extreme manifestations: the wolf represents the temptation of the sins of incontinence or concupiscence in the broadest sense. The verses convey emblematically some of the many moral variations that the temptations preying upon the sensitive soul—upon both the concupiscent and irascible parts— can display. The lines "mai non empie la bramosa voglia / . . . ha più fame che pria" signify gluttonous incontinence; the classical Latin and archaic Italian meaning of the word "lupa" as "prostitute," and the words "molti son li animali a cui s'ammoglia," ineluctably signify mercenary lewdness, and, insofar as the *lupa* is the antithesis of the *veltro*, the verse telling us that the latter "non ciberà terra nè peltro" [will not feed on land or pewter] ("terra" means both "dirt" and "territory") discloses that the *lupa* stands not merely for the temptations of *gula* and *lussuria*, but for that of cupidity, or avarice, in the most acute and severe sense—the craving for territorial possessions and wealth, "the love of money."[70] The *lupa's* raging, as the wayfarer first catches sight of her, manifests *ira*, the incontinence of the irascible soul.[71]

The problem of defining what is meant by "avarice" or "cupidity" lies in the fact that these two interchangeable terms have had a double meaning from the time of St. Augustine. First, the term "cupiditas" signifies merely a desire that has taken a wrong direction toward earthly things; as such, it is the opposite of charity and is generically equivalent to concupiscence; secondly, "avaritia" and "cupiditas" signify the capital sin deriving from that desire, an uncontrolled greed that affects others; in this sense, the sin is the opposite of justice.

St. Thomas Aquinas defines "avarice" in its generic sense as an immoderate desire for anything: "Nomen avaritiae amplicatum est ad omnem immoderatum appetitum habendi quamcumque rem" [The term avarice has been amplified to denote an immoderate desire for having anything whatever].[72] And in the *Summa Theologica* II–II, qu. 118, art. 8 (as outlined earlier in this chapter, pp. 53–54), he explains the development of generic cupidity into more serious sins, naming the latter the "daughters of avarice": *avaritia* begins, first, within the affective part of the sinning subject (= *affectu*) as an anxiety in expenditure and a certain heartlessnesss, but later breaks out to injure others (in its effect = *effectu*) as it turns into a craving that proceeds through violence, to fraud, and finally to treachery.

The wolf, when first it appears, represents the generic attractions or temptations of incontinence in their most unrestricted sense—and suggests only potentially its later role in the poem as an emblem of the more serious, specific, committed sins of avarice itself. As the poem proceeds, it waxes into a symbol of all forms of cupidity that attach man to the earth and urge his damnation.[73] From the she-wolf as temptation, we descend to hell's circle of committed avarice where the guardian monster, Pluto, is silenced as "maladetto lupo" (*Inferno* VII, 8). The severer meanings and forms of avarice's effects appear again in *Purgatorio* XX, 10–15, where in the circle of avarice, the poet is again moved to curse the wolf as the emblem of greed's relentless progression. Avarice, "il mal che tutto'l mondo occùpa," not only occasions the poet's curse but a wondering reminiscence of the prophetic and eschatological hope aroused by Virgil's prophecy of the "veltro" in the prologue scene:

Maladetta sie tu, antica lupa,
   che più che tutte l'altre bestie hai preda
   per la tua fame sanza fine cupa!

> O ciel, nel cui girar par che si creda
> le condizion di qua giù trasmutarsi,
> quando verrà per cui questa disceda?

Appropriately, in the same passage Hugh Capet recounts that the souls in purgation must rehearse each night the sins of Pygmalion: "cui traditore e ladro e paricida / fece la voglia sua de l'oro ghiotta" (*Purgatorio* XX, 104–105).

As many critics have noted, following the commentaries of Graziolo dei Bambaglioli (p. 4) and Pietro di Dante (p. 41), the more serious forms and meanings of *avaritia* are typified in Boethius's *De consolatione philosophiae* (IV, prose 3:17); "Avaritia fervet alienarum opum *violentus* ereptor: lupus similem dixeris" [Someone who robs with violence and burns with greed you could say is like a wolf]. But perhaps even more influential was the commonplace association of vicious rulers with the figure of the wolf as in the legend of Lycaon, the tyrant-turned-wolf (mentioned in Plato's *Republic* VIII, 565), whose tale was passed down to the Middle Ages primarily via Ovid's *Metamorphoses* I, 151–252.[74]

The Platonic images of the dog as guardian and the wolf as rapacious assailant are renewed in the *Commedia*'s imagery as contemporary political leaders tear savagely at the viscera of those they lead. The baneful metamorphosis of dogs into wolves ("di can farsi lupi") as the emblem of political corruption recurs through the narrative.

A number of associations linked the image of the wolf with various cities, states, and political bodies. The Guelph party, whose very name was derived from "Welf" (= wolf), supported the temporal, covetous, grasping power of the church against what Dante saw as the legitimate claims of the emperor and sought territorial aggrandizement while it caused internecine strife in Italian cities. The wolf also had associations with Guelph Florence; ironically, the wolf was the mascot of Mars, the traditional pagan patron of Florence, replaced in Christian times by St. John the Baptist.[75] Most important, as we shall note, the she-wolf mascot of ancient Rome had, in Dante's time, been adopted by the papacy. Lupine imagery appears in the poem especially when cupidity coincides with the illegitimate claims of those associated with papal rule.[76]

However, in spite of the number of these socio-political resonances, or, more precisely, because of them, it is difficult, as many critics have attempted to do, to tie the she-wolf to any single or specific political ruler, state, or entity. The *lupa* cannot, as various critics have maintained, represent merely Boniface VIII, or the Roman Curia, nor is it solely a symbol of Dante's native city; rather, it fulfills a more general negative role in the *Commedia* as a metaphor of ever-expanding greed and usurpation that involves all the particular manifestations of those evils.

Some of the image's more complex ethical and political senses as both private and public sin are exemplified in *Inferno* XXXIII, where the treacherous Guelph leader, Count Ugolino, imprisoned in the Tower of Hunger, dreams that he and his children are wolves ("lupo e' lupicini") hunted by Archbishop Ruggieri "as lord and master" and hounded by dogs tearing at their flanks. The count's narrative and the grisly ending of the episode develop the profound intricacies of the bestial symbol as the text forces the reader to re-evaluate the count's self-exculpating tale of innocence: Ugolino, the "lupo" of the dream, will be invited to gnaw the flanks of his children in hunger, just as in hell he gnaws Archbishop Ruggieri's greasy nape with his "teeth hard like a dog's upon the bone."[77]

In *Purgatorio* XIV, 29–51, Guido del Duca uses feral symbols of the Circe myth in his description of the course of the Arno; with each city that the river passes characterized by a different beast: as the river leaves the hogs of Casentino and the curs of Arezzo, it pursues its course down, like a river of hell, to the wolves of Florence:

> Vassi caggendo; e quant'ella più 'ngrossa,
>   tanto più trova di can farsi lupi
>   la maladetta e sventurata fossa.   (*Purgatorio* XIV, 49–51)

Within this passage the symbolism of wolf-and-hunter is employed again but in a way that again repels a narrow interpretation of the images. We are reminded of the basic lesson that internal cupidity grows into external injustice:

> Io veggio tuo nepote che diventa
>   cacciator di quei lupi in su la riva
>   del fiero fiume, e tutti li sgomenta.
> Vende la carne loro essendo viva;
>   poscia li ancide come antica belva;
>   molti di vita e sé di pregio priva.
> Sanguinoso esce de la trista selva;
>   lasciala tal, che di qui a mille anni
>   ne lo stato primaio non si rinselva.   (*Purgatorio* XIV, 58–66)

The "hunter" of the Florentine "wolves" is the corrupt Fulcieri da Calboli, *podestà* of the city in 1303 and fierce enemy of the Whites and

Ghibellines: the allegiances of Fulcieri's victims of beheading, torture, and confiscation extend beyond party boundaries to include both Ghibellines and Guelphs of Ghibelline leanings. From ruler of Florence, Fulcieri sinks to become one with the "ancient wolf" of avarice and rapine, an "antica belva."[78]

* * *

The biblical and patristic metaphors of the faithful-as-sheep, and the church-as-sheepfold, transferred to the empire and its governance, obviously lie as major "sunken" metaphors beneath the *lupa* sequence of the first canto. The images find overt refinement later in the poem.[79] The term "ovile" becomes narrowed nostalgically and ironically to Florence. In *Paradiso* XVI, 25, the pilgrim lovingly evokes the sheepfold of the old city sheltering its lambs as he asks Cacciaguida: "Ditemi dell'ovil di San Giovanni / quanto era allora." And later still, in *Paradiso* XXV, 1–12, the poet expresses his hope of receiving the laurel crown in the city, the "ovile ov'io dormi' agnello / nimico ai lupi che li danno guerra." But Florence's contemporary corruption contrasts with its former virtue. The images of a defiled city, ill-born of Satan, of cupidity as love of money, and of the devil's envy releasing the evil of cupidity upon the earth (*Inferno* I, 111) all combine in the imprecations of Folco da Marsiglia in *Paradiso* IX, 127–132. Love of the florin has transformed the pope from shepherd into wolf:

> La tua città che di colui è pianta
> > che pria volse le spalle al suo fattore,
> > e di cui è la 'nvidia tanto pianta,
> produce e spande il maledetto fiore
> > che ha disvïate le pecore e li agni,
> > però che fatto ha lupo del pastore.

The imagery evolves yet further in *Paradiso* XXVII, 55–57, with St. Peter's censure of the church:

> In vesta di pastor lupi rapaci
> > si veggion di qua sù per tutti i paschi:
> > o difesa di Dio, perché pur giaci?

Amid this bitter negative imagery there is one striking omission: the she-wolf as the ancient symbol of Rome and the empire. Despite the importance of the *Aeneid* as subtext for the *Commedia*, there is no hint or allusion to the ecphrasis of Aeneas's prophetic shield in *Aeneid* VIII, 626–634, in which the foundling twin brothers, founders of Rome, are suckled by a wolf: in Virgil's text, Rome, Mars's chosen city, venerated the she-wolf as its founders' nurse:

> . . . regina sacerdos
> Marte gravis geminam partu dabit Ilia prolem.
> inde lupae fulvo nutricis tegmine laetus
> Romulus excipiet gentem et Mavortia condet
> moenia Romanosque suo de nomine dicet.
>
> (*Aeneid* I, 274–277)

[. . . Ilia, the priestess queen, shall bear to Mars her twin off-spring. Then Romulus, proud in the tawny hide of the she-wolf, his nurse, shall take up the line, and found the walls of Mars and call the people Romans after his name.]

Dante, in fact, never uses the emblem of the wolf anywhere in his works as a positive image of the empire. Nor, indeed, does the poem ever mention Romulus under that name. He is "Quirino" in Charles Martel's explanation of the force of the stars and the inconstancy in human heredity: " . . . e vien Quirino / da sì vil padre, che si rende a Marte" (*Paradiso* VIII, 131–132).

This portion of Virgil's text does not appear in Dante's *Commedia* most probably because the wolf and the legend of its role in the founding of the empire had been totally discredited mythically and morally in Christian tradition. Exploiting Livy (I:4), the early Christian apologists had revelled in a scandal that dealt a blow to paganism: the twins' priestess-queen-mother was actually an adultress or a corrupt and pregnant Vestal. In book I, 20, of the *Divine Institutes*, the early church euhemerist, Lactantius, had sarcastically placed Romulus's mother first among a notorious parade of harlots deified and worshipped by the Romans:

> I come now to the religious beliefs proper to the Romans; up to this point I have been speaking of general ones. Lupa, the nurse of Romulus, has had divine honors given her, and I could accept this if she were the animal itself whose aspect she wears. But Livy [I:4] is the author of the statement that the effigy is of Larentina, and indeed, not of her body, but of her mind and customs. She was the wife of Faustulus, and be-

cause of the use of her prostitute body she was called a she-wolf, that is, a prostitute, among the shepherds; so, also, we have the name *lupanar* for a house of ill-repute.[80]

St. Augustine, quoting Lactantius some hundred years later, had the lines from *Aeneid* I more closely in mind and further adjusted the tale:

Numitor's daughter, [was] named Rhea (who was also called Ilia, the mother of Romulus), a Vestal virgin. Men claim that she conceived twins of Mars, and in this way they honour or excuse her lapse from chastity, and offer as proof the fact that a she-wolf nursed the infants when they were exposed. For they think that this sort of animal belongs to Mars, and hence the she-wolf is believed to have offered her dugs to the little ones for the reason that she recognized them as the sons of her master Mars. And yet men are not lacking who say that when the exposed infants lay wailing they were first rescued by an un-identified harlot, and that her breasts were the first to suckle them—for indeed they called harlots she-wolves, for which reason even now brothels are called *lupanaria* meaning dens of wolves.[81]

The "lupa" who had suckled the twins was merely a human whore. The symbol of the she-wolf had become too sordid for positive use in a Christian poem expressing the hope of restoring imperial justice to Italy and the world. Clearly, the *lupa* of Dante's prologue is heir to these derogatory associations. Ironically, however, the church that had once degraded the she-wolf in its literature and theology had recently usurped the beast as its own symbol: the antique statue from the Capi-toline (without, of course, the engaging twin boys sculptured by Pol-laiolo in the fifteenth century) was located, in Dante's time, near the Lateran Palace, the medieval seat of the papacy.[82]

While the poem reflects the negative assessment of Rome's pagan emblem, it does not follow St. Augustine's negative assessments of the Roman empire.[83] Books I–X of *The City of God* portray only pride and violence as the foundation of Roman rule whose expansion had come at the cost of peace. Augustine's famous anecdote recounting how a pirate had told Alexander the Great that he and the conquerer plied the same profession has no parallel in the works of Dante. For Augustine, Rome had no special mission beyond that of any other political entity or any other empire that preceded it, Assyrian, Persian, or Macedonian. Rome had been founded in fratricide with Romulus's murder of Remus, just as all worldly cities were founded in the blotted pattern of Cain's murder of Abel. There could be no right in pagan Rome, no justice where there was no love of God.[84]

However, the views of other early Christian apologists gave Dante an understanding of imperial power far more positive and righteous. In Paulus Orosius's *Adversus paganos*, especially in book V, 2, the *pax romana* was interpreted as a providential preparation for the Coming of Christ, the Savior who, as the *Monarchia* (I, 16 and II, 11) implies, asserted his human nature at the same time as he asserted his Roman citizenship.[85] Both the *Divine Institutes* and the *Monarchia* (I, 5–9) present the pattern of the empire with its single ruler as an archetype analogous to God's rule of the universe. As Lactantius had deduced the truth of monotheism from the single rule of the emperor over the world ("It is necessary for the world to be ruled by the will of one," *Divine Institutes* I, 3), so Dante had merely to reverse the process of the argument to bolster his own truth.

Against the pessimistic view of the early Christian apologists that Dante had himself once shared, the *Commedia* presents a mature theory of the providential origin of the empire that reflects ideas outlined in *Convivio* IV and argued in the *Monarchia*. The Roman empire predated the founding of the church and derived its power directly from God (*Monarchia* III, 13). In opposition to the ideas expressed in the works of St. Augustine and of his follower Orosius, the *Monarchia* treats the Romans as a chosen people[86] foreordained to gain the rule over the whole world by just contest, trial and ordeal; God's favor toward them had been attested by miracles before the Coming of Christ, and their right to world government had been sealed by his Incarnation in its midst. Government is a not symptom of cupidity, but its cure (*Monarchia* III, 4); the emperor, owning all that was bounded by the ocean, possessed all and could desire nothing; the sole monarch's rule of justice would be unsullied by greed (*Monarchia* I, 11). The poem develops this idealistic vision especially in Justinian's discourse in *Paradiso* VI.

Thus, while the *Commedia* ignores the pagan myth of the "divine" origin of Romulus and Rome, it expresses a view consonant with Vergilius Maro's belief in the eternity of Rome and in its divinely ordained mission. Rome, as the *Commedia* ultimately presents it, should be, in fact, the image of the true City of God, that Rome where Christ is Roman. Its symbol on earth and in heaven could not be the wolf, symbol of the greatest impediment to justice, but the Eagle of Justice itself, "il segno / che fé i romani al mondo reverendi" (*Paradiso* XIX, 101–102), the "bird of Jove" (*Purgatorio* XXXII, 112), and the "bird of God" (*Paradiso* VI, 4), the Eagle of St. John conjoined with the Eagle of Jupiter.[87] In *Paradiso* XVIII, 91–93, the souls of the just rulers will shape its "segno sacrosanto" out of the last "m" of the commandment to love justice: "Diligite justitiam qui judicatis terram."

CHAPTER IV

Virgil

"Ribellante a la sua legge"

Some modern Dante criticism, rejecting the traditional interpretation of Virgil as the personification of Reason or Wisdom, has begun to scrutinize the *Commedia*'s complex personage with a sharper eye.[1] For a better understanding of Virgil's role in Dante's poem let us first briefly consider the ambiguous reception of Virgil in the Christian tradition, and, secondly, examine the relationship of the wayfarer and his pagan guide within the poem.

The historical attitudes toward Vergilius Maro that underlie the portrayal of the Roman poet in the *Commedia* were varied and contradictory. Although admiration for the poet was seldom unalloyed, many early Christians and their heirs in the Middle Ages saw in Virgil's fourth *Eclogue* a prophecy of the Advent of Christ. They employed both that poem and the *Aeneid* especially as major texts for early Christian proselytizing among the pagans. Eusebius, for example, records an *Oratio* attributed to the emperor Constantine who gave a religious exposition of Virgil's poem in public assembly.[2] Dante himself cites the *Eclogue* in praise of the justice of the Augustan Age in *Monarchia* I, ii, and in the *Commedia*, following the Christian didactic tradition, he makes Virgil's poem the inspiration for Statius's conversion to the Christian faith. Statius paraphrases Virgil's lines:

> . . . "Secol si rinova;
> torna giustizia e primo tempo umano,
> e progenïe scende da ciel nova."   (*Purgatorio* XXII, 70–72)

The coming of Virgil as a messenger of God's grace and as herald of justice through his prediction of the *veltro* in *Inferno* I reflects the accepted interpretation of him in history. And this, precisely, is the paradox that Virgil embodies in the *Commedia*: exalted for his knowledge, eloquence, and prophecy, the Roman poet is nonetheless damned to hell.[3]

*   *   *

Virgil's eloquent style had, of course, been a touchstone in Roman schools. Though the popularity of the *Aeneid* waxed and waned for centuries, its reputation never flagged among the educated, and it remained the model of Latin expression through the Middle Ages down to our own day. The early Christian apologists writing against the pagans valued the epic as history and as a document of supreme eloquence, even if its explicit idolatry offended them.[4] Throughout the *Divine Institutes* (ca. 304–311), Lactantius, "the Christian Cicero," preferred to use Virgil's epic over any of the available, but less comely, Christian texts to demonstrate Christian truths. Although he was mostly antagonistic toward the pagan, he even occasionally admitted that in understanding the nature of the Godhead "Maro, the foremost of our poets was not far from the truth . . . about the supreme God," citing *Aeneid* VI and *Georgics* II and IV (*DI*, I, 5) in witness. He also cites Virgil's *Eclogue* as a millennialist prophecy of an age of justice to come when false religion is destroyed (*DI* VII, 24).

Centuries before Dante, the question of eloquence had exercised the church. The humbleness of the writing style of early Christianity had been at once a cause of concern among believers and an object of disdain among the lettered, sophisticated heathen. Early translations of the Bible, before Saint Jerome set his hand to the Vulgate, were rough and crude. Indeed, most Christian apologists, nearly all of them professional rhetoricians, used pagan texts and pagan style for the dual purposes of polemic and proselytizing.[5] Especially in Lactantius, we find a new fourth-century attitude toward the culture of the pagan world, a new desire to preserve its learning so that "the gold and silver" of the Egyptians[6] could be put to the better use of the despised Galileans. Christian theologians used the rhetoric and eloquence of pagan poetry to argue against its own matter and substance. Christianity, formerly scorned for its clumsiness and austerity of expression, would henceforth assert its truths, as Lactantius said, in "clarity and splendor of speech, so that, both equipped with its force and adorned by the light of oratory," it would convince the pagan mind.[7] Just as, one hundred years later, St. Augustine (*De doctrina christiana* IV, 1–7; *On Christian Doctrine*, pp. 117–132) realized that eloquence, though indifferent in itself and dan-

gerous if misused, lent enormous power to convincing the hearer, so
Lactantius had been particularly effective in urging the proto-humanistic
belief that pagan learning was necessary and propaedeutic for the Christian scholar. Among the early Christian apologists, Publius Vergilius
Maro, the first among pagan writers, thus held an equivocal position:
his eloquence was praised and imitated while his ignorance of Christian
truths was subjected to the harshest of attacks on spiritual grounds.[8]
Although Lactantius, like many other Christian theologians, often cited
the *Aeneid* to prove a point, he also lashed out at the historical Virgil for
his utter failure to comprehend even the central concept of his own epic
of "pius Aeneas"—that of *pietas* itself. Purposefully blurring the Christian senses of *pietas* (piety, pity, *misericordia*) with its pagan meaning
(duty, loyalty), his scathing sarcasm and censure take up the whole of
chapter 10 of book V of the *Divine Institutes*, abstracted here:

> According to Maro, what kind of examples of justice did
> [Aeneas] show us—"that king than whom no other was more
> just, nor was anyone greater in piety, in war, and in arms"?
> [*Aeneid* I, 544–545]. . . . What can be more holy than this
> piety? What more clement than to immolate human victims to
> the dead? And to feed the flame with the blood of men as
> though with oil? But perhaps *it was not his own vice, but that of*
> *the poet who defiled "a man signed with piety"* [*Aeneid* I, 10] *with*
> *the brand of crime.* Where then, poet, is that piety which you
> very often praise? . . . But this, as I said was not [Aeneas's]
> fault, who perhaps had not learned letters, but yours [O Vir-
> gil]. For although you had been trained, *you did not know what*
> *piety was, and the very thing that that hero did nefariously, detest-*
> *ably, you believed to be the function of piety.* . . . [Aeneas] was in
> no way "pious," then, who killed . . . those making supplica-
> tion to him. (my italics)[9]

The irony of the "Christian Cicero" proceeds inexorably as he
broadens his vituperation to contemplate God's judgment upon Virgil's
false, pagan piety:

> How much smoke . . . darkness and error have darkened count-
> less hearts of men who, when they think themselves especially
> pious, then, especially, do they become impious? . . . Rightly,
> therefore, does punishment follow piety of this sort, and di-
> vinity, offended with the evil crimes of falsely religious men,

pursues them with dire calamity. *Though these may live lives morally sound, . . . because, however, they worship false gods whose impious and profane rites the true God hates, they are alien to justice and the name of true piety.* (my italics) [10]

St. Augustine saw the danger of pagan letters to the Christian soul; in the *Confessions* 1:13, he equates them with lust and regrets particularly the time he had wasted over such frivolities as Dido's grief to the neglect of his own salvation.[11] Augustine's disciple, Paulus Orosius, in his *Seven Books Against the Pagans* (A.D. 418), describes Virgil's Aeneas simply as an iniquitous sower of discord:

> Furthermore, in the few intervening years, came Aeneas's arrival in Italy from Troy [*Aeneid* 1:1ff.] as a fugitive, the strifes he aroused, the wars he stirred up over a period of three years, the many people he involved in hatred and afflicted with destruction, all these have been imprinted in our minds by the instruction of the elementary school.[12]

The passages from Lactantius, Augustine, and Orosius offer insight into the darker side of Virgil's traditional place, both literary and moral, in the Christian tradition.[13] They may put into focus the current views of Dante's personal "misprision," "travisamento," or "skewing" of Virgil's text in the *Commedia*,[14] and they may also give us a doctrinal basis for a better understanding of some of the failings that critics have begun to notice in Dante's Virgil.[15]

Just as the relationship of Dante to the historical Virgil may show some strain of anxiety about the Roman poet's spiritual shortcomings, similarly, within the textual network of images and poetic narration an oscillating relation develops between the personages of the two poets, one that is on the part of the wayfarer filled with devotion mixed with intermittent doubt. Joan Ferrante has justly observed that in the *Commedia* "the language of the outlawed rebel associates Virgil with Dante, . . . although . . . Dante is in rebellion only against an unjust government of man, Virgil against the law of God" (1984, p. 138). Indeed, as we shall see, the language of the poem both suggests a certain fraternity of Virgil with Dante-wayfarer and affirms, at the same time, a certain singularity and tragic isolation for the Roman poet.

Virgil's use of the word "ribellante" to describe his own apostasy is most significant since it brings into the *Commedia* the special sense that the concept of rebelliousness holds in Christianity. Clearly, to be mean-

ingful at all, the term presupposes a knowledge and even a certain acceptance of the thing rebelled against.[16] In the Judeo-Christian tradition,
unbelief and rebellion are differentiated from idolatry insofar as they
appertain specifically to God's chosen people, the children of Israel, as
opposed to the nations. The word, in fact, applied to Virgil, defines his
special and privileged position in the world of the *Commedia.*

The Old Testament repeatedly describes the people of Israel as "rebellious," and especially at the very point at which the Law is given. In
Deuteronomy 9, Moses recounted the giving of the Decalogue to the
new generation of exiles waiting to enter the Promised Land. There, on
Mount Sinai, God had warned him that the stiff-necked Hebrews had
made for themselves the molten calf as an idol. At his descent from
Sinai, Moses burned it, broke it, and threw it into a torrent (vv. 13–22);
since the Jews did not harken to his voice, he accused them of being
"always rebellious" from the day that he had begun to know them:
"Semper fuistes rebelles a die qua nosse vos coepi." The charge was repeated, for example in Deuteronomy 31:27 as Moses gave to the Levites
the canticle commemorating the giving of the Law: "While I am yet
living, and going in with you, you have always been rebellious against
the Lord. How much more when I shall be dead?" (Cf. Deuteronomy
32:15). The Israelites' unbelief was again censured as rebellious as Moses
struck the Rock of Horeb (Numbers 20:9–10, Douay):

> Moses therefore took the rod, which was before the Lord, as
> he had commanded him, and having gathered together the
> multitude before the rock, he said to them: Hear ye rebellious
> and incredulous [(Vulg.) rebelles et increduli]: Can we bring
> you forth water out of this rock? And when Moses had lifted
> up his hand, and struck the rock twice with the rod, there came
> forth water in great abundance, so that people and their cattle
> drank.

It is essential to recognize that among the Fathers and Doctors of
the church, the Rock of Horeb was of especial importance, since it pre-
figured the sacrifice of Christ himself: the water that came forth was the
water and blood that came from his side at the Crucifixion, that is, at
the very time of the New Dispensation.[17] In Christianity, the denial of
the Deity's existence or the rejection of the Deity of Christ and the refusal of his truth constituted unbelief, but most basically, unbelief and
rebellion signified precisely the failure to credit the signs and witness of
Christ as Logos, rebellion against the Word itself. In Romans 10:21, for

example, St. Paul predicts the restoration of Israel, saying that God continues to hold his hands out to the Jews "ad populum non credentem et contradicentem." Paul treats the Jews' search for justice in the Old Law as rebellion against the Deity himself. Biblically, then, rebellion meant the questioning and refusal of God's covenants, both old and new.[18]

Perhaps the most influential *locus* of the concept of rebellion is that found in Job 24 : 13, "They have been rebellious to the light," that I mentioned earlier in the case of the wayfarer's own glance aloft (Chapter 2). I have purposely left for this chapter the lengthy discussion of the biblical verse given by St. Thomas in *Summa contra gentiles* III, 159, 2 (a treatise cited often in Dante's *Convivio*), where Thomas attributes the full responsibility for accepting God's grace to the individual:

> "They have been rebellious to the light." And since this ability to impede . . . reception . . . is within the scope of free choice, not undeservedly is responsibility for the fault imputed to him who offers impediment to the reception of grace . . . just as while the sun is shining on the world, the man who keeps his eyes closed is held responsible for his fault.[19]

This theological history of the term "rebellious" ought to inform our understanding of Virgil's self-description in the first canto.[20] In Dante's philosophical treatises, the Romans are a people chosen to found the empire as a fit place for Christ's birth, and their supreme spokesman is Virgil. But the proem of the *Commedia* implies an added degree of personal accountability; Virgil by his written prophecies was not a benighted heathen to whom God had never offered knowledge of himself. The reader must perceive certain deeper resonances of failure in faith and responsibility on Virgil's part, ones akin to those of the chosen people who rebelled at the giving of both the Old and New Dispensations.

Critics have often found Dante's judgment harsh in regard to Virgil's culpability. R. Hollander, especially, has recently moved from holding that Dante saw in the *Aeneid* a text fundamentally compatible with Christian truth to believing that for the poet, both the epic and its author were beyond salvation (1983, p. 9).[21] Hollander's opinion of Dante's judgment of Virgil is unassailable in the light of the confession placed in the sage's mouth: "quello imperador che là su regna / . . . / non vuol che'n sua città per me si vegna" (*Inferno* I, 124–126). However, although Dante "allows" Virgil ultimately to suffer the doom of second death in his poem,[22] he clearly does not view Virgil's epic with the same negativity, despite his habit of correcting and rewriting the *Aeneid* to make it conform to his own beliefs. Dante obviously considered the work as history (or almost) and as a valued record of God's providence; it was a document that could, with *Eclogue* IV, convert a heathen Statius—a reading consonant with that found in *Convivio* IV and *De Monarchia* II. As Hollander suggests, Dante's idea of the providential mission of Rome came from his reading of the *Aeneid*, as did his program of continuing the tradition of Imperial poetry.[23]

While the wayfarer of the *Commedia* expresses open admiration for Virgil's style and for his mastery of (pagan) science, the narrator demonstrates an attitude toward Virgil at once more derogatory and yet more deeply respectful. In many special ways even the erring "self" of the fiction closely parallels his pagan Roman predecessor; beginning with the prologue scene of *Inferno* I, an intimate consonance grows between them. Virgil fails shamefully before the Gate of Dis (*Inferno* VIII–IX), blunders in his conversations with the hypocrites (*Inferno* XXIII), and reacts foolishly in his confrontation with the demons (*Inferno* XXI–XXIII).[24] In the same way, the wayfarer displays his sinful weaknesses and lapses during his trials and testings in the *Inferno*. He faints with pity before the lustful Francesca (*Inferno* V); he shows anger toward Filippo Argenti (*Inferno* VIII); he indulges in an internecine quarrel with Farinata (*Inferno* X); he almost falls into the *bolgia* of Ulysses (*Inferno* XXVI, 44–45) in his distraction; and he tarries too long in the *bolgia* of the falsifiers, rapt in pity and fascination at "l'ombre triste smozzicate" (*Inferno* XXIX, 1–36, esp. v. 6). The initial apostasy of the wayfarer, with the temptations of concupiscence and idolatry in his mistaken climb involving especially the will and with the temptations of pride involving the intellect, parallels metaphorically and theologically the spiritual state of Virgil.

Virgil's confession of rebellion in *Inferno* I leaves open the possibility, *prima facie*, that, had he so wished, he could have worshipped God rightly and in due fashion even before the Coming of Christ. Describing his own state in Limbo, he is made to say:

e s'e' furon dinanzi al cristianesimo,
   non adorar debitamente a Dio:
   e di questi cotai son io medesimo.   (*Inferno* IV, 37–39)

Just as the wayfarer fails to look at the light of the sun beaming above him, so the Roman poet's failure to heed the prediction of his own fourth *Eclogue* and his blindness toward the message of his own

Aeneid bespeaks a similar refusal to face the light of faith that had come to him before the Advent. *Purgatorio* VII, 25–27, makes the parallel metaphorically explicit as Virgil confesses why he has lost the sight of the Sun of the Universe:

> Non per far, ma per non fare *ho perduto*
> *a veder l'alto Sol che tu disiri*
> e che fu tardi per me conosciuto.

Ironically and tragically, Virgil, in negligence and in the blindness of ignorance, ignored his own predictions of the coming of the Messiah, yet he was historically to become the messenger of faith to others (such as the fictionalized Statius) for whom he performed the same spiritual function that he now performs literally in the poem for his pilgrim charge:

> Facesti come quei che va di notte,
>   che porta il lume dietro e sé non giova,
>   ma dopo sé fa le persone dotte,
> quando dicesti: 'Secol si rinova;
>   torna giustizia e primo tempo umano
>   e progenïe scende da ciel nova.'   (*Purgatorio* XXII, 67–72)

It is not only Virgil's wisdom, which the traditionalists have centered on, but the very weakness of his humanity, which the revisionists have begun to recognize, that makes him a fit guide for the wayfarer's descent to humility.[25]

"Chi per lungo silenzio parea fioco"

The verses conveying the wayfarer's first glimpse of the Roman poet, "dinanzi a li occhi mi si fu offerto / chi per lungo silenzio parea fioco" (vv. 62–63), have proved to be a major crux of the poem. As R. Hollander described in his thorough history of the puzzle published in 1983, scholars have argued for centuries whether the word "fioco" here means "dim" or "faint" in appearance, or "weak" or "feeble" of body (that is, Latin "flaccus"), or "faint," "hoarse," or "raucus" of voice. Those who accepted "fioco" as a visual adjective understood the verse as a catachresis or, to use a nineteenth-century term, a synaesthesia, such as that in verse 60: "là dove 'l sol tace," or in *Inferno* V, 28: "Io venni in loco d'ogne luce muto." In this interpretation, currently the one favored by the majority of critics in Italy and elsewhere, Virgil *appears* dim because he is not a body but a shade.[26] Others, following the aural meaning, explained away the silence and consequent hoarseness with a variety of fascinating guesses: the silence was taken to signify, for example, the eclipse of Reason within Dante, or the (assumed) neglect of Virgil's works through the centuries,[27] or even the silence of death. Some scholars on both sides of the issue have adduced Dante's use of "fioco"[28] in the *canzone* of chapter XXIII of the *Vita Nuova* to win their point:

> ed omo apparve scolorito e fioco
> dicendomi: "Che fai? Non sai novella?
> Morta è la donna tua, ch'era sì bella."

But this messenger who, in Dante's delirium, brings the news of Beatrice's death, is pale ("scolorito") and "fioco" just as he is about to speak; the context leaves the meaning ambiguous; we cannot tell whether the word refers to sight or sound.

Since Virgil is a shade ("Non omo, omo già fui"), other critics compare Dante's use of "silenzio" to the adjective "silentes" that the historical Vergilius Maro applied to the shades of the underworld in book VI of his *Aeneid*: "umbrae silentes" (v. 264) [silent shades], and to the adjectival participle in the next line: "loca nocte tacentia late" (v. 265) [broad, silent tracts of night]. Still other scholars make the useful comparison with the passage in which the Roman poet describes the shades of the enemy Greeks in unforgettable lines: " . . . pars tollere vocem / exiguam, inceptus clamor frustratur hiantis" (vv. 492–493) [. . . some raise a faint voice; the cry essayed dies away in their gaping mouths].

According to this opinion—which is correct, I believe, but incomplete—the Virgil of the *Commedia* is silent and weak of voice in the very tradition of his own masterpiece.[29] Dante describes Virgil's soul from Limbo just as the pagan poet believed he would be in the afterlife; we appreciate the justice of Dante's depiction literally, morally, and artistically.

One of the most interesting of recent suggestions, if not the most persuasive or accepted, came from the pen of the late André Pézard. In 1950 he explained the adjective "fioco" by noting that in the *Vergilii vita de commentario Donati sublati* (which he unfortunately ascribed to Aelius Donatus instead of Tiberius Claudius Donatus, as Hollander has noted)[30] Virgil was described as being weak of throat and slow in speech. The French critic had not noticed, however, that the information had been available for some six hundred years in the commentary of Benvenuto da Imola: "Virgilius fuerat tardissimus in sermone, adeo ut fere indocto similis videretur ut scribit Donatus super Virgilium" [Virgil was slow of speech, so much so that he appeared quite as if he were unlearned, as Donatus writes about Virgil]. Independently of Pézard, J. Cressey (1976) discovered further evidence of Virgil's hoarseness in a work that was the actual source of T. C. Donatus's *Vita*, that is Suetonius's *Vita Virgilii*, 8: "a faucibus ac dolore capitis laborabat" [he suffered from pains in his throat and head].[31] If "fioco" means "hoarse" because Virgil really did have difficulty speaking, the crux seems to be simply and readily solved in its literal significance; or it does so until we look at the text closely again and see that the "fiocaggine" there results from—or is in some other way related to—"long silence": "chi *per lungo silenzio* parea fioco."

Later, in 1957, Pézard claimed that he had solved the problem of Virgil's speech impediment in a different way, one which, we might add, did nothing to bolster his earlier suggestion. Gathering an exhaustive number of classical and medieval texts to reinforce his point, the critic found an answer in the "lupus in fabula" tradition (alluded to amid the bestiary lore in Chapter 3), that is, in the odd legend that the wolf could cut off the human voice if the animal saw its victim before the latter saw the wolf. The critic, however, did not grasp the full theological ramifications of his point and revealed his own discomfort with the explanation. Arguing that Dante might indeed have used such an "élément vulgaire," but that the legend was nonetheless beneath the dignity of the *Commedia* (p. 20), Pézard concluded that the poet would have us understand the presence of the wolf fable only "à demi mot."[32]

Pézard's observations do not give a coherent interpretation of the literal sense. First, we might object, it is the wayfarer, and not Virgil, who, without any apparent loss of voice, is seen, challenged, and put to flight by the wolf. Secondly, no matter whether Virgil was "fioco" because he was physiologically weak of throat or because he was the (unlikely) victim of lupine magic, the cause of his long silence previous to the encounter would still go unexplained. However interesting the historical information and the legend may be, they do not clarify the problem of the verse or relate it to the context of the *Commedia* as a whole.

There remains a major contradiction in the text that demands a solution: why does the poem baffle the reader by describing Virgil's silence and weakness of voice and then almost pander to his expectations by having the wayfarer launch into a flattering, indeed, gushing, praise of the Roman poet as "quella fonte che spandi di parlar sì largo fiume"

(vv. 80–81)? We must recognize that the strategy of such a disrupting juxtaposition is deliberate. The larger textual and intertextual links that can solve the puzzle are still to be explored.

Hollander's recent study of the question in the light of theological patterns makes strides toward a resolution. Dismissing the traditional arguments over sight or sound, he argues persuasively that the terms "fioco" and "silenzio" compose a catachresis where *both* the visual and auditory hold. The appearance of Virgil on Good Friday 1300 coincides with the darkness of the sun at the time of Christ's death: the profound sense of the term "silenzio" points not only to Virgil's state as a shade but also to his disobedience, for though he was eloquent and filled with all the knowledge that could be gained without grace, he failed to recognize the Light, the Sun of Christ, the Word. Hollander argues that the images "il sol tace" and "per lungo silenzio parea fioco" signify that both poets dwell in a realm of shadows, ignorant of the true Sun. Virgil (as Pézard had noted also [1950], p. 341), who precedes Beatrice in the work of Dante's salvation, is a figure of John the Baptist, the "vox clamantis in deserto."[33]

Too complex to be given justice within the confines of this *lectura*, Hollander's position is the best analysis of the problem to date. Building upon his work we can adduce further evidence that, I believe, will prove conclusive.

In the first chapter of this study I emphasized that the problem of apostasy was a major theme toward which all the biblical allusions and actions of the first sixty-one lines pointed. The fictional date of the *Commedia*'s first day, Good Friday, as we see also in Petrarch's handling of the theme in the *Canzoniere*, is, in Christian tradition, the very day of apostasy, the day of St. Peter's denial of Christ, the day, in fact, on which all mankind abandoned the Redeemer, all that is, except the Blessed Virgin, who never wavered in her belief in the resurrection and redemption of her son. In the *Commedia* she is made, correspondingly, the first agent in the wayfarer's salvation. These pre-Easter themes clearly join the apostasy of both poets in a poetic pattern, linking it to other related biblical images of the silence of God and man.

In the canto, the sun, the figure of the Godhead, falls silent in his anger at unbelief as he so often does in the Bible. In Ezechiel 3:26, God ceases to speak to the people through his prophet as punishment for their faithlessness and backsliding. The silence of the Deity is part of the trial in the victory over impiety in Habacuc 1:2 and 1:13; God does not respond to Job's prayers (for example in Job 30:20), and is silent as the Psalmist begs him to speak in Psalm 83:2 (Vulgate 82:2). In Psalm 27:1,

his silence is damnation: "Ad te Domine clamabo Fortis meus ne obsur-
descas mihi *nequando taceas a me et adsimilabor descendentibus in lacum*"
[Unto thee will I cry, O Lord: O my God, be not thou silent [deaf] to
me; *lest if thou be silent to me, I become like them that go down into the pit*].
This last verse is, of course, one of the major biblical patterns for *Inferno* I, 60–63:

> *mi ripigneva là dove'l sol tace.*
> *Mentre ch'i' rovinava in basso loco,*
> dinanzi a li occhi mi si fu offerto
> chi per lungo silenzio parea fioco.

The wayfarer's recidivism and alienation from God have brought him
to the very pass feared by the Psalmist.

Concomitant with the biblical recognition of the silence of God is
the silence of man expressed in the familiar injunction of Ecclesiastes 3:7: "A time to keep silence, and a time to speak." In the Judeo-
Christian tradition, man is enjoined to bear witness to the Godhead;
not to speak signifies a failure of trust, the sin of unbelief; man cannot
be silent in acknowledging God's power: the formula "non taceo" "non
tacere" is common in the Vulgate. Jeremiah will not hold his peace in
his call to the repentant of Jerusalem: "Non tacebo" (4:19). In Isaiah
62:1–6, the watchmen of Jerusalem's walls shall never hold their peace:
"Non tacebunt." In Luke 19:40, Christ chides the Pharisees who re-
buked him for permitting his disciples to bless and hail him as king:
"Si hii tacuerint lapides clamabunt" [If these shall hold their peace the
stones will cry out]. God orders Saint Paul, "Noli timere sed loquere et
ne taceas" (Acts 18:9) [Do not hold thy peace].

The conceptual alliance of the images of silence ("tacere," "silenzio") in the poem, reflecting biblical tradition, help us to understand
not only the auditory but also the spiritually darkening senses of the
verse, "chi per lungo silenzio parea fioco." As we have noted, Virgil's
own confessions in the poem reflect his having failed to bear witness to
his own predictions. Both by the examples of the Old Testament prophets and patriarchs (*Inferno* IV, 55–63) and by the fictional salvation of
Trajan and Ripheus (*Paradiso* XX, 46–48, 68), Dante stresses the orthodox belief that in God's unfathomable plan, salvation was always
possible by faith in Christ to come ("quei che credettero in Cristo ven-
turo," *Paradiso* XXXII, 24). Theologically (and on this point we can cite
St. Thomas Aquinas's *Summa contra gentiles* III, 159), those alone are
deprived of grace who offer within themselves an obstacle to grace; man
can impede grace and ensure his own damnation.

As we have seen, the historical Virgil had come under the scrutiny, praise and indictment of the early Christian euhemerists and apologists, and the personage Virgil of the *Commedia* is made to bring that whole context into the poem by his own (unhistorical) self-identification and confession: born "*sub Julio*," under Julius Caesar, he lived under Augustus at "the time of the false and lying gods."[34] Later, he will tell the wayfarer often of his own fallibility and limitations concerning things *de fide* and here, at his first appearance, he foretells his own leave-taking: another guide will lead the pilgrim in heaven (*Inferno* I, 122–126).

The wayfarer responds to Virgil's clues with immediate understanding. Although he zealously describes his constant study of the *Aeneid*, naming the poem with an honorific title "*volume*," addressing Virgil as his "autore," his author and authority (*Inferno* I, 85),[35] he makes no mention of the *subject* of the poem but only of "*lo bello stile*" that he has taken from Virgil and by which he has brought himself worldly honor. Given the centuries-old tradition of lavish praise of Virgil's style and the ambiguous position that eloquence held in the early struggle between idolatry and true religion, the wayfarer's encomium rings hollow and even self-serving in stark, poignant and tragic contrast to Virgil's anguished regrets.[36]

The concepts of rebellion, eloquence, and silence are filled with grim portents for this shade who did not worship God aright. An examination of the writings of the early Fathers of the church clarifies his situation. In book V of the *Divine Institutes*, Lactantius rails against those who defended paganism but were silent about its true nature: "Rightly do [the pagans] not dare teach anything about [their own] divine matters, lest they be mocked by our people and deserted by their own. . . . Hence, '*faithful silences in religious matters*' have been instituted by clever men, so that the people may not know what they worship" (book V, ch. 19, trans. McDonald, p. 379; my italics).

The line that Lactantius cites comes, tellingly, from Virgil's *Aeneid*, book III, 112: "fida silentia sacris" [the faithful silence of mysteries].[37] Indeed, Lactantius refers to a long historical tradition concerning the "keeping of silence" about the inconsistencies of paganism; the idea was a topos of blame among Christian euhemerists as it had been previously a topos of praise and caution among the pagans. The Christian writer Minucius Felix, for example, has his interlocutor, Caecilius, take the pagan side in his euhemeristic dialogue, *Octavius* (a work, by the way, often thought to be "Octavus" or "book VIII" of Arnobius's *Seven Books Against the Pagans*). In chapter 6 of the work's prologue, Caecilius warns Octavius, the Christian: "You would be better advised if you did not pronounce any opinion of your own on deities; you should rather trust your forebears who in a still uncultured age at the very infancy of the world were blessed with gods."[38] The tradition of reverential silence, termed "faventia," stems from the order of silence proclaimed at Roman pagan rites: "favete linguis" (or "faves lingua"), "curb your tongue," a tradition that was known to the Middle Ages. Compare Paul the Deacon in his eighth-century epitome of Festus the Grammarian: "*Faventia* bonam ominationem significat. Nam praecones clamantes populum sacrificiis favere iubebant. Favere est bona fari, at *veteres poetae pro silere usi sunt favere*" [*Faventia*, the keeping of silence, means a good omen. For shouting heralds used to order the people at sacrifices to be silent. *Favere* is to say only well-omened things; *thus the ancient poets used favere for silere, to be silent*] (my italics).[39]

In contrast to Christianity, whose worship is the liturgy, the *leitourgia*, the pious "work of the people," pagan piety commanded silence at its rituals and on the subject of faith.[40] The *silenda* were the very mysteries or rites of divination that were above discussion among pagans. In augural language, *silentium* itself meant, specifically, "freedom from disturbance," that is, "faultlessness," "perfection" of the rites performed. As Cicero recounts in the *De Divinatione* II, 34, 71 (*On Divination*, pp. 450–453):

> In our forefathers' time the magistrates on such occasions used to call in some expert person to take the auspices—but in these days anyone will do. But one must be an expert to know what constitutes "silence," for by that term we mean "free of every augural defect" [id enim silentium dicimus in auspiciis, quod omni vitio caret]. . . . After the celebrant has said to this assistant, "Tell me when silence appears to exist" [Dicito, si silentium esse videbitur] the latter, without looking up or about him, immediately replies, "Silence appears to exist" [Silentium esse videri].

Cicero's words are also preserved in Paul the Deacon's epitome of Festus: "hoc enim est proprie *silentium, omnis vitii in auspices vacuitas*" [This is silence proper: the absence of any defect in the auspices].[41]

A textual and intertextual pattern begins to emerge. The "silence" of paganism signified the very *perfection* of rites in the works of pagan classic writers and in those of the early Christian euhemerists, the *sinful failure* to criticize the true nature of those pagan rites. Both senses are joined in the first identification of Virgil in *Inferno* I. Though the Roman poet had predicted the coming of Christ and had demonstrated the greatest eloquence in the history of literature, he had been mute not only in true praise of God but in his criticism of idolatry. Indeed, among pagans, Virgil was a renowned authority on all aspects of divination and worship of the gods. Macrobius, in the *Saturnalia*, for example, extolled the poet's thorough expertise in pagan religious rites and his supreme accuracy and excellence of vocabulary in describing them.[42] Virgil's association with the "false and lying gods" resulted, historically, from far more than the mere accident of the time of his birth. Thus, we may find that the lines attributed to him in *Purgatorio* VII, 7—"Io son Virgilio; e per null'altro rio / lo ciel perdei che per non aver fé"—may be the kindest of understatements.

Other passages of the *Institutes* can also help us elucidate Dante's strategy in *Inferno* I. Lactantius discourses on those who, by cleaving to the obvious falsity of idolatry, recognize nothing of the truth of Christianity; the doctrine expressed by Lactantius is the most likely key to Dante's text:

> For he *who is ignorant of the nature and existence of the divinity is truly speechless and dumb [vere elinguis et mutus est], although he be the most eloquent of men.* When the tongue begins to speak the truth, that is, virtue, and to interpret the majesty of one God, then, at last, it is performing the function of its nature. But as long as it speaks false things, it is not working according to its own usefulness, and, therefore, of necessity *he is but incapable of speech [infans] he who is not able to speak of divine things.* (p. 310; my italics)

Elsewhere he emphasizes that paganism is mute and is practiced by the mute (*DI* IV, 3):

> Where, therefore, is wisdom joined with religion? There, namely, where one God is adored, where life and every act is referred to one head and the Supreme Being, and, finally, the same ones are the doctors of wisdom who are also the priests of God. Let it not, however, disturb anyone, that which has often happened and can take place, that some philosophers undertake the priesthood of the false gods. For when that happens, philosophy is not joined with religion, but both the philosophy will cease among the sacred things, and the religion, when philosophy will be treated. *For that religion is mute, not only because it is of the mute*, but because its rite rests upon the hand or

in the fingers, not in the heart or tongue, as does ours which is true. (p. 249; my italics) [43]

The "metaphor" of being "faint of voice because of long silence" turns out to be a doctrinal truth, *litera et sensu*. When we examine the text of *Inferno* I, 61–81, grammatically, we recognize that it is indeed the poet-narrator in retrospect—and not the wayfarer through immediate experience—who recounts the appearance of Virgil.[44] Note the preterit: "dinanzi a li occhi mi si *fu* offerto. . . . Quando *vidi* costui nel gran diserto" (vv. 61, 64). The event has been completed and given context by the wayfarer's subsequent journey, with, and beyond, Virgil. The poet writing from greater knowledge can truthfully describe Virgil as "weak of voice because of long silence." Indeed, as we contemplate the poem as a whole and with hindsight, we see that the words presenting Virgil are no more or less grammatically ambiguous as an identification nor less literally "true" than Dante's identification of the shade (most probably Celestine V) in *Inferno* III. The affinity in the choice of words is instructive. Compare:

vidi e conobbi l'ombra di colui
che fece per viltade il gran rifiuto.   (*Inferno* III, 59–60)

with

dinanzi a li occhi mi si fu offerto
chi per lungo silenzio parea fioco.

The poet recounts how he as *viator* on both occasions caught sight of a lost shade; the formula is basically the same. An indefinite pronoun, "chi," "colui che," acts as subject of a verb, "parea," "fece," and, in each case, a clause introduced by "per" gives the *cause* of the shade's sinful action or non-action: "out of, because of, through cowardice," "out of, because of, through silence." The final, terrible realization of this comes to us again in retrospect with Virgil's own confession in *Purgatorio* VII, 7–8, of his sole wickedness, his lack of faith: "'Io son Virgilio; e *per* null'altro rio / lo ciel perdei che *per* non aver fé.'" Just as in the Bible man's silence could signify the failure of belief and God's silence could represent his wrath at unbelief, so in Christian euhemerism, the idolatry of paganism, the ultimate in unbelief, was characterized by *silentium*. The very silence prized by the pagans signified, for the Christians, faithlessness and rebellion against God. "Per lungo silenzio" is a synonym for "per non aver fé."[45]

Throughout the *Commedia* Dante creates his moral vision of the realms of the afterlife in just such a blending of varied traditions, drawn from pagan, biblical, and patristic texts and their commentaries to form a synchretic, polysemous image. Virgil, who ignored pre-redemptive grace in life reveals in the *Commedia* his fallibility when we first behold him: though he is "a fount that pours forth so broad a stream of speech," he is indeed weak of voice in matters of faith.

Yet the important matter is not the past silence of Virgil, but that this silence is broken in the prologue of the *Commedia*. Dante has Virgil "correct" his own failure for, in his sublime role as a bearer of grace, his "largo fiume di parlar" will now be in the service of Christ.[46] With this realization, we glimpse the real affection that Dante had for the Roman poet: the breaking of silence is one with entrusting to him the altruistic agency of conversion; this, too, is "il ben che vi trovai," for, in a sense, it is one of the most charitable of inventions ("trovare," "trobar," "trouver") in the history of poetry.[47]

CHAPTER V

"Il veltro"

The Early Commentators

Prophecies, particularly those in, and based upon, the biblical apocalyptic tradition, arise from two forces, or, rather, aim at two objectives: first, a recapitulation of historical fact disguised as vaticination ("vaticinium ex eventu"), or second, an intended eschatological prediction whose outcome would be unknown to the author.[1] In the *Commedia* many of the prophecies at the fictional date of the narrative, 1300, were, of course, past events at the time of composition—chronicles written in the future tense—such as Farinata's and Cacciaguida's "foretelling" of Dante's exile in *Inferno* X, 79–81, and *Paradiso* XVII, 49–99, or the dire punishment to be meted out to "le sfacciate donne fiorentine" that Forese "predicts" in *Purgatorio* XXIII, 101, punishment already provided for in legislation approved by the Bishop's synod in Florence and Fiesole by 1310.[2] History can permit us to see the meaning of the poem in the many cases where we know of or discover evidence that the specific catastrophe, ill, or wrong has occurred, been cured, or surpassed; yet there are, likewise, instances in which the text expresses the Christian virtues of hope and faith in exhortations and prayers for which there could be no possibility of realization within any foreseeable time, or for which only the barest traces of fulfillment could be imagined.

The major critical question about the *veltro* is whether to categorize Virgil's prediction as "vaticinium ex eventu" or as real prophecy. The history of opinion is sharply divided, with the early commentators aligned with the notion of genuine apocalypticism, and the nineteenth and twentieth century, generally, on the side of consummated fact. Critics have wrangled for centuries over the poet's intention, and each has seen a different message encoded in the prognostication: either a generic prophecy, or a specific individual; either a present redeemer or one yet to come; either a pope or an emperor—or simply a "leader" or a reformer of some mysterious provenance.[3]

For many critics the key to the riddle of the *veltro* has appeared to hinge on verse 105, "e sua nazion sarà tra feltro e feltro." The line has been the subject of controversy since the earliest commentaries; and the various identifications of the "veltro" have both colored and have been colored in turn by the meanings given to the words "tra feltro e feltro." We can, in the main, distinguish four principal categories of interpretation of the verse, but these categories are not mutually exclusive nor are they without their own peculiar refinements and variations, both ancient and modern. The fact that many scholars adopted two or more interpretations simultaneously, depending upon the nature of the meaning that they were discussing, makes the history of the discussion difficult to outline either thematically or chronologically.

First, perhaps both in time and importance, were the astrological constructions of the ancient glossators. For most of these, "tra feltro e feltro" meant "tra cielo e cielo," "amid the heavens," and thus the words signified the influence of a constellation. It is difficult to decide whether an understanding of "filtra" ("filtre") for "feltro" was actually entertained by the early exegetes or not, but the logic of the leap from "feltro" to "cielo" is otherwise by no means immediately apparent to the modern reader.[4] A major hybrid and inventive variant dating from our own century derives, in turn, from the astrological interpretation: "feltro" referred to the felt caps of Castor and Pollux, and, thus, to the constellation of Gemini, the birth sign of the predicted reformer who was to be identified with the poet himself.[5]

Second, interpreters saw in the word "felt," a symbol of poverty and thus a sign of the deliverer's humble birth; some modern scholars have seen it (for various reasons) as a specific reference to the humble garments of the mendicant orders,[6] and have theorized that Dante might have anticipated a social reform originating with the Franciscans. Earlier, still others had seen the "vile," matted cloth as signifying the bastardy of the future redeemer.

Third, the geographical interpretation of "Feltro e Feltro" construing the words as the names of two cities, Feltre in the Marca Trevigiana and Montefeltro in Romagna, was first recorded in the fourteenth century, mocked during the Renaissance, espoused in the early part of this century and, thereafter, regarded again with the disfavor that is still largely current.

Fourth came the twentieth-century suggestion that the verse referred to an actual fourteenth-century process of voting or electing candidates for high office.[7]

Scholars have observed that the earliest commentators were hesitant to make any identification of the "veltro" with specific historical personages.[8] Jacopo di Dante (com 1322) was, perhaps, the first to give the interpretation an astrological bent, attributing the future restoration of man to the "velocissima variazione delle stelle" personified by the *veltro* in opposition to the figuration of contemporary vices, "the cupidity of avarice," symbolized by the *lupa* (p. 50). The expression "tra feltro e feltro" signified "tra cielo e cielo," since the origin of this renewal would come from the heavens. Jacopo reported and rejected the opinion of others, however, who, believing "feltro" to signify "a vile kind of cloth," saw in the prophecy just some virtuous redeemer, "alcuno virtudioso," of humble birth who would cure all men of vice.

Jacopo della Lana (com ca. 1324–1328; pp. 112–115) descried in Dante's lines an echo of the astrologer Albumasar for whom the world was divided into seven ages, just as the week was divided into seven days, each with a reigning planet; since the seventh fell under the avaricious influence of the Moon, the next expected age, the returning golden reign of Saturn, would be characterized by generosity and benevolence. Lana explained "tra feltro e feltro" in two ways: that it meant, first, "tra cielo e cielo," that is, that the cure would be effected by means of a heavenly constellation, or, secondly, that the restorer would be of low birth, "chè feltro è vile panno." Shortly thereafter, in 1333, the Ottimo was to repeat substantially the same ideas (com pp. 9–12).

Other early glossators gave minor variants on the astrological explanation. Boccaccio (com 1373) frankly admitted his uncertainty as he espoused the theory of a generic stellar influence: "E, per quello che io abbia potuto comprendere, sì per le parole dell'autore, sì per li ragionamenti intorno a questo di ciascuno il quale ha alcun sentimento, l'autore intende qui dovere essere alcuna costellazione celeste, la quale dee negli uomini generalmente imprimere la virtù della liberalità" (pp. 87–88). Then, adducing the prophecy of *Purgatorio* XX, 15, "quando verrà per cui questa disceda," he narrowed his explanation to the coming of *one* man: "E costui mostra dovere essere virtuosissimo uomo." For the sense of "tra feltro e feltro," he again confessed his perplexity ("confesso ch'io non intendo") while rejecting two opposing views: first, that of those who believed it to signify the humble, virgin birth of Christ and, thus, his Second Coming, and, secondly, of those who interpreted the line as the prediction of the coming of a Tartar emperor because at their death the Khans were customarily buried in felt wrappings (pp. 90–91).[9] Boccaccio sided, however, with those who saw "feltro" as signifying the low birth of one who, by example, would cast avarice into oblivion (p. 90).

Francesco da Buti (com 1385–1389) and, a century later, Landino (com 1481) continued to view "tra feltro e feltro" as meaning "tra cielo e cielo." The former again took the view of a general celestial influence that would "dispose the world to wisdom, virtue and love" (pp. 46–47), while the latter contemplated this influence once more as being embodied in a single ruler. Meanwhile, the Anonimo Fiorentino (com ca. 1400), rejecting the idea of "feltro e feltro" as signifying either base birth or two cities, had returned simply to the interpretation of the phrase as "costellazioni superne"—supernal constellations that would drive avarice from the world (p. 25).

In the three different versions of his glosses on his father's poem (com 1340–1341; 1348–1350),[10] Pietro di Dante made the astrological interpretation more specific: the prophecy referred to the auspicious conjunction of Saturn and Jupiter (p. 52). But the prediction would find fulfillment in a "vir virtuosus et dux" born "tra feltro e feltro," that is, of both low and bastard birth, for felt was not a duly woven textile but a base cloth merely matted together. This *veltro* would become, according to the Ottobonian version of Pietro's *Commentarium*, not merely leader of Italy but emperor of the whole world, "qui regnum mundi praesens et gubernationem habebit" (p. 55). Citing Virgil's *Eclogue* IV and *Aeneid* VI, 849–853, Pietro claimed that the prophecy legitimately referred both to "Octavianum Augustum," that is, to an emperor, and to Christ (p. 53). In the Ashburnham version of the glosses, Pietro further suggested an identity with the pseudo-Methodius's prediction of the last of the Roman emperors, the "rex Christianorum," who was to vanquish the Ishmaelites, that is the Muslims, before the coming of the Antichrist and, thus, herald the Second Coming of Christ.[11] In all three versions of his commentary, Pietro compares the prediction with the coming of the "novus homo" of Alain de Lille's *Anticlaudianus*: both Alain and Dante's heroes were to combat avarice and restore the world. In Pietro's later two versions of the *Commentarium*, the *veltro* is specifically identified with the "515" prophecy of *Purgatorio* XXXIII, 43.

Some among the earliest commentators preferred an eschatalogical interpretation, or at least combined it with one or more of the astrological versions. Graziolo (com 1324), followed, as we have seen, by Pietro but rejected by Boccaccio, had interpreted the *veltro* both as a prophecy of the Second Coming of Christ and as the prediction of a Roman pontiff or an emperor or "some other man of lofty prudence, sublime virtue and humble birth" (pp. 9–10) who would come to lead mankind onto the path of virtue. Guido da Pisa (com 1327–1328), surely basing his reading on Dante's *Monarchia*, gave the *veltro* prophecy several meanings: he interpreted it first as symbolizing the "nobility of the Roman people" that held primacy among all kingdoms, and, secondly, not only as that nobility bodied forth as an emperor in the mold of Scipio Africanus come to cure the world of avarice, but also, anagogically, as Christ at his Second Coming (p. 33).[12] Among the strangest of explanations for the sense of "tra feltro e feltro," however, is Guido's idea that "feltrum" was the armpit: "The heart is midway between the two armpits. And the armpit in the Spanish language is called *feltrum*. And so he says: 'la sua nazion sarà tra feltro e feltro'; that is, his actions . . . will come from a pure heart." I have found no evidence that Guido's "armpits" founded any interpretive school.

More single-mindedly, the Anonimo Selmiano (com ca. 1337) held that the *veltro* was Christ at the Last Judgment, "Cristo figliuolo di Dio" (p. 7), and the Codice Cassinese (com ca. 1350) followed suit: "Veltrus, id est Christus" (p. 13).

Benvenuto da Imola (com 1373–1380) followed Guido da Pisa and Pietro di Dante: he considered the prophecy both (p. 55) as an imitation of Virgil's *Eclogue* IV and also as a dual prediction of Christ's coming to judge the avaricious and of a future "Roman prince" who would curtail the greed of prelates: " . . . dico quod illud, quod Dantes dicit de veltro, potest intelligi de Christo, et de quodam principe futuro" (p. 56) [I say that what Dante says of the *veltro* can be understood of Christ and of some future ruler]. He accepted the astrological interpretion of "feltro e feltro" as "cielo e cielo" and ridiculed those who explained it geographically. Like his peers, the "falso Boccaccio" (pp. 17–18), too, relied heavily upon the opinions of others and duly recorded them: some, he writes, held that the "veltro" would be an emperor who would actually dwell in Rome and chase out the false shepherds of the church; others that it was Christ "quando verrà al dì del giudicio." The view that it would be a pope he dismisses with a curt "io nol credo."

Serravalle (com 1416–1417, p. 34) mocked the geographical interpretation of "feltro e feltro" as Feltre and Montefeltro as "opinio ridiculosa et vana" and dismissed the explanation that "feltro" was felt: "Hec opinio ridiculosior est prima."[13] He reported the astrological view disinterestedly, citing, without credit, Pietro's reference to Albumasar and tied the *veltro* to the "515" prophecy of *Purgatorio* XXXIII, 43: the influence of a constellation would produce "unum dominum, quem aliquando vocat ducem" who was to usher in a golden age. Serravalle's personal preference was, instead, for the coming of a "Summum Pontificem" who would contemn temporal dominion and riches, appoint to the cardinalate only good and virtuous men, and slay the wolf of avarice. But, undogmatically, he allowed that it could also be a single emperor or prince, it mattered not: "vel forte erit unus Imperator vel Dux. Non est cura."

Modern Interpretations

While most of the earliest commentaries did not see the prophecy as identifiable with a known specific personage, later critics have not always been so reticent.[14] Nineteenth- and twentieth-century interpretations generally can be categorized into three main streams. First, those who believe the predicted reformer to be an emperor;[15] second, those who see him instead as a pope;[16] third, those who, harking back to the tradition of the fourteenth century, prefer to view the prophecy more generically: the *veltro* is simply a reformer yet to come of some unknown affiliation.[17] Still others have seen Dante's prediction as changing and developing in the course of his completion of the *Commedia*. To this last position perhaps V. Cian (1897, p. 18; 1945, esp. pp. 4, 49 et passim) and E. G. Parodi (1920, pp. 367–492) contributed most. Parodi, in particular, saw Dante's hopes clinging ever more closely to Henry VII of Luxembourg as the poet wrote the last cantos of the *Purgatorio*—until they were dashed by the death of the monarch on August 24, 1313.

The twentieth century has been rich in development of a variety of ideas. Several critics have evolved new interpretations by giving new emphasis to various details that were already present in the critical history but that had been ignored by the majority. Following the interpretation reported but rejected by Boccaccio, A. Bassermann (1901) and H. Matrod (1914) argued that the *veltro* prophecy signified the coming of the Great Khan of the Tartars. Following some suggestions of L. Tondelli (1940; 2nd ed. 1953) that he ultimately rejects, R. E. Kaske (1961) and, in his wake, J. B. Friedman (1972), viewed the prophecy as embodied in the two preaching orders of the Franciscans and Dominicans; such a view had also been propounded earlier by P. Caligaris (1951). Ungaretti (1952, rpt. 1962) saw the prophecy as heralding the return of the Age of Gold. Similarly, G. Ferretti (1935, p. 434) viewed it as the incarnation of justice; he, R. Roedel (1959), and A. Vallone (1954; rprt. 1955), following in the tradition of the ancient commentaries, did not give it any specific historic referent. M. Sampoli Simonelli (1954) interpreted it as an "ordinatore supremo" who would bring peace and justice to Italy.

Other, more traditional views, such as that of *veltro* as the Second Coming of Christ, found defenders in F. M. Torricelli (1865) and P. Chistoni (1905 a and b). P. Cassel (1890), L. Filomusi-Guelfi (1911, p. 41), G. Papini (1933, pp. 367–390), and M. Colacci (1947, p. 79) viewed the prophecy as the coming of the Joachite Age of the Holy Spirit.

Vellutello (com 1544), who accepted the geographical interpretation of "tra feltro e feltro" rejected by Pietro and the Anonimo Fiorentino, seems to have been the first to give written testimony of the *veltro*'s identification as Can Grande della Scala (with the "515" of *Purgatorio* XXXIII, 43, identified as Henry of Luxembourg), an interpretation taken up by Lorenzo Magalotti (com 1665),[18] U. Foscolo (com 1842–1843; *Discorso* [1842], p. 396), G. Todeschini (1872), and E. Soprano (com 1955); many others, such as K. Witte (1869–1879, vol. 1, pp. 137–139), F. Kampers (in several articles), and T. Casini (1905; 1913), agreed. Other critics have suggested other joint identifications: R. Hollander (1969, pp. 181–190) proposed Can Grande and Christ; and E. Auerbach (*Dante, Poet* [1929; Eng. trans. 1961], p. 129), Can Grande and the Great Khan or the Phoenix.[19] Indeed, the flattering mention of Can Grande, the emperor's vicar and captain of the Ghibelline forces in Italy, that Cacciaguida gives in *Paradiso* XVII, 76–93, makes the Lord of Verona a candidate not to be dismissed out of hand; Cacciaguida compares the Scaligera crest to the Imperial eagle ("the Holy Bird upon the Ladder," v. 72), lauds Can Grande's future generosity to the poet, and extols his future deeds and magnificence; however, the wayfarer is carefully told *not* to speak of these things, for they would not be believed:

> "e portera'ne scritto ne la mente
> di lui, e nol dirai"; e disse cose
> incredibili a quei che fier presente.   (vv. 91–93)

The poem suggests its own poetic and narrative motives in concealing the sense of the prophecy.

V. Cian (1897; 1945), G. Gentile (1918; 1921), A. Solmi (1922) and, most recently, F. Mazzoni (com 1967) have all supported the identification of the *veltro* with Henry VII. L. Arezio (1931; 1939) also accepted this identification and suggested, in support, the derivation of *"veltro"* from German "welt-herr" "world ruler" (Weltherr). Although ingenious, his etymology inspired no following. There has been no lack of other important choices for imperial candidates. In a long essay of 1826, Troya (pub. 1932) put forth Uguccione della Faggiola,[20] and Joan Ferrante (1984) has recently given interesting and cogent reasons for supporting Ludwig of Bavaria (pp. 119–121, 129–130).

L. Pietrobono (1929; rprt. 1959) understood the *veltro* prophecy more generally as a prediction of an emperor who would renew society; in a similar vein, B. Nardi (*Il Preludio* [1963], pp. 3–17) saw in the *veltro*'s pursuit of the wolf the coming of a universal monarch who would rescind the Donation of Constantine and restore the ideal of poverty to the church. G. R. Sarolli (1963) identified the *veltro* with the "515" prophecy, understanding them as two "simboli cristomimetici" to be embodied in a Holy Roman emperor springing from the people.[21]

In contrast to these "Ghibelline" interpretations came those who held that the work of earth's restoration would be undertaken by a particular pope (for example, M. Porena, com 1946–1948, rprt. 1961; 1953): Benedict XI found supporters in S. Betti (1865), G. B. Giuliani (1861), G. M. Cornoldi (com 1887, p. 14), and Renucci (1954, p. 94; 1965a). Others have rejected the identification as being unlikely, not only on the usual thematic and philosophical grounds, but because it would assume an impossibly early date for the writing of the *Inferno*; Benedict died in 1304.[22]

Dante *poeta-veltro*

Critics have put forth other identifications even more surprising or strained. Ruggero Della Torre reported a letter from Pompeo Azzolino to Gino Capponi, published in 1837, in which Azzolini had identified the *veltro* with Dante himself; R. Della Torre himself defended the thesis warmly in two volumes entitled *Poeta-Veltro* (1887–1890);[23] he was followed in this by S. Scaetta (1896, esp. pp. 15–18), R. Petrucci (1901), C. Borromeo (1901), R. Benini (1919; rprt. 1952), and L. Olschki.[24] Olschki, having interpreted the words "tra feltro e feltro" in his *Myth of Felt* of 1949 as a reference to the felt caps of Castor and Pollux, the twins of the zodiac, published a second short treatise in 1953 entitled *Dante "poeta veltro,"* which, as the title proclaimed, again proposed the poet himself as the longed-for messiah, born under the sign of Gemini. Olschki's views have been espoused by S. Falchitto (com 1952) and, most recently, by G. Getto (1960; rprt. 1967). Even ignoring the minor objections that the Dioscuri's caps could be made from other materials (such as leather) and that felt could be made into garments other than the "pilleus" worn by the twins (as Porena and others saw), however, this strain of criticism is not convincing: it ignores Dante's epistolary pleas for reform from imperial sources and makes light of his view of the empire as central to man's earthly happiness and perfection.[25]

Other critics have developed a more plausible, but not widely accepted, thesis of a "poema-veltro": G. Crescimanno's thorough study of 1905 was followed by those of C. G. Hardie in 1961, 1963, and 1964: the *veltro* was the *Commedia* itself.[26]

"Tra Feltro e Feltro"

The interpretation of the enigmatic verse 105 has continued to be divided mainly between the geographical and astrological, even in modern times. The controversial capitalization of the words "Feltro e Feltro"[27] as place names in the Società Dantesca Italiana edition of 1921 helped garner converts to identify the *veltro* with Can Grande, despite the obvious imprecision of using the two cities to delimit the boundaries of the Scaligera realm. But, in fact, the aroused opposition won: Petrocchi's new edition expunged the society's liberties; on this side of the Atlantic, Singleton adopted the reading "tra feltro e feltro" and translated "between felt and felt," leaving the riddle enveloped in its mystery.

In the very year that the Società Dantesca attempted to make "tra Feltro e Feltro" the canonical reading, Aurelio Regis, prompted by the early commentators' acceptance of "feltro" as signifying a "cloth of a vile sort," made a suggestion that, at first blush, seemed quite seductive: "tra feltro e feltro" referred to the felt linings of election boxes, "bossoli foderati di feltro" used throughout the fourteenth century in many of the communes of Italy to deaden the sound of the lead ball, "pallotta" or "ballot," as it was dropped within. Orders for such boxes for secret elections are found recorded in the statutes of many cities, including Siena, Treviso, Brescia, Cremona, and Casale; and the practice of electing high officials by "bossolo e pallotta," "box and ballot," is recorded in many other cities, including Padua, Rome, Ascoli-Piceno, Venice, and Florence among many others. Although Regis adduces the widespread Italian custom to support an imperial interpretation,[28] his explanation, in fact, does little to resolve the choice between a pope or an emperor since both positions were elective. The scholar does not, furthermore, ascertain whether the German imperial electors actually chose the emperor using lead ballots and felted boxes. The main stumbling block to acceptance of his theory, however, is its foundation: his departure from the text in reading "nazion"—a word signifying "birth," "nation," "race," "stock," "lineage" "clan," or "people" for Dante and his contemporaries—as "election." One's "nazion" could not be changed by subsequent vote.

The Ambiguity of the Prophecy

Let us again examine closely the text of the prophecy:

Molti son li animali a cui s'ammoglia,
  e più saranno ancora, infin che'l Veltro
  verrà, che la farà morir con doglia.
Questi non ciberà terra né peltro,
  ma sapïenza, amore e virtute,
  e sua nazion sarà tra feltro e feltro.
Di quella umile Italia fia salute
  per cui morì la vergine Cammilla,
  Eurialo e Turno e Niso di ferute.
Questi la caccerà per ogne villa,
  fin che l'avrà rimessa ne lo 'nferno,
  là onde 'nvidia prima dipartilla.
Ond'io per lo tuo me' penso e discerno
  che tu mi segui, e io sarò tua guida,
  e trarrotti di qui per lo loco etterno.   (vv. 100–114)

To argue, as some exegetes have, that the trinitarian "sapienza, amore e virtute" is more applicable to an ecclesiastical than to a temporal ruler is to ignore the christological and trinitarian language that Dante himself applies, for example, to Henry VII in his epistles. He terms the emperor another Moses who will lead Italy from its oppressors; Henry is the Bridegroom "the most clement . . . Elect of God and Augustus and Caesar" and is flattered most remarkably with an intimate confession: "Tunc exultavit in me spiritus meus, quum tacitus dixi mecum: 'Ecce Agnus Dei, ecce qui tollit peccata mundi'" [Then my spirit exalted within me, when I said silently within myself: "Behold the Lamb of God which taketh away the sins of the world"].[29]

Yet, let us resist identifying the *veltro* with any specific candidate and make two primary textual observations: first, the prophecy comes between the description of the baleful habits and effects of the threatening *lupa* and Virgil's first statement of the ordained plan to guide the wayfarer through the first two realms of the hereafter; second, Virgil foretells that the *veltro* will bring the salvation only of "umile Italia."[30] We can apply the sense of the *veltro*'s redemptive office to the Roman empire as a whole only figuratively—by synechdoche, or by some extra-textual knowledge of the *Aeneid*, that is, of the outcome of the struggles between the Trojans and Rutilians for possession of Latium. There is no actual mention of the hound's having kingly (or even papal) dignity in the text of *Inferno* I; nor is there any mention of his rule after he has defeated the embodiment of greed in all of the "ville" of the peninsula. Likewise, Virgil implies that it is because this hound has *not yet come* that the wayfarer should follow him on a journey to knowledge. It seems best, therefore, to consider this prophecy as something different from Beatrice's "cinquecento diece e cinque, messo da Dio" of *Purgatorio* XXXIII, 43.[31]

In fact, neither here in *Inferno* I nor in *Purgatorio* XX, 10–15, where the *lupa* and her adversary are arcanely alluded to, is there any specification of the exact form or office that the hound/hunter will have. The text is ambiguous. Nothing in *Inferno* I, verses 100–114, or anywhere else in the poem, would forbid identification with a military leader, such as that near-traditional, though tentative, identification with the Ghibelline Captain in Italy, Can Grande. But there is, likewise, nothing to compel it.[32]

The Prophecy

The *veltro* of *Inferno* I, 101–102, actually constitutes the first of three major prophecies in the *Commedia*[33] of a cure for the temporal corruption of church and state. At the end of *Purgatorio* (XXXIII, 34–45) comes Beatrice's even more puzzling prophecy of a "cinquecento diece e cinque," one who will come to slay the thievish whore and become heir to the imperial eagle. And in *Paradiso* XXVII, 61–63, St. Peter, the first bishop of Rome, predicts God's imminent intervention through imperial power to end ecclesiastical corruption[34] just as his providence had used Scipio "to defend the glory of the world for Rome."

> Ma l'alta provedenza, che con Scipio
>   difese a Roma la gloria del mondo,
>   soccorrà tosto, sì com'io concipio.

In the same canto Beatrice's railing against "cupidigia" again ascribes the corruption of man to the fact that the imperial throne is empty:

Tu, perché non ti facci maraviglia,
    pensa che 'n terra non è chi governi;
    onde si svia l'umana famiglia.   (vv. 139–141)

Clearly, given the whole political philosophy of the *Commedia*, the salvation of the temporal world could only come from a secular ruler. The differences in emphasis among the three prophecies and the auxiliary predictions may, indeed, be due to an attempt to account for changing political contingencies at different times during the composition of the poem.[35]

In both the *Convivio* and the *Monarchia*, Dante had argued that only a world monarch could bring lasting peace and true justice, for only by possessing all worldly goods could the ruler be truly without greed. Universal monarchy cannot by definition be split; thus, the Donation of Constantine and other such later gifts of temporal power to the papacy are illegitimate. Secular power in the church is, therefore, *prima facie*, corruption; for the "heirs of Levi" (for Dante the priesthood) are excluded from the division of the lands of Canaan, that is, from temporal rule (*Purgatorio* XVI, 131–132). As Marco Lombardo is made to express it: "The shepherd who leads may chew the cud but does not divide of the hoof" (*Purgatorio* XVI, 98–99), the pope can meditate on spiritual matters but not judge earthly ones. Dante had asserted in the *Monarchia* that governments were set up as a remedy for sin; but in the *Commedia* the argument becomes more strident in attributing the world's error not to the corruption of human nature but to the evil consequences of the papacy's meddling in temporal affairs. Existing laws have been set as a curb on human appetites, but they are ignored (*Purgatorio* XVI, 97). If the world goes astray, it is because there is no monarch who can discern "the tower of the true city" (v. 96).

Despite the indeterminacy, there is a constant inducible both from the imagery in which the three major predictions are couched and from Dante's thought expressed in his other works: the reform sent by heaven will not be ecclesiastic or, even less, papal.[36]

As in the case of most genuinely intentioned prophecies or prophetic hopes, history may prove them wrong, or the true character, or time, of their fulfillment may never be known: in the *Commedia*, St. Peter and Folco da Marsiglia merely say that an imperial savior will come "soon," "tosto" (*Paradiso* IX, 139–142; XXVII, 63). The text reflects Christian faith in the face of worldly uncertainty in what appears to be a repetition of the *veltro* prophecy in the poet's apostrophe of *Purgatorio* XX, 10–15:

> Maladetta sie tu, antica lupa,
>   che più che tutte l'altre bestie hai preda
>   per la tua fame sanza fine cupa!
> O ciel, nel cui girar par che si creda
>   le condizion di qua giù trasmutarsi
>   quando verrà per cui questa disceda?

Imprecation and promise typical of biblical prophecy in both ancillary and major predictions give a clue to their significance; lexical choice expresses meaning while maintaining ambiguity concerning any referent external to the text: the prophetic iterations act as an emblematic creed, an expression of faith in the justness of God's providential plan for a new world order. For Dante's contemporaries the prophecies stood as a source of hope amidst a picture of earthly desolation.

Analogous Prophecies

Some of the most important attempts to understand the prediction of the *veltro* have derived from a comparison with other historical prophecies predating and coeval with the *Commedia*. Vittorio Cian, in his *Oltre l'enigma* of 1945, a *rifacimento* of his original 1897 study, and Marjorie Reeves (1969) gave ample listings of some contemporary prophecies, especially those concerning imperial hopes.

Increased scholarly attention to the influence of the seventh-century pseudo-Methodian prophecies[37] upon medieval apocalyptic and messianic literature has revived interest in Pietro Alighieri's view of the *veltro* (given in the Ashburnham version of his *Commentarium*) as the advent of an emperor at the end of time. The prophetic tradition of a Last World emperor had entered the West by the seventh or eighth century; by the eleventh it had been conflated with the apocalyptic oracle of the Tiburtine Sybil: before the Day of Judgment there would arise a great emperor who would vanquish all before him, rule the Christians, and convert the Jews and Saracens. After a period of halcyon reign, the Antichrist would appear; the emperor would then surrender his insignia of authority and his very life on Golgotha in Jerusalem. Then St. Michael or Christ at his Second Coming would vanquish the Antichrist, and Dies Irae would immediately follow.

I agree with Marjorie Reeves's assessment that the connection between the *Commedia* and this tradition is actually rather slim, particularly because the association ill agrees with a *veltro* who "non ciberà terra né peltro." Earthly conquest, ultimate capitulation to evil and then Judgment are not the themes of Dante's theory of monarchy, and they contradict the optimistic, historical hope for the restoration of man upon which the *Commedia* is built.[38]

Since Gioachino da Fiore (ca. 1132–1202), the great Cistercian seer and writer of apocalyptic works, is allotted a place in *Paradiso* and is lauded with the very verses taken from the Antiphon to Vespers with which his followers were permitted to honor him ("di spirito profetico dotato" [*Paradiso* XII, 141]), the question of his influence and place in the poem is unavoidable. From the end of the 1800s until the late 1940s, a body of literature grew up devoted to the thesis that Dante had absorbed the later and more extreme Joachite opinions of the Spiritual Franciscans.[39] Thus, even before the landmark discovery and publication of the manuscripts of Gioachino's book of *Figurae*, much had been made of the supposed influence that Pier Giovanni Olivi and Ubertino da Casale had upon the young poet when they were in Florence between 1285 and 1290. In 1929, A. Dempf, for example, asserted that the *Commedia* was itself "a Joachite apocalypse."[40] L. Filomusi-Guelfi (1911) in a well-researched, if perhaps misguided, chapter (defended by Papini in 1933) identified the *veltro* with the Holy Spirit of the third age expected by the Joachite Franciscan Spirituals. This view, however, was ably refuted by F. Foberti (1939; pp. 153–171), M. Barbi (1939), and Tondelli (1940; 1953, p. 297).

Conservative opinion warned that although Dante wrote in the genre of contemporary apocalyptics and with a knowledge of Joachite prophecy, he did not absorb or agree substantially with either the original Joachite writings or with the variants evolved by the Spiritual Franciscans.[41] Against the exaggerations of some critics holding the extreme Joachite view, M. Barbi (1934) noted that Dante began to frequent the philosophical schools of the Dominicans and Franciscans only after the death of Beatrice in 1292, when both Pier Giovanni Olivi and Ubertino da Casale were far from Florence.[42] Since Monsignor Tondelli's publication of the magnificent *Liber figurarum* in 1940 and its definitive edition by Tondelli, Reeves, and Hirsch-Reich published in

1953, there can be no doubt at all that Dante used the beautiful illuminated manuscript diagrams of Gioachino's "figurae" for the imagery of the Tree of Justice, the Eagle, and the Trinity in the *Paradiso*.[43] Yet, as Reeves and Hirsch-Reich observe in their careful joint study (1972), great as Gioachino's influence was, Dante remained eclectic and independent before the great seer's mystical construct: "Dante was impressed by shapes and artistic details rather than influenced by the complex structures of thought behind the *figurae*."[44] These scholars have meticulously revised the work of their predecessors, carefully expunging the over-enthusiastic notions of Dante's Joachite dependence.

Unfortunately, especially in regard to the *veltro*, Tondelli's chapter, "L'enigma svelato del veltro," along with Crocco's synopsis, I believe, must also be relegated alongside other exaggerated claims of derivation.[45] In plate XII of the *Figurae*, amid a grand diagram of Gioachino's plan of the world under the coming Age of the Holy Spirit, beneath one marked in block letters "VITULUS" [calf] and above another designated "OVIS" [sheep] below, one finds a tiny box labeled "CANIS" [dog] representing an "oratorium" of pastoral friars who govern the "oves" [the sheep] below; within the "CANIS" box the following description is found:

> In this oratorium will be gathered together the priests and clerks of the DOG who want to live chastely in a community, but who do not wish to abstain completely from eating meat and wearing animal pelts. They will fast in winter on the fourth and sixth days of the week [i.e., Wednesdays and Fridays]. They will also be obedient to their prior, according to the disposition and judgment of the spiritual father who will be in charge of all. These men will not use cloaks, but cowls, so that there may be a distinction between their clothing and that of the laity. Among them there will be the pursuit of art and grammar, and boys or youths will be placed among them so that they may learn to speak and write Latin and to commit to memory, as far as possible, the writing of the Testaments. They will give a tenth of their labour and a tenth of their tenth that they receive from those joined with them into the hands of their spiritual father for sustaining the poor of Christ, if, perchance any should be in need.[46]

According to Tondelli, Dante's *veltro*, therefore, should be identified not as Gioachino's Holy Spirit, as Filomusi-Guelfi and Papini had claimed, but as a scion of this "dog" subcategory, that is, as a member of a monastic, priestly order; the description of special garments, differentiated from those of the laity ("non utentur palliis sed tantum cappis"), which the governing priests would wear, explained away for him all the problems of "felt and felt"; the rule of poverty, which applied to all those orders for which Joachism was a concern, was the true significance of the verse "non ciberà terra né peltro."

Tondelli wisely did not push his claim for derivation too far. Later in the same chapter, he sees "tra feltro e feltro" extending beyond an ecclesiastical order to include the whole of society "saturated" with the ideal of poverty; the *veltro* is an extension of the conventional "dog" symbol of the Dominicans that Andrea di Buonaiuto was to use so strikingly in the later frescoes (1365) of Sta. Maria Novella's Spanish Chapel. Tondelli's argument ultimately rests on the Joachite hope of a "papa angelicus" to be elected by the influence of monastic orders, just as Celestine V and Benedict XI had been. Then, perhaps seeing the weakness of his own reasoning (the "angelic" pope who founds the Celestines is, after all, consigned to the vestibule of hell in *Inferno* III, vv. 58–60), he ultimately avoids assigning any name to Dante's *veltro* (1940, p. 306; 1953, p. 360).

Even with his attenuations, however, Tondelli's views simply do not square either with the thought Dante expressed in any of his works or with the context of verses 100–102. The surrounding lines bristle with images of empire deriving from the *Aeneid*—even to the extent that God's realm in the empyrean is itself couched in imperial terms (vv. 124–129, "imperador," "impera"). The repeated antipapal and anticlerical excoriations throughout the poem argue against any possibility of the restoration of earthly justice by ecclesiastical authorities. (I will take up his especially jaundiced view of the state of contemporary monks and friars again later.)

The discovery of the box labeled "canis" in the manuscript diagram of the *Liber figurarum* really marked no step forward in our understanding. There is no mention in the description of the *canis* oratorium that its priests would do any reforming or, in fact, anything other than teaching Latin and the Bible to children. Given the common metaphor of the dog's "healing tongue," which predates St. Dominic by centuries, it is not surprising that the Abbot of Fiore, or his follower, would use the time-worn image of a dog for a preaching order. Had Dante wanted for *locus*, he could have found one in a legion of religious and encyclopedic works.[47] The poet, however, never uses that image anywhere in his poem.

The *veltro* of the *Commedia* cannot be reduced to the "canis" of the *Liber figurarum*.

Why a *veltro*?

Two central literary questions still remain in interpreting the *Commedia*'s first prophecy: how is the prediction of Italy's liberator affected by the canine terms in which it is expressed and, most especially, what does the word "*veltro*," "greyhound," imply for the sense of the prophecy?[48]

The dog, generically, was a Christian symbol of faith and fidelity (both senses of *fides*), and in many medieval bestiaries, such as that of Rabanus Maurus's *De universo* VIII, 1 (*PL* III, col. 223), the dog was reputed to be an animal of great sagacity and wisdom, "Nihil autem sagacius canibus."[49] *Paradiso* XII, 60, refers to an episode in the legend of St. Dominic in which the saint's mother is said to have dreamt of her son as a dog.[50] In further facile extensions of conventional dog-preacher imagery, the saint's followers were called "the dogs of the Lord," "Domini canes," and "Dominicani," and depictions of Dominic himself in Christian art are accompanied by the emblem of a dog with a torch in its mouth. St. Francis's description of the Dominicans' decadence in *Paradiso* XI, 124–129, however, seems to discourage any identification of the *veltro* with this order:

> Ma'l suo peculio di nova vivanda
> è fatto ghiotto, sì ch'esser non puote
> che per diversi salti non si spanda;
> e quanto le sue pecore remote
> e vagabunde più da esso vanno,
> più tornano a l'ovil di latte vòte.
> Ben son di quelle che temono 'l danno
> e stringonsi al pastor; ma son sì poche,
> che le cappe fornisce poco panno.

In contrast to G. Tondelli's vision of a society "saturated" by the ideals of the preaching orders, the St. Francis of the poem laments how very few indeed have chosen, or respect, the Dominican "cappe." The Dominicans are lost sheep, not sagacious shepherd dogs.

In contrast with the traditional Platonic symbol of the dog as defender of the *polis*, the six uses of the word "cane" in the *Commedia* ("can," twice; "cani," four times), are found in totally negative contexts.[51] Most important, "cane" is not "veltro," and in order to find more convincing reasons behind the choice of the word we must seek other possible cultural influences and traditions.

As many critics, such as E. J. Boehmer (1869, pp. 363–366), I. Samuel (1947), C. G. Hardie (1964, pp. 158–172), and A. Pézard (1978) have noted, in the *Chanson de Roland* Charlemagne has two pairs of prophetic dreams concerning a greyhound, "un veltres," that would come to protect the interests of the empire.[52] Even more striking, in a *sirventese* of ca. 1277, discovered in 1896 and published by T. Casini in his *Scritti danteschi* (1913; pp. 39–44), we find the very rhymes *feltro, veltro,* and *peltro*; also, in a counter-parallel to our poem, a lion attacks a greyhound: "e'l leone asalíu el veltro." The use of the greyhound image both in a political *sirventese* and in an epic so widespread and important might reasonably have suggested it to Dante for his own enigmatic prediction of an earthly savior.

The greyhound, specifically, as most glosses have it, is characterized by its speed and its enmity to wolves. Guido da Pisa speaks of the "laudable qualities that the greyhound possesses . . . for the greyhounds among all dogs are nobler and more generous" (p. 33). The wisdom of the greyhound ("Canis veltris, vetrahus, vertragus, etc.") is stressed in Du Cange's *Glossarium* (ed. 1883–1887), 2:89, col. 3, where it is described as "canis sagax, vel odorisequus, leporarius." Basing their interpretations on these descriptions and on the verb "caccerà," Dante scholars have tended to emphasize the qualities of the greyhound as a hunting dog.[53]

In addition to being prized for its hunting, however, the *veltro* was the common Italian shepherd dog, as can be readily observed in many medieval and, especially, fourteenth-century paintings depicting scenes from the birth of Mary and of the nativity of Christ where its slender, unmistakable form regularly accompanies shepherds and sheep.[54] Giovanni Pisano's adoration of the shepherds on the pulpit of the parish church of San Andrea in Pistoia (1301) depicts a resting greyhound, and an altar predella of the nativity and adoration by Bernardo Daddi (1332–1334) in the Accademia in Florence contains several greyhound figures; the dog accompanies the shepherds in the legend of Mary's father, Joachim, in Giotto's frescoes in the Scrovegni Chapel of the Arena in Padua (ca. 1305–1306).[55] Surely this image, forming an introductory metaphor to the poem's biblical imagery of sheepfold, flocks, and shepherds, strongly influenced the choice of vocabulary in *Inferno* I.

It seems likely, therefore, on various grounds—from the repetition of the very rhymes from a political *sirventese*, from the possible echo of a well-divulged literary work, from the reflection of contemporary practices of husbandry and from the use of a familiar iconography: (1) that the *veltro* predicts an earthly liberator of the imperial party; (2) that the *veltro* is to be some sort of attendant of the "pastore," that is, a subaltern of the earthly ruler to come and, thus, also the directly ordained servant of Christ, the Good Shepherd, and not an actual emperor or Christ himself;[56] and (3) that the prognostication of *Inferno* I was conceived independently or arose from a set of circumstances different from those of the "515" in *Purgatorio*, and that it was originally unassociated with the prophecy placing "the Lofty Henry" in the empyrean (*Paradiso* XXX, 137–138: "l'alto Arrigo, ch'a drizzare Italia / verrà in prima ch'ella sia disposta").

*   *   *

In conclusion, although some literary critics might argue that the question of referentiality and intention may, perhaps, lie outside the realm of textual criticism, some excursus on Dante's strategy seems unavoidable: perhaps, indeed, the poet's hopes, so often raised and dashed, may have led him to modify his expectations and perhaps he reflected these modifications darkly in the poem's various repeated prophecies of an earthly savior. Most probably he created a purposeful obscurity to give the widest possibility to some fulfillment of the record of these hopes preserved indelibly in his poem.[57] We can be sure that he did not seek unplanned obsolescence for a work "to which both heaven and earth had set their hand."[58]

Textually, the prediction of the *veltro* comes in the mode of biblical prophecy and and has the outward effect of a ritual-liturgical *credo* upon the reader; spiritually it is a profession of faith in the substance of things unseen and as yet unknowable. I noted earlier that Dante's Jeremiah-like pessimism about humanity was not so extreme as that of St. Augustine, for whom empires were but gangland spheres of influence. The earth would eventually have the perfect functioning for which it was created, and Dante cites Aristotle to this effect in the *Convivio* IV, iv, 1–5. God would provide earthly justice as he had provided the earthly peace necessary for Christ's birth and man's salvation. Unlike the *Commedia*'s myriad prophecies uttered *post factum*,[59] the *veltro* prophecy truly concerns not humanity's present but its unknown future: "infin che il veltro *verrà*," "la sua nazion *sarà* tra feltro e feltro."

That the verses are couched in the mode of true *vaticinium* seems to me to be the real core of Dante's message here. The *veltro* will be the salvation of "umile Italia,"[60] and if different candidates can be discerned darkly behind the veil, they are clearly to be ranked with those heroes and heroines, "Cammilla, Eurialo e Niso e Turno" (vv. 107–108), who had given their lives for Rome and its founding. As the names of the valiant from opposing sides in the *Aeneid* are intertwined in Dante's verses, so shall future heroes' names, in turn, come to form part of that historical intermeshing of a progress toward justice ordained by God.[61]

The later apostrophe concerning the vanquisher of the *lupa* in *Purgatorio* XX, 15, "quando verrà per cui questa disceda?" again stresses futurity and, in turn, implies that the figure of the poet-narrator in the *Commedia* is in an analogous position to that of Vergilius Maro before his fourth *Eclogue*. Yet that very situation underlines the distance between the poet of the *Commedia* and the poet of the *Aeneid*. The difference hinges on their acceptance of their own prophecies: the bucolic prediction of the coming of the Redeemer spoken, yet disbelieved and disregarded by Virgil, contrasts with the second, heard and embraced in faith by the wayfarer—most surely uttered and embraced in faith by the historical Dante.

CHAPTER VI

Shadows of Conversion

"Questo male e peggio"

Verses 1–61 of *Inferno* I present a disordered world whose total values are allegorically, and quite literally, reversed in the course of the poem after the entrance of Virgil.[1] Isolated, constituent parts of the poem elicit interpretations that ultimately require correction when the whole fabric of the narrative has been compassed. The text not only invites but compels the reader's participation. Images derived from differing, disparate, and even antithetical traditions of metaphoric language, from the Bible, patristic writings, the classics, and vernacular poetry, may at first imply conventional and comforting readings that only later reveal their inconsistency and their need of correction. Our later understanding often proves quite different from, or even antithetical to, our first construction.

The themes related to conversion in *Inferno* I seem, at first glance, familiarly positive. We draw on our ready repository of stereotypes to interpret a number of binary oppositions that the text presents, each with its own apparent hierarchy: up/down (*colle/selva*), light/darkness (sunlight/shadowed wood), forward/backward, persistence/fear. Each term of the first category we assume to be superior to the second: light, upward, forward, and persistence all hold an apparent moral value over downward, darkness, backward turns, and crippling fear.

When the three beasts confront the wayfarer, constraining him to retreat from his goal of ascent, we commit the logical fallacy, *post hoc propter hoc*, and interpret his failure to climb the shining mountain as the moral cause of his fall to the depths. The savagery of the beasts we accept literally and metaphorically as negative impediments to a goal apparently so nearly reachable; the wayfarer's turning from them we construe negatively as the result of the frailty and timidity of his human condition.[2]

In addition, the circumstances of those early lines, although their action takes place "in the midst of the path of our life," all seem at a time and space removed, a sense aroused not only by the preterit in which they are recounted but even more because symbolic evocation substitutes for descriptive mimesis. Although it is morning and broad daylight, the text conjures events that are perceived in a twilight haze where nothing seems palpable or convincing. The dark wood, the valley, and the mountain all lack physicality; we are aware that they are not natural images but supernatural emblems. Indeed, when we look back from the "realism" of mid-*Inferno*, we are struck fully by the lack of any sense of physical density in the prologue scene: as most critics have rightly observed, everything seems to exist there for the purpose of signifying, without concreteness. Yet this shadowy reality is also essential to the opening dilemma of the poem: the reader must experience the wayfarer's sense of dismay and perplexity, the sense of shifting ground, of moral and religious wandering as the planes of reality slip without warning from the literal into the metaphoric; he experiences also the sense of renewed bewilderment as the narrator relives in memory the uncertain steps of the wayfarer-protagonist; sudden swings of emotion betray spiritual instability. As some scholars have correctly seen, the first canto of the *Inferno* is a study in Augustinian psychology.[3]

It has become a commonplace to say that the secondary significances immediately overpower any literal meaning of the setting or the adventure. Since the earliest commentators, readers have spoken of their bafflement at the peculiar quality of the poetry. Compare the comments of Francesco da Buti, for example, "Qui si dimostra che l'autore ebbe altro intelletto, che solo letterale" (com vol. I, p. 35); and of a modern critic, Luigi Pietrobono (1915), in the same context: "Ora ci basti osservare che *valle*, *piaggia* e *monte*, posti come sono, ordinatamente, nell'oscurità, nella penombra e nella luce, *portano quasi congenito il loro significato morale*: più che simboli si potrebbero chiamare metafore" (my italics).[4] That things both are and are not what they seem is a conclusion of critics as different as Croce and Singleton.[5] Gaetano Ragonese sums up the majority view: "la lettera del testo . . . assorbe in sé il suo significato simbolico."[6] Given the discord that attends so much of the poem's interpretation, critical agreement on the unreal quality of the poetry of the *Commedia*'s opening scene is somewhat unusual.[7]

Yet, there is the regrettable fact that critical appreciation of *Inferno* I has often been marred by a misunderstanding of, and even at times

impatience with, its shadowy and insubstantial nature. In a primal failure of the critical act, a few scholars have given neither the author nor
his text their receptive sympathy; they have assumed *a priori* that Dante
simply was not in perfect control of his poetry. In 1901, F. D'Ovidio
(p. 315), for example, vigorously voiced his antipathy toward the canto:
"È questo un dei casi in cui il simbolismo sforza la lettera, eccedendo i
confini del reale, e nuoce a quel po' di bello, un bello sempre di medi-
ocre lega, che può essere nella poesia allegorica." For D'Ovidio (p. 325),
the wayfarer's trials in the prologue are one of "le parti meno estetiche
del capolavoro."[8] Guido Mazzoni (1918) shared his prejudice: "Ricono-
sceremo, senza titubanza alcuna, che Dante, nel primo canto, non fu
sempre quel perfetto artista che già, è vero, si rivela in esso, ma che, nel
processo del poema, più splendido di mano in mano e più glorioso si
afferma."[9] Particularly in the first decades of this century, those who
had fallen under the aesthetic influence of Benedetto Croce saw the very
use of allegory as a failure on the part of the poet. In his *Poesia di Dante*,
Croce himself dismissed the possibility that allegory could be part of
true poetry ("Nella poesia, l'allegoria non ha mai luogo," p. 14). There
are cases, he claimed, where

> l'allegoria non lasci sussistere la poesia o non lasci nascere, e al
> suo luogo ponga un complesso d'immagini discordanti, poeti-
> camente frigide e mute, e perciò non sono vere immagini ma
> semplici segni; e in questo caso, non essendoci poesia, non c'è
> neppure oggetto alcuno di storia della poesia, ma solo l'avver-
> tenza del limite di questa, del poeticamente fallito e nullo, del
> brutto. . . . Se l'allegoria c'è, essa è sempre, per definizione,
> fuori e contro la poesia.   (p. 15)

The beginning of the *Commedia* he condemned with his harshest
censure:

> I primi canti dell'Inferno sono, in generale, i più gracili; o che
> appartennessero a un primo abbozzo, poi ritoccato e adat-
> tato . . . o che ritenessero dell' incertezza di tutti i comincia-
> menti, accresciuta in questo caso dalla difficoltà di costruire e
> mettere in moto una macchina così grande. Specialmente il
> primo canto dà qualche impressione di stento.   (p. 67)

Even so sensitive a reader as Attilio Momigliano (com 1946–1951; F.
Mazzoni, com 1972–1973), failed to appreciate the special qualities,

technique, and effects of the first canto; his first gloss is especially negative:

> La qualità del luogo, la selva, è suggerita a Dante dall'intenzione allegorica: questo è il germe che corrode il canto. . . . Il I canto è il più incertamente concepito dell'*Inferno* . . . si svia nell'allegoria. . . . Il complesso manca di sicurezza e, relativamente, di stile.

Fortunately, the aesthetic and Crocean prejudices against allegory have gradually faded as a new understanding of the *Commedia* has flourished, mainly through the writings of Auerbach, Singleton, and their students and followers.

In his influential essays, Charles Singleton claimed that the poet strove precisely for a "double vision" in which the literal and allegorical hold at once,[10] where the visible, spatial world shadows forth the spirit, the spiritual truth of the interior soul that occupies no space.

One must, of course, remark that allegory does not have to be so bewildering as it appears in the prologue of the *Commedia*. The oscillation between the literal and the allegorical senses permits neither the literal nor the allegorical a stable or privileged status in the prologue scene; the text evokes conflicting reactions. The attentive reader is rightly ill at ease when he finds that, at verses 19–27, the metaphor of landscape fades into seascape, that the mountain and forest he had accepted now mysteriously transmute into a sea and shore not present before. The focus of the metaphor's equation shifts and changes from the compared to the comparison. Thus, the first part of the metaphor, the literal (as Singleton noted), is made to accommodate the actual presence of a formerly metaphorical and hypothetical body of a panting, shipwrecked sailor coming forth—from the lake of his own heart.[11] Only fleetingly, though, do we grasp the fact that the metaphor has become embodied, for there comes another shift that seizes us from that watery escape from sin and thrusts us back to the earthly mountain where the wayfarer begins to limp upward yet again: "ripresi via per la piaggia diserta / sì che 'l piè fermo sempre era'l più basso" (vv. 29–30).

The ruptures in the narrative portray mental aberration with an unparalleled effectiveness. The wayfarer's groping repeats itself in the persona of the poet as he struggles for expression: "quanto a dir qual era è cosa dura." Yet the rhetoric of the text is self-conscious, masterful, and deliberate. The narrator's pained interjection "ahi!" recalls the terror of a moral nightmare.[12] Litotes seeds doubt in the reader's mind and betrays the wayfarer's unreliability as an observer: "*non* sì che paura *non* mi desse.*" A catachresis (the classical "abusio" of language) imitates the chaos of senses: "là dove il sol tace." The anadiplosis of verse 5, "esta *selva selvaggia* e aspra e forte," and the confusing homonymic and internal rhymes of verses 34–36, "dinanzi al volto . . . fui per ritornar più volte vòlto" compel re-reading and interpretation.[13]

The protagonist himself flounders and fluctuates amid contradictory responses and inconsistent desires. The site and the appearance of the three wild beasts oddly arouse in him both terror (vv. 4–6; 14–15; 35–36; 44–48; 49–61) and attraction (37–43).[14] Fear vies intermittently with sin:

> lethargy and habit: sleep of sin at entering wood
>   fear, *pietà*: remorse, *il cor compunto*
> rest, quieted fear: *la paura un poco queta*
>   fear: *l'animo mio, ch' ancor fuggiva*
> allure of the *lonza*
>   fear: *leone*
>   fear redoubled: *lupa*

The first sixty-one lines of the text recount the bewildering alternation in the wayfarer's manic sways of will and passion until he "ruins" down to a place of non-being and damnation. The fluctuating instability of his mood and direction, his chaotic swings of passion, recall St. Augustine's revelations of his sinful distance from God in the *Confessions* XI, 29:

> But I have been spilled and scattered among times whose order
> I do not know; my thoughts, my innermost bowels of my soul,
> are torn apart with the crowding tumults of variety, and so it
> will be until all together I can flow into you, purified and mol-
> ten by the fire of your love.

The nightmare of tumult is broken only after the arrival of Virgil, the last link in the chain of grace: the wayfarer has uttered his *De profundis*, literally from the depths, finally admitting his own helplessness: "*Miserere* di me!"

The prologue embodies both narratively and structurally a didactic theme that was a favorite not only of Augustine but also of Lactantius, who, in the *Divine Institutes* VI, 7–8, described the correction of those considered wise by their fellows. Following a false way to wisdom without a guide, "wise men" grasp at shadows and images of the truth so that God places obstacles in their way to guide them to the right path. All the elements Lactantius describes of the "seeming" quality of a *via non vera*, later to become traditional, are present also in the poem:

> All those who through the acknowledged folly of others are believed to be wise, *led on by the appearance of virtue, grasp shadows and images, but nothing real.* This comes about in this way, because that deceitful road which leads to a fall has many by-paths on account of the variety of studies and disciplines which are varied and diverse in the life of men. Just as the way of wisdom holds something of folly . . . *so this way, although it is entirely one of folly, has some likeness of wisdom which those who understand the general folly snatch at.* And as it holds manifest vices, so it holds something which seems like virtue; and as it holds open crime, so it holds *a certain image and species of justice. For how could the precursor of that way [Satan], whose entire force and power lie in deceiving, lead all into fraud, unless he were showing men likeness of the truth?* (my italics) [15]

The doctrinal idea of grasping at shadowy images of truth informs not only the narrative of the wayfarer's actions at the start of the *Commedia*, but also the mysterious quality of the verses in which those actions are presented—the unreality, the lack of literality, that critics have not only correctly noticed but have, at times, blindly censured.

The opening lines of the *Commedia* recount the poet's memory of an experience lived by a wayfarer "sì pien di sonno," full of the sleep of sin, with a mind clouded by pride and anguish, and recalled in fear by the *persona* of the poet. But *Inferno* I not only depicts the instability and ambiguity of the wayfarer's psychology, it also evokes it in the reader. Allowed to glimpse only shattered fragments, we too are placed in the position of those "wise," proud philosophers, such as Lactantius describes, and we are also allowed to experience their failure. The unreality of the prologue scene is an integral part of the artistic and moral message. Readers who have failed to grasp the true nature of its "shadowy" structure, interpreting the climb and the glance as positive, have fallen into that very error with which Beatrice will charge the sinning wayfarer in *Purgatorio* XXX, 130–132:

> e volse i passi suoi per via non vera,
> *imagini di ben seguendo false,*
> che nulla promission rendono intera.

The canto challenges the reader with the ambiguity of truths at once revealed and concealed: the text is simply not transparent upon events. The poetry figures "the manner of seeing permitted us in this life," the mode of vision reflected in a puzzle that St. Paul describes in I Corinthians 13 : 12, "per speculum in aenigmate"; it belongs to that special form of "obscure" theological allegory "hard to discern" and actually defined as "enigma" by St. Isidore and St. Augustine.[16] The *sensus litteralis* of *Inferno* I, 1–61, is no "falsehood" or "allegory of poets." It has its poetic foundation in Christian truth: in the struggle of the unaided human mind, clouded by sin, to see and comprehend within, and beyond, the *saeculum*.

"Il ben che vi trovai"

In the course of the *Commedia*, the pilgrim is three times directed to set forth the moral lesson of the poem: by Beatrice in *Purgatorio* XXXII, 103–105, by Cacciaguida in *Paradiso* XVII, 124–142, and by St. Peter in *Paradiso* XXVII, 64–66. Lines 8 and 9 of Canto I express the narrator-poet's intention to fulfill of these fictional commissions, describing both the composition of his poem and his method: "ma per trattar del ben ch'i' vi trovai, / dirò de l'altre cose ch'i' v'ho scorte." Recounting the "good" found in the shadowy forest of the prologue is, in fact, the stated purpose of the poem: to share and divulge what was learned and enacted in the wood, the lesson of humility and the reversal of direction—the conversion—that made possible the journey through the three realms to attain the ultimate promise of salvation. To a twentieth-century reader, the choice of the simple phrase "l'altre cose" may seem, at first glance, generic or even uninspired, but, on the contrary, it represents a precise fourteenth-century description of an artistic process. The words indicate that the "good" will be understood by means of allegory, that is, the "alieniloquium" (literally, "other speech") of St. Isidore or, to quote the *Epistle to Can Grande,* by allegory: "Allegoria dicitur ab *alleon* graece, quod in latinum dicitur alienum, sive diversum" [the word "allegory" is so called from the Greek *alleon*, which in Latin is *alienum* ("other") or *diversum* ("different")]:[17] "In order to treat of the good that I found there, / I will speak of *other* things that I descried there."

Similarly, the verbs "trattar" and "dirò" represent a careful lexical choice centering on the practice of literary composition; they define exactly the scope of the work: that is, first that it will be a philosophical treatise (since "trattare" meant "to treat philosophically"), and secondly ("dirò"), that it will be an autobiographical verse narrative in the vernacular.[18]

The text, however, presents the "ben" and the "other things" so obliquely in *Inferno* I that even the earliest commentators disagreed on what exactly was meant.[19] Like Jacopo di Dante (com 1322), many of them believed, indeed, that "the good" lay in the setting forth of the wayfarer's experiences in the next world, that is, in the didactic effect of the poem: "Per questo bene di che egli trattare intende il dichiarare al mondo, la passione de' rei e la gloria de' buoni si considera, la qualità loro secondando per dare correzione e lode a chi n'è degnio" (p. 46). However, for Graziolo de' Bambaglioli (com 1324), the "ben" was somewhat more narrow: it meant the setting forth of vice and error that man commits in this life: "Auctor offert hic se monstraturum et dicturum de hiis que invenit et vidit in ipsa silva, hoc est de vitiis et erroribus que per vitam humani generis perpetrantur" (p. 3) [The author shows here that he is going to set forth and talk about these things that he finds and sees in the wood itself; that is, about the vices and errors that are committed during human life]. Jacopo della Lana (com 1324–1328) also concentrated on the negative example that the first part of the poem would afford: "Qui mostra come lo uomo si dovrebbe partire da pensare e adoperare tale vita: ma acciò che si possa prendere esemplo per saperla schifare, è da farne trattato" (p. 108). The Ottimo (com 1333) followed suit: hell's punishments were the lesson: "Per trattare del bene, che seguita della detta cognizione de' vizj, tratterà delle pene inflitte ad essi" (p. 4).[20] In a second redaction he specified those on whom the lesson would have its effect; those inclined to sin would avoid it out of base, servile fear: "acciò che quelle [anime] le quali non odiano peccare per amore di virtù, almeno cessino di mal operare per timore de la pena."[21]

There was some difficulty or unwillingness on the part of other commentators to treat the sins of hell or the tribulations of the wayfarer as "goods." We find this reticence particularly in the commentaries of Pietro di Dante (for whom the "ben" is the arrival of a renewed sense of Divine Justice), of Boccaccio, and of Francesco da Buti. In his *Esposizioni* (com 1373, p. 69), Boccaccio suggests that by "il ben" we must not fail to "intendere altro che la misericordia di Dio."[22] Francesco da Buti gives an explanation first of the letter, explaining the good as "l'apparimento, conforto et ammaestramento di Virgilio: non che queste cose desse la selva per sua natura; ma a lui sopravvenneno per grazia"; the other things "furono li animali ch'elli finge che impedissono lo suo salimento del monte" (p. 23). Then, in his exegesis of the allegory, he clarifies his interpretation that the "ben" is grace: "Dubiterebbesi che cosa di bene può essere nella vita mondana viziosa, a che si può rispondere che è la grazia preveniente da Dio che fa desiderare d'uscire di tale vita" (p. 26).[23] Recently, A. Limentani has understood "il ben" as "assistance sent from Heaven" (1985, p. 4).

An examination of the narrow letter of verses 8 and 9 reveals that the adverbial "vi," repeated twice for emphasis ("*vi* trovai" "io *v'*ho scorte") does, in fact, restrict the site of the "ben" to the referent, the "selva oscura." The key, therefore, must lie in some positive central action of the first two cantos that takes place within the forest itself: literally, it can only be the change of direction, allegorically signifying the "turning of the will," the first of the triple conversions recounted in the *Commedia*.[24] All actions ("l'altre cose") contribute to this result: first the negative events, the wayfarer's glance aloft; his climb; the appearances of the three beasts that hinder him, drive him back, and finally force him down to the "basso loco" of darkness and despair; and, then, at last, the positive, the appearance of Virgil who, after the wayfarer's demurring, effects the backward journey, the "fatale andare" down again through the darkened wood into hell itself ("intrai per lo cammino alto e silvestro," *Inferno* II, 142). The wayfarer's pattern of action reflects exactly the concept of conversion in the Old Testament: Hebrew "šūb," like its Latin translation "conversio," means precisely to "change route, to come again, to retrace one's steps." Not yet does he attain Greek "metanoia," Christian repentance, change of mind, and inward change, or "epistrephein," the return to God, that his journey will become in *Purgatorio* and *Paradiso*.[25]

The action taking place in the "selva oscura" is a microcosm of the course of human salvation in history. Although it may sound fanciful to modern ears, the theological concept of "speculum salvationis," the "mirror" of salvation, was in fact precise, for salvation was understood to reverse the order of damnation in a mirror image: "Eva," emblem of the Fall, was transformed in a kind of palindrome into the "Ave" of the Annunciation. To explain the Old Testament as a process toward the fullness of time promised through the coming of the messiah and to clarify the coming of Christ as the fulfillment and recapitulation (*anakephalaiosis*) of that promise, the Fathers and Doctors of the church pushed biblical texts as far as they could to demonstrate the inverse consonance of the Fall and Salvation: Christ was the second Adam; thus, the creation of Adam and the Incarnation were both dated and commemorated on March 25; Jesus was crucified on a Friday, the same day of the week as Adam was created; Jesus died exactly where Adam was buried, and his blood flowed over Adam's skull. The Creation and the Annunciation were believed to have occurred on the same site. Thus Creation and the re-creation of Redemption possessed chronological and geographical identity.[26]

The corollary of the notion of recapitulation was that the history of all mankind, as we noted earlier, was reflected in the life of the individual. Just as mankind had to fall ("O felix culpa") in order that the Redeemer would come for his salvation, so the individual fell into personal sin to be tried and tested for his own correction and instruction. The path that led to sin led, in reverse, to grace, virtue, and salvation. Such a pattern, deriving from the Bible, became a theological matrix of thought.

The rhetorical devices of chiasmus and hysteron-proteron were major characteristics of theological language. Ideas of prefiguration and fulfillment fused with other, eschatological ideas of reversal so common in Gospel passages discussing entrance into the kingdom of heaven (e.g., Matt. 19:30, "Many that are first shall be last: and the last shall be first"; 20:16: "So the last shall be first and the first last"; also Mark 10:31 and Luke 10:28, 13:30).

Upon this process Dante builds the major structures of the *Commedia*.[27] In *Inferno* I the wayfarer climbs the "colle" in pride[28] only to fall toward ruin ("mentre ch'i' rovinava in basso loco"). At the brink of his destruction rescue comes; the wayfarer in the "fullness" of his time ("nel mezzo del cammin di nostra vita")[29] receives the grace of God made possible in the fullness of historical time by Christ's sacrifice; the path into sin must be re-traversed in the opposite direction as a lesson. The wayfarer reverses his way to follow a downward path through hell, yet without further change in direction, he will climb upward upon a path that will ultimately lead to heaven.[30]

Compare the traditional exhortation to the sinner to retrace his steps expressed by Lactantius in book VI, 24, of his *Divine Institutes*: "Therefore let whoever has wandered astray *retrace his path*, and as soon as possible recover and reform himself" (p. 464). Eight hundred and fifty years later, St. Bernard described the steps of ascent to pride and descent to humility in similar terms in chapter 9 of his *Steps of Humility* (*De gradibus*):

[In Psalm 1:1, 6] David seems to speak of two ways. In fact, there is only one, but there is a distinction and a reason for the two names. The same ladder is for those who come down, the way of iniquity, for those who go up, the way of truth. By the same steps one goes up to the throne and one comes down from it; by the same road one goes to the city and one departs from it; by the same gate one enters and one leaves the house. . . . *It is that when you wish to return to the truth there is no need to seek an unknown road: it is the same one by which you came down.* . . . Now that you are humbled you will climb by the self same steps you trod on as you came down in your pride.

(trans. Conway, p. 56; my italics)

Perhaps St. Thomas Aquinas gives the most cogent exposition of the idea in a treatise that Dante cites both appreciatively and extensively in his *Convivio*, the *Summa contra gentiles* III, 158, 1:

> Now the movement by which one moves away from something is contrary to the movement whereby one approaches it. . . . Consequently, the will must abandon sin by moving in a contrary direction from those movements whereby it was inclined to sin.[31]

The two verbs "ritrovare" and "trovare" in the opening lines of the poem also reflect the reversal of conversion; the first verb of the poem with its repetitive prefix, "mi *ri*trovai" (v. 2), contrasts with the second, "il ben ch'i' vi *trovai*" (v. 8), which expresses a single, completed act. The stubborn ascent in pride up the shining mountain receives its initial correction in temptation. The reverse journey is necessitated by these didactic trials and temptations and is accomplished, at last, as a result of grace. The first verb, "mi ritrovai," introducing the last acts of habitual sin, is reversed in the *finding* of the "ben"; the wayfarer ruins down to the depths at verse 61, nearly falling into the jaws of "second death,"[32] but in the very next line his success begins with outside aid. And thus commences the salutary effect on the sinning wayfarer of the journey through hell, the consequent purgation of his sin, and the foretaste of glory in the supernal realm of Paradiso promised at the end of the canto (vv. 118–120).

The reversal of direction heralds the retrospective patterns, noted incisively by C. S. Singleton, of the whole poem.[33] For just as Dante wayfarer retraces, and must retrace, his steps, so, as the poem progresses, and especially as it ends, the reader must look back from the final perspective in order truly to understand the poem and its workings. Only from there can he comprehend the significance of all that has gone before; he returns to these early lines and sees a providence taking shape. From the divine perspective the "rovinare in basso loco," though it results from a fault of the sinner, will be seen more truly as a personal lesson sent by God in preparation for *gratia gratis data*, "grace given freely"—the inexplicable generosity of the Deity self-moved, bestowed upon the sinner. All the events that led to the wayfarer's temporary failure have an ultimately beneficial effect, for it is fitting that the newly converted be tried and proven by temptation; evil is a corrective lesson on the path of life. As Hugh of St. Victor explains in the *De sacramentis* I, viii, 2: "The world is the place of erring and of those who are to be restored, and so good and evil simultaneously were ordered in it, that through good indeed they might receive consolation, but through evil, correction" (p. 142).

This paradoxical effect of sin and failure is a central theme of church dogma. In the *City of God* XIV, 13, St. Augustine gives a grimly comical explanation of why a fall to the depths is a lesson and a cure: "It is useful for the proud to fall into some patent and obvious sin by which they may become displeased with themselves after they had already fallen by being pleased with themselves."[34] God leaves man to himself in order that he may experience his own weakness and ignorance and realize that he is in need of counsel and aid.[35] To be assailed by sin is actually a merciful dispensation to cure any self-satisfaction or proud elation in a Christian's progress.[36] The wayfarer's personal failure in Canto I, 1–61, ironically leads to the ultimate fortunate outcome of the prologue; he falls without God's grace, but that failure is part of God's mysterious providence preparing him to accept that grace when it is given. In the tradition springing from the book of Job, though Satan sends temptation, he does so with God's permission.[37] As even the portal of hell proclaims:

FECEMI LA DIVINA PODESTATE,
LA SOMMA SAPÏENZA E'L PRIMO AMORE.

(*Inferno* III, 5–6)

ABBREVIATIONS

Articles and books are listed in the text and notes under the author's name, the date and page number; full bibliographical listings are found in the bibliographies at the end of the volume. The abbreviation "com" indicates a commentary or translation of the *Divina Commedia*.

ACW	Ancient Christian Writers
AHR	*American Historical Review*
ARDS	*Annual Report of the Dante Society* (until 1965)
BAR	*Biblioteca dell'Archivum Romanicum*
BI	*Bulletin Italien*
BSCI	*Biblioteca delle Scuole Classiche Italiane*
BSDI	*Bullettino della Società Dantesca Italiana*
CeS	*Cultura e Scuola*
CFS	Cistercian Fathers Series
CJ	*Classical Journal*
CODIR	Collezione di Opuscoli Danteschi Inediti o Rari
CSEL	Corpus Scriptorum Ecclesiasticorum Latinorum
CUA Press	Catholic University of America Press
Dante Studies	*Dante Studies and the Annual Report of the Dante Society*
DBT	Léon-Dufour, ed.: *Dictionary of Biblical Theology*
DCD	Augustine: *De Civitate Dei*
DDJ	*Deutsches Dante-Jahrbuch*
DI	*Divine Institutes* (Lactantius)
ED	*Enciclopedia Dantesca*
FC	Fathers of the Church
GD	*Giornale dantesco*
GSLI	*Giornale Storico della Letteratura Dantesco*
LCC	Library of Christian Classics
LCL	Loeb Classical Library
LF	A Library of Fathers of the Holy Catholic Church Anterior to the Division of the East and West
LI	*Lettere Italiane*

LLA	Library of Liberal Arts: Bobbs-Merrill
MLN	*Modern Language Notes*
MRTS	Medieval and Renaissance Texts and Studies (series; Binghamton, N.Y.)
NGD	*Nuovo Giornale Dantesco*
NPNF	The Nicene and Post-Nicene Fathers
PG	Migne: *Patrologia graeca*
PL	Migne: *Patrologia latina*
PMLA	*Publications of the Modern Language Association of America*
REI	*Revue des Etudes Italiennes*
RN	*Romance Notes*
RR	*Romanic Review*
RTAM	*Recherches de Théologie Ancienne et Médiévale*
SCG	St. Thomas Aquinas: *Summa Contra Gentiles*
SD	*Studi Danteschi*
SEI	Società Editrice Internazionale
SIR	*Stanford Italian Review*
ST	St. Thomas Aquinas: *Summa theologica*
SUNY Press	State University of New York Press
YIS	*Yale Italian Studies*

Lecturae

LDA	*Lectura Dantis Americana* (Dante Society of America)
Lect. Fiorentina	*Lectura Dantis . . . in Orsanmichele*
Lect. Genovese	*Lectura Dantis Genovese*
Lect. Neapolitana	*Lectura Dantis Neapolitana*
Lect. Romana	*Lectura Dantis Romana*
Lect. Scaligera	*Lectura Dantis Scaligera*
Lect. Virginiana	*Lectura Dantis [Virginiana]* University of Virginia
Lett. Classensi	*Letture Classensi* (Ravenna)
Nuove Lett.	*Nuove Letture Dantesche* (Casa di Dante in Roma)

NOTES

1. All quotations from the *Commedia* are from the Petrocchi text (com 1966) as reprinted by C. S. Singleton (com 1970–1975).

2. As part of his discussion of "cano," the first verb in the *Aeneid*, Servius had observed that the opening verse of Virgil's poem had a vast array of meanings: "polysemus sermo est." Servius is, therefore, the probable source of the term "polysemos" that appears in the *Epistle to Can Grande* XIII [X], para. 7. The choice of the word clearly places the *Commedia* on a par with the great Roman epic. The word and its implications seem typical of Dante's authorial pride and may be an additional reason for attributing the letter to him.

Since specific allusions to this epistle do not appear until the 1500s and because it saw publication only as late as 1700, many critics have held it to be a forgery. Colin Hardie, in an article of 1960, outlined the reasons for excluding the letter from the canon (see also the bibliography in his 1966 revision of Toynbee's edition of Dante's *Epistolae*, pp. 256–257), and G. Brugnoli's "Introduzione" in the Frugoni-Brugnoli edition of the *Epistole* in *Opere minori*, vol. 2 (1979), pp. 512–521, repeated the reservations while discussing the dating and giving an ample bibliography on both sides of the issue. Acceptance or rejection of the epistle seems to be grounded more on the individual scholar's critical interpretation of the *Commedia* than on an unbiased interpretation of the historical facts of the letter's transmission.

Many recent critics, and not only those on this side of the Atlantic, have been inclined to accept the epistle as genuine, or, at least, to believe that the ideas it contains are consonant with Dante's own. F. Mazzoni believes that Dante composed the letter in Verona; Pagliaro also accepts its authority in his criticism. My own belief that Dante was indeed the author is primarily based on the fact that various paragraphs of the letter (except, mainly, the dedicatory paragraphs 1–4 that are, however, the best preserved in the oldest manuscripts [but see B. Nardi (1960b), pp. 31 36]) were paraphrased by Jacopo della Lana (com 1324–1328 ca.), Guido da Pisa (com 1327–1328), the Ottimo (com 1333), Pietro di Dante (com 1340–1341), Giovanni Boccaccio (com 1373), Franscesco da Buti (com 1385–1395), and Filippo Villani (who, in his commentary of ca. 1400, knew the entire thirty-three chapter-paragraphs of the letter, including the dedication to Can Grande). See also N. Mineo (1968), esp. p. 88. D. Costa (1985) has recently made some persuasive arguments both for the consistency of the first four chapters with the rest of the letter and for its attribution to Dante; Costa provides a useful bibliography (pp. 5–6).

3. Compare, for example, Dante's statements on the pleasures of hidden meaning in *Convivio* I, ii, 17 and discussion of vv. 53–61 of his first *canzone* in *Convivio* II, xi, 5–10, where he urges those who cannot understand the poem's sense at least to admire the beauty of its construction.

See J. J. Wilhelm (1982) on "the cult of the difficult."

4. C. S. Singleton (*Dante Studies 1*, p. 89) stressed that Dante's allegory has a "this-and-that" rather than a "this-for-that" structure and significance.

See also R. S. Haller, "Introduction" to *Literary Criticism of Dante Alighieri* (Lincoln: University of Nebraska Press, 1973), p. xliv.

The changes in the reader's perspective have a major source in the alternation and dialectic between the views of the wayfarer and the poet-narrator. Leo Spitzer's useful distinction (succinctly set forth in his article of 1946, p. 416) between the two personas is now recognized by the majority of Dantisti: the morally lost protagonist, "Dante-wayfarer," is distinct from the narrator, "Dante-poet," who has glimpsed the face of God.

From the perspective of the end of the poem, however, it will be the wayfarer who is spiritually privileged and the poet-narrator who is depicted in a dramatic human struggle to express the ineffable. This problem has been ably discussed by F. X. Newman (1967), pp. 56–78, and M. Chiarenza (1972), pp. 77–91. Recently, J. Gellrich (1985, p. 165) has also observed "the structure of temporal distance between the originary *liber* of God, envisioned in the sky at the end of the poem, and the book of written efforts to explain the experience of its meaning." It is ironical, yet artistically fitting, that the narrator's struggle to express what was seen in "nostra vita" "through a glass darkly" in the prologue scene of the poem will be almost as arduous as describing what has been seen "face to face."

In the following study I have also taken care to separate the self-conscious, historical artist from the two fictional personas within the text.

5. In *Paradiso* XVII, Cacciaguida plainly sets forth the didactic effect of the journey's account: the poem contains "vital nodrimento" (v. 131) for the restoration of society. The *Epistle to Can Grande* (para. 6, 8, 90 et passim) returns several times to the didactic, moral and practical nature of the *Commedia*'s message.

CHAPTER 1: The First *Terzina*

1. "In this canto the author gives his general and universal proemium to the *Commedia*."

2. Both the first and second cantos have a proemial function: some critics, though not all, believe that Canto I acts as proem for the poem as a whole, while Canto II introduces the first of the three canticles, the *Inferno*. See R. Jacoff and W. Stephany, *Lectura Dantis Americana:* Inferno II, forthcoming.

In the usage of this *Lectura*, "the prologue scene" refers to vv. 1–61 of *Inferno* I.

3. *Exempli gratia* we might point out also St. Augustine's definition in his *Sermon* on Luke 12:56–58: "Via, vita ista dicta est: finisti istam vitam finisti viam. Ambulamus; et ipsum vivere, accedere est" [This life is called "the way"; when thou hast ended this life, thou hast ended "the way." We are going on and the very living is advancing]. *Sermo* CIX, 4 (*PL* 38, col. 638); *Homilies on the Gospels*, Sermon LIX, [Benedictine ed. no. CIX]. Select Library of the Post-Nicene Fathers, vol. VI [1974], p. 443.

Boccaccio (com 1373), p. 63; G. Pascoli (1913), p. 364.

4. P. Vinassa De Regny (1942), pp. 405–413. R. Elisei (1952), pp. 9–25.

5. F. Mazzoni (com 1967), pp. 14–23, gives an ample bibliography on the various interpretations. See also S. Battaglia, *Esemplarità* (1966), vol. 1, pp. 66–72.

G. B. Bronzini (1978) expresses reservations about the importance of the chronological references, p. 161.

6. Boccaccio, *Esposizioni* (1373), p. 20.

7. C. S. Singleton (com 1970–1975); G. Petrocchi, *Itinerari* (1969a), pp. 257–275, esp. pp. 260–262; G. Contini, *Un'idea* (1976), pp. 117–120; F. Mazzoni (com 1967), pp. 23–24; F. Masciandaro (1976), esp. pp. 14–37.

On the important aspect of time references and the dating of the vision within the fiction of the *Commedia*, see E. Moore, (1887). See also E. H. Plumptre (com 1886), vol. 1, p. 1; F. Palleschi (1905), pp. 8–9; F. Angelitti (1897); R. Benini (1919, pp. 65–96; rprt. 1952); M. A. Orr, who has clear charts and graphs (1914, pp. 358–367; rprt. 1956, esp. pp. 235–244, 275–288); A. Camilli (1950a, pp. 61–84); and W. Anderson (1980, p. 282). B. Basile, "viaggio," *ED*, vol. 5 (1976), pp. 995–999.

Like Angelitti, W. and T. Parri (1956) supported 1301 as the year of the fictional journey.

8. C. S. Singleton (1965). See the works on numerology referred to in n. 14 below.

9. *Commentarium*, p. 27 (Pietro's first redaction).

10. In his discussion of the ages of man, Dante interprets Christ's death and the redemption of man as occurring as close as he can calculate to the midpoint of human life (*Convivio* IV, 23 and 24; Busnelli-Vandelli ed., vol. 2, pp. 287–319).

11. Among other passages, N. Mineo (1968, pp. 168–169) points to Isaiah 6:1: "In the year that king Ozias died, I saw . . . "; Jeremiah 1:2: "The word of the lord which came to him in the days of Josias the son of Amon king of Juda, in the thirteenth year of his reign . . . "; St. Paul in II Corinthians 12:2: "I know a man in Christ above fourteen years ago . . . caught up to the third heaven." R. Hollander has noted to me personally an observable difference between biblical time references and Dante's: the Bible's are specific; Dante's are implicit. The reader himself must supply the date 1300 and assume the responsibility for making the poet-narrator a prophet.

12. Guido wrote, "Per istud dimidium nostre vite accipe somnum, in quo, secundum Macrobium super *Somnium Scipionis* quinque visionum species sive

genera contemplantur; hoc est: oraculum, visio, somnium, insomnium et fantasma. Cuiusmodi autem speciei vel generis fuerit ista visio quam habuit ipse Dantes, transcurrendo ista quinque genera visionum videbimus manifeste" (p. 18).

13. Cf. A. Pagliaro, *Ulisse* (1961a; 1967, p. 4). F. Mazzoni (com 1967, pp. 14–15), cites the second and third redactions of the Ottimo, unavailable to me, and on p. 18, refers to L. Rocca (1891, pp. 34–35) for the unpublished *Chiose ambrosiane*. Guido da Pisa (com 1327–1328), p. 18.

14. R. Fornaciari, "Il passaggio dell'Acheronte e il sonno di Dante" (in *Studj* [1900], pp. 25–44), sees sleep as a symbol of the wayfarer's moral weakness and as "fomite del peccato." A. Pagliaro, *Ulisse* (1961a; 1967), pp. 5–6: "Ovviamente, non è possibile pensare che il poeta volesse fare passare la sua grandiosa costruzione come una visione di sogno, quando ogni sua cura è riposta nella storicizzazione del viaggio. . . ." See also his page 6, note 4. Perhaps the best arguments against the interpretation of the *Commedia* as a dream were advanced by C. S. Singleton in *Dante Studies 1*, "The Substance of Things Seen," pp. 61–83, and in his essay, "The Irreducible Dove" (1957). R. Hollander (1980) points to Filippo Villani's rejoinder in the same vein: "Non enim in somniis, sed per venam divini subsurrii, spiritu revelante et aperiente os poete, divinum hoc opus prolatum est. Unde qui eum in somniis tanta suscepisse dogmatizzant, meo videre, sompniant." (See Hollander's discussion of the question, p. 77, especially his note 81.)

F. Villani's position was taken up in 1572 by Giacopo Mazzoni during the Renaissance Aristotelian debate on Dante: "Nel poema di Dante vi è vera imitazione d'attione, e non semplice narratione d'un sogno, come molti hanno creduto" (1898, p. 61).

See also N. Mineo (1968), pp. 195–201 (Mineo's notes contain a useful bibliography). G. B. Bronzini (1978), pp. 161–177. A. Mariani, "cammino," *ED*, vol. I (1970), pp. 777–778 (unfortunately without bibliography). F. Mazzoni (com 1967), pp. 16–19.

For T. Wlassics, the episode of the three beasts is a "visione" (1975, p. 170) and also the "compiuto ritratto dello stato mentale straniato."

15. Noted in F. Mazzoni (com 1967), pp. 14–15, with no citation from the *Chiose marciane* text. The *Chiose* probably remained unknown to most later commentators.

16. Boccaccio fully understood the connections of the metaphor: "Il sonno mentale, allegoricamente parlando, è quello quando l'anima, sottoposta la ragione a' carnali appetiti, vinta dalle concupiscenze temporali, s'adormenta in esse e oziosa e negligente diventa . . . e questo è quel sonno dal quale ne richiama san Paolo, dicendo: '*Hora est iam nos de somno surgere.*' E questo sonno può essere temporale e può esser perpetuo. . . . Perpetuo è quel sonno mentale, il quale, mentre che ostinatamente ne' nostri peccati perseveriamo, ne sopragiugne l'ora ultima della presente vita e, in esso adormentate, nell'altra passiamo, là dove, non meritate la misericordia di Dio, in sempiterno co' miseri in

tal guisa dimoriamo: li quali si dicon dormire nel sonno della miseria, in quanto hanno perduto il poter vedere, conoscere e gustare il bene dello 'ntelletto, nel quale consiste la gloaria de' beati" (*Esposizioni*, pp. 60–61). F. Villani (p. 99) gives a long list of references to sin as sleep.

17. That numerological interpretations are controversial I am well aware, but perhaps the observation may be worth the hazard. Eleven exceeded 10, the number of perfection; it went beyond the Decalogue, but was deficient of 12. M. Hardt (1973), p. 180. R. A. Peck (1979), pp. 47–80.

Dante has Virgil discuss the sins of all hell (as the pagan poet understands them) in *Inferno* XI.

18. My translation.

19. See the bibliography in F. Mazzoni (com 1967), pp. 14–23. A. Frugoni (1950), pp. 1–121. C. T. Davis, on the jubilee (1957), pp. 21–23; on "Dante and the Papal City" (1957), pp. 195–235. F. Masciandaro (1972, pp. 1–26, esp. pp. 2–5; 1976).

20. See Bruni's *Vita* and the quotation from the letter in Solerti, ed. (1904), p. 100; Thompson and Nagel (1972), p. 62.

21. "Ché la diritta via era smarrita": I read "ché" as a causal conjunction along with G. Petrocchi (com 1966a, p. 3, n. 3; "Il primo canto." 1966, rprt. 1966–1967, pp. 1–16; 1969a, pp. 263–264) and G. Padoan (com 1967). C. S. Singleton (com 1970–1975) prints it without an accent.

Pagliaro and S. A. Chimenz read "che," giving the conjunction a modal value ("di modo che"). For an examination of the varied interpretations and a bibliography, see F. Mazzoni (com 1967), p. 31. See also G. B. Bronzini (1978), p. 175.

22. Boccaccio, *Esposizioni*, p. 63: "Egli è il vero che le vie son molte, ma tra tutte non è che una che a porto di salute ne meni, e quella è esso Idio, il quale di sè dice nell'*Evangelio*: '*Ego sum via, veritas et vita*'; e questa via tante volte si smarrisce—dico 'smarrisce,' perché poi chi vuole la può ritrovare, mentre nella presente via stiamo—quante le nostre iniquità da' piaceri di Dio ne trasviano, mostrandoci nelle cose labili e caduche esser somma e vera beatitudine."

23. St. Thomas Aquinas cites John Chrysostom in *ST* II–II, 72, art. 6: "The Devil is allowed sometimes to speak true things, in order that his unwonted truthfulness may gain credit for his lie." The concept is, of course, a topos.

24. In his *Commentarius* XI, 38 (*PL* 24, col. 393) on Isaiah 38:10, St. Jerome glosses: "In medio vitae cursu, et in errorum tenebris ducentur ad tartarum." A. Steiner (1937), pp. 259–260. F. Mazzoni (com 1967), p. 21. G. Getto, *Lect. Scaligera* (1960), p. 5. See also A. Pézard (1965), esp. pp. 224–225, for a different explanation of the meaning of the allusion to Isaiah.

Dante refers to Hezekiah later in *Paradiso* XX, 51, placing the monarch in the eye of the Eagle.

25. See Chapter 6, pp. 120–125, above on "il ben che vi trovai."

26. Dante gives a long discussion of the ages of man in *Convivio* IV. Particularly, he discusses the fittingness of Christ's dying in his thirty-third year: "Ed io credo che se Cristo fosse stato non crucifisso, e fosse vivuto lo spazio che la sua

vita poteva secondo natura trapassare, elli sarebbe a li ottantuno anno di mortale corpo in etternale transmutato" (*Convivio* IV, xxiv, 6; Busnelli-Vandelli, ed., pp. 310–311). The idea is based on the rest of the line from Psalm 89 [90], 10: "If in the strong they be fourscore years: and what is more of them is labour and sorrow." Dante gives the opinion that it would have been unfitting for Christ to have lived beyond the apex of his years until they began to decline. *Convivio*, ed. Busnelli-Vandelli, p. 292, n. 10; B. Nardi *Saggi* (1930), p. 136.

Dante placed the "arco" of man's life at its very center because he had learned from Aristotle that the waxing of man's life equaled the time of waning. See Aristotle's "The mental processes of passing away and coming to be occupy equal periods of time." *On Generation and Corruption*, book II, chapter 10, in Aristotle, *Complete Works*, vol. 1, p. 551. See commentary on the *Convivio* by Busnelli-Vandelli, vol. 2, p. 310, n. 4, and the very detailed essay by B. Nardi (1930), esp. pp. 133, 136, 142; C. S. Singleton (com 1970–1975), pp. 3–4. See also the Gospel of Mark 15:33–37; Matthew 23:45–50. P. Priest (1982, pp. 92–93) emphasizes the Christological and Trinitarian pattern.

27. B. Nardi (1930), p. 136.

28. The Italian term "smarrito" is difficult to render into English. Literally it means "bewildered" when applied to persons and "mislaid" when applied to objects. It has the effect of a transferred epithet. The pilgrim in fact returns to "la perduta strada" in *Purgatorio* I, 119, thus underlining the appropriateness of the second reading here.

29. Jacopo della Lana (com 1324–28 ca.), I, pp. 107–108.

J. B. Fletcher's intelligent remarks in his article of 1926 (pp. 66–67), asserting that Dante is speaking here both of poetics and spiritual growth, have been too long neglected: "Augustine's story [in the *Confessions*] is a *spiritual* comedy. Beginning in the misery of sin, by intervention of a 'god'—the true God—he is ending in the felicity of virtue. . . . [Augustine] finding out himself, he *re*found himself—the true self he had so nearly lost . . . Dante too, finding out himself, *re*found himself. 'Mi *ri*trovai,' he says. But by definition a right comedy cannot so *begin* prosperously" (Fletcher's italics). The critic clearly saw the problems attending a Pelagian reading of the text.

C. Stange (1938, pp. 164–172) compares the first lines to Egidio Colonna's commentary on Guido Cavalcante's "Donna me prega." He does not deal with the meaning of "ritrovarsi."

30. While nodding courteously to the historical interpolations imposed upon the opening lines, G. Padoan (com 1967) interprets "mi ritrovai" stressing the moral and psychological intensity with both theological accuracy and sensitivity: "E il doloroso stupore di chi si è avveduto solo allora, per la prima volta, di essere in luogo pericoloso. La consapevolezza dello stato di peccato è il primo necessario passo per la salvezza." As I point out in the text (p. 11), however, such "consapevolezza" is not in itself sufficient for conversion in a Christian context; the Old Law gave knowledge of sin but gave no means of surpassing it. The sinner-wayfarer must confess his powerlessness in a "De profundis" (v. 65) before his journey in grace can begin. A. Scrocca glosses the verb: "Il ritrovarsi,

quindi non vale *accorgersi di essere*, ma, semplicemente, *imbattersi, incorrere*" (1908), p. 2.

31. As we shall note, Jacopo Alighieri omits any evaluation of the "ri-" prefix of "mi ritrovai."

32. Thus Scartazzini-Vandelli (com 1929), ad loc.

Compare Landino (com 1481): "E dice mi ritrovai, . . . perchè cominciandosi a destare in lui la ragione, *s'accorse* che fin'allora era stato signoreggiato dall'appetito." Note also the pluperfect "era stato," suggesting that the victory over the disordered appetite has been accomplished through the wayfarer's own powers.

A. Pagliaro (*Ulisse*, p. 13) comments: "Già il Landino acutamente rilevava che il 'ritrovarsi' è qualcosa di diverso che un trovarsi materiale un entrare puro e semplice." The main problem is that critics have gone to the other extreme and have ignored the material, literal meaning, failing to keep in mind the polysemousness of the poem. "Ritrovarsi" signifies that the wayfarer has re-entered the wood.

Concerning further ideas for the essentiality of "mi ritrovai" to Dante's poetics and his meaning here, Judson B. Allen in *The Ethical Poetic* (1982, p. 13) cites some interesting observations by R. A. Shoaf on the use of the verb to signify literary (self-)creation: "The category [ethics-hyphen-poetry] is enacted in a complex of Dantean puns, of which R. A. Shoaf has kindly informed me. At the very beginning of the *Commedia*, Dante found himself ('mi ritrovai' *Inf.* 1:2); etymologically the word connects his act to that of the trouvères, and names a poetic invention, of which Dante's use of the word 'per' makes the dark wood an agent or means as well as a location. Dante then promises to treat ('trattare') of the good he found there. What results from such a treating, verbally, is a tractate or a commentary—in this case, Dante's poem, which treats his invention, himself."

Shoaf himself deals with the matter at length (1983, pp. 49ff.). I quote in part: "When Dante 'finds' himself, in a sense he 'poets' himself; underwriting this sense is the Latin equivalent of 'trov-' or 'inventio,' the rhetorical term for that process by which a poet 'finds' or 'invents' or 'discovers' his matter."

His remarks are acute. As for the "discovery" of matter for poetry, in *Paradiso* X, 27, the poet-narrator indeed claims (within the fiction) that he is the scribe, not the "inventor," in the modern sense, of his material. As for Dante Alighieri, he, of course, invents, but would have us believe that he only "finds."

See A. Niccoli, "ritrovare," *ED* 4 (1973), p. 995, and, "trovare," *ED* 5 (1976), pp. 745–747; F. Tateo, "inventio," *ED* 3 (1971), pp. 489–490.

33. Compare C. S. Singleton's words about location and the necessity of keeping the text's polysemy in mind as we read: "The poet is deliberately leading the reader into double vision, to place him on what he had every right to assume would be the most familiar of scenes. There is this about that landscape at the beginning: we may not mark its whereabouts on any map. . . . But that is not the important point. The point is that the scene was designed to locate us" (*Dante Studies 1* [1954], p. 7).

34. *Confessions* XIII, 7, "cui dicam? neque enim loca sunt, quibus mergimur et

emergimus." Singleton (*Dante Studies 1* [1954], pp. 7, 17, n. 3) cites the F. J. Sheed translation (New York, 1943). J. Freccero (1966a; rprt. 1986), pp. 1–15.

35. In spite of claims of precedence and priority by other scholars, the earliest specific statement that I have been able to discover on the dichotomy of the *poeta-viator* is L. Spitzer (1946), p. 416: "Dante the protagonist is quite distinct from Dante the narrator."

36. See, for example, L. Pietrobono's "Argomento" to *Inferno* I (com 1946), vol. I, p. 3. F. Masciandaro (1972, p. 8) sees in line 2 the "risveglio spirituale del pellegrino." P. Priest (1982, p. 92) interprets the action as Dante's "coming to himself."

37. F. Figurelli in "*Inferno*: Letture degli anni 1973–1976," *Nuove Lett.* (1977), pp. 21–22. Figurelli's interpretation of the canto is Pelagian or semi-Pelagian: "Redentosi dallo smarrimento figurato nella selva selvaggia, Dante *ha cominciato a salire il monte* della vita virtuosa non solo né tanto, come il racconto per ora ci ha lasciato credere, per la propria salvezza, ma 'a pro' del mondo che mal vive,' come sarà orgogliosamente proclamato nel corso del poema, cioè per la redenzione della società" (p. 21). For this critic, the Dante of the poem is a superhuman figure, savior of himself and other men.

G. Mazzoni expresses a contrary view (1907), p. 249: "[Dante] si accinge di purificarsi; ma con le sole sue forze non avrebbe potuto, chè di necessità poggiava sulla sua propria condizione umana; onde presto *si troverà a tornare* nella miseria di prima (ruinava in *basso loco*)."

S. Pasquazi's (1985, p. 54) view is similar.

38. *De spiritu et littera*, esp. cap. 4–7, 13–16, 23–26.

39. St. Augustine believed that free choice alone, if the way of truth was hidden, availed for nothing but sin; see *De spiritu et littera*, cap. 5. Compare also St. Thomas, *SCG* III, 155, 9: "We set aside the error of the Pelagians, who said that free choice is sufficient for man to persevere in the good, and that he does not need the help of grace for this purpose" (trans. Vernon J. Bourke, vol. III, pt. ii, p. 252).

And *SCG* III, 160, 4: "The opinion of the Pelagians is evidently stupid, for they say that man in the state of sin is able to avoid sin, without grace. The contrary to this is apparent from the petition from the Psalm (70[71]:9): 'When my strength shall fail, do not thou forsake me.' And the Lord teaches us to pray: 'And lead us not into temptation, but deliver us from evil'" (trans. pp. 262–263).

On the vanity of striving for the summit of contemplation without prevenient grace, see Richard of St. Victor, *The Twelve Patriarchs*, LXVII, trans. Zinn, p. 135.

Dante's clearest anti-Pelagian statements are made to come from the mouth of Beatrice in *Paradiso* VII, 97–102: "Non potea l'uomo ne' termini suoi / mai sodisfar, per non potere ir giuso / con umiltate obedïendo intese ir suso; / e questa è la cagion per che l'uom fue / da poter sodisfar per sé dischiuso." Later she adds (vv. 118–120): "e tutti li altri modi erano scarsi / a la giustizia, se'l

Figliuol di Dio / non fosse umilïato ad incarnarsi." R. Kirkpatrick (1987, p. 9) observes the "virtiginous confusion" of the first sixty one lines before Virgil's arrival and sees the wayfarer's helplessness in awakening "to the knowledge of his own involvement in sin."

40. A. Pagliaro (*Ulisse*, p. 13) paraphrases Dante: "Nel percorrere il cammino della vita, dice Dante, giunto a metà di quello che è il percorso normale, *mi accorsi che mi trovavo ad aggirarmi per una selva oscura* senza una direzione." V. Vettori (1963), p. 10, glosses: "Ritrovai me . . . cioè, mi svegliai." Cf. R. Lansing (1977), p. 98.

"To find oneself again" does, of course, presuppose consciousness or awareness, but so does many another verb—all verbs, perhaps, except those that imply or express its loss; we cannot reduce Dante's poetry to such an anachronistic Cartesian tabula rasa. We miss too much of the poetic sense when we substitute for the original verb another that implies only the fact of consciousness, while omitting the more important locational-spiritual ideas of the "regio dissimilitudinis" [the region of unlikeness to God] and the idea of repeated failure so important in the traditions of conversion theology.

41. Dante uses the verb "ritrovare" only six times in the poem: twice reflexively and once transitively in the *Inferno*, and three times transitively in the *Paradiso*. For the one transitive use in *Inferno* VI, 97, "ritroverà la trista tomba," C. S. Singleton (com 1970–1975) translates "will find again." In each case in the *Paradiso* (II, 99; V, 69; XXXIII, 134), the verb clearly means "to locate" or "find after seeking."

42. A. Scrocca (1908), pp. 1–2. G. B. Bronzini makes a firm case for this point in his article (1978), pp. 166–167.

43. Cf. II Corinthians 4:16 and 5:14–17. See C. S. Singleton's discussion in *Essay on the Vita Nuova* (1949), pp. 114–116.

44. Again diametrically opposed to mine is F. Figurelli's interpretation (1977, p. 22), which views the wayfarer-poet as a kind of messiah in D'Annunzian dress: "Così alto carisma e così eccezionale missione non potevano ovviamente essere largiti ad un peccatore recidivo, quale sarebbe stato Dante se nuovamente sopraffatto dal male dopo d'esserne redento, ma solo a chi possedesse straordinarie virtù e le esercitasse in perfetta armonia coi fini trascendenti della vita, con eroica volizione e col personale sacrificio d'ogni legittimo bene." The critic forgets the cases of St. Paul, Mary Magdalene, and St. Augustine; he similarly ignores the question of the wound of original sin in the will and the consequent impossibility of ascent without prevenient grace (*gratia gratis data*). There is no question of "self-redemption" fulfilled in the prologue section of Canto I (vv. 1–61); it is not given or implied in the narrative of the poem, nor is it possible in the teachings of Christianity that support the poetics of the text.

More accurate, I believe, is the position of R. Giglio (1973), p. 154: "Se Dante è riuscito a mettersi in salvo, uscendo dalla selva e fuggendo la lupa *con l'ausilio di Virgilio*, come poi dimostra in seguito, *il merito non è suo*" (my emphasis).

On the orthodox necessity of grace, see St. Augustine, *De correctione et gratia*

(*PL* 44, col. 942). J. Freccero (1959; rprt. 1986, pp. 29–54) comments: "Without God's help, man can only stagger *repeatedly* out of the forest by his own power, only *to return again* to the misery out of which he has come" (p. 280; again my emphasis).

St. Cyprian comments on the *Pater noster*: "When, moreover, we ask that we come not into temptation, we are reminded of our infirmity and weakness, lest someone extol himself insolently, lest someone proudly and arrogantly assume something to himself" (*De Dominica oratione*, ed. W. Von Hartel, CSEL 3. 1. 3: 286; *The Lord's Prayer* [*De Dominica oratione*], ch. 26, in *Treatises*, trans. R. J. Deferrari, *FC*, p. 150).

On the positive aspects of a fall into sin as a corrective, and of the repeated humbling lessons of sin, see, for example, St. Augustine, *DCD* XI, 31, where he discusses Proverbs 24:16.

45. St. Augustine, *De Sermone Domini* II, 9, 35 (*PL* 34, cols. 1284–1295); *Commentary on the Sermon on the Mount*, trans. Kavanagh, pp. 143–144.

46. St. Gregory's whole commentary on Job is based upon the concepts of attempted conversion, recidivism, temptation as correction, and re-conversion: "We can never be free from sin so long as we are held fast in a body of mortality" (*Moralia* VIII, 56; *Morals*, vol. I, p. 461). Cf. Job 7:1: "The life of man upon the earth is a warfare." See *Moralia* XX, 8; *Morals*, vol. II, p. 452, and *Moralia* XXVI, 65; *Morals*, vol. III, p. 183. No one except Christ is so perfect so as not to have sinned in some degree (cf. *Moralia* XIV, 21; *Morals*, vol. II, p. 219).

The notion of the helplessness of man left to himself is addressed in *Purgatorio* XI, 19–21, as the souls recite a paraphrase of the Pater noster: "Nostra virtù che di leggier s'adona, / non spermentar con l'antico avversaro / ma libera da lui che sì la sprona."

47. Concerning the problem of the meaning of "per" in verse 2, I find convincing the view of G. Contini, F. Mazzoni, and Bosco-Reggio, who interpret the word as "entro" (within), adducing Guido Cavalcanti's verse 20 from the canzone "Io non pensava": "l'anima sento *per* lo cor tremare" (G. Contini, *Poeti del Duecento*, 2:500, n. 20).

48. Such a positive view of Dante's poetic effects is shared neither by neo-Croceans nor by critics who read only for aesthetic appreciation, ignoring the power of allegory. Compare Momigliano: "Ma la qualità del luogo, la selva, è suggerita a Dante dall'intenzione allegorica: questo è il germe che corrode il canto. . . . Il I canto è il più incertamente concepito dell'*Inferno*. . . . Il complesso manca di sicurezza e relativamente, di stile" (T. Casini-S. A. Barbi and A. Momigliano, ed. F. Mazzoni [com 1972–1973], pp. 4–5). C. Ballerini (1953) gives a particularly sensitive and un-Crocean reading, although I differ with his views on many points concerning the theology reflected by the text. See also E. Ragni, "selva," *ED*, vol. 5 (1976), pp. 137–142.

49. For the *Chiose marciane* and the Ottimo's third redaction, see F. Mazzoni (com 1967), p. 27.

50. Typical, and, I believe, correct, is the T. Casini-S. A. Barbi (F. Maz-

zoni com 1972–1973) interpretation: "*selva*: raffigura la vita viziosa, propria dell'uomo peccatore." Cf. Pagliaro, *Ulisse*, I, p. 12.

G. Marchetti (1819) saw the *selva* as representing Dante's exile, a view opposed by Foscolo (*Discorso* [1842], p. 385). See also G. Casella's remarks in his *Opere* (1884) 2, pp. 377–380. I. Sanesi (1902), pp. 1–16; Ballerini (1953), p. 39; P. Giannantonio (1980), p. 6.

51. Bernardus Silvestris, *Commentary*, ed. Jones and Jones (1977), p. 62; their text and that of G. Riedel (1924, p. 62) differs from that quoted by Silverstein (1932, p. 81), reading "inviam" for "immensam." The Riedel and the Jones and Jones readings present a text even closer to Dante's concept. Bernardus Silvestris gives the same meaning to "lucos": "bona temporalia" (Jones and Jones, p. 53). See also Singleton (com 1975–1980) on "selva."

52. See Augustine, *Homilies on the Gospel According to John*, LF trans., vol. 1, p. 256.

E. R. Curtius (1963), pp. 194–195, E. Auerbach (*Mimesis*, esp. pp. 107–124), and F. Mazzoni (com 1967), p. 29.

53. The parallel is fairly striking, but we must note the difference. Dante is speaking in the earlier treatise of the sins that beset particular age groups: as gluttony affects children, lust affects adolescents, and so on. But clearly the wayfarer "nel mezzo del cammin" is, according to Dante's own calculations, some ten years beyond adolescence (adolescence ends at 25), and there is in the specific lines of the poem nothing to link the forest simply with the sole sin of lust. *Convivio* IV, xxiv, 12, deals not with the interior struggles of moral choice and the necessity of the correction of temptation and grace, but with the *paideia* of elders. In the *Commedia* the *selva* takes on a broader poetic and moral scope.

S. Battaglia (*Esemplarità* [1966], vol. 2, p. 29): "Tutta la vita si configurò come una 'selva' selvaggia, che rappresenta con evidenza pittorica il caos dei sensi: e come tale, dominata dalla confusione, dalla tenebra, dalla cecità." See also F. Mazzoni (com 1967), p. 27.

See J. Daniélou (1956), pp. 276–278, on the five ages of the *saeculum*, and A. Cassell (1984), pp. 62–65, for other reflections of the tradition in the *Commedia*.

For the first seven verses of the *Commedia* as representing the seven ages of man's life from "vita" to "morte" (v. 7) see F. W. Locke (1967), pp. 62–63.

54. A. Pagliaro agrees with Landino (*Ulisse* I:11).

For "silva" as *hyle*, see E. R. Curtius (1963), p. 109. J. Whitman (1981), pp. 63–86, esp. pp. 68–69; S. Battaglia, *Esemplarità* (1966), vol. 1, p. 69.

E. Vance sees the "silva" as the corrupting factor of chaos (1980), pp. 137–155. R. A. Shoaf has explored the idea that one of the senses of "selva" is language itself (1983, p. 49).

55. Notable here also is the fact that while *selva* occurs in line five, the first use of the word "paura" occurs in verse 6, the number associated with the renewal of the sixth age in Christ, with the initiation into the Christian faith, and with the new spiritual age as opposed to the five senses and the "saeculum" asso-

ciated with the number five. Fear is the beginning of wisdom in the Judeo-Christian tradition, and it is no accident that "paura" here applies to the persona of the poet whose soul, fresh from the sight of God, is now in righteous order. Since the commentary tradition has, for the most part, viewed fear only in its negative, physical aspects, in Chapter 2, "La paura un poco queta," I have tried to correct this imbalance by dealing with the traditional, positive values of "paura" in Judeo-Christian theology and in the poem.

Cf. G. Getto, *Aspetti* (1966, p. 3): "Non si tratta più di un tremore della carne, ma di una esperienza angosciosa e disperato di peccato, dove la paura semmai è paura della morte seconda, della morte dell'anima."

56. Pagliaro, *Ulisse*, p. 11.

57. As the reader will note, I assume the adjective "amara" is conjoined to "selva." Different views have been held and defended: (1) that "tanto è amara" modifies "cosa dura," (2) that "amara" cannot refer to "selva" because the forest is the provenance of "il ben," and (3) that "amara" refers to "paura." I believe Dante is calquing his verse on Augustine's "amara silva" in the *Sermo in Joannem* XVI, 6, that I cited earlier in the text, just as I also believe he calques his evaluation of climbing mountains on Augustine's preceding *Sermo* XV, 25. See L. G. Blanc (1865), pp. 1–4; M. Barbi, *Problemi* (1941), 2ᵃ serie, p. 46, n. 3; S. Battaglia, *Esemplarità* (1966), vol. 1, p. 65; F. Mazzoni (com 1967), pp. 26–31; C. S. Singleton, *Inferno: Commentary* (com 1970–1975), p. 6.

58. Dante warns us about the siren effect of bad reading—or hearing—in *Purgatorio* II, 106–133, where attention only to sound and literal senses makes souls listen "come a nessun toccasse altro la mente." See C. S. Singleton (com 1970–1975); J. Freccero (1973, rprt. 1986), pp. 186–196; R. Hollander (1980, pp. 91–205) makes the case that Lady Philosophy is herself the siren.

59. Pagliaro, *Ulisse*, p. 12.

Cf. also Ecclesiastes 7:27 [26]: "I have found a woman more bitter than death"; Ecclesiaticus 41:1: "O Death, how bitter is the remembrance of thee." C. S. Singleton (com 1970–1975).

60. St. Augustine, *In Ioannis Evangelium* XV, 25 (*PL* 35, col. 1519); trans. *Homily* XV, 25, *Homilies, LF* trans. vol. 1, pp. 244–245.

61. Vandelli (Scartazzini-Vandelli [com 1929; rpt. 1983], p. 4) saw the "dilettoso monte" as a symbol of the presumption of anyone who believed that he could gain salvation under his own, unaided powers. Vandelli was one of the very few who recognized the real implications of Dante's Christian beliefs here. G. Getto (*Aspetti* [1966, p. 2]) also quite clearly understood the problem of the direction taken in *Inferno* I, 1–61: "Il ritrovarsi di Dante in un luogo, fuori strada, in una selva, in una direzione falsa, segna uno spazio che è fisico e metafisico insieme, un luogo che è del corpo e dell'anima."

62. Cf. A. Pagliaro: "Una volta lasciata la giusta via, questa non esiste più; e il viandante si ritrova perduto nel selvaggio intrico . . . ma si affanna verso il monte della vita contemplativa, che all'improvviso gli si scopre dinanzi come l'unica salvezza" (*Ulisse*, p. 13). On p. 14, Pagliaro recognizes that the path

through the wood and the path up the mountain are identical: "Se dovessimo rappresentarci la situazione topografica della vicenda, dovremmo, a me sembra, immaginare una via diritta, che da una sorgente di luce è guadagnata dentro una fosca valle selvosa e, al di là di questa, un colle ridente, pieno di sole." Although the mountain symbolizes contemplation or philosophy, it must be understood that this is, in the context of the *Commedia*, a secondary good to be used and that to rest in or "enjoy" philosophy is as much a sin as to rest in or "enjoy" any other thing in the *saeculum*; cf. the famous paragraphs on "uti" and "frui" in Augustine's *De doctrina christiana* I, 3–5.

Critical views, however, have misapprehended the mountain and the climb as a primary good. Mattalia saw it as all "elements of perfection of man's journey to God." The commentaries of Casini-Barbi, Porena, Sapegno, and Chimenz all concur that the shining mountain is "the virtuous life" or grace itself. D. Consoli ("colle," *ED*, vol. 2 [1970], pp. 51–52) writes "Il c[olle] si presenta quindi sin dalle prime battute del poema come una delle mete, *se non la meta suprema*, dell'itinerario dantesco." For I. Del Lungo (1925, p. 15), it represents Purgatory; for Pagliaro (*Ulisse*, pp. 15–17), it is contemplation. See F. Mazzoni (com 1967), pp. 58–60, and Consoli ("colle") for a discussion and bibliography.

63. The following is a synopsis of the assumptions and conclusions of my argument in the chapters to come: 1. The wayfarer at first sees the "colle" as a positive goal. 2. Dante leaves ambiguous Virgil's statements concerning the "dilettoso monte / ch'è principio e cagion di tutta gioia" (vv. 77–78). If Virgil is meant to refer to the "colle" and imply that the climb signifies a philosophical ascent possible to the wayfarer without outside help, then Dante is portraying Virgil as a pagan, alien to Christian beliefs. If "monte" refers to the Mount of Purgatory, the implications of Virgil's question would be doctrinally correct— we will learn retrospectively in *Inferno* II of Beatrice's tutoring that included this information. (One might note, in passing, that no useful, consistent theological distinction is made in Latin patristic writings between "colles" and "montes," "hills" and "mountains," although there are some isolated attempts not germane to our argument here.) 3. At first reading we are led by the text itself to view the "colle" as positive. 4. At later readings, contemplating the "colle" from further on in the poem, we realize that the choice and means of the initial climb is mistaken. We should see also, in retrospect, that there were negative signs in the verses when the "colle" was first presented. The text has, meanwhile, revealed many limitations and failings on the part of the wayfarer and, more surprisingly, of his guide. We can see, in hindsight, that the ambiguity serves a didactic function: it calls attention to the fundamental discrepancies between pagan and Christian philosophies, and it teaches the basic Christian belief of man's helplessness without God's grace. In fact, both possibilities implied in the ambiguity of the word "dilettoso" hold true in the poem.

As I shall point out in Chapter 6, "Il ben che vi trovai," this is not the last of the interpretive reversals imposed by the structure of the poem itself.

CHAPTER 2: "Al piè d'un colle"

1. Compare, for example, Francesco da Buti (com 1385–1395), p. 23 "lo rag-guardamento del pianeta sopra il monte." Castelvetro (com ca. 1570), p. 10: "gli fu mostrato il sole." H. F. Dunbar (1929), p. 159: "Dante's first progress from the terrible forest of moral and political chaos . . . was initiated at dawn by an up-ward look toward that planet that leads men straight on every path." O. M. Johnson (1926), p. 42: "The sun seen by Dante from the dark forest is a symbol of Paradise." G. Ungaretti (1952, rprt. 1962), p. 10. Nancy H. Rosenberg (1962), pp. 101–102. U. Limentani (1985), p. 2: the "sun [is] glimpsed from the lowest slopes of the hill."

See also H. D. Austin (1943), pp. 71–74, on "il pianeta."

On the identification of the "colle" with the Mount of Purgatory, see I. Del Lungo, *Prolusione all'Inferno, Lect. Romana* (1901), p. 27: "Il dilettoso monte, il colle, è l'immagine similare del Purgatorio." In 1925 he repeated the assertion (pp. 14–15): "La selva è l'imagine dell'Inferno; il Colle è l'imagine del pur-gatorio." That the images are proleptic of the two realms seems clear, but to view the hill of the prologue as identical with the mountain of Purgatory ig-nores the geography, cosmology, and theology of the poem. Cf. L. Filomusi-Guelfi (1917), p. 62. E. G. Parodi disagreed with the identification, expressing surprise that anyone could, without qualms, attribute to Dante such a rough and feeble construction (1918), p. 97. A. Masseron (1922) tentatively agrees with Parodi, pp. 119–120.

Jacopo della Lana saw the path up the mountain as the life of virtue; the Ot-timo believed it signified virtue and the knowledge of true happiness; Ben-venuto viewed it as "ardua virtus"; the Anonimo Fiorentino as true knowledge and the perfect understanding of all things. Serravalle (com 1416–1417) saw the "colle" as the "via virtutum" and a "penitentia." For Daniello (com 1568) the mountain was virtue; the light, the light of grace. In 1905, F. Palleschi saw a clear dichotomy: "Ossia la selva [è] la colpa . . . il colle, erto e difficile, è in contrapposizione della selva" (pp. 11–12). T. Casini (1913, p. 25) interpreted the wayfarer's glance as "una luminosa visione consolatrice"; B. Nardi (1930, p. 318) agreed that it was "il simbolo della virtù e della felicità terrena." R. Elisei (1952) believed the ascent to be "la via del perfezionamento": the hill represented the active life (pp. 13, 16). G. Petrocchi (*Lett. class.*, 1966a, p. 166) identified the hill as "la via di salvezza." For Padoan (com 1967) the "colle . . . simboleggia la via del riscatto spirituale." P. Giannantonio (1980, pp. 8–10) read the journey with-out a guide as a successful rediscovery of the "itinerario salvifico": "L'errante ritrova il sentiero del riscatto . . . vicina è la via della salvezza ed allora mi-surando la singolarità della grazia divina il pellegrino rinasce di nuova vita." Cf. F. Masciandaro (1972), p. 11. For a résumé of positive assessments of the way-farer's choice of the "colle," see T. Bolelli (1973), pp. 165–168.

Other critics, however, in the wake of Parodi, have begun to see the inade-quacy and inconsistency of such interpretations: J. Freccero (1966a; rprt. 1986, pp. 1–28) confirmed the negative symbolism of the shining mountain. C. Hardie

(1970), pp. 81–100, expressed the view that to interpret the climb up the "colle" as positive or as being one with the ascent of Mount Purgatory "seems to turn the symbolism of the Antipodes into nonsense" (p. 90).

2. I agree with the near-consensus that the sun here symbolizes the Deity. For an earlier use of the symbol by the poet, see *Convivio* III, xii, 6–7. See also J. Freccero (1959; rprt. 1986), pp. 278–279; C. S. Singleton (1960), p. 1.

3. A. C. Mastrobuono (1979, p. 47) likewise paraphrases "il monte vestito già dai raggi" as "a mountain flooded by sunlight."

There are seventeen instances of the verb "vestire" in the *Commedia*: in each of the other sixteen cases, the verb signifies the clothing or cloaking of the exterior of a body, shade, or form, that is, the covering of the total exterior; in *Paradiso* XXV, 91–92, for example, the verses refer to Isaiah and the "double garment" of the shining soul and glorified body. In no case does it mean "outlined" or "silhouetted"; thus, in *Inferno* I, 17, if the light of the rising sun falls directly on the mountain/hill, it must come from behind the wayfarer. As I point out, a silhouetted mountain would, obviously, be black against the light, not floodlit by it. One could compare the situation in *Purgatorio* XXVII, 65–66, where, as the wayfarer goes straight forth from Purgatory into Eden, his body intercepts the rays of the setting sun.

4. *Divine Institutes* VI, 8; trans. p. 412.

5. *Divine Institutes* VI, 8; trans. p. 411. The sea receives its traditional gloss also in the *Moralia*, XVII, 45 (*Morals*, vol. II, p. 307) as St. Gregory comments on Job 26:12: "What else is denoted by the title of *the sea* save *the present world*, wherein the hearts of men seeking after earthly things swell with the varied billows of thought?" See also Singleton (1948), "Sulla fiumana." Emile Mâle (*The Gothic Image*, p. 30) cites the bestiary attributed to Hugh of St. Victor, where, under "columba," we read that its color recalls the storms of the unquiet sea and thus the desires and passions of the flesh (*De bestiis*, PL 177, col. 19).

6. *Divine Institutes* VI, 4; trans. p. 402.

7. *Divine Institutes* VI, 8; trans. pp. 411–412.

8. C. S. Singleton (com 1970–1975), note to *Inferno* I, 13–18.

9. The usual gloss on the word "altrui" (v. 18) is "l'uomo," "homo" [man] (cf. Benvenuto da Imola, "ducit hominem recte" [com 1373–1380, p. 30]; Padoan, "guida sicuramente l'uomo per ogni via" [com 1967]), "ognuno," "tutti" [everyone] (cf. Guido da Pisa, "qui omnem hominem per omnem callem via recta deducit [com 1327–1328, p. 11]; G. Padoan, com 1967; and P. Caligaris [1969, p. 20]) or "chiunque" [whomever] (cf. L. Cassata [com 1987–1988], p. 4). In the history of the criticism of this verse the power of repeating over the centuries an "accepted" interpretation has made itself felt.

The meaning in the context is initially unclear. At our first reading, we surmise that the wayfarer's climb is righteous; our puzzlement first makes us reject the normal sense of "others." Similarly, those who have not realized the transvaluating process of the imagery as the poem progresses and who see Dante wayfarer's climb here only as a positive ascent, have been forced to say that "altrui" does not mean "others" but that it has a quite different meaning—one, in fact, that ignores the literal sense of the text. When we recognize that the first sixty-one lines of the poem recount a failure, we realize that "altrui" has a meaning that *excludes* rather than *includes* the wayfarer. The events of the first sixty-one lines will prove that the pilgrim is not included in the pronoun: the sun does not lead him aright on his path; rather, the sun is silent and the unaided wayfarer falls to the depths. It will take God's grace with the coming of Virgil to turn the wayfarer in the right direction—the direction of the "verace via."

"Altrui" is used 54 times in the poem. In every other case, "altrui" means "other(s)" or "Another" (God), or is used as a Latinism to mean "of others," (cf. *Paradiso* XVII, 59), "to others" (cf. *Paradiso* VI, 132), and so on. It always refers to those beyond and outside a given frame of reference, usually independent of the self, not including it. I submit that "altrui" in verse 18 clearly excludes the wayfarer and emphasizes his total alienation: at this point the sun leads "other men," not him, straight along their paths. As the poem will reveal, the wayfarer in *Inferno* I, 1–61, is journeying backwards on his own path; that is, he is one of those Christians who have erroneous "fidanza . . . ne' ritrosi passi" (*Purgatorio* X, 123).

In the following pages I hope to demonstrate that Dante's imagery follows theological metaphor very closely; the sun's guidance for the sea voyage of life, and the ascent of mountains as a philosophical journey of contemplation both appear, as we would expect, in some of the earliest Christian apologetic texts and form the firm traditional nexus of figures from which the poet drew.

10. *Divine Institutes* VI, 3; trans. p. 398.

11. The duplicitous Ulysses reverses the metaphor to confuse his men—and, perhaps, the less careful reader: he *follows the sun* ("di retro il sol")—not the *rising* sun, but the *setting* sun; he sails *west* not *east* (*Inferno* XXVI, 124). He also sails to the left, in the "sinister" and wrong direction, "sempre acquistando dal lato mancino" (*Inferno* XXVI, 126). In classical cosmology Aristotle had made the east the absolute "right" and followed ancient tradition in believing that the heavens also moved to the right (cf. J. Freccero, 1961a; rprt. 1986, p. 73).

12. On the negative value of "poppa" meaning "poop" see the amusing observations by T. Wlassics, *Lect. Virginiana* (1987), p. 62.

13. *Moralia* XVI, 70; *Morals*, vol. II, p. 268.

14. Compare J. S. Carroll (1903), p. 11; the Scottish critic's perceptive comments have been too long neglected: "Nothing is more unsatisfactory than the summary way in which this hill is usually dismissed by a quotation from the Psalms—'I will lift up mine eyes unto the hills,' or a reference to the 'delectable mountains' of the *Pilgrim's Progress.*" The rest of Carroll's argument is intelligently reasoned: "If we say that the mountain Dante first attempted to climb was Philosophy, it fits in sufficiently well with all the facts. . . . For a time he thought her sunlit heights sufficient, not knowing that he had a far loftier mountain to climb. . . . Dante found it beyond his power to climb . . . even Philosophy is beyond the man who has not conquered the beast in himself" (p. 12).

Obviously, in Christianity, the negativity of an object does not lie in its essence—an object is not bad in itself; its value rests on human choice. Cf. St. Augustine in the *De natura boni*, chapter 36: "Sin is not a seeking of something evil, but an abandonment of what is better. So the deed is the evil thing, not the thing of which the sinner makes evil use. Evil is the bad use of a good thing" (*The Nature of the Good*, ed. and trans. J. H. S. Burleigh, *Augustine: Earlier Writings*, LCC, vol. 6, p. 338).

As I indicated earlier in Chapter 1, p. 141, n. 63, the problem for the reader becomes even more puzzling at this point with Virgil's question concerning a mountain "perché non sali il dilettoso monte?" (*Inferno* I, 77). Does the sage refer to the "colle" or to Mount Purgatory—and why should he choose either as a good? He could easily be referring to Purgatory, since he knows not only of its existence but also of its punishments: "e vederai color che son contenti / nel foco, perché speran di venire / quando che sia a le beate genti" (vv. 118–120).

Later the realization of Virgil's fallibility in the poem begins to frame the crux differently and our suspicicion that the "monte" is to be identified with the "colle" of verse 13 receives further confirmation. There may be some irony in the adjective "dilettoso": as a pagan, Virgil may still see a mount of contemplation as the source of ultimate delight, much as he sees Beatrice as Philosophia (on this latter point see C. S. Singleton, 1956, pp. 29–38, and J. T. Chiampi, 1981, p. 173). Note the negative use of "delight" in *Inferno* V, 127 ("Noi leggiavamo un giorno per diletto") and Brunetto Latini's disquisition on "délit" in *Li Trésors* II, 40 (Carmody, ed., p. 206).

What is obvious is that we cannot, at verses 77–78, reject either of the possible explanations; both must hold in the polysemousness of the poem.

On Virgil's "imperfetta conoscenza," see S. Pasquazi (1985), p. 55, who identifies the "monte" with "uno stato di felicità naturale" (p. 56) whose attainment must be only an illusory hope for man unaided. While I agree totally with Pasquazi's interpretation, there are further aspects of the wayfarer's proud, presumptuous, dogged pursuit of this illusion that he neglects.

15. A. C. Mastrobuono (1979), p. 53, equates the mountain here with Mount Sinai and Golgotha. A. E. Wingell (1981, p. 17) discusses Augustine's distinction between the "montes Dei" and the "montes saeculi," and notes that "his rule of exegesis included a warning that the same sensible thing in different places in the sacred writings could signify opposite spiritual values." Wingell gives a well-chosen anthology of "wicked mountains" (p. 32).

The church fathers were well aware of the negative meanings of "Sinai" and "Sion." St. Cyprian's *De montibus Sinai et Sion* 2, for example, translates their names thus: "Haec est interpretatio de Hebraica lingua in Latinam. Sinai mons interpretat 'aeterna temptatio et odium': aeque et Sion interpretat 'temptatio exacerbationis et speculatio.'" *Opera omnia*, ed. Hartel, pars III (1871), p. 105.

Like the "selva," the "colle" is indeed the place of temptation, as I shall explore in Chapter 3.

A skewing of the traditional ambiguity of the mountaintop as a holy place is also found in Boccaccio's *Decameron*, where in the comic "papere" tale of the Introduction to Day IV, Filippo Balducci retires as a hermit with his son to Monte Asinaio ("Mount Asinine")—usually glossed as a variant form of Monte Senario, a mountain north of Florence, yet for Boccaccio a comic "-sinai-" with a waggish alpha and omega at its beginning and end.

16. That the song is Satan's is Tyconius's interpretation in *Regula* VII (*Liber de septem regulis, PL* 18, col. 55–56) repeated by St. Augustine in *De doctrina christiana* 3, 37, 55 (*PL* 34, col. 88); *On Christian Doctrine*, pp. 115–116; *DCD* 11:15; *De Genesi ad litteram*, 11:24 (ed. Zycha, CSEL, pp. 356–357); *The Literal Meaning of Genesis*, trans. J. H. Taylor (1982), *ACW* vol. 2, pp. 155–156.

17. Cf. Hosea 4:13: "On the mountain they offer sacrifice. . . ." There is frequent mention of the "high places" in Deuteronomy, I and II Kings (I and II Samuel), Isaiah, Hosea, and Amos. See especially the Deuteronimic passages in II [IV] Kings 18:4; 23:8; 23:13, 14, 19. Jeremiah 19:5; 32:35. Through the prestige of Jerusalem, Deuteronomy's program of destruction of "high places" in both the south and the north (II [IV] Kings 23:4–20) was finally accomplished by Josiah who destroyed the rest of the many mountaintop cultic sites in 621 B.C. and left the Temple at Jerusalem as the sole place of Jahweh's worship from then on. Jeremiah 2:20 and 3:23 speak of the danger of idolatry associated with these "bamoth" because of their very dispersion.

On the question of "bāma," "bahmot"—also transliterated "bahmoth"— ["excelsa" or "high places"] in the Old Testament, see L. H. Vincent (1948), pp. 245–278, 438–445; W. F. Albright (1957), pp. 242–258; R. de Vaux (1961), esp. pp. 284–288, 331–344; H. J. Kraus (1966), pp. 99, 134–178, esp. 150, 168–169; P. H. Vaughan (1974), esp. pp. 10–11.

18. Hezekiah is named in the genealogy of Jesus in Matthew 1:9–10; however, his reputation as a ruler was not always so solid as Dante makes it out; he was reviled for his submission to the Assyrians (II[IV] Kings 18:9–22; 20:16–19).

19. St. Augustine, *In Joannis Evangelium* tract. XV, cap. 25 (*PL* 35, col. 1519); trans. *Homilies on the Gospel*, XV, chapter 25, p. 245.

20. Cf. Boccaccio, com p. 71, and note 13 above.

21. In the *Enarratio in Psalmum* 35 (*PL* 36, col. 347); trans. Hebgin-Corrigan, *ACW*, vol. 2, p. 234.

22. *Enarratio in Psalmum* (*PL* 36, col. 347; trans. Hebgin-Corrigan, *ACW*, vol. 2, p. 234. St. Augustine makes the identity of the foot of mountains with the foot of pride explicit in his *De spiritu et littera* 19; *The Spirit and the Letter*, trans. Burnaby, *Augustine: Later Works*, LCC, vol. 8, p. 209. St. Gregory in his *Moralia* XXX, 1, gives more negative identifications for mountains, suggesting Satan "angelus apostata" (*PL* 76, col. 669) and "the loftiness of the proud" (*PL* 76, col. 586).

Some of the earlier commentators made similar, anthropomorphic interpretations of Dante's "colle," but *in bono*. The Anonimo Fiorentino (p. 13) comments: "Le spalle sue s'intende li excellentissimi uomini addottrinati per scienza et chiarissimo conoscimento." Cf. F. Villani (com p. 106).

23. W. M. Green discusses the shining mountain in *De beata vita* thoroughly in the context of the sin of pride and Pelagianism (1949), esp. p. 407.

We recall that the mount of true beatitude, Purgatory, is "bruna per la distanza" for the unworthy Ulisse (*Inferno* XXVI, 133–134).

24. *De beata vita* (*PL* 32, col. 960–961); *The Happy Life*, II, pp. 44–47. Wingell also cites the passage (1981), p. 18.

25. D. Thompson (1974, pp. 62–73); J. Freccero (1966a; rprt. 1986), pp. 1–25. R. Hollander has dealt with Dante's reprobation of his former devotion to philosophy in "Cato's Rebuke"; he identifies Lady Philosophy with the siren (1980, pp. 91–105). See also A. E. Wingell (1981), p. 39. On the problem of philosophy and religion, *philosophia creata* and *increata* and the influence of Boethius, see also M.-Th. d'Alverny (1965), pp. 5–24, esp. 9–24.

26. See, for example, Jean Radermakers's entry on "Error" in Léon-Dufour, ed., *DBT*, pp. 144–145.

27. Pietro di Dante alludes to Daniel 4:29–30 (p. 35) in the Ashburnham version of his commentary.

On the mad, vagabond Nebuchadnezzar and his tradition in medieval literature, see P. Doob (1974).

28. Lactantius speaks of the falseness, foolishness, and failings of philosophical schools at length in book III of the *Divine Institutes*. Cf. St. Augustine *De beata vita*, I, 3; *Confessions* VII, 20, 26; *DCD* X, 29; XIX, 4. On baptism and the "languor naturae," see G. Pascoli, "L'umana colpa" (1902–1913), pp. 321–339.

29. On the "scuola," see G. Busnelli (1918), p. 86, and his notes.

30. The metaphor receives its corollary in Statius's description of his conversion and Virgil's role in it. Virgil, too, refused to see the light in not recognizing Christ as Savior of the world; the ancient poet, with his works pointing to the coming of the Redeemer, is therefore like one who bears a lamp behind him, deriving no benefit from it yet aiding others: "Facesti come quei che va di notte, / che porta il lume dietro e sé non giova, / ma dopo sé fa le persone dotte" (*Purgatorio* XXII, 67–69).

31. The metaphor, predicated of Florence, as it is of Satan and of Dante himself, demonstrates that the political and spiritual implications are inextricably intertwined.

32. For the traditional cosmography accepted and used by Dante, almost the reverse of that assumed by the twentieth century, see J. Freccero (1961a; rprt. 1986), pp. 70–92.

33. See St. Augustine, *De trinitate*, XV, 15–16 (*PL* 42, cols. 1068–1069).

34. C. Ballerini (1953) concentrates on the physical, negative aspects of fear. See also V. Russo (1965), pp. 391–408.

35. For G. Pascoli (1900; rprt. 1912, p. 109) the wayfarer's fear suggested no metaphysical meaning: "Ora se la paura è lo stato dell'animo privo della prudenza, e perciò delle altre tre virtù, è naturale che cessi al finir della notte, s'ella era connessa a quella notte."

Pascoli's criticism was vitiated by his failure to realize that values and directions are reversed in *Inferno* I, 1–61. G. Ragonese declared fear in the prologue to be "quasi esclusivamente fisiologica, istintiva," but he allowed also that it had a modicum of theological value, too, "una sua carica morale-religiosa, una sua risonanza spirituale, metafisica" ("fiera": "le tre fiere," *ED,* vol. 2 [1970], pp. 857–861).

G. Getto (1960; rprt. *Aspetti* [1966], p. 3) has, perhaps, seen the problem of fear in *Inferno* I most clearly: "'Tant'è amara che poco è più morte' (v. 7), acquista un significato diverso e sembra affermare qualcosa di meno incontrollato rispetto alla paura, trasferendosi dall'ordine dell'emozionale su di un piano di precisa responsabilità razionale e morale. Non si tratta più di un tremore della carne, ma di una esperienza angosciosa e disperata di peccato, dove la paura semmai è paura della morte seconda, della morte dell'anima." See F. Salsano, "paura," *ED,* vol. 4 (1973), pp. 350–351.

36. St. Augustine, *In Epistolam Joannis Evangelium,* XLVI; *PL* 35, col. 1732.

37. Since I first noted the positive value of fear in an article entitled "Fear, Pride and Conversion" (1976), the proposition has been researched anew and defended by R. Spraycar (1978).

On Dante's "lago del cor" (v. 20), see Spraycar's article for a definitive gloss and bibliography.

38. Ecclesiasticus [Sirach] 1 : 11–28, esp. 25.

39. St. Augustine, *In Epistolam Joannis ad Parthos* IX, 5; *PL* 35, col. 2049; cf. also IX, 2, 3, and 4.

40. *Moralia* XXII, 48; *Morals,* vol. II, p. 588.

41. *ST* II–II, qu. 21, art. 1.

42. *Moralia* II, 77; *Morals,* vol. I, p. 119. Cf. St. Thomas, *ST* II–II, qu. 162, art. 3.

43. Cf. St. Thomas, *ST* II–II, qu. 21, art. 3: "Presumption, then, is obviously in opposition to fear, especially servile fear and the preoccupation with punishment coming from God's justice; it is confident this will be withheld. Still on the basis of specious resemblance, it is more against hope, being a sort of unwarranted hope in God." See also *ST* II–II, qu. 22, art. 1.

St. Augustine had used the same formula in his *Confessions* X, 36, "Compressasti a timore tuo superbiam meam," and his *Enarratio in Ps.* CXIX, cap. 2 (*PL* 37, col. 1599). St. Bernard, *Sermo* XXIII, 13–14. *In Cantica Canticorum, Opera* I, pp. 147–148; *Sermo* XXXVII, 4–6, pp. 11–12. St. Thomas cites St. Gregory (*Moralia* II, 49), where the latter opposes pride to the gift of fear (*ST* II–II, qu. 162, art. 3).

44. *Moralia* XXIV, 27; *Morals,* vol. III, p. 69.

45. C. S. Singleton, *Dante Studies 2,* pp. 31–34 and 43–54, for the significance of Virgil and his role as bearer of grace.

St. Thomas treats of fear both as a vice and as one of the *charismata,* or the Gifts of the Holy Spirit. Fear is a principal passion for St. Thomas; as a human vice, it is also termed timidity; it concerns worldly *bodily harm,* corporal death, or, for example, death in battle, and is opposed to the virtue of fortitude (*ST*

II–II, qu. 125, art. 2). Cf. C. S. Singleton (com 1970–1975, note to *Inferno* I, 6): "Fear, which always besets the sinful life and enslaves the sinner, proves to be the main impediment at the start of the journey." J. Freccero (1959, rprt. 1986), p. 43. Cf. St. Thomas, *ST* I–II, qu. 44, art. 1–4: "De effectibus timoris."

Beneficial fear is a gift of the Holy Spirit (*ST* II–II, 19, 1–12: "De dono timoris"). Beginning as a "servile fear" (the fear of punishment, particularly of damnation), it may grow into "filial fear" (fear of blame or guilt; the fear a son owes to a father; the fear of Christ on the cross) that is always part of charity and faith. St. Thomas puts both values of fear into focus in *ST* II–II, qu. 19, art 2: "We are speaking of fear now, in so far as it makes us turn, so to speak, to God or away from Him. For, since the object of fear is an evil, sometimes, on account of the evils he fears, man withdraws from God, and this is called human or worldly fear [dicitur timor humanus vel mundanus]; while sometimes, on account of the evils he fears, he turns to God and adheres to Him. . . . Accordingly if a man turn to God and adhere to Him, through fear of punishment, it will be servile fear; but if on account of committing a fault, it will be filial fear."

In *DCD* XIV, vii, St. Augustine speaks of the positive sense of fear: "The term for fear, 'timor,' is used in a good sense in the passage where the Apostle says: 'With fear and trembling work out your salvation.'" The concepts of fear as human vice and servile fear as a preparation for the divine gift of filial fear form a tension in Dante's narrative.

46. St. Bernard, *De diligendo Deo* XIV, 38, ed. Leclerq, *Opera*, 3, p. 152; *Works of St. Bernard*, vol. 5, *Treatises* II, *CFS* 13, p. 130.

F. Villani (com ca. 1400, p. 117), in an interesting variation, identified the "piè fermo" with the affections and the "fear of the Lord" that kept man from sin.

47. Fear, piety, and compunction ("il cor compunto") are linked in theology as they are in Dante's lines. Piety forces the convert to "lament his own situation. For the knowledge of a good hope thrusts a man not into boasting but into lamentation." *De doctrina christiana* II, 7, 9–11; *On Christian Doctrine*, p. 39. On this and the Seven Gifts, see E. Gilson (1960), pp. 124, 305, n. 24. See R. Spraycar (1978), p. 7, for fear as prerequisite for purgation.

See also the interesting examination of "pietas," though from a totally different approach from mine, by R. Ball (1981), pp. 59–79. Cf. E. Glässer (1943); H. D. Goldstein (1965), pp. 316–327. J.-P. Callu (1978), pp. 161–174.

48. On compunction's mental effects, see St. Gregory, *Moralia* XXIII, 40–43; *Morals*, vol. III, pp. 34–38.

49. On Virgil's fallibility, the idea of "pietas" in the *Aeneid*, and the attitude of the early church fathers, see Chapter 4, p. 79.

50. Virgil's recognition of Beatrice is treated by C. S. Singleton (1956), pp. 29–38. J. T. Chiampi notes that Beatrice's lesson is recalled in *Purgatorio* XXX, 50–57.

My colleagues, William Stephany and Rachell Jacoff, who have collaborated on the excellent second volume of this series, have also interpreted Virgil's impatience here as an encouragement to fortitude in the face of the dangers of the journey. Since fortitude is also one of the political, pagan virtues, I believe them to be correct.

We might recall that the Sibyl encourages Aeneas as he enters Avernus (*Aeneid* VI, 257), but the hero does not require such urging since he enters with fearless steps: "ille ducem haud timidus vadentem passibus aequat." St. Thomas, *ST* II–II, qu. 125, art. 2. St. Thomas deals with the martial quality of fortitude in *ST* II–II, qu. 123, art. 5.

51. D'Ovidio gave a brief synopsis of views in his essay "Il piè fermo" in *Nuovi studii* ([vol. 2], 1907, pp. 447–469). A. Masseron (1922, pp. 124–128) examined early twentieth-century theories somewhat lightheartedly, if not dismissively. F. Mazzoni (com 1967, pp. 91–99) gives a thorough discussion of the important bibliography to about 1965. As Mazzoni observes, among the earliest commentators, only Boccaccio interprets the verse in an entirely literal manner, seeing it merely as a description of a climb, but he was followed by Gelli, Daniello, and more recently by Scartazzini (in his *Enciclopedia Dantesca* 1, p. 772), and, in their commentaries by Tommaseo (see also his *Nuovi Studi* [1865], pp. 291–315, 317–318), Casini-Barbi, Del Lungo, Scarano, Rossi [Rossi/Frascino], Vandelli, D. Guerri (1905, pp. 177–189), Momigliano, Sapegno, Mattalia, and Chimenz. Others, however, have even seen in Dante's lines the description of a man walking on the flat (Magalotti [com], F. Scolari, Andreoli [com], E. Bittanta [1952], pp. 732–735). Biagioli believes that the wayfarer is mounting in a spiral motion, as does A. Buscaino Campo (1877, pp. 19–88; 1894, pp. 7–39). Some commentators believe that Dante is describing a climb to the right, or that his "firm foot" designates not the left but the right foot: A. Buscaino Campo (1877, p. 47; 1894, p. 37), Casella, Filomusi-Guelfi (1911, pp. 30–31), R. Montano, *Storia* (1962, vol. 1, p. 327); while still others have interpreted the verse as describing a running, or slow, gait.

See also P. Caligaris (1950), pp. 241–243. A. Niccoli, "piede," *ED,* vol. 4 (1973), pp. 482–485. G. Mazzoni, *Lect. rom.* (1914; 1918).

52. *Enarratio in Psalmum* IX, 15–16 (*PL* 36, col. 124); *On the Psalms,* trans. Hebgin-Corrigan, *ACW,* vol. 1, p. 123.

53. Richard of St. Victor, *De statu interioris hominis* II, p. 65.

54. *De statu interioris hominis* V, p. 68.

55. Richard's Latin in *De statu interioris hominis* V, p. 68, reads: "Sed, sicut nichil utilius prudenti consilio, sic nichil inferius, nichil infirmius carnali desiderio eo quod, juxta pedis similitudinem, infimum locum teneat et per delectationem carnis terrenis inhereat. Quid, queso, infirmius, quid abjectius quod nec illis quidem plene resistimus in quibus erubescimus? Quanta, queso, vilitas, quanta ve infirmitas mente quidem consentire legi Dei quia bona est, cotidie tamen *videre aliam legem in membris meis, repugnantem legi mentis mee et captivantem in lege peccati*? Vides ex his adhuc quam recte intelligatur per caput liberum arbitrium, per cor consilium, per pedem carnale desiderium."

56. *Commentarium,* pp. 37–38: "Et sic procedendo dicit, quod 'pes firmus in-

fimior erat.' Hic est figura; nam sicut corpus humanum habet duos pedes, per quos vadit ad bonum vel malum, ita anima habet duos pedes, per quos bene vel male incedit, idest duos affectus. Nam dicit Augustinus: 'pes animae amor est, qui directus est, dicitur caritas; si curvus, dicitur cupiditas.' Et psalmista: 'pes enim meus stetit in directo.' Ubi glosa dicit: 'in directo,' idest, 'affectio mea, quae facile labi solet, non recessit a rectitudine, sed firma stetit et processit.' Et alibi: 'qui perfecit pedes meos tamquam cervorum, et super excelsa statuit me.' Igitur ad propositum, pes auctoris, id est affectio, in quo magis adhuc fir-mabatur, erat infimior, quod adhuc ad infima terrana relicta aliquantulum magis inclinabatur, quamquam superior pes ad superiora ascenderet, et sicut claudus ibat." Pietro is probably referring to St. Augustine's *Enarratio in Psalmum* IX, 15 (*PL* 36, col. 124); *On the Psalms*, pp. 123–124.

J. Freccero (1959; rprt. 1986), pp. 38–39, 282.

Francesco da Buti (com 1385–1395, p. 31) identified the two feet of man as "due effetti che erano in lui"; the rest of his gloss at this point garbles Dante's text. For F. Villani (com ca. 1400, pp. 116–117), the "firm foot" signified fear: "talis pes ponitur pro timore, qui fermat hominem, ut non peccat . . . et pri-mum est timor Domini, qui homo removet a peccato." Cf. B. Basile (1971), pp. 219–220. For D'Ovidio (1907, vol. 2, pp. 447–469), Fraticelli, Porena, and Sapegno the "firm foot" represented fear and/or a slow gate. Torraca (com 1905), however, believed that the wayfarer was running: "Accenna all'andar frettoloso."

57. *Enarratio in Psalmum* XXXV (*PL* 36, col. 353–354); *On the Psalms*, trans. Hebgin-Corrigan, *ACW*, vol. 2, p. 245–247 (my italics).

In his *De spiritu et littera* 19, Augustine ties the metaphor of the foot of pride to the "foot of the hill of pride" and to the darkness of the proud soul: "Emp-tiness is the peculiar disease of men who deceive themselves in the belief that they are something, when they are nothing. They enter into the shadow of that swelling hill of pride, of whose foot the holy singer prays that it not come against him, saying, 'In thy light we shall see the light.' Thus they have turned away from the very light of changeless truth and their foolish heart is dark-ened" (*The Spirit and the Letter*, trans. Burnaby, *Augustine: Later Works, LCC*, vol. 8, p. 209).

58. *De gradibus superbiae tractatus* IX, 24 (*PL* 182, col. 955). See also *The Steps of Humility*, Latin text and trans. G. B. Burch (1940; 1963), pp. 172–173. A. Bozzoli (1967), pp. 518–529, esp. 527. In "Les douze degrés de l'orgueil," in *Dante et St Bernard* (1953), pp. 197–222, A. Masseron dealt only with the purgatorial circle of pride and denied that Dante was following St. Bernard there, arguing with-out evidence that the poet would have been, at most, only indirectly influenced by him. I believe, on the contrary, that the large numbers of parallels between Bernard's works and the poem, and the choice of Bernard as the ultimate guide in the journey, indicate that Dante most probably knew and used the *De gradibus*.

59. *De gradibus superbiae tractatus* IX, 26 in *Opera* (1963), vol. 3, p. 36; also *PL*

182, col. 956. *The Steps*, Latin text and trans. G. B. Burch, pp. 174–177.

60. *Sermo LXXXV Super Cantica Canticorum*, 5; ed. Leclerq, *Opera* (1958), vol. 2, pp. 310–311; *Sermons on the Song of Songs*, pp. 519–520.

61. Elsewhere, St. Bernard, in a letter to a recipient identified only as "N" (*Epistola* CDLXXXVIII; *Works* III, pp. 236–237), lists twenty-four precepts for separating oneself from the desire of worldly things to attain true blessedness; he makes concrete his precepts by contrasting the delusion of worldly "hills" with the "hills" of eternity: the passage may help put into theological perspective the wayfarer's choice of the *colle* in Dante's prologue scene and the contrast between that "hill" and the goal of the Mount of Purgatory: "Let *a desire for the everlasting hills* be perfected in us. These virtues, then, are many in number, and form, as it were, a ladder of salvation, by which those who are influenced by earnest faith, and sacred modesty, in all their words and actions, are able, without doubt, to reach the summit . . . *when thou shalt have begun to use thy feet*, as it were, *upon the path of the new man, upon the footpath which is fixed between fear and the love of humility*, you may be able to obtain greater heights (of virtue), and to move freely upon loftier eminences." St. Bernard's images in this passage provide a further example of the traditional matrix within which we may understand the meaning of the *piè fermo* in *Inferno* I: the beneficial effects of fear, the images of feet, the path, humility, and righteous ascent combine with positive and negative "hill" metaphors.

62. As other critics have seen for similar reasons, the unsuccessful ascent of the first canto, like Ulysses' last voyage, is an allegory of philosophical pride; through it the wayfarer was led to a sinful sense of self-sufficiency and had departed from Christ's charity as embodied in his love for Beatrice. B. Nardi (1949), esp. pp. 161–162. D. Thompson (1967; rprt. 1974), p. 72. J. Freccero (1973; rprt. 1986), pp. 180–194.

63. Using different examples, C. S. Singleton outlines the retrospective ways of the poem in his "Vistas in Retrospect" (1965b; 1966, pp. 55–80).

64. C. S. Singleton, *Dante Studies 2* (1958), pp. 254–287.

65. The "loco spatioso" omitted is the opposite of the "basso loco" of *Inferno* I.

On the question of the inappropriateness of the rest of the psalm, see J. Freccero, "Adam's Stand" (1961b), pp. 115–118, and R. Hollander (1973; 1980), pp. 107–113.

66. *Enarratio II in Psalmum* XXX (*PL* 36, col. 238–239); *On The Psalms*, trans. Hebgin-Corrigan, *ACW*, vol. 2, p. 27.

The *Allegoriae in Universam Sacram Scripturam* once attributed to Rabanus Maurus but now considered to be by Garnier de Rochefort glosses the word "pedes": "Per pedes, illi sancti, qui in patria coelesti sunt, ut in Psalmis: 'Statuisti in loco spatioso pedes meos' quod in latitudine gratiae sunt qui hinc exeuntes in coelesti patria consistunt" (*PL* 112, col. 1025). The exegetical definition points to the conventionality with which the term "feet" could evoke analogical ideas of justice.

67. *Enarratio II in Psalmum* XXX (*PL* 36, col. 230); *On the Psalms*, trans. Hebgin-Corrigan, *ACW*, vol. 2, p. 10.

68. See G. Alessio and C. Villa (1984), pp. 1–21.

69. That this is no lapsus but a skillful maneuvering of the reader is, of course, made explicit in the following canto, where Dante-wayfarer, by denying that he is Aeneas, makes a rather strong case that he actually could be.

70. "Superbo Ilión" echoes Virgil's usage in the *Aeneid* III, 2–3. Dante will use "Troia" or "Ilión" as the major example of pride brought low in *Inferno* XXX, 13–14, and in *Purgatorio* XII, 25–63: in the first case he will use the term "altezza" to signify pride, and, in the second, he will place the city significantly in the lines directly following the anaphorical acrostic "VOM" (= "UOM," "man") symbolizing the sinful pride of man and its consequences.

71. *Epistola* CCCXCIII ad W. Patriarcham Jerosolymorum (*PL* 182, col. 602). *Letters*, trans. S. J. Eales in *Life and Works of St. Bernard*, vol. 3, pp. 84–85. J. Freccero (1966a; rprt. 1986), p. 10. R. Spraycar (1978), p. 8.

72. *Epistola* CCCXCIII ad W. Patriarcham Jerosolymorum (*PL* 182, col. 602). Trans. *Life and Works of St. Bernard*, vol. 3, p. 85.

CHAPTER 3: Three Beasts

1. On the agreement of ancient commentators, see F. Flamini (1904), p. 117; (1916), p. 33. A. Masseron (1922), pp. 136–137. R. Giglio (1973), p. 140. G. Bonfante discusses various identifications (1946), pp. 69–72.

2. F. D'Ovidio notes (1901), pp. 302–303, that "vanagloria" was used in three ways, first, as a subspecies of pride, secondly, as a capital sin (one of the seven mortal sins taking pride's place among the seven, while *superbia* stood outside the seven as cause of them all), and thirdly, as a venial form of pride. In *Purgatorio* XI, 91, Dante uses the term as an alternate for pride.

3. Cf. F. Flamini (1904), p. 117: "Chi sappia la loro usanza di copiarsi l'un l'altro, non darà gran peso a questo consenso." A. Masseron (1922), pp. 136–137, gave a positive assessment and saw some justice in the consistency of early commentators' views. It must be admitted that the tendency to transmit opinions unquestioned is still a major feature of modern Dante scholarship—as it is, regrettably, of many exegetical traditions.

4. On these political identifications, see also D'Ovidio, *Studii* (1901), p. 304; I. Del Lungo (1921), pp. 18–19. J. S. Carroll (1903) held to the political interpretation of Florence = *lonza*, House of France = *leone*, and Papal Curia = *lupa*, but also saw a moral meaning with "the panther" as sensuality, the lion as pride or ambition, and the wolf as avarice (p. 17). Cf. G. Ragonese, "fiera": "le tre fiere," *ED*, vol. 2 (1970), pp. 857–861, esp. p. 859. Recently, O. Filipponi (1983), echoing F. Villani, has attempted to create a variation on the political explanation by seeing in it a reference to the beasts of the Apocalypse (Revelation 13: 1–18): the lion is political power, the *lonza*, ecclesiastical power (p. 23), and the wolf the "antico serpente, Satana, il diavolo" (p. 24).

5. In his *lectura* of *Inferno* I, "Il Preludio" (1963), B. Nardi did not make his

position on the *lonza* clear, i.e., that he considered the beast a combined figure of lust and fraud. In his polemical essay against Pasquazi, "Il 'getto della corda' e Gerione" (in *Saggi e Note*, 1966), pp. 332–354; however, he did elucidate his view, seeing a parallel in the girded lustful and deceitful Venus, "la dolosa ciprigna," the "wily Cyprian."

Since lust is a specific mode of sin, and fraudulence a *degree* to which any sin can be amplified or aggravated, my position has no basic disagreement with Nardi's solution. I believe, however, that the beasts represent earthly and infernal temptations, and that, therefore, they have more than a mere social or political meaning for, and effect on, the wayfarer. See also M. Colacci (1947), pp. 7–100.

6. A. Scrocca (1908), pp. 13, 28, saw the beasts as primarily political; he denied that they represented the vices of Dante himself, yet he admitted that Dante was guilty of pride and lust, though not of avarice. Cf. G. Busnelli, 1909, p. 52. F. D'Ovidio (1901), p. 310: "Le fiere che gl'impediscono di salire a una vita onesta e pacifica . . . devono simboleggiare tre vizii comuni nel mondo e nella sua città, che frastornino l'uomo volto al ravvedimento e desideroso del bene. Non è poi necessario che quelli siano in tutto o in parte i vizii suoi individuali, quadra anzi meglio che siano i vizii dell'ambiente." Compare I. Sanesi (1902), p. 70: "Queste benedette fiere non possono già raffigurare, come par che comunemente ed erroneamente si creda, tre vizi già posseduti da Dante, ma bensì tre vizi diffusi fra gli altri uomini e nei quali egli pare avrebbe facilmente potuto incorrere."

F. Figurelli (1977, p. 22) also took an extreme position: "Le colpe simboleggiate nelle tre fiere non sono nel personaggio assalto, ma a lui esterne, e a lui al proposito di bene operare irriducibilmente avverse." Figurelli's extreme Pelagian views, however, ultimately vitiate his understanding of the canto. We shall note that the beasts, insofar as they represent external temptations and not internal, committed sins, actually can be interpreted as a lesson bringing the wayfarer back to the road of righteousness. A. Pézard ("Les loups," 1957, p. 9) traces the wolf's corruption of the Roman Curia, its corruption of the Florentine Black Party, of the the Capetians and of all the enemies of the empire and of the peace of God.

Compare, however, P. Nicosia (1969), p. 27: "Che Dante volesse rappresentare con essi delle potenze politiche (comuni, casa di Francia, curia papale) . . . non lo si pensa, credo, più."

A. C. Mastrobuono identified the leopard and lion with original sin and the she-wolf as death (1979, p. 56).

7. Chalcidius, *Timaeus a Calcidio translatus commentarioque instructus*, ed. J. H. Waszink, with P. J. Jensen, in *Plato Latinus*.

8. St. Thomas, *In decem libros Ethicorum* V, Lectio xvii, n. 1106; ed. Spiazzi, p. 302; trans. Litzinger, p. 476.

9. Philo, *De opificio mundi* 28; *On the Creation* 28, *LCL*, ed. and trans. Colson and Whitaker, pp. 66–67. St. Ambrose's *Hexaemeron* VI, ch. 9, 55 (*PL* 14, col.

265); *Hexameron*, trans. J. J. Savage, *FC* 42, p. 268; St. Augustine, *Expositio quarundum propositionum ex epistola ad Romanos* 53 (*PL* 35, cols. 2074–2076); and *De diversis quaestionibus* 83, qu. 67 (*PL* 40, col. 66); St. Gregory the Great's *Homiliarium in Evangelia libri duo*, hom. 29, n. 2 (*PL* 76, col. 1214). J. Pépin (1961), p. 222.

10. Bernardus Silvestris, *De mundi universitate libri duo, sive Megacosmus et Microcosmus*, ed. C. S. Barach and J. Wrobel (1876; rprt. 1964). See also P. Delhaye (1951).

11. Richard de Saint-Victor, *De statu interioris hominis*, ed. J. Ribaillier, "Etude littéraire," pp. 14–31, esp. 15. I follow Ribaillier's lucid essay closely here. See also P. Delhaye (1949), pp. 155–160; and (1951), p. 77.

12. J. Ribaillier, ed., *De statu interioris hominis*, p. 16.

13. G. Casella's views are found in his *Opere* (1884), vol. 2, p. 384.

14. F. D'Ovidio (1901, p. 324) substitutes *invidia* for *lussuria* in regard to the *lonza*; both he and I. Sanesi (1902, pp. 37–90) reject Pietrobono's inverting the interpretation of *lonza* with that of the *lupa*.

15. See G. Ragonese, "fiera": "le tre fiere," *ED*, vol. 2 (1970), pp. 857–886.

16. It will suffice to cite Grandgent (com 1909–1913; rprt. 1933) "Inasmuch as the sins of Hell fall under the three heads, Incontinence, Violence and Fraud, it is natural that the ravening beasts should stand for corresponding practices: the ravening wolf is Incontinence of any kind, the raging lion is Violence, the swift and stealthy leopard is Fraud" (p. 11).

17. St. Thomas defines the two parts of sin, *culpa* and *poena*: the latter is not itself an evil since it is administered by God; the guilt or fault of man, however, is: Thomas cites the pseudo-Dionysius, "Punishment is not an evil, but to *deserve* punishment is" (*ST* I–II, qu. 87, art. 1 reply obj. 2).

18. The heresiarchs are omitted in the penal system of hell outlined by Virgil in *Inferno* XI. I. Sanesi (1902, pp. 55–57), however, believed that the heretics were those guilty of "bestialità," which he interprets as "stupidity" according to Dante's censure of unbelief in the afterlife in *Convivio* II, viii, 7: "Dico che intra tutte le bestialitadi quella è stoltissima, vilissima e dannosissima, chi crede dopo questa vita non essere altra vita." Sanesi's opinion gained little following and most commentators continue to equate "matta bestialitade" (*Inferno* XI, 82–83) with force or violence; see, however, A. Triolo (1968), pp. 247–292.

19. *ST* II–II, 116, art. 2, reply obj. 1: "Now, other things being equal, it is more grievous to harm a person openly, by violence as it were, than secretly. Wherefore robbery is a more grievous sin than theft." Cf. *ST* II–II, qu. 66, art. 9.

20. Cf. W. H. V. Reade (1909), pp. 348–350. Reade does not note St. Thomas's inconsistency regarding the relative seriousness of force and fraud.

21. Compare Richard of St. Victor, *De statu interioris hominis post lapsum* XL, p. 111. Busnelli (1909) deals with the *impedimenta*, p. 31. J. Freccero (1959; rprt. 1986), pp. 38–52.

22. Casella (1884), vol. 2, p. 384. F. Flamini (1904), p. 144. J. Freccero (1959;

rprt. 1986), pp. 29–54, for the beasts, the "vulneratio naturae," and the firm foot. On the beasts as *impedimenta*, see G. Busnelli (1909), p. 31. F. Mazzoni (com 1967), p. 101, cites several patristic texts. C. S. Singleton preferred to see the beasts as reflecting the Exodus pattern of temptations, impediments, and backslidings that had plagued the Isrealites after they had crossed the Red Sea and entered upon the way of the desert (1960), 1–24, esp. p. 3. See also A. S. Bernardo (1963), p. 15.

23. G. Lajolo (1906, p. 45) and G. Busnelli (1909, p. 57) do deal with the inter-relation of sins. Cf. A. Triolo (1968), esp. pp. 279–289. R. Manselli (1970, pp. 307–325) traces the theme of avarice leading to betrayal, with the expansion of *cupiditas* and the destruction it causes. G. Lajolo (1906) puts the case clearly: "La distribuzione delle pene non è fatta secondo i principii del peccato, ma secondo il vario grado di colpevolezza; e tale distinzione è di capitale impor-tanza" (p. 45).

24. With Frate Alberigo and Branca Doria in *Inferno* XXXIII, we have the examples of souls already in hell before death; demons possess their bodies for the remainder of their earthly term. The paradigm of sin can be exhausted and exceeded on earth in Dante's view.

25. See the illustrations of the trees of virtues and vices in A. Katzenellen-bogen (1939; rprt. 1964), esp. pp. 63–74, plates 64–67.

26. Dante's depiction of Pier della Vigna (*Inferno* XIII), for example, closely follows St. Thomas's doctrine: by placing Piero among the lesser sins of vio-lence, Dante, of course, schematically exonerates Piero of treachery or betrayal; yet, he nonetheless has Piero's guilt reflect St. Thomas's view of Judas's para-digmatic descent into culpability: Piero's covetousness, his historically attested merciless tyranny against others, and his ambiguous vigilance in Frederick's ser-vice, identical in history to his restlessness in obtaining greater riches, were all eventually to drive the Grand Seneschal to a final, violent self-destruction, pre-cisely in the manner of Judas's suicide, as Dante's son, Pietro, recognized in his commentary on *Inferno* XIII (p. 231). Similarly, we see deeper in *Inferno*, among the fraudulent of Canto XXVI, that Ulysses' culpability accretes by his pitiless insensibility to family, friends, and allies, by the theft of the Palladium, by a restless burning for worldly experience, by the fraud and falsehood of the Trojan Horse, the perjury to Deidamia, and by the fraudulence of his *piccola orazione* urging the last voyage upon his men. Cf. A. Cassell (1984), pp. 48, 86, 171.

27. Ciacco damns himself by inveterate (habitual) gluttony; Francesca is con-demned not by one simple act of lust, as she claims, but by her enduring unre-pentance; both she and Ciacco renew their obduracy in their interviews with the wayfarer.

Among the violent, for example, Brunetto falls not only through pride of life and lust of the flesh, but through his submission to the "progeny" of those sins: vainglory (in respect to his writings) and, as we know from his position in hell, homosexual violence. As we noted in n. 26 above, Pier della Vigna's historical career and Ulysses' crimes, for example, go through the Thomistic paradigm of the "daughters of avarice."

28. This is a commonplace of criticism; two representatives will suffice: C. S. Singleton (com 1970–1975), re. vv. 31–60, and F. Mazzoni (com 1967), p. 103.

29. C. Hardie (1964), p. 166. A. S. Bernardo (1963), pp. 15–24. While I am concerned here mainly with the spiritual significances of Dante's verses, J. Demaray's studies (1974) of the historical sources of the events of the pilgrimage in the *Commedia* should be noted here. Contemporary accounts of the Great Circle route to Sinai and Jerusalem tell of lions blocking the path of travelers, of leopards attacking even knights, and of wolves infesting the deserts and mountains (pp. 138–143). Conditions had not changed since biblical times.

30. The major exception to this is G. Busnelli (1909), who carefully traced the exegetical tradition of the text, pp. 32–52.

31. Hugh of St. Cher, in his commentary on Jeremiah 5:6 (1732 ed., tom. IV, f. 190ᵛ), identifies the trio with the tyrant idolater Nebuchadnezzar for three reasons: "scilicet, per Leonem propter ejus superbiam, et fortitudinem; per Lupum propter ejus fraudulentiam; per Pardum propter ejus malitiosam sollicitudinem" [to wit, with the Lion on account of his pride and boldness; with the Wolf on account of his fraud; with the Pard on account of his vigilant malice]. He also identifies all three beasts as the devil: "Mystice leo est diabolus inquantum est superbus et inquantum de superbia tentat, lupus ipse idem, inquantum de luxuria, quia lupus gaudet de effusione sanguinis; pardus inquantum de avaritia, quia variat, et turbat cor et inquantum de dolositate et fallacia" [Mystically the lion is the devil insofar as he is proud and insofar as he tempts with pride; he is also the wolf insofar as he tempts with lust, for the wolf gloats over the spilling of blood; he is the pard in so far as he tempts with avarice, for he is particolored (is fickle) and troubles the heart, and insofar as he tempts with wiles and falsity]. Hugh's text is useful for an idea of the beasts' chthonic-satanic origins, but his assignment of symbolic meanings to the beasts does not square directly with Dante's. See G. Busnelli (1909), p. 35.

32. *Moralia* XX, 66; *Morals*, vol. II, p. 501; see also *Moralia* XXIII, 51; *Morals*, vol. III, i, p. 45 ("We learn by our sins which tempt us, what we are of ourselves"); *Moralia* XXXIII, 25; *Morals*, vol. III, ii, p. 580.

33. On the three temptations of Christ as repeating and curing the Fall, see D. Howard (1966), pp. 43–75. B. O. Murdoch (1974); both these critics deal brilliantly with the temptation of Christ as a fundamental, informing pattern in medieval literature. On the temptation in patristics, see K. P. Köppen (1961).

34. On the theme of Christ's temptation and its mystic sense in a Christian exodus from sin, see J. Daniélou (1950; trans. 1960), pp. 153–174, esp. 158–159. Notable is C. Ballerini's (1953, p. 35) impression of the wayfarer's plight as reflecting Christ's agony in the Garden: "Il primo canto comincia dallo stesso stato d'animo che Nostro Signore provò nell'Orto del Getsemani: 'Tristis est anima mea usque ad mortem.' Nel Vangelo la passione di Cristo, di Dio: nella *Divina Commedia* la passione dell'uomo."

35. As F. Mazzoni notes (com 1967, p. 104), it may also echo Isidore, *Etymologiae* XII, ii, 20: "bestia maculis distincta ut pardus sed similis lupo." Pietro di Dante, p. 39; Benvenuto, (com 1373–1380), vol. 1, p. 34; F. D'Ovidio (1901), p. 321; E. Moore, *Scripture and Classical Authors in Dante* (1896), pp. 180–181. J. Camus (1909), pp. 1–40.

36. Benvenuto (vol. I, p. 34) conflates the leopard with the hunting leopard (i.e., with the cheetah or *ghepardo*): "Pardus, quamvis familiariter domesticetur, saepe fallit et prodit, imo saepe vincit leonem fraude." Similarly, Buti's "lepre" may be a copyist's error for "leporarius," "levereri," meaning the cheetah; the word may be derived from "leopardus" and conflated with the "levrier" or hunting dog of Europe. J. Camus (1909), pp. 1–40, remarks on the confusion between "leporarius" and "leopardus" and "pardus" (signifying the cheetah, "ghepardo," "guépard") in translating documents concerning hunting in the medieval Middle East (esp. p. 31). See also P. Renucci (1937).

37. E. Proto (1907), p. 3. K. McKenzie (1901), pp. 18–30, cites E. G. Parodi (1895, pp. 24–25), that, apart from the linguistic derivation of the "lonza" from the word lynx, the lynx has absolutely nothing to do with Dante's *lonza*.

38. E. Proto (1907); J. Camus (1909). G. Busnelli (1909), pp. 37–45. Such considerations must rule out, further, the allegorical arguments resulting from this identification of the *lonza* with the lynx: that the beast represents envy is without basis; the bestiary legend that the lynx's urine forms a precious gem called "lyncurium" and that it enviously guards this stone from man has no connection with Dante's prologue.

Again here, J. Demaray's demonstration (1974, esp. pp. 139–141) that the wayfarer's experiences in the *Commedia* parallel those of contemporary pilgrims in the Holy Land can help our identification: medieval accounts attest to the fact that leopards actually roamed the desert along the whole of the Exodus route and posed a mortal danger.

39. *Consulte*, ed. A. Gherardi (1896–1898), I, p. 257. F. Cipolla (1895), pp. 103–114. F. D'Ovidio (1901), p. 323; (1894–1895), p. 117. T. Casini (1895), 116–120. F. Torraca (1899), pp. 6–8. The keeping of mascots by Italian communes and princedoms was common; in the previous century Frederick II had kept a large private zoo at Lucera dei Pagani that included not only raptors but other species such as lions, leopards, dromedaries, giraffes, and elephants. On Frederick's procuring an elephant from "Prester John of India," see *Trésors*, I, 187: "Des olifans"; Carmody, ed., pp. 164–165.

40. I. Del Lungo (1901), p. 15. F. D'Ovidio (1901), p. 323.

41. R. Davidsohn, *Storia* (1956–1968), vol. 7, p. 513; G. Villani, *Cronica* Lib. 6, cap. 69; Lib. 8, cap. 62 (1823; rprt. 1980, vol. 2, p. 95; vol. 3, pp. 106–107). J. Ferrante (1984), p. 66.

42. P. Chistoni (1903), pp. 817–848. E. Proto (1907), p. 5, and F. D'Ovidio (1901), p. 323, list many occurrences of the word "lonza" in contemporary medieval literature. In *Il detto del gatto lupesco*, first published by T. Casini ("Rime inedite dei secoli XIII e XIV," in *Il Propugnatore* [1882], p. 339; now in *Poeti del Duecento*, vol. 2, a cura di Gianfranco Contini [Milano-Napoli: Ricciardi, 1960],

p. 292), the leopard is mentioned along with the *lonza*: "e vidivi quattro leopardi / . . . una lonça e un tinasso. . . ."

G. Casella (1865; 1884), II, p. 387, sees the "leggerezza" and "prestezza" of the *lonza* as a reproof of Florence: the circles of fraud are filled with Florentine hypocrites, yet no Tuscan is found in the area of lust. The "pelle dipinta," as Casella observes, is echoed in the circle of the hypocrites, "una gente dipinta." See D'Ovidio's reservations (1901), p. 306. We might also remark that the allegorical proclivities of the *lonza*, lust and ferocity (not attributes that the *Commedia* specifically gives the beast), in Thomas of Cantimpré's *Liber de natura rerum* IV, 86–87 (ed. Boese, p. 159), are united as cause and effect.

43. However, as E. Proto (1907), p. 2, P. Chistoni (1903), pp. 819–820, and F. Flamini (1916a, pp. 94–103; 1916b, vol. 2, pp. 74–77) have noted, in the *Historia orientale* of Jacques de Vitry and other medieval bestiaries we do meet with the term "lonzanus" in a context that differentiates it from "pardus": "Sunt ibi leones, pardi, ursi, dami, capri silvestris, et aliud quoddam saevissimum quod appellatur *lonzani*, a cuius saevitia nullum animal potest esse tutum: et ut dicunt, terret leonem." Cf. Albert the Great on "lauzany" in *De animalibus* 22 : 113 (trans. Scanlan, pp. 155–156), and the entry "lanzani" in *De natura rerum*, where Thomas of Cantimpré cites Solinus and Jacques de Vitry: "Lanzani est animal, ut Solinus et Jacobus dicunt, sevissimum, a cuius crudelitate nulla bestia potest esse tuta. Nam, ut dicunt, ipsum leonem deterret, qui tamen omnibus formidabilis perhibetur. Grassatur in bestias non sui generis; suo autem generi parcit. Illa animalia insectatur implacabili odio, que reliquas bestias depredantur. Et cum hoc scelus in aliis persequatur, proprie tamen iniquitatis non meminit. Hominem miro modo persequitur, et hoc forte divino iudicio, ut qui deberet esse omnium animalium placidissimus in natura, omnium est sevissimus vitiose iniquitatis malitia" (IV, 570; p. 142). While the "lanzani" may have given added notions about the savagery of the "lonza," and most especially about its allegorical associations with "malitia," the bestiary entry is generic enough to be applied to almost any predatory beast whatsoever: we are not told of its speed or alertness nor that it had a dappled hide. There is no evidence that Dante actually believed that the "lanzanus" was the "lonza" so familiar to him.

The best synopsis of Dante's use of medieval bestiaries is given by A. Scolari (1982), pp. 1–14.

44. On the "panthera" in bestiaries, see F. McCulloch (1960), pp. 148–150. Unlike the pard or leopard, however, that are not found in many versions of the *Physiologus* fables, the "panthera" figured in its earliest manuscripts of that work and remained as a mainstay down through the centuries. Indeed its allegorization was the longest in the collection: the "quiet and exceedingly mild" beast, after eating its fill, slept three days in a cave and then came forth to utter a great roar with a breath so sweet that it attracted all other beasts except the dragon, which fled in terror. By its varied colors the panther signified the attributes of the incarnate Christ who drew mankind to himself; the dragon was the devil; the three-day sleep in the cave represented Christ's death and man's redemption; the sweet odor of its breath was Christ's call to man after the Resurrec-

tion. Cf. Thomas of Cantimpré, *Liber de natura rerum* IV, 86–87, ed. Boese, p. 159. *Il Bestiario toscano*, pp. 42–43. *Il Libro delle nature degli animali*, ed. Segre (1959), p. 207. *Il Bestiario moralizzato*, pp. 768–769.

Amidst the shadowy reality of the poem's prologue, perhaps we cannot entirely exclude some distant resonance of the panther. However, the theme of the animal's attractiveness *in bono* in the *Physiologus*, makes, at best, for a tenuous comparison with the attraction of the *lonza, in malo*, in the *Commedia*: it is, after all, the beast's hide that is alluring in the poem, not its breath, and where the presence of Christ is discerned, it is not in the animal itself but in the paschal season and early-morning hour that bring the wayfarer cause for hope.

As we will note elsewhere, however, in the perspective of the "altro viaggio," the divinely ordained journey of the poem through hell, the beasts who make the wayfarer turn back are actually making him face in the ultimately correct direction: in this way, as temptations, they are sent for instruction to the backsliding wayfarer.

45. *De animalibus*, trans. Scanlan (1978), p. 156. Cf. E. Proto (1907), p. 9.

46. Cf. Theobaldi, *Physiologus*, ed. P. T. Eden (1972); trans. M. J. Curley (1979).

47. The pseudo-Hugh of St. Victor, *De Bestiis, PL* 177, col. 83; Albert the Great, *De animalibus* 22:131, 89; trans. Scanlan (1987), pp. 170–171.

48. Isidore cites Pliny: "Sicut et Plinius in *Naturali Historia* (8:42) dicit, leonem cum parda, aut pardum cum leaena concumbere et ex utroque coitu degeneres partus creari, ut malus et burdo" (*Etymologiae* XII, 2, 11).

Scholars have pointed out that "leo-pard" may itself have originated as a folk etymology, much as the forms "leofante" for "elephant" and "leocorno" for the "unicorn."

49. *Liber de natura rerum* IV, 55, pp. 141–142. Thomas of Cantimpré quotes the pseudo-Ambrose's equation of the "varietas" of the animal's hide with mutability of mind: "Hee bestie crudelissime sunt naturaliter; unde dicitur: 'Si mutare potest Ethiops pellem suam et pardus varietatem suam,' id est mutabilitatem animi"—an interesting observation for those critics who see a pun in Dante's description of his female beast ("leggiera molto") and associate it with lust, particularly with the lustful Francesca and Paolo swept along, light ("leggieri") on hell's winds symbolic of their own fickle ("leggieri") storms of passion (*Inferno* V, 75).

50. *Liber de natura rerum* IV, 86, p. 159. Thomas's entry is a conflation of Isidore's two entries, 10 and 11 on the pard and leopard in the *Etymologiae* XII, 2; in fact the "e pardi procreari dicuntur" appears to be a deformation of Pliny's "ex utroque coitu degeneres *partus* creari" (*NH* 8:42), cited by Isidore, *Etymologiae* XII, 2, 11.

51. *Il Bestiario toscano*, pp. 86, 97–98.

52. The cruelty and ferocity of the *lonza* is also mentioned in *Proverbia quae dicuntur super natura feminarum*, and in a sonnet of Rustico Filippi; see F. Mazzoni (com 1967), pp. 99–103; A. Scolari (1982), p. 3, n. 6.

53. Cf. Thomas of Cantimpré, *Liber de natura rerum* IV, 86–87, p. 159. See n. 10, above.

54. *De eruditione*, lib. III, cap. XI (*PL* 196, col. 1358). Garnier de Rochefort identifies the pard with dissemblers: "per pardum hypocritae" (*Allegoriae in Sacram Scripturam*, *PL* 112, col. 1022).

55. Ibid.

56. Compare F. D'Ovidio (1901), pp. 9–10: "Ripugna al buon gusto e al solito metodo dantesco che due simboli notevolmente diversi stiano a rappresentare un identico peccato" (pp. 309–310). See also E. Proto (1900), pp. 65–105.

57. See G. Petrocchi (com 1966), p. 10; (1966a); *Lett. Classensi* (1969), pp. 161–162, for reasons to choose *tremesse* over *temesse*.

58. Albertus Magnus, *De animalibus* 22:107 [58], trans. Scanlan, pp. 150–151. Pseudo-Hugh of St. Victor, *De bestiis*, *PL* 177, col. 150; Vincent of Beauvais, *Speculum naturale*, XX, cap. 68. See also Garver-McKenzie, ed., *Il Bestiario toscano*, pp. 80–81.

59. For the unbent neck as a symbol of pride, cf. Isaiah 3:16 and Deuteronomy 31:27. Cf. Garnier de Rochefort's *Allegoriae in universam Sacram Scriptorem* (once attributed to Rabanus Maurus): "cervix est superbia" (*PL* 112, cols. 1023–1024).

The "marzocco," the leonine symbol of Florence, is a heraldic device earlier represented by mascot lions in cages (see R. Davidsohn [1929], pp. 476–477).

60. In the bestiary tradition the lion is said to haunt the peaks of mountains: cf. the *Physiologus* (ed. Eden, pp. 26–27): "Nam leo stans fortis super alta cacumina montis, / Qualicunque via descendit vallis ad ima." The pseudo-Hugh of St. Victor gives it as the lion's first "natura": "Prima est, quod per cacumina montium amat ire" (*PL* 177, col. 57). If we are to read into the appearance of the lion his descent from the "altezza" of the hill in the prologue, the spiritual negativity of the wayfarer's climb becomes even clearer.

61. *ST* II–II, qu. 162, art. 3. G. Casella (1865; 1884), vol. 2, p. 385, saw the lion as both violence and *superbia*. D'Ovidio saw the beast as heresy and violence (1901, p. 305). G. Ferretti (1932, rprt. 1950, pp. 87–94), however, contends that the *matta bestialitade* of *Inferno* XI is to be connected exclusively to heresy. The majority of critics, such as G. Busnelli (1907, esp. pp. 45–49), B. Nardi (1950; rprt. 1962), and J. Freccero (1959, rprt. 1986, p. 48), identifies violence with *matta bestialità*. In his thorough essay of 1968, A. Triolo attempted to show that the "*malizia*" of *Inferno* XI was the plausible description for all the sins of *basso inferno*; he contended that there was no reason why *matta bestialità* could not refer to the worst sins of fraud and treachery in Cocytus. I believe, however, that there is sufficient evidence in patristics to show the causal relation of *malitia* to *fraudulentia*, and also to connect them metaphorically not with the lion but more narrowly with the "lonza," the female of the "pardus" of the Bible (see the section "Una lonza," pp. 59–65 in this chapter).

62. *ST* II–II, qu. 118, art. 8. Also concerning the interrelationship of sins, it is noteworthy that pride, the love of one's own excellence, and lust are conjoined in theology: Isidore of Seville, in his *De summo bono*, quoted by St. Thomas Aquinas in *ST* II–II, qu. 162, art. 6, makes lust a corrective of pride: "Pride is the worst of all vices; whether because it is appropriate to those who are of highest and foremost rank or because it originates from just and virtuous deeds,

so that its guilt is less perceptible. On the other hand, carnal lust is apparent to all, because from the outset it is of a shameful nature: and yet under God's dispensation, it is less grievous than pride. For he who is in the clutches of pride and feels it not, falls into the lusts of the flesh, that being thus humbled he may rise from his abasement." In the bestiary tradition, the *leone*, like its companions the *lonza* and the *lupa*, is said to breed wantonly and indiscriminately with other animals, the lion especially with the *pardus* or *leopardus*.

63. See the essays and bibliography on the *lupa* in M. Apollonio (1951; rprt. 1964, vol. 1, pp. 695-697, 701-702), and especially in F. Mazzoni (com 1967, pp. 109-111, 126-131).

Unfortunately, L. Vanossi's article on "lupo e lupa" in the *ED*, vol. 3 (1971), pp. 742-743, gives no bibliography.

64. Isidore means that "λύκος," "wolf," derives from "λυσσα," "rage." Among the most influential examples of works that absorbed the *Etymologiae* was the *De bestiis* (*PL* 177), attributed erroneously to Hugh of St. Victor; many manuscripts of the work helped keep alive the commonplace of the wolf's avidity: "rapax est bestia, et cruoris appetens." Cf. Albertus Magnus, *De animalibus* 22:114 [68]; Scanlan trans., pp. 156-159. The *Bestiario toscano* (p. 24) puts it thus: "è nominato rappace cioè rapitore." According to the pseudo-Hugh, prostitutes are termed "lupas" because they lay waste the goods of their paramours. See also Segre's partial edition of this bestiary under its more correct title *Libro della natura degli animali* (1959), pp. 300-302. The wolf also is a figure of the devil, for Satan can take that form; cf. the pseudo-Hugh of St. Victor: "Ejus figuram diabolus portat" (*PL* 177, col. 67). The *De bestiis* of the *Clavis* repeats the same idea: "Lupus diabolus . . . lupi daemones" (ed. Pitra, vol. 3 [1855], pp. 62-63). F. Villani stresses the idea of the *lupa* as *signum Dyaboli*, citing Revelation 11:7: "Ioannes in Apocalipse: 'Et vidi bestiam exeuntem de abisso.'" See also B. Basile (1971), p. 221.

Cf. F. McCulloch (1960), p. 189. O. Filipponi (1983), p. 30.

65. Thomas of Cantimpré, *Liber de natura rerum* IV, 60, 1-2; ed. Boese, pp. 143-144. Vincent of Beauvais, *Speculum naturale* XIX, 85. Albertus Magnus, *De animalibus* 22:114; trans. Scanlan, p. 157. A. Scolari (1982), p. 5.

66. "Ciberà terra": that wolves actually eat dirt is found in Pliny, *Natural History* VIII, xxii, 34 [83] (LCL, vol. III, pp. 58-61); in Albertus Magnus, *De animalibus* 22:114; trans. Scanlan, p. 157; in Thomas of Cantimpré, IV, 60:29; ed. Boese, p. 144; in Bartholomaeus Anglicus, *De proprietatibus rerum* XVIII, 69; and in Brunetto Latini, *Tresor* I, 190 (ed. Carmody, p. 167). Cf. F. McCulloch (1960), p. 189.

As will become clear, "terra" signifies not only "earth" or "dirt," but "land" and "territory." Insofar as the wolf gulps dirt, gluttony is obviously signified; insofar as the beast symbolizes the insatiable desire for possession, "terra" points to the seizing of territory.

67. Plato mentions the wolf's cutting off a man's voice in the *Republic* I, 10 336d (trans. Cornford, p. 15); Virgil, in his *Bucolics* IX, 53-54. The legend is attested in Isidore's *Etymologiae* XII, ii, 23, and in St. Ambrose's *Hexameron* VI, iv, 26. Cf. F. McCulloch (1960), p. 189. *Il Bestiario toscano*, p. 24. Indeed, St.

Ambrose in the *Hexameron* VI, iv, 26, seems to be a major source for this extension of the *lupus in fabula* legend: "A wolf takes away a man's power of speech by first staring at him." Ambrose continues in his next paragraph to make the wolf a symbol of the tempting devil, emphasizing that the allegorical *sententia* of the legend outweighs the letter. Indeed the identification of the wolf with the devil as temptor became a topos, one which we cannot ignore in approaching the chthonic origins of the she-wolf—unleashed from hell upon the world by an envious devil. Cf. Albertus Magnus, *De animalibus* 22:114; trans. Scanlan, p. 156.

A number of critics have used the tradition to explain Virgil's silence at verse 63: Holbrook (1902), p. 116, Grandgent (com 1909–1913; rprt. 1933), p. 15, A. Pézard (1957; 1978), and M. Dozon (1969), pp. 5–33. See Chapter 4, under "per lungo silenzio," pp. 84–93.

Ignoring the essential allegorical and moralistic nature of the bestiary tradition, A. Scolari (1982) supposed that this evidence of *physical* distress gave the lie to the various glosses that attribute the wayfarer's reaction to a spiritual or psychological dismay, torment, fear, or "affanno."

68. D. W. Robertson (1962), p. 6; cf. D. Howard (1966), p. 27.

69. Cf. *ST* I, qu. 63, art. 2, reply obj. 2; II–II, qu. 118, 1.

70. See Flamini (1904), II, p. 140.

Avarice, "il mal che tutto il mondo occupa," is memorably tied to the *lupa* on the purgatorial terrace (*Purgatorio* XX, 10–15) where penance is done for avarice. There the poet is prompted to exclaim: "Maledetta sie tu, antica lupa, / che più che tutte l'altre bestie hai preda / per la tua fame senza fine cupa! / O ciel, nel cui girar par che si creda / le condizion di qua giù trasmutarsi, / quando verrà per cui questa disceda?" Clearly the poet intends the recall of Virgil's prediction and curse here in *Inferno* I. In *Inferno* VII, 8, Virgil addresses Pluto, guardian of the avaricious, with "taci maledetto lupo"—where only that part of vice reducible to incontinence, lack of just measure, is punished. Cf. D'Ovidio (1901), p. 315.

71. St. Thomas states that "the irascible understood in a broad sense is not distinct from the concupiscible power" (*ST* II–II, qu. 162, art. 3; cf. *ST* I, qu. 59, art. 4; qu. 82, art. 5, ad. and 2).

72. *ST* II–II, qu. 118, art. 2.

73. A. Pézard (1957), p. 9: "La louve est un symbole de toutes les convoitises qui attachent l'homme à la terre, et causent sa perdition."

74. In the *Republic* VIII, 565, Plato has Socrates say: "How does the transformation of the people's champion into a despot begin? You have heard the legend they tell of the shrine of Lycaean Zeus in Arcadia: how one who tastes a single piece of human flesh mixed in with the flesh of the sacrificial victims is fated to be changed into a wolf. In the same way the people's champion, finding himself in full control of the mob, may not scruple to shed a brother's blood. . . . Is it not thenceforth his inevitable fate either to be destroyed by his enemies or to seize absolute power and be transformed from a human being into a wolf?" (trans. Cornford, p. 285).

Although Dante would not have known Plato's lycanthropic legend directly, he learned from Ovid's *Metamorphoses* I, 222–315, that the early king of Arcadia had fed on human flesh and had tried to feed it, boiled and roasted, to his guest Jove; by such wickedness, Lycaon had become a wolf and precipitated the destruction of the world by a flood. The tale is synopsized in the popular mythographies used widely in the Middle Ages: the first of the Latin mythographers published by Bode (1834), I, 189, explains: "Juppiter propter audacium Lycaonis ceterorumque mortalium . . . orbem terrarum . . . inundavit" [Jupiter, because of Lycaon's audacity and that of other mortals, flooded the earth's globe].

75. A little after Dante's death, Pierre Bersuire, or "Berchorius," a friend of Petrarch, was to describe the Roman god of war in his *De formis figuresque deorum* and comment on the god's received iconography: Mars was depicted as a raging man seated upon a chariot accompanied by a wolf; he was the symbol of the corrupt ruler who favored the "wolves," his unjust and derelict stewards and officials (ed. Engels, p. 15): "The image of Mars was that of a raging man sitting in a chariot. He had a helmet on his head. In front of him a wolf was depicted because that animal was especially consecrated to him by the ancients" (*Ovidius moralizatus*, trans. Reynolds, p. 53). Later in the work (p. 54) he defines the meaning of the "wolf": "Wolves are said to be consecrated to Mars because of the fact that, wolf-like and derelict, stewards and servants are held in favour by cruel, evil soldiers and rulers to whom they are especially devoted" (trans. Reynolds, p. 54). Such wolves, then, are the mascots of evil rulers; Bersuire expatiates on the idea (ed. Engels, pp. 15–16): "A wolf in which is designated their grasping, wolf-like household is pictured in front of them because such princes of the world and tyrants always have with them wolves—that is, cruel and wicked officials—who have the knowledge and desire to ravage the sheep—that is, to afflict their rulers' subjects—so that they can have the opportunity to wage war" (trans. Reynolds, p. 54). Mars himself "signifies the sin of discord which sits in the chariot of an evil soul which four wheels draw—that is, the four vices, avarice, pride, detraction and injustice" (p. 55).

It is to Mars's baleful influence, and most particularly to the shattered statue of the pagan god at the Ponte Vecchio, that Dante (*Paradiso* XVI, 146) attributes the beginning of internecine strife in Florence.

76. C. S. Singleton (*Commentary: Inferno*, p. 17; *Commentary: Purgatorio*, p. 806), among others, has allied the verse "molti son gli animali a cui s'ammoglia" (*Inferno* I, 100) with the whore of Babylon who fornicates with the kings of the earth in Revelation 18:2–3, and to the whore and the giant fornicating on the *carro* in *Purgatorio* XXXIII, 100. Compare Apocalypse 18:3: "De vino irae fornicationis eius biberunt omnes gentes, et reges terrae cum illa fornicati sunt" [All the nations have drunk the wrath of her immorality, and the kings of the earth have committed fornication with her]. Dante knew that cupidity was the poison of civilization, that its disease spread in the souls of rulers to engulf the body politic, and that it spread among the temporal as it spread among the leaders of the church. His she-wolf and all that she signifies cannot be applied solely and narrowly to the avarice of the Roman Curia. Although the she-wolf was the classical symbol of Rome, within the *Commedia* many other political entities are associated with lupine imagery.

See "Wolf" and "Wölfin" in *Lexikon der christlichen Ikonographie*, ed. E. Kirschbaum (1972), vol. 4, pp. 535–539, for representations of the wolf as the devil and as "rapacitas" in the figurative arts predating Dante.

77. J. Freccero (1977, rpt. 1986, pp. 152–166) and R. Herzman (1980, pp. 53–78) have examined the liturgical and theological implications of Ugolino's cannibalism. For a review of the contrary view, see R. Hollander (1985b), pp. 64–81.

78. Unconvincing is the interpretation that begins with Benvenuto da Imola, who attributes the singular "antica belva" to the plural "li" referring to the Florentines: "Sicut bos innocens in senectute securi percutitur" (com vol. 3, p. 384). He is followed by many, among them Del Lungo, Chimenz (vol. 1, p. 435), Musa, and Mandelbaum.

More consistent with the poem's imagery is Pietro Alighieri's interpretation: "Dicendo deinde dictus Dominus Guido dicto domino Rainerio de Fulcerio suo nepote, quomodo crudelizzavit ut belva inter illos lupos, idest Florentinos, dum eorum rector fuerit tempore expulsionis Blancorum." Pietro is followed by Scartazzini-Vandelli: "come vecchia belva, abile per lunga esperienza e sicuro nel suo inferocire," and Casini-Barbi, "vecchia, e però adusata all ferocia."

Not only is the grammar of the line and the consistency of the poem's imagery in favor of Pietro's interpretation, but history is as well. G. Villani writes in his *Cronica* VIII, 59 (vol. 3, pp. 100–101) that Fulcieri was "uomo feroce e crudele."

79. "Beware of false prophets who come to you in the clothing of sheep, but inwardly they are ravening wolves" (Matthew 7:15). In Matthew 15:24, Jesus is the shepherd of the lost sheep of Israel (cf. Mark 6:34). The apostles are sent out as sheep amd shepherds among wolves (Matthew 10:16). The flock of the faithful is persecuted by wolves from without (Romans 8:36). See the interesting comments on this imagery by J. T. Chiampi (1981), pp. 141–143.

80. Livy, *Ab urbe condita*, ed. and trans. B. O. Foster, LCL, vol. 1, pp. 18–21. Lactantius, *Divine Institutes* I, 20; trans. McDonald, p. 75.

81. *DCD* XVIII, 21; LCL, vol. V, pp. 436–437. Paulus Orosius, St. Augustine's follower, also ridicules the divine founding of Rome by pagan "gods," recording Rhea, Romulus's mother, "as convicted of defilement," and agrees with Augustine on the parricidal and fratricidal nature of the founding of Rome: "Romulus continually stained his rule by parricide . . . after first killing his grandfather, Numitor, then his brother, Remus, seized power and founded the city" (*Adversum paganos*, II, 4; VI, 1. *Against the Pagans*, FC, vol. 50, trans. Roy J. Deferrari, pp. 48, 230).

82. F. Lanza (1965), pp. 258–259; J. Ferrante (1984), p. 66.

83. *Convivio* IV, 5; *Monarchia* II, i, 2. Cf. C. T. Davis (1957), p. 46.

84. See C. T. Davis's fundamental treatment of the influence of St. Augustine and Orosius on the poet (1957), pp. 40–73.

85. C. T. Davis (1957), p. 59.

86. In *Convivio* IV, v, 12, where Dante discusses the "divine election of the Roman empire" and in IV, v, 13, its divine inspiration; in IV, v, 17–19, he sees

God's hand and inspiration in all Roman history. Cf. *Monarchia* II. On St. Augustine, see P. Brown (1965), esp. his bibliography, pp. 18–21. G. Papini's observations are important for the history of the canto (1933), p. 321.

87. For possible Joachite influences of this image in the *Paradiso*, see L. Tondelli (1940; rprt. 1953); A. Crocco (1961; rprt. 1965); A. Piromalli (1966); M. Reeves and B. Hirsch-Reich (1972), pp. 317–329.

CHAPTER 4: Virgil

1. In 1918 G. Busnelli contrasted Virgil with Beatrice: "Beatrice si palesa in un'aureola di superiorità e di gloria, a cui non può approssimarsi la pallida ombra del fioco Virgilio" (p. 66). Among the recent studies that have addressed Virgil's inadequacies in the poem, see: G. Baglivi and G. McCutchan (1977), pp. 250–262; M. Chiarenza (1983), pp. 25–35; S. Guyler (1972), pp. 25–42; R. Hollander (1980, 1983a, 1984, and 1985a and b); C. Ryan (1982a), pp. 16–31, and (1982b), pp. 1–38; T. Barolini, (1984); see especially Barolini's discussion (pp. 205–206) of the articles by A. P. MacVay (1948) and R. V. Schoder (1949).

On the question of the historical personage in the poem—i.e., that the Virgil of the poem is not a mere personification see E. Auerbach, "Dante und Vergil," trans. "Dante e Virgilio," in *San Francesco Dante Vico* (1970); R. Bacchelli (1954; 1965), pp. 1–32. The Bosco-Reggio (1979) commentary, however, maintains that Virgil is indeed a personification.

For an interesting study of the perception in the late Empire of Aeneas's and Virgil's failings see J.-P. Callu (1978), pp. 161–174.

2. On the *Oratio* preserved as an appendix to Eusebius, *Vita Constantini* IV, 32, see D. Comparetti (1895, p. 134; trans. p. 100) and P. Courcelle (1957), pp. 294–319. On *Eclogue* IV in early Christian proselytizing see also G. Radke (1978), pp. 147–160, and Courcelle. The latter gives a historical bibliography for the authenticity of Eusebius's text (p. 296, n. 1) and also deals with other important commentaries on the *Eclogue*: the *De promissionibus et predictionibus Dei* attributed to Quodvultdeus, a commentary ascribed to Philargyrius, and the *Scholia Bernensia*.

For modern interpretations of *Eclogue* IV, see W. Berg (1974), esp. pp. 46–51, 155–177, and *Présence de Virgile*, R. Chevallier ed. (1987). In the *DCD* X, 27 (LCL, vol. 3, pp. 374–375), St. Augustine explains the lines "Tu duce. . . . terras" from the *Eclogue* as a figure, or adumbration of Christ. He believes in the absolute fact of Virgil's *Eclogue* as a prophecy, but, echoing Lactantius (*DI* VII, 24), states that the poet is repeating it from the Cumaean Sibyl. Augustine never cites the truly relevant verses of Virgil's text, as though to keep its ready convertibility away from any Christian scrutiny. St. Jerome ridicules the idea of a proto-Christian Virgil: "Quasi non legerimus Homerocentonas et Vergiliocentonas; ac non sic etiam Maronem sine Christo possimus dicere Christianum qui scripserit: Iam redit et Virgo etc. Puerilia sunt haec et circulatorum ludo similia, docere quod ignores" (Hieronymi, *Epistola 53 ad Paulinum*, c. 7, *Opera*, CSEL 54, pars 1, p. 454).

See Comparetti's chapter on the Christian reception of Virgil's *Eclogue* IV (1895), pp. 129–138; trans. pp. 96–103.

Among the many essays treating the relation of Dante with the historical Vergilius Maro, and/or dealing with the persona of Virgil in the poem, some of the most important are the following:

L. Pietrobono (1915), I, pp. 199–203. K. McKenzie (1930), pp. 11–21. E. Auerbach (1929; It. trans. 1963b), pp. 214–216 et passim. H. T. Silverstein (1932), pp. 51–82. A. Fiammazzo (1933), pp. 138–147. G. Mazzoni (1914; rprt. 1918). M. Rossi (1942), pp. 112–128. R. V. Schoder (1949), pp. 413–422. J. H. Whitfield (1949; 1965).

U. Leo (1951), pp. 41–64. G. L. Bickersteth (1951). D. L. Sayers (1954b), esp. pp. 54–57. R. Vivier (1954). C. S. Singleton, *Dante Studies 2*. F. Schneider (1958), pp. 126–127. G. Getto (1959), pp. 11–20. G. Fallani (1959), pp. 51–63. F. Montanari (1959), pp. 117–133.

G. B. Townend (1960), pp. 67–77. H. de Lubac (1959–1964), vol. 2, pp. 233–262. R. Bacchelli (1965), pp. 5–28. E. Esposito (1965). R. Bezzola (1965), pp. 379–395. F. N. Girardi (1965), pp. 237–242. B. Nardi (1965; rprt. 1966), pp. 220–337. E. Paratore (1965), pp. 3–50; (1968), pp. 25–121; (1982). M. Santoro (1965), pp. 343–355. F. Cento (1967), pp. 1–19. D. Consoli (1967).

K. Foster (1977), esp. pp. 156–253. R. Hollander (1968, pp. 142–146; 1969; 1980; 1983a). J. Petrie (1981), pp. 130–145. T. Barolini (1984), pp. 201–269. J. Ferrante (1984).

See also D. Consoli, "Virgilio," *ED*, vol. 4 (1976), pp. 1043–1044.

3. In a curious passage, D. Comparetti (1895), p. 132, hedges concerning the true damnation of Virgil: "Egli è il primo fra coloro che Dante, fedele e profondo interprete del sentimento religioso del medio evo, *non osò riporre fra i dannati*, ma collocò nel luogo destinato a chi avea *la sola colpa involontaria* di non essere nato alla fede di Cristo." On the contary, Limbo is in hell; those there are among the damned. (I note that the English version of Comparetti's study is unfaithful at this point.)

In favor of the contrary view, H. Urs von Balthasar (1962; It. trans. 1973, p. 109) is equally hesitant, yet, I believe, both closer to Dante and closer to Christian doctrine on this point: "Esiste per Dante il battesimo di desiderio, partecipazione alle virtù teologali anteriore alla comparsa di Cristo; questa partecipazione non viene rigidamente separata dalla moralità naturale, per cui il passaggio dall'Inferno [cioè di Rifeo] ai regni superiori appare motivato dall'una e dall'altra insieme. . . . Non si può documentare che Dante abbia lasciato aperta una *chance* a Virgilio, ritenendo segretamente che, come tutti i nobili spiriti dell'antichità, fosse degno della salvezza, ma non si può neppure dimostrare il contrario."

4. Minucius Felix, Fermicus Maternus, Arnobius, Lactantius, and St. Augustine of Hippo all had thorough training in rhetoric.

5. E. Auerbach, "Sermo humilis," in *Literary Language* (1958; Eng. trans. 1965), pp. 27–66.

6. The expression is from St. Augustine, *De doctrina christiana* II, 40; Robertson trans. *LLA*, p. 75. G. L. Ellspermann (1949). D. C. Allen (1970), esp. pp. 14–20.

7. Lactantius, *DI* I, i; trans. McDonald, *FC* 49, p. 17.

8. For St. Augustine in the *Confessions* IX, 4, rhetoric itself was the "school of pride." The destructiveness of rhetoric in the Brunetto episode in *Inferno* XV has recently received a most interesting treatment by E. Vance (1980), pp. 137–155. For Virgil's reputation among churchmen in the fourth century and later see chapters 5 and 7 of D. Comparetti (1895, pp. 66–98, 129–138; trans. pp. 50–74, 96–118).

9. Lactantius, *DI* V, 10; trans. McDonald, pp. 351–353. My emphasis.

10. *DI* V, 10; trans. McDonald, pp. 352–353. My emphasis.

In a recent article, M. Frankel (1985) has alluded to the revisionist position of the "School of Harvard" that has, in the last few decades, begun to see Vergilius Maro no longer as an uncritical, optimistic celebrator of the Roman Empire (p. 408). The critics of this group see Aeneas as finally overcome by the anger and madness of war, finally losing the justness and piety that had made him an attractive hero. Vergilius Maro writes more out of despair and pessimism. Fearing to "superimpose modern sensitivity on a medieval poet," Frankel attributes Dante's own detection of this negativity that lies beneath the surface of the Roman epic, however, to his own, autonomous "analytical and reflective reading of the Latin poem," a reading that led the Florentine poet to change his evaluation of Virgil between the composition of the *Monarchia* (which she dates prior to the *Commedia*) and the *sacro poema* itself (p. 410). Frankel's fear is unfounded. Dante's negative assessment of the *Aeneid* is probably due to his reading of the early Christian apologists and euhemerists such as Lactantius. The negative evaluation of Aeneas and his creator is part of the Christian tradition and it is that which allowed Dante to come to his colder, more analytic reading of Virgil.

11. See E. Vance (1973), pp. 18–22. Sara Sturm-Maddox deals with Petrarch's use of Augustinian models in *Petrarch's Metamorphoses* (1985), esp. pp. 95–126, "The Confessional Subtext": "In the *Confessions*, the abuse of the senses and the abuse of words are clearly identified: the vice of lasciviousness is promoted by the matter of rhetoric, and the reading of pagan letters is repeatedly correlated with the temptations of the flesh" (p. 97).

12. Paulus Orosius, I, 18; *Against the Pagans*, trans. Deferrari, p. 38. We might note the allusion to Aeneas's strife in Virgil's question to the wayfarer: "Ma tu perché ritorni a tanta noia" (v. 76); see my remarks above in Chapter 2, under "il piè fermo," pp. 34–44.

13. P. Nicosia (1969), pp. 47–67, gives an excellent overview of the early commentators glosses on "lo bello stilo" (v. 87).

14. "Misprision" is H. Bloom's term (1973) for an author's purposeful, creative misreading of his predecessor; Bloom cites a conversation with J. Freccero concerning Dante's "skewing" of Virgilian texts on pp. 122–123. For "travisamento" see R. Hollander (1983a, pp. 9, 81–116).

15. See n. 2 above, for a bibliography.

16. Cf. K. Foster (1977), p. 251: "Presumably, this false-worship-rebellion must have involved some culpable omission of an act of faith, tantamount to a refusal of grace; since grace and faith go hand in hand, and faith is the primary condition of access to the Christian God (Hebrews 11:6)." The pagan belief of those in Limbo is not merely negligence but entails "some act on their part impeding faith." Father Foster held that if Virgil were unconscious of his personal sin it was because he lacked the Law that would have given him that knowledge (p. 252). I cannot agree with T. Barolini's view of Virgil's essentially "passive role throughout the poem," or that "Virgil is always a medium, never an agent." T. Barolini (1984), p. 253.

The hindering of the reception of grace, available at all times to all men, is not a passive hindering but an active one; St. Thomas presentation of this in *SCG* III, 159, is, like much of Christian orthodoxy, unequivocal and harsh.

17. On this tradition see H. Rahner (1941), pp. 367–403. On Dante's use of the image in the *Commedia*, see A. Cassell (1984), pp. 58–60.

18. Idolatry and rebellious apostasy are not the same thing in theology. Apostasy is unbelief in that it is "a backsliding from God" (*ST* II–II, 12, 1); idolatry is the worship of false gods and can co-exist with imperfect belief in God (*ST* II–II, 94, 1–4). Virgil and the wayfarer are guilty of both—Virgil, in the last case literally, the wayfarer metaphorically. St. Augustine had realized and taught that resting in things of the world—his famous passage in the *Confessions* X, 35, on the hound, the hare and the spider—was in itself a kind of idolatry (cf. *De doctrina christiana* I, 3–5; *On Christian Doctrine*, pp. 8–10); there was, he wrote, "more than one way to make sacrifice to the fallen angels." As C. S. Singleton ("Symbolism," *Dante Studies*, pp. 19–29) showed, Dante was to dramatize this concept of idolatry in *Purgatory* II, 106–123, where the souls attend to Casella's song, "as if nothing else touched their minds." Instantly, there, the anti-idolater, Cato, scolds them and turns them once again on their path to God. See also J. Freccero (1973; rprt. 1986), pp. 186–194; R. Hollander (1975; 1980), pp. 91–105. A. Cassell (1984), pp. 71–72, 104, 113, 151.

19. *SCG* III, 159; trans. Bourke, book III, pt. 2, pp. 260–261.

20. T. Bottagisio recorded his extensive research on the damnation of Virgil in his *Limbo dantesco* (1898); see also G. Busnelli, "La colpa del non fare" (1938), pp. 79–97.

Concerning ideas on the possible salvation of Virgil see: A. Fiammazzo (1933), pp. 138–147; F. Torraca (com 1905), vol. 1, p. 14 (re: *Inferno* II, 74). F. Schneider (1958), pp. 126–127. Compare S. Pasquazi (1985, p. 62), for whom Virgil's "'non fare' . . . significa non omissione ma impotenza, non negligenza ma frustrazione." While I cannot agree with this position intellectually, I must, however, admit that I sympathize with Pasquazi and admit sentimental solidarity with those who "root for" Virgil, so to speak, in the face of implacable doctrine. Surely, herein lies the real tragic effect of Virgil's fate in the *Commedia*: the emotional dilemma is the result of Dante's careful plan.

See also T. Barolini (1984), esp. pp. 253–254. R. Hollander examines the possible meaning of "ribellante" (1983a), pp. 126–127.

21. The self-exaltation of Dante, as champion of the Christian cause, over Virgil because of the latter's lack of Christian faith is a problem that we must confront—"Chrestiens unt dreit, païens unt tort" as the *Chanson de Roland* teaches. If such an assumption of superiority is conjoined with the harsh spiritual and psychological verities of imitation and rivalry so intelligently and keenly examined in modern literature by René Girard (*Deceit, Desire*, 1965), and later applied to authorial mediation and influence by Harold Bloom (*The Anxiety*, 1973), this literary filiation ("dolcissimo padre") might be revealed as more vehemently partisan and Oedipal than most critics (including the present author) now believe.

22. While hailing Beatrice's arrival, Dante also seals Virgil's departure in *Purgatorio* XXX, 21, 49–50, by echoing the funereal prophecy from the *Aeneid* VI, 883, "*Manibus*, oh, *date lilia plenis!*" See R. Hollander (1980), pp. 74, 87. On Dante's citation of *Aeneid* VI, 883, in *Purgatorio* XXX, 21, 49–50, see also C. S. Singleton (com 1970–1975).

23. R. Hollander (1983a), p. 8.

24. Cf. C. J. Ryan (1982a), pp. 16–31; (1982b), pp. 1–38; R. Hollander (1984).

25. The fundamental ambiguity of Virgil's confession-protestation lies not only in the Pauline subtext from Romans 7:19, but in the significance of "tardi" and "conoscere." Does "tardi" mean "late in life" or "too late": "too late in life" or "too late, in death," that is, nineteen years after his death at Christ's Harrowing? Is "conoscere" "to know" or "to recognize"? I cannot help but believe that Dante's ambiguity is intentional and significant in itself.

26. Among many, Scartazzini (com 1874–1882) and Grabher (com 1934–1936). Since both G. Brugnoli (1981) and, more especially, R. Hollander (1983a) have meticulously traced the history from the earliest commentators to the present, there is no need for me to duplicate their work here. See Hollander's "Nota Bibliografica," pp. 13–21 (and charts, pp. 78–79); Hollander's study supersedes that of F. Mazzoni (com 1967), pp. 114–115.

Some critics have tried to explain this and other major cruxes by assuming a lack of authorial control on Dante's part; compare B. Porcelli (1970, p. 20), for example, citing Sapegno: "'La *Commedia* s'intende assai meglio quando la si prende come un'opera *in fieri*,' in cui siano possibili ingenuità ed incertezze iniziali." Cf. N. Sapegno (1960), p. 6.

27. G. Brugnoli (1981, pp. 1170–1174) notes that Benvenuto da Imola's five explanations (com 1373–1380) encapsule many of the major *prises de position* of commentators and critics before and since his time: Virgil is "fioco" or "hoarse" (1) because he has not spoken for a millenium (a position untenably held, for example, by Graziolo de' Bambaglioli: within the fiction of the *Commedia*, Virgil has conversed for centuries with his colleagues in the Nobile Castello); (2) allegorically, because his works were neglected (similarly, a false proto-humanistic and humanistic assumption asserted by Jacopo della Lana, the Ottimo, the Anonimo Fiorentino, Francesco da Buti, Cristoforo Landino and Alessandro Vellutello and Bernardo Daniello); (3) because Virgil is human reason that is seldom used; (4) because Dante's reason, personified by Virgil is "rauca"

(found, with minor variations in Pietro di Dante, and, among the moderns, in Scartazzini-Vandelli, Sapegno, Dragonetti, Getto, F. Mazzoni, and L. Cassata); (5) because Virgil was historically physiologically weak of throat (Suetonius and Donatus; "rediscovered" by Pézard).

Thus, for example, for I. Del Lungo in 1925, p. 16, the silence of Virgil still signifies the darkness or eclipse of Dante's Reason (although P. W. Spillenger speaks for many modern critics when he insists that Virgil "cannot be construed simply as human reason personified" [1983, p. 55]). G. Casella (1884, vol. 2, p. 382) comments: "Virgilio, ossia la Ragione e la Sapienza latina, che sebben *fioca* per il lungo silenzio dei secoli barbari, cominciava a farsi udire di nuovo." Cf. R. V. Schoder (1949), pp. 415–416.

28. While Scartazzini (com 1874–1882) and Dragonetti (1961), pp. 47–74, for example, assume that the meaning is auditory, Pagliaro (*Ulisse*, pp. 23–43) and Aglianò ("fioco," *ED*, vol. 2 [1970], pp. 892–893) consider it visual; cf. G. Brugnoli (1981), pp. 1175–1176; R. Hollander (1983a), pp. 28, n. 8; 61.

29. Tommaseo (com 1837; rprt. 1934) *ad loc.* also cites this passage from the *Aeneid*; E. Moore, Series 1 (1896), p. 181. Between them, G. Brugnoli (1981) and R. Hollander (1983a) give a complete schematic listing of commentators' and critics' views of the problem.

30. R. Hollander (1983a), pp. 56–57 and notes.

31. R. Hollander (1983a) also rejects A. Pézard's 1957 study in a footnote (p. 57, n. 63). However, I must point out that, unknown to himself, Pézard was on a track that led him very close to the real answer. The "lupus in fabula" was used by the church fathers in adjunct to the notions of the "silence" of unbelief, as I point out below in note 43.

Suetonius, trans. Rolfe, *LCL*, vol. 2, pp. 466–467.

32. Cf. R. Hollander (1983a), p. 57, n. 63.

33. See Hollander's discussion and evaluation of earlier critics (1983a), pp. 125–127. H. Flanders Dunbar (1929) also came close to the true sense of "silenzio" in the intelligent pages she devoted to the Veltro (pp. 163–171); however, she construes the silence as blame ascribed to the pope and emperor: "The equivalence of voice and light in the Word is of primary importance. The silence or the lack of the true voice of pope or emperor had plunged the world into a chaos from which redemption was possible only through the living Logos. The wolf is in definite opposition to the sun" (p. 165).

We should also note the role of doctrinal language in describing pride, for it can cast further light on one of the senses of "il sol tace." In his *Morals on the Book of Job*, St. Gregory warns many times that pride is a "silent" sin arising from "cogitatione tacita," "silent cogitation." "Superbia," "pride," the beginning of all sin in the Bible, does not begin as a sin of action, but as a sin of thought. Pride is the conceit of the new convert waxing arrogant after the first movements of his conversion; pernicious, devious *superbia* steals into secret, silent thoughts to work its evil (cf. *Moralia* XXIII, 25 [*PL* 76, col. 688] and XXXIV, 51 [*PL* 76, col. 746]).

G. Brugnoli, arguing that both the visual and auditory meanings of "fioco" must hold together (a position that I share), examines the minor differences in meaning between Latin and Italian "silere" and "tacere," "not to speak" and "to cease speaking" (1981, p. 1177).

34. M. Wigodsky (1975), 177–183, discusses the historical discrepancies in the dates assumed in verse 70. On *Inferno* I, 67–87, see G. Alessio and C. Villa (1984), pp. 1–21.

35. Concerning the question of authority, see *Convivio* IV, vi, 5; cf. C. S. Singleton (com 1970–1975), *ad loc.*

36. There is little in Dante's works before the *Commedia* that really reflects Virgil's influence. Is Dante referring to his own *canzoni* of the *Convivio* even though they show little influence of Virgil? On the question of Virgil as "fonte" of Dante's style, see U. Leo (1951), pp. 41–64, R. Fitzgerald (1952; rprt. 1957), and R. Hollander (1980), pp. 39–89, esp. pp. 86–89.

The description of Virgil's words as "parola ornata" (*Inferno* II, 67) is undercut by the "parole ornate" used to describe Jason's seduction and deception of Hypsipyle in *Inferno* XVIII, 91. On this see G. Mazzotta (1979), p. 158, and R. Hollander (1985a), pp. 30–31.

37. In these lines from the *Aeneid* III cited by Lactantius, the idea of "faithful silence," as we shall note, formed part of the traditional core of the religion of the Romans. Servius in his commentary on the *Aeneid* (III, 112) glosses, "Fida silentia sacris hinc, inquit, inventum est servare sacris *fidele silentium*" (Harvard ed., vol. 3, p. 56) [From here came the reverential silence at sacrifices—he says that here began the keeping of reverential silence at sacrifices]. It is worth noting that at the point where Anchises is made to use the term in the *Aeneid*, he is describing the island of Crete, the place where the rites of paganism (idolatry to the Christians) were supposed to have derived from the birth of Jove. Though Anchises will ironically and ultimately be proved wrong in his choice of Crete as the final destination of Aeneas and his men, the old man rejoices and proclaims that the island must be their goal: "Hear, O princes, and learn of your hopes. *In mid-ocean lies Crete the island of great Jove, where is Mount Ida*, and the cradle of our race. . . . Not yet had Ilium and the towers of Pergamus been reared . . . [when] from here came *the Mother* the patron of Cybele, *the cymbals of the Corybantes, the grove of Ida, the faithful silence of mysteries.*"

Clearly the description cited here is echoed in Dante's account of Ida in *Inferno* XIV, which occurs as part of Dante's very treatment of idolatry and the Veglio di Creta. I have recently shown the connection of idolatry and the Veglio in two chapters of *Dante's Fearful Art of Justice* (1984). As Lactantius (*Divine Institutes* I, 11–14; V, 5) had made Crete and Jove the sources of idolatry, sin, injustice, warfare, and bloodshed, so Dante has the Cretan statue of Jove on Ida form the source of the sinful waters of hell in the *Commedia*.

38. Marcus Minucius Felix, *Octavius* 1, 6; trans. G. W. Clarke, *ACW* 39, p. 59.

39. Paul the Deacon's dictionary-epitome *De significatione verborum* is found in W. M. Lindsay, ed., Sexti Pompei Festi, *De verborum significatu quae supersunt cum Pauli Epitome* (1913); "faventia," p. 78.

40. I omit any discussion here of the silence of monastic orders (cf. St. Bene-dict's *Regula* VI), since I believe it is a tradition external to the meaning of Dante's text in *Inferno* I. Silence in the context of the cloister was usually termed *taciturnitas* or *quies* (cf. Adam Scot: "Vigor claustralium quies eorum"); *quies* was always accompanied by the *voiced praise* of psalmody (*Regula* IX–XVIII).

On the question of the Psalter and monastic silence, see P. F. Gehl (1984), pp. 219–244; I thank Paolo Cherchi for drawing my attention to Gehl's article.

41. *Festi fragmenta . . . Pauli excerpta*, ed. W. M. Lindsay (1913); "silentium," p. 474. The Latin dictionary of Forcellini and that of Lewis and Short give the same references, s. v. "faveo" and "sileo," "faventia" and "silentium."

42. "Our poet so habitually uses the proper word that such exactitude of ob-servance ceases to be a ground for praising him, but it is worth noting that this propriety of usage is nowhere more in evidence than in his use of words that relate to religious rites or sacrifices," Macrobius, *Saturnalia* III, cap. 2.

43. St. Ambrose, for example, in an age when the church was no longer in danger of external pagan persecution but from rifts from within, in his *Expositio in Evangelium secundum Lucam*, VII, 51, joins "silence" not to pagan idolatry but to heresy as he speaks of the effect of heretics who cut off the voice of the faithful, preventing them from confessing their faith in God: "If by a ruse, en-closing [a sheep, i.e., one of the faithful] in the circles of their disputations, they succeed in anticipating him, they reduce him to *silence*: for *mute* is he who can-not confess the word of God in the glory that is due to Him. Take care that a heretic does not take away your voice if you are not the first to catch him in error. Cruel are the bites of heretics, plunderers more terrible than raging beasts whose voracity knows no respite" (*PL* 15, col. 1712).

Pézard (1957), p. 17, cited this passage but was concerned only with the legend of the wolf's cutting off the voice of its victim; he did not refer to the wide-spread religious and sacramental meanings of muteness and silence.

44. B. Porcelli makes the same observation (1970), p. 22: "La perifrasi non è l'equivalente di un'immediata percezione di Dante attore, ma il consapevole re-soconto di Dante narratore."

45. That Dante's Italian "per" has the value of the Latin "per" seems born out by Richard of St. Victor in his *De statu interioris hominis* XL (ed. J. Ribailler, p. 112), as he concludes his discussion of the sins against the Trinity: "Peccare itaque in Patrum, ut dictum est, est *peccare per impotentiam*, peccare in Filium est *peccare per ignorantiam*, peccare in Spiritum Sanctum est *peccare per mali-tiam*." Statius's confession of how he became a Christian reveals a tragic irony: "*Per te* poeta fui, *per te* cristiano" (*Purgatorio* XXII, 73).

(We might note, in passing, that Richard's categories roughly parallel Dante's three areas of hell, though not in order: force [second in Dante], incontinence [first], and malice [third in both works].)

Virgil's failing is made clear in *Inferno* IV, 37–39, where he explains that he and the other inhabitants of the "Nobile Castello" failed to worship God aright: "e s'e' furon dinanzi al cristianesimo, / non adorar debitamente a Dio: / e di questi cotai son io medesmo." Virgil, in fact, makes two confessions of similar wording concerning that one sin that damns him to Limbo. In *Inferno* IV, 37–42, he insists, "Per tai difetti, non per altro rio / semo perduti." And he echoes himself in *Purgatorio* VII, 7–8: "per null'altro rio / lo ciel perdei che per non aver fé." When he claims that the shades of the ancient worthies "non peccaro" (*Inferno* IV, 34), he refers to personal sin, not original sin; of the latter, he, as a pagan, seems to have poor understanding; he similarly seems not to grasp in what way unbelief is itself a personal sin. C. S. Singleton (com. 1970–1975; *Purgatorio: Commentary*, p. 58) remarks, "Virgil's understanding of a specifically Christian truth—even one such as this, by which he himself is judged—is veiled and dim." Indeed, the words "non peccaro" and "per null'*altro* rio" are self-contradictory. On the question of faith and salvation, see *ST* II–II, 2, arts. 3–10.

Though Virgil's sin is "through silence," he obviously could not have been expected to spread the good news in Pauline fashion. However, that Dante understood that an awareness and expression of the truth of God was possible to the pagans is clear in the *Epistle to Can Grande* 22–23, where, arguing the ubiquity of God's goodness, wisdom and virtue, Dante cites Cato's words in Lucan's *Pharsalia* IX, 580, where the general refuses to make idolatrous trial of the oracle of Ammon-Zeus: "Iuppiter est quodcumque vides, quocumque moveris" [Jupiter is whatever thou seest, wherever thou goest]. Cato, as the censorious adviser to the shades on Mount Purgatorio's shore in the *Commedia*, is one of the elect. P. Renucci (1954), pp. 296–310, deals with Cato's place in Purgatory. See also S. Pasquazi (1966), pp. 99–126, and G. Padoan (1969), pp. 372ff.

46. See Benvenuto da Imola's comparison of Virgil's *Eclogue* IV to the *veltro* prophecy: "Dantes, qui studuit imitari Virgilium, voluit facere similem passum ambiguum . . . quod Dantes dicit de veltro potest intelligi de Christo, et de quodam principe futuro" (com 1373–1380, p. 56).

T. K. Seung (= Swing) (1965; 1976, pp. 35–37) has argued that Virgil's flood of speech makes him a Trinitarian figure of Christ, the Logos. P. Priest (1982, p. 93) suggested that Virgil symbolizes the Holy Spirit.

47. Compare Shoaf's comments cited on p. 135, n. 32, Chapter 1 above.

The question of "silenzio" and the exchange of salutations between the wayfarer and Virgil in *Inferno* I connects closely with the question of Beatrice's "salute" in the *Vita Nuova*. "Salve," the classical and Christian greeting, and the whole concept of "salutation" have wide semantic and social implications: the possibility of exchanging discourse, communication, greeting, the charitable wish for the well-being of another, thus love itself, concern for the welfare of the body, the welfare of society's members, and the salvation of the soul. The removal of greeting, silence, is the sign of a breakdown in this communication, a symbol of actual or perceived transgression of a social, moral, or religious bond or contract. It is used as corrective punishment to humble and reintegrate the transgressor (viz. excommunication by the church, Mennonite shunning, or, *se parva licet*, much as English schoolboys place a fellow "in Coventry" to reprove him). Beatrice's silence in the *Vita Nuova* is analogous to God's silence toward his recalcitrant chosen people in the Old Testament. In the *Commedia* the first exchange of salutation brings about the possibility of the salvation of Dante-wayfarer.

CHAPTER 5: "Il veltro"

1. P. J. Alexander (1968).

2. V. Cian (1945), pp. 119–32. A. K. Cassell (1978), pp. 75–82.

3. For a history of the problem, see E. Moore (1896), p. 167, and (1903), pp. 253–283; E. G. Parodi (1920), pp. 367–532; M. Barbi (1938), pp. 29–39; V. Cian (1945); R. E. Kaske (1961); A. Vallone (1954; rprt. 1955; 1961, pp. 85–87); F. Mazzoni (com 1967); Singleton (com 1970–1975). C. T. Davis, "veltro," *ED*, vol. 5 (1976), pp. 908–912.

4. It has, at least, been entertained among the moderns: cf. L. Pietrobono (1915), vol. 1, p. 204: "I cieli sono i feltri o i filtri che piovono nei viventi le virtù divine di cui sono i dispensatori." And it has been rejected: L. Olschki (1953), p. 42. On the question of the planetary conjunctions of Saturn and Jupiter in 1325, see K. M. Woody (1977), pp. 119–134.

5. L. Olschki (1949; 1953).

6. Cf. G. Papini (1933); R. E. Kaske (1961).

7. See this chapter, "Tra Feltro e Feltro," pp. 102–103.

8. Perhaps the best bibliographies on the subject from the earliest commentators to the present are found in V. Cian (1897; 1945), and in C. T. Davis's article, "veltro," in the *ED*, op. cit.

9. G. Villani in his *Cronica* attests to the fact that the Khans were raised on rough felt. See 5:29, "Come i Tartari scesono le montagne di Gog e Magog" (vol. 1, pp. 245–247), concerning "Cangius, il quale in su un povero feltro fu levato imperadore, e come fu fatto signore, fu chiamato il sopranome Cane, cioè in loro lingua imperadore." (My thanks to R. Hollander for this point.)

10. For the dating of Pietro's three redactions, see L. Rocca (1891), pp. 350–352; J. P. Bowden (1951), pp. 21ff.; F. Mazzoni (1963), pp. 279–360; L. Jenaro-MacLennan (1974), pp. 19–20; esp. Egidio Guidubaldi's "Nota introduttiva" (1978) to Pietro di Dante, *Commentarium* (com 1340), pp. xxi–xxv.

11. Pietro di Dante, *Commentarium* (1978), p. 54. For the complete text of the pseudo-Methodius in Latin, see E. Sackur, ed., *Sibyllinische Texte* (1898), pp. 59–96.

12. Guido da Pisa (com 1327–1328): "Per istum leporarium accipere possumus Christum, qui venturus est ad iudicium, cuius natio, id est apparitio, erit inter feltrum et feltrum, hoc est inter bonos et reprobos" (p. 33).

13. For R. Benini (1919, p. 100), the *veltro* was Dante himself and "tra feltro e

feltro" meant the "Val di Pado," the original seat of the Alighieri family. See also L. Olschki (1953), p. 45, n. 3.

14. Davis notes ("veltro," *ED*, vol. 5 [1976], pp. 908–912), however, the adulation given by the court grammarian, Summacampagna, to his lord, Can Grande della Scala, as the "the one who puts the false wolf to flight." See the various earlier prophecies listed by V. Cian (1945), pp. 11–24. M. Reeves (1980), pp. 44–60.

15. Among those who believe it to be an emperor are G. Pascoli (1913, pp. 226–240), J. Döllinger (1888, pp. 78–117), V. Cian (1897; 1945), R. Fornaciari (1883, pp. 25–29; rprt. 1900, pp. 18–21), A. Medin (1889, pp. 287–304), G. Gentile (1921), pp. 253–296, F. Ercole (1921; rprt. 1928, vol. 2, pp. 314–407), A. Solmi (1922), M. Barbi (1938; 1939), B. Nardi (1921; 1930), L. Pietrobono (com 1946), A. Momigliano (com 1946–1951), O. Castellino (com 1946), H. Gmelin (com 1954–1957), G. Mazzoni (1914; rprt. 1918, pp. 31–32), S. Frascino (1954–1957, pp. 5–37), E. von Richthofen (1956; 1966), B. Töpfer (1964), C. S. Singleton (com 1970–1975), G. R. Sarolli (1971), C. T. Davis (1957; 1975), and J. Goudet (1981), pp. 136–137.

16. Those who believe the *veltro* to be a pope include I. Del Lungo (1873; rprt. 1879, vol. 2, pp. 554–555; [1901], p. 33; [1925], p. 14), G. Lajolo (1906, esp. p. 105, with the "DXV" as an emperor), V. Grazzani (1921, p. 125), F. Torraca (com 1905), R. Davidsohn (1902), E. Rivalta (com 1946), A. Dempf (1929; Ital. trans. 1933), L. Tondelli (1940; 1953), M. Porena (com 1946–1948; rprt. 1951), pp. 17–18; (1953), pp. 230–237, esp. p. 236; and A. Crocco (1961; rprt. 1965).

17. Critics who view the *veltro* more generically as a "reformer" include A. Vallone (1954; rprt. 1955; 1957; rprt. 1961), N. Sapegno (com 1955), A. Pézard (1978), and G. Petrocchi (1966, pp. 1–16).

18. "Questi è messer Cane della Scala veronese, onde la sua patria, dice Dante, che sarà tra Feltro e Feltro, perché tra Monte Feltro dello Stato d'Urbino e Feltro del Friuli si ritrova in mezzo Verona." L. Magalotti (com 1665; 1819, p. 13). G. Todeschini believed that Can Grande's name was the inspiration for the *veltro* and all the animal imagery of *Inferno* I (1872), vol. 1, pp. 155–169, esp. p. 160.

However, far less specific still is the poet's own apostrophic question of *Purgatorio* XX, 15, about one who will come to rout the "ancient wolf" of greed; the identity there is left as an abstract pronoun: "quando verrà per cui questa disceda?"

19. See the opposing argument of L. Filomusi-Guelfi, "Per Can Grande della Scala" (1911), pp. 83–87.

20. Troya was followed by B. Bianchi (com 1868), p. 12: "Non potrebbe essere che Uguccione della Faggiuola, valoroso e audace capitano ghibellino." But he was contradicted by G. Todeschini (1872), vol. 1, p. 160: "No, dunque, risolutamente no: il Veltro di Dante non ha nulla che fare con Uguccione della Faggiuola." For the history of Carlo Troya's essay on the *veltro*, see Costantino Panigada's "Note," in his edition of Troya's works (Troya, 1932), esp. pp. 352–

372. C. Balbo (com 1853), p. 408. I. Del Lungo (1873; rprt. 1879, vol. 2, p. 528). G. Lajolo (1906), p. 91.

21. Both G. R. Sarolli (1963) and R. E. Kaske (1961) interpreted the "515" as "DXV" as a reflection of the monogram for "vere dignum," common in liturgical books of the time, symbolizing and depicting Christ. While Kaske leans to the ecclesiastical, Sarolli prefers a "Ghibelline" interpretation.

22. For P. Renucci (1954; pp. 89–94), the fact that Benedict XI's humble birthplace lay on the very road between Feltre and Montefeltro made that pope a candidate for the *veltro*'s mantle. See also the nineteenth-century discussions by B. Giuliani (1861), p. 243, and V. Marchese (1855), pp. 291–316. A. Crocco (1961; rprt. 1965), esp. pp. 33–37. For contrary views see A. Vallone (1954; rprt. 1955), pp. 10–11; C. T. Davis, "veltro," *ED*, vol. 5 (1976), p. 910.

O. Filipponi (1983) has recently identified the *veltro* with the "messo" of *Inferno* IX, whom he believes is St. Michael, the conqueror at Armageddon.

23. "Il Poeta è il Veltro, cuore generoso, che muore peregrino e mendico, benefacendo all'Italia col suo Poema." R. Della Torre (1887–1890), vol. 1, p. 103. Even V. Cian (1897; 1945) saw Dante "non soltanto annunziatore, ma precursore e collaboratore del Veltro." See also G. Busnelli (1909), p. 114, and the objections of M. Colacci (1947), pp. 14–19.

24. For R. Petrucci (1901), pp. 460–461, the *veltro* was Dante garbed in the rough clothing ("entre bure et bure") of the Order of St. Francis; "questi non ciberà terra nè peltro" referred to Dante's *Convivio*. See also C. Borromeo (1901). R. Benini identifies the "515" prophecy with Dante also.

See A. Santi (1918), pp. 81–82; V. Cian (1945), p. 96; T. Ventura (1953), p. 191; A. Vallone (1954; rprt. 1955), p. 13, n. 2; C. G. Hardie (1963), esp. pp. 277–278; A. Crocco (1961; rprt. 1965), p. 34.

25. L. Olschki (1949; 1952; 1953). M. Porena (1953) and F. Mazzoni (1964) rejected Olschki's interpretation. M. Sampoli Simonelli (1954, pp. 101–105) also disagreed, preferring to see in the *veltro* a "supreme organizer" who would bring peace and justice. S. A. Chimenz (com 1962) labels Olschki's view "assurdo" and identifies the *veltro* with a prophet or pope, and the "515" with the prediction of an emperor.

26. "Dante does not claim to be a new savior but only to have been saved." C. G. Hardie (1961), p. 162. "To write the *Comedy* is Dante's crusade." Hardie (1963), p. 286.

27. For G. Todeschini (1872, vol. 1, pp. 161–162), "nazion" signifies the "generazione d'uomini nati in una medesima provincia." "Feltro e Feltro" signified "Feltre della Marca Trivigiana" and "il monte Feltro." For R. Benini (1919; rprt. 1952, p. 102) and C. G. Hardie (1963, pp. 290–292), "nazion" meant lineage or clan; "tra Feltro e Feltro" signified the "val di Pado," or the city of Ferrara, the original seat of the Alighieri family.

28. Regis's suggestion (1921), pp. 85–97, received enthusiastic support from F. Foberti (1939, esp. pp. 158–159) and S. Frascino (1954–1957), pp. 5–37. Following some suggestions of Castelvetro, E. Crivelli (1939; pub. 1941) put

forth the view that the word "peltro" ("questi non ciberà terra nè peltro," v. 103) signified the pewter chargers or trays upon which food was served rather than simply signifying wealth or riches. The contrast with the wolf identified as incontinence and cupidity would thus be brought into greater relief: the *veltro* would feed on spiritual food, not earthly luxury.

29. *Epistola* VII in *Epistole: Opere minori*, vol. 2, p. 564.

30. Glossing "umile Italia," *Inferno* I, 106–108, most critics refer to *Aeneid* III, 522ff.; some see the phrase as a calque keeping the Virgilian sense. Others note the "misprision": Dante does not mean "low-lying Italy" but "misera Italia" that has become a "serva." See C. Rossi (Rossi/Frascino, com 1923–1948, vol. 1, p. 49); S. A. Chimenz (com 1962), p. 12; C. S. Singleton (com 1970–1975). See also G. Crescimanno (1905), pp. 81–91; F. Torraca (com 1905); G. Rossetti (com 1826–1827), vol. 1, p. 14 ("bassa Italia"); A. Pézard (1950), p. 353, and com 1965; Gmelin (com 1954) translates it "das schlichte Land Italien"; G. P. Small Stuart (1959), pp. 295–301; R. M. Haywood (1959), pp. 416–418 ("below the horizon"); A. Ronconi (1964), pp. 5–44, esp. p. 31; A. Pagliaro, *Ulisse*, pp. 45–46, 766, n. 16.

For a discussion and bibliography, see F. Mazzoni (com 1967), pp. 135–136. See also Chapter 5, "The Prophecy," pp. 104–106.

31. For recent interpretations of the "515" prophecy see: R. E. Kaske (1961); P. Mazzamuto, "Cinquecento diece e cinque," *ED*, vol. 2 (1970), pp. 10–14; C. H. Grandgent (com 1909–1913; rprt. 1933), p. 11; C. G. Hardie (1961; 1964); Singleton (com 1970–1975); R. Kay (1979); Kearney and Schraer (1982); J. Ferrante (1984), pp. 115–121.

32. See L. G. Blanc (1865), pp. 17–18, who sees wisdom in not identifying the *veltro*. C. H. Grandgent (com 1909–1913; rev. 1933), p. 11: "It is possible that [Dante] so constructed his prognostication as to make its application to Can Grande evident in case those hopes should be realized, but not obtrusive in case they were not." M. Barbi (1938), p. 30, saw no identification possible with any historical personage: "È però inutile cercar di identificare questo liberatore con un determinato personaggio, dal momento che il poeta ha voluto soltanto designarlo genericamente come oggetto della sua ferma speranza, senza riferimento ad alcuna persona." For A. Vallone (1954; rprt. 1955, pp. 127–142), the *veltro* is "una profezia vera e propria."

33. C. G. Hardie (1964), p. 170; R. Hollander (1969), pp. 181–191; C. T. Davis, "veltro," *ED*, vol. 5 (1976), p. 908; cf. J. Ferrante (1984), pp. 115–116.

For a list of all the prophetical passages in the *Commedia*, see V. Cian (1945), pp. 119–132; see also N. Mineo (1968). O. Filipponi's *Le profezie* (1983) is only of marginal interest.

34. The idea of imminence is expressed similarly in *Paradiso* IX, 139–142, by Folco da Marsiglia: the coming savior will specifically reform the church, referred to in synechdoche as the tomb of Peter: "Ma Vaticano e l'altre parti elette / di Roma che son state cimitero / a la milizia che Pietro seguette / tosto libere fien de l'avoltero."

35. As we noted in treating the image of the *lupa*, the poem abounds in images of popes and clerics who lead their flock astray. Cf. J. Ferrante (1984), pp. 112–113.

36. Persuasive is R. Hollander's argument (1969), pp. 89–90, for a calque on *Aeneid* I, esp. v. 294, that is, Jupiter's prediction of Caesar Augustus who "will close the doors of war and shackle furor forever."

37. First published in their medieval Latin form by Sackur in 1898 (rprt. 1963), and studied in their original Greek and historical importance by Paul Alexander (1971), Marjorie Reeves (1961; 1969; 1972), and B. Hirsch-Reich (1972).

38. M. Reeves (1980), pp. 51–52.

39. See, among others, F. X. Kraus (1897), U. Cosmo (1898, pp. 112–117), A. Dempf (1929), G. Papini (1933), H. Grundmann (1928; 1932), J. C. Huck (1903; 1938, pp. 183–189), and to a minor extent the Russian D. Merejkowski (Ital. trans. 1938; rprt. 1940, pp. 338–351) and M. Colacci (1947, pp. 17–19).

F. Mazzoni has wisely warned against insisting on Joachite interpretations (com 1967), as has A. Vallone (1955).

40. For A. Dempf (1929, pp. 472–491), the Beatrice of the *Vita Nuova* signifies Franciscan spirituality: her absence from the earth would be brief and she would return when the "DUX" (the "515" interpreted in Roman numerals as "DXV" and rearranged as letters) had annihilated the false popes and the royal house of France, and the *veltro*, the angelic pope, would come to chase the wolf of greed back to hell. For a concise and convincing rebuttal, see M. Barbi (1934), pp. 209–211.

41. Dante, in fact, expressly warns against going outside of Holy Writ or Catholic orthodoxy in questions of salvation: "Avete il novo e 'l vecchio Testamento, / e 'l pastor della Chiesa che vi guida; / questo vi basti a vostro salvamento" (*Paradiso* V, 76–78).

42. Barbi (1934), p. 210, and L. Cicchitto (1947), pp. 217–231. But see L. Tondelli (1944, pp. 107–121); F. Russo (1966, pp. 219–220) believes that Dante is a follower of Gioachino's original thought but not of the heterodox modifications of the Franciscan Spirituals, yet he writes: "L'Alighieri . . . era imbevuto di ideali gioachimiti, non solo per la sua estrema facilità ad assimilare tutto lo scibile del suo tempo, ma anche per essere stato a Santa Croce tra gli uditori di Pier di Giovanni Olivi e Ubertino da Casale."

See especially L. Tondelli (1940), p. 297; (1953), p. 351; and M. Reeves's discussion of Gioachino's orthodoxy (1969), pp. 126–132.

43. L. Tondelli (1940; 1953); A. Crocco (1961; rprt. 1965); A. Piromalli (1966); M. Reeves and B. Hirsch-Reich (1972), pp. 317–329; M. Reeves (1980), pp. 44–60, esp. 54–55.

44. M. Reeves and B. Hirsch-Reich (1972), p. 329.

45. Tondelli does not consider any of the early commentaries in his arguments; thus, for example, he attributes the interpretation of "tra feltro e feltro" as "tra cielo e cielo" erroneously to Pietrobono and ends his attribution with a quizzical exclamation mark (1940, p. 299; 1953, p. 353).

46. The Latin of the description of the the the oratorium reads as follows: "In hoc oratorio erunt congregati sacerdotes et CANIS clerici qui volunt continenter et communiter vivere, sed tamen ab usu carnium et [ab usu] pelliceis nolunt penitus abstinere. Isti ieiunabunt in yeme quarta et sexta feria. Et erunt obedientes priori suo secundum dispositionem et arbitrium patris spiritualis qui preerit omnibus. Hii non utentur palliis, sed tantum cappis, ut inter habitum illorum et laicorum differentia sit. Apud istos erit studium artis gramatice, et instituentur apud eos pueri sive adholescenties ut sciant loqui latine et scribere, et litteram utriusque testamenti pro posse memorie commendare. Isti dabunt decimam operis sui et decimam decime eorum que accipient a coniugatis in manus patris spritualis pro sustentatione pauperum Xristi si forte aliqui indiguerint."

47. Cf. (pseudo-Rabanus Maurus), Garnier de Rochefort, *Allegoriae in Universam Sacram Scripturam* (*PL* 112, col. 883): "Per *canes* praedicatores boni, ut in Evangelio, 'canes lingebant ulcera Lazari' [Luke 16:21], quod sancti praedicatores sanabant peccata gentilis populi." Similarly, in the *De bestiis* (*PL* 177, col. 65–66), popularly attributed to Hugh of St. Victor, we find the same "dog" image explained: "Cujus figuram in rebus quibusdam praedicatores habent, qui semper admonendo atque exsequendo quae recta sunt, insidias diaboli propellunt, ne thesaurum Dei, id est Christianorum animas rapiendo ipse auferat. Lingua canis dum lingit vulnus, sanat, quia peccatorum in confessione emundatur vulnera sacerdoti facta confessione." See also col. 87, ibid.

48. This is the only occurrence of the term "*veltro*" to designate a future reformer. In *Inferno* XIII, 126, the black bitches who chase and punish those guilty of avarice's opposite, prodigality (the destruction of one's material substance), are compared to "veltri" unleashed from a chain.

49. Rabanus Maurus, *De universo* VIII, 1 (*PL* 111, col. 223); the entry is repeated verbatim in the *De bestiis* attributed to Hugh of St. Victor in *PL* 177, col. 86–87. Cf. also the pseudo-Rabanus Maurus's *Allegoriae in universam Sacram Scripturam* (now attributed to Garnier de Rochefort), *PL* 112, col. 883.

50. The tale is recounted by Jacopo della Lana and the Ottimo. See also R. E. Kaske (1961), esp. p. 232.

51. For the guardian of the *polis* compared to the watchdog, see *Republic* II, 374; trans. Cornford, pt. II, chapter VIII, p. 62.

The concordance of Rand and Wilkins (1912) reports no use of "canis" in Dante's Latin works. The use of "cane" ("can," "cani") is always negative in the *Commedia*.

If the "veltro" were to be identified with Can Grande (or to any future liberator), it would at least distinguish him with a term nobler than the one debased everywhere else in the poem—one, perhaps, embarrassingly identical with the name of Verona's lord.

The Scaligera family, indeed, cultivated the canine pun; beside Can Grande, its members bore such names as Mastino and Cansignorio.

52. In the comparison of the *Chanson* with the *Commedia* in his study, *Tant que vienne le Veltre* (1978), A. Pézard brings in every minute detail to make a case

for a direct inspiration. See also F. Koenen (1936), p. 189; H. Gmelin, *Kommentar* (com 1954–1957), pp. 40–41; P. Renucci (1954), p. 90, n. 532; E. Von Richthofen (1956), esp. pp. 11–20, and (1966), pp. 117–127; U. Limentani (1985), p. 14.

53. Cf. R. E. Kaske (1961), p. 232; B. Nardi (1966), p. 153.

54. Naturally, various kinds of dogs are so described in the bestiaries; cf. the pseudo-Hugh of St. Victor, *De bestiis* (*PL* 177, col. 65): "Canum sunt plura genera. Alii enim ad capiendum feras silvarum investigant . . . alii ab infestationibus luporum greges ovium cum pastoribus custodiunt."

55. Galleria dell'Accademia Inv. no. 271; G. Schiller (1971), pl. 191.

Other outstanding later examples among many are Stefano da Verona's *Adorazione dei Magi* on a panel, signed and dated 1435, now in the Pinacoteca Brera in Milan: in the background, as part of the annunciation to the shepherds, are two beautifully depicted greyhounds. The *Presepio* of Giovanni della Robbia from the Chiesa di San Girolamo delle Poverine, now in the Bargello in Florence (cat. no. 25), has several "veltri" guarding sheep.

56. J. Ferrante (1984, p. 119, and n. 53; p. 285) allies Can Grande to the prophecy of the *veltro*.

57. V. Cian's words bear repeating: "A seconda delle occasioni, dei varii momenti e condizioni, dell'attimo fuggente della storia, anche a seconda delle disposizioni dell'animo suo, il poeta si illuse di vedere incarnato nell'uno o nell'altro quelli che furono i protagonisti sulla scena storica del suo tempo" (1897, pp. 12–13); cf. Busnelli (1909), p. 115.

58. *Paradiso* XXV, 2. In the tradition of the earliest commentators many modern critics, such as L. Malagoli (com 1955–1956), N. Sapegno (com 1955–1957), A. Pézard (1978), and G. Petrocchi (1966), refuse to give a specific identity to the *veltro*.

C. Ballerini (1953), p. 45, seems to see "la spada folgorante di un arcangelo" pointed at the she-wolf's spine, but he finally gives no identification for the *veltro*.

59. C. Hardie (1964), however, does argue for a prophecy *post eventum*, since for him the "veltro" is the *Commedia* itself.

60. Cf. Pagliaro, *Ulisse*, I, pp. 57–60; A. Vallone (1954; rprt. 1955) likewise does not believe the *veltro* is identified anywhere in the poem. E. N. Girardi (1965, p. 240) sees the "unknowing" of Virgil (*Purgatorio* XXII, 67–69) as parallel to the ignorance of the identity of the *veltro* in *Inferno* I, 110–111.

61. On the significance of intertwining the names of these heroes from opposing sides, see G. Ungaretti (1952; rprt. 1964, pp. 22–23). On Camilla, see E. Auerbach, "Camilla, or, the Rebirth of the Sublime" (1958; trans. 1965, pp. 181–234); G. P. Small Stuart (1959), pp. 295–301; A. Pézard (1950), p. 353. For a discussion and bibliography, see F. Mazzoni (com 1967), pp. 136–137; C. Kraus, "Camilla," *ED*, vol. 1 (1970), p. 774; "Eurialo," *ED*, vol. 2 (1970), p. 766; "Niso," *ED*, vol. 4 (1973), p. 50; "Turno," *ED*, vol. 5 (1976), p. 760.

CHAPTER 6: Shadows of Conversion

1. In "Dante's Prologue Scene," Freccero (1966; rprt. 1986, pp. 4–5) put the case eloquently: "The descent into Hell, whether metaphorical as in the *Confessions*, or dramatically real as in Dante's poem, is the first step on the journey to the truth. It has the effect of shattering the inverted values of this life (which is death, according to Christian rhetoric) and transforming death into authentic life. The inversion of values is represented in Dante's poem by the curious prefiguration in the first canto of the ascent of the mountain of Purgatory: the light at the summit, the mountain itself, the attempted climb. Although the landscape is analogous to the scenery that comes into sharper focus in the second *cantica*, all directions are reversed. What seems up is in fact down; what seems transcendence is in fact descent. Just as the reversed world of Plato's myth in the *Statesman* [*Republic*] represented a world of negative values, so the reversed directions of the prologue stand for spiritual distortion. Augustine alludes in the seventh book to Plato's myth when he describes his spiritual world before his conversion as a 'regio dissimilitudinis.'"

2. Even U. Limentani's perceptive reading ignores the problematic transvaluation of the various elements of the prologue scene: "The hill is in contrast to the wood; it is high, while the wood is low, and leads on higher" (1985), p. 2.

3. J. Freccero (1966; rprt. 1986), pp. 1–15.

4. L. Pietrobono, "Il prologo," *Il poema sacro*, vol. 1 (1915), p. 160. See also S. Battaglia, "Linguaggio reale e linguaggio figurato nella *Divina Commedia*," (1962), pp. 21–44; rprt. in *Esemplarità* (1967), I, pp. 51–82.

5. B. Croce (1920; rprt. 1952), p. 67; C. S. Singleton, *Dante Studies 1*, p. 6. J. Freccero (1966; rprt. 1986), p. 1.

6. G. Ragonese, "fiera," "le tre fiere," *ED*, vol. 2 (1970), p. 858.

7. In his chapter "Through Shadowy Realms of the Living," J. Demaray (1974, pp. 138–143) has shown that Dante's imagery here, for all its symbolic literary quality and textual structure, is not pure fiction (as, for example E. Gilson supposes [1963, pp. 291–293]), but has a basis in historical reality. He cites many contemporary and near-contemporary pilgrim accounts that attest to the dangers of attack from leopards, lions, and wolves in the deserts and on the mountains of the Holy Land. Demaray's study goes far in demonstrating that the poetry here cannot be "allegory of poets": "Both aesthetically and in the perspective of the pilgrimage tradition, the three beasts can be regarded as 'real,' their physical presence in turn supporting varying symbolic values."

8. D'Ovidio compares the three beasts to hierogylphs.

9. G. Mazzoni, "Il canto I dell'*Inferno*," *Lect. romana* (1918), p. 15.

10. C. S. Singleton, *Dante Studies 1*, pp. 6–7.

11. C. S. Singleton, *Dante Studies 1*, pp. 9–10; cf. also J. Freccero (1966; rprt. 1986, p. 6) who cites Singleton's observation to stress the incarnational aspects of Dante's poetics.

12. "Ahi" is not attested in all manuscripts. See Petrocchi (com 1966), vol. 2, pp. 3–4, for a historical discussion and the reasons for preferring this reading.

13. P. Nicosia points to Dante's self-conscious use of rhetorical figures, par-

ticularly *amplificatio* and *iteratio* (1969), pp. 54–61. R. Roedel notes "un'abilità strutturale tutto nuova" in the canto (1959), pp. 1–12. See also T. Wlassics (1975), esp. pp. 69–90.

14. Cf. E. H. Plumptre (com 1886), vol. 1, p. 3: "The leopard did not alarm the wanderer. . . . The lion and the wolf . . . unlike the leopard are simply deterrent."

On the theme of tumult and variety in poetry after Dante, see G. Warkentin (1975), esp. p. 15, and S. Sturm-Maddox (1985), p. 157, n. 28.

15. *Divinae institutiones* VI, 7; trans. McDonald, p. 410.

16. St. Augustine, *De Trinitate* XV, 16, 26 (*PL* 42, col. 1068): "Aenigma est autem, ut breviter explicem, obscura allegoria." I believe that it is in the prologue that Dante is consciously applying this form of theological allegory; when the scene changes from "our life" to the realm beyond, immediately a firmer solidity or "irreducibility" (to use Singleton's term) takes over. Concerning our discernment on earth Augustine tells us: "There need be no surprise that in the manner of seeing permitted us in this life, 'through a mirror in an enigma,' our struggle to see at all must be a hard one" (*The Trinity*, in *Augustine's Later Works*, LCC, trans. Burnaby, p. 143).

Cf. S. Battaglia, *Esemplarità* I, pp. 73–74, n. 2.

In 1979, A. C. Mastrobuono argued for the prologue as "an allegory of theologians" (pp. 9–10; 41–79). However, in spite of the fact that he claimed that both Montano (1962, I, p. 326) and Singleton (*Dante Studies 1*, p. 97) had declared *Inferno* I an "allegory of poets," any casual examination of the passages to which Mastrobuono referred reveals that no such statement was made by either critic. In effect, Mastrobuono argued against those with whom he agreed.

In 1948 Singleton examined the first canto thus: "Had Jeremiah not spoken of the *three beasts*? Had not a *hill* and a *valley* been mentioned by others? These things have meaning outside the poem, like words. But they are not *mere* metaphors, if by such a qualification one means that they do not denote real things. The 'road of life' is not less real (I speak as the poem speaks) for not being found on any map. Such words and metaphors do not point to fictions but to realities. And *if we speak here of allegory, it may not be of that kind of allegory that begins in a fiction, that is an acknowledged creation of poets*. Beatrice is not urged here by Lucia to look down upon that kind of world, from heaven" (p. 273, some italics added). As for the presence of the allegory of poets anywhere in the *Commedia*, Singleton wrote, "I believe that the correct answer can be given in the negative" (*Dante Studies 1*, p. 97).

17. Isidore, *Etymologiae* I, 37, 22. *Epistola* XIII, 7, ed. G. Brugnoli, p. 610; numbered *Epistola* X, 7, in Toynbee-Hardie, ed., p. 174; Eng. trans. p. 199. See R. Hollander (1969), pp. 235–236.

The usual gloss identifies "le altre cose" not with a metaliterary statement of procedure but with the three beasts, or the spectacle of evil that Virgil will show the wayfarer; compare, for example, Pasquini-Quaglio (com 1982), vol. 1, p. 2.

18. On the technical significance of the verb "trattare," see E. R. Curtius, *European Literature* (Eng. trans. 1963), p. 222.

"Dire [in rima]" meant to "write poetry." As a title, "le dit de . . . ," "il detto di . . . ," was common in French and Italian. (Compare "Il detto del gatto lupesco" [*Poeti del Duecento*, ed. Contini, vol. 2, pp. 285–293], for example, that may have had an influence on Brunetto Latini [*Tesoretto*] and on Dante, especially in this first canto.)

19. Recently P. Nicosia (1969), pp. 17–33, has identified the "ben" with the beasts. His interpretation has some merit. I might add that the beasts, as temptations, do lead the wayfarer to realize his powerlessness, and only when they force him to turn back does the wayfarer face in the direction that Virgil will later impose. I cannot, however, construe "il ben" of the poem so narrowly. The "good" that the wayfarer finds is the whole process of conversion; the beasts only provide a lesson leading to that ultimate benefit.

20. Graziolo, the Ottimo, Landino, Gelli, Daniello, Magalotti, Fraticelli, and Cornoldi express similar thoughts in their commentaries; that "il ben" is the lesson of evil is suggested in the editions of Torraca, Pietrobono, and Grabher. For F. Palleschi (1905), p. 11, it is "l'apparenza di Virgilio." F. Mazzoni (com 1967, pp. 54–55) gives a thorough history of the critical problem; I disagree, however, with his view that the "ben" is a "presa di coscienza da parte del poeta" in verses 2–3. Knowledge of evil does not imply the ability to avoid evil; such knowledge was gained by Adam and Eve at the Fall. I have argued in earlier chapters that I do not believe a neo-Pelagian interpretation would be acceptable to Dante or that it squares with the text; it is not until Virgil arrives as the bearer of the first movement in grace that the wayfarer begins to make progress in the right direction; of himself he can do nothing. See the synopsis of P. Nicosia (1969), pp. 19–26, and the entry of D. Consoli, "bene," *ED*, vol. 1 (1970), pp. 569–572, unfortunately without bibliography.

21. Cited in F. Mazzoni (com 1967), p. 52.

22. Boccaccio is followed by Lombardi (com 1791) and G. Fallani (com 1965), among others; cf. also P. Nicosia (1969), p. 22.

For Benvenuto (com 1373–1380; vol. I, p. 27), as for Jacopo della Lana and the Ottimo, the good is to be seen in the punishment of the damned: "Sed quid est istud bonum? Dicunt aliqui: certe virtutes et bona moralia reperiuntur in isto mundo inter vicia, sicut rosa inter spinas. Tu vero dic et melius quod bonum, quod hic reperitur, est multiplex; nam per istam inspectionem et considerationem viciorum et suppliciorum eorumdem apparet punitio malorum, emendatio multorum, et perfectio bonorum. Poena etiam in se bona est, ratione justitiae quae bona est, ut testatur Boetius in quarto [*Consolatio* IV, 4]."

Serravalle (com 1416–1417) echoes Benvenuto: the "ben" is divine justice and its effects: "Que sunt illa bona? Dicit quod est divina iustitia et etiam humana, conversio sepe peccatorum, abiectio peccatorum, et conversio ad virtutes" (p. 28). For Stefano da Ricaldone (com 1474; vol. I, pp. 9–10) it is the return to virtue from vice; for Scartazzini (2nd ed. com 1896, followed by F. Mazzoni, com 1967), it is the "risveglio, principio della salute . . . nella selva." For I. Del Lungo (1921, p. 103), the good is salvation, as it is for Flamini (1916b), vol. 2, p. 6. For Chimenz it is "la sua liberazione dal peccato e dell'errore, la salvezza della sua anima" (com 1962, p. 4). Cf. Siebzehner-Vivanti, *Dizionario* (1954),

s. v. "bene." For Sapegno (com 1955; rprt. 1957) and Porena (com 1946; rprt. 1951, p. 8), it is the meeting with Virgil.

P. Venturi (com 1732; ed. 1826, vol. I, p. 32) believed that it was the teaching that Dante received and also "la strada, che vi trovai per salire al cielo." With this last I substantially agree.

23. Vellutello and Castelvetro echo him. The thesis and its modifications was pursued in the nineteenth century by Andreoli, G. Rossetti, B. Bianchi, Palmieri, and Scartazzini, and in the twentieth century by Rossi (com Rossi/ Frascino), Casini-Barbi, G. A. Venturi, Vandelli, Porena, Momigliano, Montanari, and Sapegno. See F. Mazzoni (com 1967), p. 53.

24. C. S. Singleton, "The Three Conversions," in *Dante Studies 2* (1958), pp. 39–56. R. Roedel (1959, pp. 1–12) also saw the dominant motif of *Inferno* I as the "cammino della redenzione."

25. See the article on "conversion" by Jean Giblet and Pierre Grelot in Léon-Dufour, *DBT*, p. 486. I do not imply that Dante necessarily knew or was consciously using these Hebrew and Greek terms. Lactantius discusses the question of retracing the path of sin and "metanoia" in the *Divine Institutes* VI, 24 (pp. 462–464).

26. W. Staerk, "Anakephalaiosis," in *Reallexikon für Antike und Christentum*, vol. 1 (1950), 411–414. E. Scharl, *Recapitulatio mundi* (1941). Brian O. Murdoch, *The Recapitulated Fall* (1974). Freccero, "Terza Rima" (1983, p. 11; rprt. 1986, p. 317), refers to St. Augustine, *De doctrina christiana* III, 30 (*On Christian Doctrine*, pp. 104–106), where the sixth of the seven *Rules* of Tyconius, "Of Recapitulation," is mentioned (*Regula* VI, "De recipulatione" [*PL* 18, cols. 53–55]). H. Urs von Balthasar (1973), p. 59. E. Mâle (1958), p. 191. For many examples of the traditional prefiguration-fulfillment pattern of exegesis between the two Testaments of the Bible, the reader might consult the *Pictor in carmine*, a medieval guide for painters (text ed. by M. R. James), and Schmidt, *Die Armenbibeln* (1959). See also J. Daniélou (1951; 1956 and 1950; 1960).

27. Singleton, "The Vistas in Retrospect" (1965b; rprt. 1966). A. S. Bernardo noted that the beasts tempting the wayfarer come in an order reversed from the order of the areas they represent in hell; in fact they come in an order perceived by Satan from the bottom of Cocytus ("The Three Beasts and Perspective," 1963, pp. 15–24).

28. On the question of the climb in pride, see Chapter 2, esp. pp. 19–30 above.

29. According to Dante, thirty-five was the "arc" or high point of life (*Convivio* IV, xxiii, 8–10).

30. I realize it could be objected that the wayfarer's twisting around on Satan is a change in direction, but the reverse is true: the turning at that point is made to preserve the ultimate single direction of the "altro viaggio." See J. Freccero (1961a), pp. 168–181; rprt. 1986, pp. 70–92.

31. St. Thomas repeats this idea many times: "Since man cannot return to one member of a pair of contraries without moving away from the other extreme, he must, in order to return to the state of rectitude *by means of grace, move away*

from the sin whereby he had swerved from rectitude. And because man is chiefly directed toward the ultimate end, but, by his own will, is also turned away from it, it is not only necessary for man to abandon sin in the external act, but also to renounce it in his will, *for the purpose of rising again from sin*" (*SCG* III, ch. 158, 1–3; p. 256; trans. adapted). St. Benedict's *Rule*, cap. 7, uses the same scriptural axioms of humiliation in proud exaltation and exaltation in humility.

I should emphasize that Dante's wayfarer is not at a *bivium*, or crossroads, in a classical, or even modern, sense (see, however, M. Dozon [1969], pp. 7, 18, who perceives the dilemma as a "carrefours"). It is central to Christian thought that there be one path in Christ. The "ben," the first step of conversion in *Inferno* I symbolized by the reversal of direction, corrects the "ritrosi passi" of aversion and sin (cf. *Purgatorio* X, 123).

32. As a gloss on *Inferno* I, 117, C. S. Singleton (com 1970–1975), following Pietro di Dante, points to the biblical use of "second death" for "spiritual death" or damnation in Revelation 20:14 and 21:8. St. Lucia refers to death with the same metaphor in *Inferno* II, 107: "Non vedi tu la morte che'l combatte . . . ?"
Cf. N. Tommaseo (1865), pp. 76–102.

The cry of the wastrels in *Inferno* XIII, 118, "Or accorri, accorri, morte" simply demonstrates that they are fixed in their earthly self-destructiveness; they parody such petitions as those of Psalm 69:2 (70:1): "O Lord make haste to help me," or of Psalm 70:12 (71:12): "O my God, make haste to my help." Graziolo, Boccaccio, and Benvenuto believe that it is a wish for the annihilation of the soul; while this cannot be denied as a possible desire on the part of those who have destroyed "their substance," it cannot be fulfilled in a Christian universe where the soul is immortal. For a fuller discussion of the question and a bibliography, see F. Mazzoni (com 1967), pp. 139–145, esp. pp. 142–143, and L. Cassata, "morte," esp. "seconda morte," *ED*, vol. 3 (1971), pp. 1040–1041.

33. Singleton, "The Vistas in Retrospect" (1965b; rprt. 1966).

A failure to understand this process hindered, for example, comprehension of the relation of the beasts with the three areas of Hell, because, they were in the opposite order in the prologue, *Inferno* I. See A. Masseron (1922), p. 142.

Dante has Virgil use the same reverse technique throughout his discussion in *Inferno* XI; note especially the sins of violence, vv. 28–33. We might remark also that the normal tendency in Italian is to reverse the former-latter pattern usual in English.

34. *DCD* XIV, 13; LCL ed., vol. IV, pp. 342–343.

35. Hugh of St. Victor, *De sacramentis*, Lib, pars viii, cap. 3; *PL* 176, col. 307. *On the Sacraments*, p. 143.

36. *Moralia in Job* XXIII, 51; *Morals*, vol. III, i, p. 45. "All the devil's will is unjust and yet while God permits it, all his power is just." *Moralia* XVIII, 4; *Morals*, vol. II, p. 319.

37. *Moralia in Job* XXXIII, 25; *Morals*, vol. III, ii, p. 580; *PL* 76, cols. 688–689.

BIBLIOGRAPHY

EDITIONS, COMMENTARIES, AND TRANSLATIONS OF THE
DIVINA COMMEDIA CONSULTED

Works from this bibliography are cited in the text with the prefix "com." For a listing of early commentaries and a selection of the more important modern ones see R. Hollander, "A Checklist" (1983b).

Andreoli (1865). *La Divina Commedia di Dante Alighieri* col Commento di Raffaello Andreoli. Firenze: G. Barbèra, 1887.

Anonimo Fiorentino (ca. 1400). *Commento alla Divina Commedia d'Anonimo Fiorentino del secolo XIV, ora per la prima volta stampato a cura di Pietro Fanfani*. Bologna: G. Romagnoli, 1866–1874.

Anonimo Latino (ca. 1330?). "Edited from the longer forms of the commentary in the British Library and the Pierpont Morgan Library, and from the shorter forms in the Munich, Seville, Florence Libraries, together with Italian translations." Ed. Vincenzo Cioffari. Forthcoming.

Anonimo Selmiano (ca. 1337). *Chiose anonime alla prima Cantica della Divina Commedia di un contemporaneo del Poeta, pubblicate . . . da Francesco Selmi*. Torino: Stamperia Reale, 1865.

Balbo (1853). *Canto I e II dell'Inferno con un commento critico*. In *Vita di Dante scritta da Cesare Balbo con le annotazioni di Emmanuele Rocco*. Napoli: Presso Gabriele Rondinella, 1853.

Benvenuto da Imola (1373–1380). *Benevenuti de Rambaldis de Imola Comentum super Dantis Aldighierij Comoediam, nunc primum integre in lucem editum sumptibus Guilielmi Warren Vernon, curante Jacopo Philippo Lacaita*. Florentiae: G. Barbèra, 1887.

Bianchi (1868). *La Commedia di Dante Alighieri, novamente riveduta nel testo e dichiarata da Brunone Bianchi*. Firenze: Successori Le Monnier, 1868. [This is the 7th ed. of the commentary of Paolo Costa that Bianchi first made substantially his own in the 3rd ed. of 1844 (Firenze: Le Monnier), *La Divina Commedia di Dante Alighieri col comento di P. Costa notabilmente accresciuto dall'abbate Brunone Bianchi*.]

Binyon (1933–1943). *Dante's Inferno Translated into English Triple Rhyme by Laurence Binyon*. London: Macmillan and Co., 1933. *Purgatorio*, 1943. *Paradiso*, 1943. *The Divine Comedy*, rprt. *The Portable Dante*. With notes from

C. H. Grandgent. Ed. with intro. Paolo Milano. New York: The Viking Press, 1947; rprt. Penguin Books, 1970. [Several reprintings.]

Boccaccio, Giovanni (1373). *Esposizioni sopra la Comedia di Dante,* a cura di Giorgio Padoan. Vol. VI of *Tutte le opere di Giovanni Boccaccio,* a cura di Vittore Branca. Milano: Mondadori, 1965.

Bosco/Reggio (1979). *La Divina Commedia a cura di Umberto Bosco e Giovanni Reggio.* Firenze: F. Le Monnier, 1979.

Buti, Francesco da (1385–1395). *Commento di Francesco da Buti sopra la Divina Commedia di Dante Allighieri . . . per cura di Crescentino Giannini.* Pisa: Fratelli Nistri, 1885–1862.

Butler (1880–1892). *The Hell of Dante Alighieri. . . .* Notes by A. J. Butler. London and New York: Macmillan, 1892. [1st ed.]

Caligaris (1969). *La Divina Commedia di Dante Alighieri a cura di Pietro Caligaris.* Roma: De Luca, 1969.

Carlyle-Wicksteed (1932). *The Divine Comedy of Dante Alighieri. The Carlyle-Wicksteed translation.* Intro. C. H. Grandgent. Bibliog. Ernest Hatch Wilkins. The Modern Library. New York: Random House, 1932.

Cary (1805). [Trans. of *Inferno* finished in 1805.] *The Vision: or Hell, Purgatory, and Paradise of Dante Alighieri.* Trans. H[enry] F[rancis] Cary. [Many printings.] London, New York, Chicago, and Toronto, 1814. *Dante: The Divine Comedy.* Trans. H. F. Cary. Intro. Edmund G. Gardner. London: J. M. Dent and Sons Ltd.; New York: E. P. Dutton and Co. Inc., 1908; rprt. 1945.

Casini (1889). *La Divina Commedia commentata da Tommaso Casini.* 4th ed. Firenze: G. C. Sansoni, 1896.

Casini/Barbi (1921). *La Divina Commedia di Dante Alighieri con il commento di Tommaso Casini. 6ª ediz. rinnovata e accresciuta per cura di S. A. Barbi.* Firenze: G. C. Sansoni, 1944; rprt. 1973–1976. [See also F. Mazzoni (1972–1973).]

Cassata (1987–1988). "Il canto I della Comédia: Testo e Commento. Esercitazioni di Letteratura Italiana." Ed. Letterio Cassata. Università della Calabria. Dipartimento di Filologia. Anno Accademico 1987–1988. Mimeograph.

Castellino (1946). *La Divina Commedia a cura di O. Castellino.* Torino: Società Editrice Torinese, 1946.

Castelvetro (ca. 1570). *Sposizione di Lodovico Castelvetro a XXIX Canti dell'Inferno dantesco, ora per la prima volta data in luce da Giovanni Franciosi.* Modena: Società tipografica: Antica Tipografia Soliani, 1886.

Chimenz (1962). *La Divina Commedia di Dante Alighieri a cura di Siro A. Chimenz.* Torino: UTET, 1962.

Chiose marciane. Cited in F. Mazzoni (com 1967).

Ciardi (1954). *The Inferno. A Verse Rendering for the Modern Reader by John Ciardi.* Historical intro. Archibald T. MacAllister. New Brunswick, NJ: Rutgers University Press, 1954; rprt. Mentor Books, New American Library, 1982.

Codice Cassinese (1350?). *Il codice cassinese della Divina Commedia . . . per cura dei monaci benedettini della badia di Monte Cassino.* Tipografia di Monte Cassino, 1865. [1326–1378?] [See pp. xii, xl of this edition for conjecture on dating.]

Cornoldi (1887). *La Divina Commedia di Dante Alighieri col comento di Giovanni Maria Cornoldi.* Roma: A. Befani, 1888 [– 1887].

Costa (1819–1821). *La Divina Commedia con brevi note di Paolo Costa.* Bologna: Cardinali e Frulli, 1816–1827.

Costa-Borghi (1840). *La Divina Commedia di Dante Alighieri con le note di Paolo Costa e gli argomenti dell'Ab. G. Borghi, adorna di 500 vignette designate ed incise in legno da A. Fabris ed una vita appositamente scritta dal Prof. Ab. Melchior Missirini. Seconda Edizione Originale Italiana eseguita sotto la direzione dei sigg. Proff. G. B. Niccolini e G. Bezzuoli.* Firenze: Nello Stabilimento Artistico Tipografico Fabris, 1840. 4 vols. [Missirini's *Vita* is not found in these volumes.]

Daniello (1568). *Dante con l'espositione di M. Bernard[in]o Daniello da Lucca sopra la sua Comedia dell'Inferno, del Purgatorio, & del Paradiso.* . . . Venetia: Pietro da Fino, 1568. Rprt. University Press of New England, 1988.

Del Lungo (1926). *La Divina Commedia commentata da Isidoro del Lungo.* Firenze: F. Le Monnier, 1926.

Dolce (1555). *La Divina Commedia di Dante con gli argomenti, allegorie, e dichiarazioni di Lodovico Dolce.* Venezia: G. Giolito de Ferrari, et fratelli, 1555.

Fallani (1965). *La Divina Commedia a cura di Giovanni Fallani.* Messina-Firenze: G. D'Anna, 1965.

"falso Boccaccio" (1375). *Chiose sopra Dante: Testo inedito ora per la prima volta pubblicata* [da G. G. Warren, Lord Vernon]. Firenze: Piatti, 1846.

Foscolo (1842–1843). *La Commedia di Dante Alighieri illustrata da Ugo Foscolo.* [Ed. G. Mazzini.] Londra: P. Rolandi, 1842–1843.

Fraticelli (1852). *La Divina Commedia di Dante Alighieri col comento di P[ietro] Fraticelli. Nuova ediz. con giunte e correzioni.* . . . Firenze: G. Barbèra, 1886.

Gelli (1541–1563). *Commento edito e inedito sopra la Divina Commedia* [di Giovan Battista Gelli]. Ed. C. Negroni. Firenze: Bocca, 1887. [Lectures on *Inferno* I–XXV delivered 1553–1563.]

Giacalone (1968). *La Divina Commedia a cura di Giuseppe Giacalone.* Roma: A. Signorelli, 1968.

Giuliani (1861). *Metodo di commentare la Commedia di D. Allighieri proposto da Giambattista Giuliani.* Firenze: F. Le Monnier, 1861. [Commentaries to *Inferno* I–IV.]

Gmelin (1954–1957). *Die Göttliche Komödie, übersetzt von Hermann Gmelin. Kommentar.* Stuttgart: Klett, 1954–1957.

Grabher (1934–1936). *La Divina Commedia, col commento di Carlo Grabher.* Firenze: La Nuova Italia, 1934–1936. [See also 3rd ed., Bari: Laterza, 1964–1965.]

Grandgent (1909–1913). *La Divina Commedia di Dante Alighieri.* Ed. and annotated by C[harles] H[all] Grandgent. Heath's Modern Language Series. Boston: D. C. Heath, 1909–1913. [See also the revised ed. of 1933.]

Graziolo de' Bambaglioli (1324). *Il commento dantesco di Graziolo de' Bambaglioli, dal 'Colombino' di Siviglia con altri codici raffrontato. Contributi di Antonio Fiammazzo all'edizione critica.* Savona: D. Bertolotto e C., 1915.

Guido da Pisa (1327–1328). *Guido da Pisa's Expositiones et Glose super Comediam Dantis, or Commentary on Dante's Inferno*. Ed. with notes and intro. Vincenzo Cioffari. Albany, NY: State University of New York Press, 1974.

Guiniforto delli Bargigi (ca. 1440). *Lo Inferno della Commedia di Dante Alighieri col comento di Guiniforto delli Bargigi, tratto da due manoscritti inediti del secolo decimo quinto con introduzione e note dell'avv°., G. Zac[c]heroni*. Marsilia: L. Mossy & Firenze: G. Molini, 1838.

Jacopo Alighieri (Jacopo di Dante) (1322). *Chiose alla cantica dell'Inferno di Dante Alighieri, scritte da Jacopo Alighieri, pubblicate per la prima volta in corretta lezione con riscontri e facsimili di codici, e precedute da una indagine critica per cura di Jarro* [Giulio Piccini]. Firenze: R. Bemporad e figlio, 1915.

Jacopo della Lana (ca. 1324–1328). *Comedia di Dante degli Allaghieri col Commento di Jacopo della Lana bolognese, a cura di Luciano Scarabelli*. Bologna: Tipografia Regia, 1866–1867.

Landino (1481). *Comento di Christophoro Landino fiorentino sopra la Comedia di Danthe Alighieri Poeta fiorentino*. Firenze: Nicholò di Lorenzo della Magna, 1481.

Lombardi (1791). *La Divina Commedia, novamente corretta, spiegata e difesa da F. B. L. M. C.* [i.e., Fra Baldassare Lombardi, minore conventuale]. Roma: A. Fulgoni, 1791[–1792].

Longfellow (1867). *The Divine Comedy of Dante Alighieri translated by H. W. Longfellow*. Boston: Ticknor & Fields, 1867.

Magalotti (1665). *Comento sui primi cinque Canti dell' Inferno di Dante, e quattro Lettere del conte Lorenzo Magalotti* [1637–1712]. Milano: Imp. Regia Stamperia, 1819.

Malagoli (1955–1956). *La Divina Commedia, note e commento di Luigi Malagoli*. Milano: "La Prora," 1955–1956.

Mandelbaum (1980). *The Divine Comedy of Dante Alighieri: Inferno. A verse translation by Allen Mandelbaum. Notes by Allen Mandelbaum and Gabriel Marruzzo, with Larry Magnus. Drawings by Barry Moser*. Berkeley: University of California Press, 1980; rprt. New York: Bantam Books, 1982.

Mattalia (1960). *La Divina Commedia a cura di Daniele Mattalia*. Milano: A. Rizzoli, 1975.

Mazzoni, F. (1967). *Saggio di un nuovo commento alla "Divina Commedia": Inferno—Canti I–III. Quaderni degli "Studi Danteschi"* 4. Firenze: G. C. Sansoni, 1967.

———. (1972–1973). *La Divina Commedia con i commenti di T. Casini/S. A. Barbi e di A. Momigliano. Introduzione e aggiornamento bibliografico-critico di Francesco Mazzoni*. [*Inferno* and *Purgatorio*.] Firenze: G. C. Sansoni, 1972–1973.

Momigliano (1946–1951). *La Divina Commedia commentata da Attilio Momigliano*. Firenze: G. C. Sansoni, 1946–1951. [See also F. Mazzoni (1972–1973).]

Montanari (1949–1951). *La Divina Commedia* [a cura di Fausto Montanari]. Brescia: "La Scuola" Editrice, 1954–1958.

Musa (1971–1984). *Dante's Inferno, Translated with Notes and Commentary by*

Mark Musa. Bloomington and London: Indiana University Press, 1971. [*Purgatorio*, 1981; *Paradiso*, 1984.]

Norton (1891–1892). *The Divine Comedy of Dante Alighieri*. Translated by Charles Eliot Norton. Boston and New York: Houghton Mifflin and Co., 1891–1892; London: Constable and Co., 1901; Cambridge: The Riverside Press, 1901; rprt. 1902; rev. ed. 1903.

Oelsner (1899–1901). *The Temple Classics Translation of Dante*. London: J. M. Dent, 1899–1901. [Notes by H. Oelsner to *Inferno* (1900) and *Purgatorio* (1901).]

Ottimo (1333). *L'Ottimo Commento della Divina Commedia* [Andrea Lancia]. *Testo inedito d'un contemporaneo di Dante* . . . [ed. Alessandro Torri]. Pisa: N. Capurro, 1827–1829.

Nidobeato (1477). *La Comedia di Dante Aldighieri, excelso poeta fiorentino*. Milano: [Ludovicus & Albertus Pedemontani for Martino Paolo Nidobeato & Guido Terzago], 1477–1478.

Padoan (1967). *La Divina Commedia: Inferno [I–VIII] a cura di Giorgio Padoan*. Firenze: F. Le Monnier, 1967.

Palmieri (1898–1899). *Commento alla Divina Commedia di Dante Alighieri di Domenico Palmieri, S. I.* Prati: Giachetti, 1898–1899.

Pasquini/Quaglio (1982). *Commedia di Dante Alighieri, a cura di Emilio Pasquini e Antonio Quaglio*. Milano: Garzanti, 1982.

Passerini (1897–1901). *La Divina Commedia di Dante Alighieri novamente annotata da G. L. Passerini*. Firenze: G. C. Sansoni, 1897–1901.

Petrocchi (1966–1967). *La Commedia secondo l'antica vulgata a cura di Giorgio Petrocchi*. Milano: A. Mondadori, 1966–1967.

Pézard (1965). *Oeuvres complètes de Dante Alighieri, traduction et commentaires par André Pézard*. Paris: Gallimard, 1965.

Pietro Alighieri (Pietro di Dante) (1340–1341; 1348?–1355?). *Petri Allegherii super Dantis ipsius genitoris Comoediam Commentarium, nunc primum in lucem editum* . . . [ed. Vincenzo Nannucci]. Florentiae: G. Piatti, 1845.

––––––. *Il "Commentarium" di Pietro Alighieri nelle redazioni ashburnhamiana e ottoboniana*. Ed. R. della Vedova & M. T. Silvotti. Nota introduttiva di Egidio Guidubaldi. Firenze: L. S. Olschki, 1978. [*Inferno* only.]

Pietrobono (1946). *La Divina Commedia di Dante Alighieri, commentata da Luigi Pietrobono*. 3rd ed. [1st 1924–1930]. Torino: S.E.I., 1946. 4th ed. rev. 1944; rprt. 1964.

Plumptre (1886–1887). *The Commedia and Canzoniere of Dante Alighieri: A New Translation with Notes, Essays and a Biographical Introduction by E. H. Plumptre, D.D., Dean of Wells*. London: Wm. Isbister, 1886–1887.

Poletto (1894). *La Divina Commedia di Dante Allighieri con commento del prof. Giacomo Poletto*. Roma & Tournay: Desclée, Lefebvre, 1894.

Porena (1946–1948). *La Divina Commedia di Dante Alighieri commentata da Munfredi Porena*. Bologna: N. Zanichelli, 1946–1948. Rprt. 1951; new ed. rev. 1961.

Ricaldone (1474). *La Commedia di Dante Alighieri col commento inedito di Stefano*

Talice da Ricaldone. Pubblicato per cura di Vincenzo Promis, Bibliotecario di S. M. e di Carlo Negroni, Socio della R. Commissione dei Testi di Lingua. 2ª ed. Vol. I: *Inferno*. Milano: Ulrico Hoepli, 1888.

Rivalta (1946). *La Divina Commedia . . . col commento di Ercole Rivalta*. Firenze: E. Vallechi, 1946.

Rossetti, G. (1826–1827). *La Divina Commedia di Dante Alighieri con commento analitico di Gabriele Rossetti*. Londra: John Murray, 1826–1827. [*Inferno* only.]

Rossi. See Rossi/Frascino.

Rossi/Frascino (1923–1948). *La Divina Commedia commentata da Vittorio Rossi e Salvatore Frascino*. Milano-Roma: Società Editrice Dante Alighieri, 1941–1948. [Rossi's commentary to *Inferno* published Napoli: F. Perella, 1923 (rprt. here 1941).]

Salinari-Romagnoli (1980). *La Divina Commedia a cura di Carlo Salinari, Sergio Romagnoli, Antonio Lanza. Inferno*. Roma: Editori Riuniti, 1980.

Sapegno (1955). *La Divina Commedia a cura di Natalino Sapegno*. Milano-Napoli: R. Ricciardi, 1957. [See also 2nd ed. Firenze: La Nuova Italia, 1968.]

Sayers (1949). *The Comedy of Dante Alighieri the Florentine. Translated by Dorothy L. Sayers*. Harmondsworth, Middlesex: Penguin Books. *Cantica* I: *Hell* (*L'Inferno*), 1949.

Scarano (1924–1928). *La Divina Commedia di Dante Alighieri commentata da Nicola Scarano*. [Palermo]: R. Sandron, 1924–1928.

Scartazzini (1874–1882). *La Divina Commedia di Dante Alighieri, riveduta nel testo e commentata da G. A. Scartazzini*. Leipzig: Brockhaus, 1874–1890. 2nd ed. 1896. [And see the greatly revised 2nd ed., 1900, rprt. Bologna: Forni, 1965.]

Scartazzini/Vandelli (1929). *La Divina Commedia col commento scartazziniano rifatto da Giuseppe Vandelli, 9ª ed*. Milano: Ulrico Hoepli, 1929. [20th ed. rprt. 1983.]

Serravalle (1416–1417). *Fratris Johannis de Serravalle Ord. Min. Episcopi et Principis Firmani. Translatio et Comentum totius libri Dantis Aldigherii, cum textu italico Fratris Bartholomaei a Colle eiusdem Ordinis, nunc primum edita* [a cura di Fr. Marcellino da Civezza & Fr. Teofilo Domenichelli]. Prati: Giachetti, 1891.

Sinclair (1939). *The Divine Comedy of Dante Alighieri with Translation and Comment by John D. Sinclair. Inferno*. Oxford: The Bodley Head; New York: Oxford University Press, 1939. Rprt. 1946, 1961, 1977.

Singleton (1970–1975). *The Divine Comedy, Translated, with a Commentary, by Charles S. Singleton*. 6 vols. Princeton: Princeton University Press, 1970–1975.

Soprano (1955). *La Divina Commedia nell'interpretazione e nel commento di Edoardo Soprano*. Firenze: E. Vallecchi, 1955.

Steiner (1921). *La Divina Commedia commentata da Carlo Steiner*. Torino: G. B. Paravia, 1921.

Tommaseo (1837). *La Divina Commedia con le note di Niccolò Tommaseo e introduzione di Umberto Cosmo*. Torino: UTET, 1927–1934. [Rprt. of 2nd, definitive ed., Milano: F. Pagnoni, 1865.]

Torraca (1905). *La Divina Commedia di Dante Alighieri nuovamente commentata da Francesco Torraca*. 4th ed. Milano-Roma-Napoli: Albrighi, Segati, 1920.

Vandelli. See Scartazzini/Vandelli.

Vellutello (1544). *La Comedia di Dante Alighieri con la nova espositione di Alessandro Vellutello*. Vinegia: Francesco Marcolini, 1544.

Venturi, G. A. (1924–1926). *La Divina Commedia commentata da Giovanni Antonio Venturi*. Milano: C. Signorelli, 1924–1926.

Venturi, P. (1732). *La Divina Commedia di Dante Alighieri . . . col Commento del P. Pompeo Venturi*. Firenze: L. Ciardetti, 1821. Rprt. 1826.

Villani, F. (ca. 1400). Filippo Villani. *Il comento al primo canto dell' "Inferno."* *Pubblicato ed annotato da Giuseppe Cugnoni*. Collezione di opuscoli danteschi inediti o rari 31–32. Città di Castello: S. Lapi, 1896.

PRIMARY SOURCES

Alain de Lille. *Anticlaudianus*. Ed. R. Bossuat. Texte critique avec une introduction et tables. Paris: Librairie Philosophique J. Vrin, 1955.

———. *Anticlaudianus of the Good and the Perfect*. Trans. and comm. James J. Sheridan. Toronto: Pontifical Institute of Mediaeval Studies, 1973.

[Albert the Great] Albertus Magnus. *Opera omnia*. Ed. B. Geyer. Aschendorff: Monasterii Westfalorum, 1972.

———. *Man and the Beasts: De animalibus (Books 22–26)*. Trans. James J. Scanlan. Binghamton, NY: MRTS, 1986.

Albumasar [Ja' far ibn Muhammad (Abu Ma'shar) al-Balkhi]. *De Magnis Coniunctibus*. Venetiis: expensis Melchiorem Sessa per Jacobum Pentium de Leucho, 1515. (In the University of Illinois Library, Urbana.)

Alexander von Roes. *Die Schriften des Alexander von Roes*. Ed. and trans. H. Grundmann and H. Heimpel. Weimar: H. Böhlaus Nachfolger, 1949.

Allegoriae in Sacram Scripturam. See Garnier de Rochefort.

[St. Ambrose] Ambrosius. *Expositio in Evangelium secundum Lucam*. PL 15, cols. 1527–1850.

———. *Hexaemeron*. PL 14, cols. 125–274. *Hexameron, Paradise, and Cain and Abel*. Trans. John J. Savage. FC. New York: Fathers of the Church, Inc., 1961.

[Aquinas, St. Thomas] S. Thomae Aquinatis. *In decem libros Ethicorum Expositio*. Cura et studio Raymundi M. Spiazzi. Taurini-Romae [Torino-Roma]: Marietti, 1949.

———. *Sententiae libri ethicorum Aristoteles*. In *Opera omnia*. Ed. Fratrum Praedicatorum Scta. Sabinae. Roma: Sancta Sabina, 1969. Vol. 47, pt. 1. *Commentary on the Nicomachean Ethics*. Trans. C. I. Litzinger. 2 vols. Chicago: Henry Regnery Company, 1964.

———. [*Summa contra gentiles*] *On the Truth of the Catholic Faith: Summa contra gentiles*. Trans. Anton C. Pegis, J. F. Anderson, Vernon J. Bourke, et al. Garden City, NY: Doubleday, 1955–1957. Rprt. as *Summa contra gentiles*. Notre Dame, IN: Notre Dame Press, 1975.

———. *Summa Theologica*. Ed. Ottawa Institute of Medieval Studies. 4 vols. Ottawa: Impensis Studii Generalis Ordinis Praedicatorum, 1941–1944.

Summa Theologica. Trans. Fathers of the English Dominican Province. 3 vols. New York: Benziger Brothers, 1947–1948.

Aristotle. *The Complete Works of Aristotle*. The Revised Oxford Translation. Ed. Jonathon Barnes. Bollingen Series. Princeton: Princeton University Press: 1984.

——. *On Generation and Corruption*. In J. Barnes, ed. *The Complete Works*. Vol. 1, pp. 512–554.

——. *Historia animalium*. 2 vols. *Parts of Animals*; *Generation of Animals*. Trans. A. L. Peck. LCL. Cambridge: Harvard University Press; London: William Heinemann, 1965–1970.

——. [*De iuventute et senectute*] *On Youth and Old Age*. In *The Complete Works of Aristotle*. Vol. 1, pp. 745–763.

——. *Nicomachean Ethics*. Trans. Martin Ostwald. LLA. Indianapolis-New York: Bobbs-Merrill, 1962.

[Augustine of Hippo, St.]. *Augustine: Earlier Writings*. Trans. John H. S. Burleigh. LCC, vol. VI. London: SCM Press, 1953.

——. *Augustine: Later Works*. Trans. John Burnby. LCC, vol. VIII. London: SCM Press, 1955.

——. *De beata vita*. PL 32, cols. 959–976. *The Happy Life*. Ed. and trans. Ludwig Schopp. St. Louis, MO, and London: B. Herder, 1939. (Facing Latin text.)

——. [*De civitate Dei*] *The City of God Against the Pagans*. Ed. and trans. G. E. McCracken, et al. LCL. Cambridge: Harvard University Press; London: William Heinemann, 1957–1972.

——. *Confessions*. Trans. William Watts [1631]. LCL. Cambridge: Harvard University Press; London: William Heinemann, 1912; rprt. 1946.

——. *The Confessions of St. Augustine*. Trans. Francis J. Sheed. New York and London: Sheed and Ward, 1943; rprt. 1951.

——. *De correctione et gratia*. PL 44, cols. 917–959. *Admonition and Grace*. Trans. John Courtney Murray. In *Writings of St. Augustine* 4. FC 4. New York: CIMA, 1947.

——. *De diversis quaestionibus*. PL 40, cols. 11–147.

——. *De doctrina christiana libri IV*. PL 34, cols. 15–122. *On Christian Doctrine*. Trans. D. W. Robertson. LLA. Indianapolis, IN: Bobbs-Merrill, 1958.

——. *Enarrationes in Psalmos*. PL 36–37. *On the Psalms*. Trans. Dame Scholastica Hebgin and Dame Felicitas Corrigan. ACW, vols. 29–30. Westminster, MD: The Newman Press, 1960. *Expositions on the Book of Psalms*. Ed. A. Cleveland Coxe. NPNF, vol. 8. Grand Rapids, MI: W. B. Eerdmans, 1974.

——. *In Epistolam Joannis ad Parthos*. PL 35, cols. 1977–2062. *On the Epistle of John to the Parthians: Ten Homilies*. In *Homilies on the Gospel According to John and his First Epistle*. Trans. with notes and indices. LF. Oxford: John Henry Parker, 1849.

——. [*Exposition on the Epistle to the Romans*] *Expositio quarandum propositionum ex epistola ad Romanos*. PL 35, cols. 2063–2088.

——. *De Genesi ad Litteram*. Ed. Joseph Zycha. CSEL 28 (Sect. 3, pars 1).

Prague-Vienna-Leipzig: F. Tempsky and G. Freytag, 1893. *The Literal Meaning of Genesis*. Trans. John Hammond Taylor. 2 vols. ACW 42. New York: Newman Press, 1982.

———. *In Joannis Evangelium tractatus CXXIV*. PL 35, cols. 1379–1976. *Homilies on the Gospel According to John and his First Epistle*. Trans. with notes and indices. 2 vols. LF. Oxford: John Henry Parker, 1848–1849.

———. *De natura boni*. PL 42, cols. 551–572. *The Nature of the Good*. Trans. Burleigh in *Earlier Writings*. Pp. 324–348.

———. *De sermone Domini in monte*. PL 34, cols. 1229–1308. *Commentary on the Lord's Sermon on the Mount*. Trans. D. J. Kavanagh. FC, vol. 11. New York: Fathers of the Church Inc., 1951.

———. *Sermones*. PL 38, cols. 23–1484. [*Homilies on the Gospels*] *Sermons on Selected Lessons of the New Testament*. A Select Library of the Post-Nicene Fathers of the Christian Church. Ed. Philip Schaff. Vol. 4. Grand Rapids, MI: W. B. Eerdmans, 1974.

———. *De spiritu et littera*. PL 44, cols. 199–246. *The Spirit and the Letter*. In *Augustine: Later Works*. Trans. John Burnaby. Pp. 182–250.

———. *De Trinitate libri XV*. PL 42, cols. 819–1098. *The Trinity*. In *Augustine: Later Works*. Trans. John Burnaby. Pp. 17–181.

———. *De vera religione*. PL 34, cols. 121–171.

Bartholomaeus Anglicus [Bartholomaeus de Glanville]. *De proprietatibus rerum*. Nürnberg: A. Koberger, 1483. (In the University of Illinois Library, Urbana.)

[St. Benedict, Abbot of Monte Cassino]. *Sancti Benedicti Regula monasteriorum*. Ed. Dom Cuthbertus Butler. 3rd ed. Freiburg im Breisgau: Herder, 1935.

———. *St. Benedict's Rule for Monasteries*. Trans. Leonard J. Doyle. Collegeville, MN: The Liturgical Press, St. John's Abbey, 1948.

Berchorius, Petrus [Pierre Bersuire]. *De formis figurisque deorum: Textus e codice Brux., Bibl. Reg. 863–9 critice editus*. Ed. J. Engels. Utrecht: Instituut voor Laat Latijn der Rijksuniversiteit, 1966.

———. *Ovidius Metamorphoseos moralizatus*. Ed. Fausto Ghisalberti. *Studij Romanzi* 13 (1913): 5–132. "The Ovidius Moralizatus of Petrus Berchorius: an Introduction and Translation." Ed. and trans. William Donald Reynolds. Diss. University of Illinois, Urbana-Champaign, 1971.

———. *Reductium morale, Liber XV, cap. ii–xv*: "*Ovidius moralizatus*." Ed. J. Engels. Utrecht: Instituut voor Laat Latijn der Rijksuniversiteit, 1962.

[St. Bernard of Clairvaux]. *De consideratione*. See *Five Books on Consideration*.

———. *De diligendo Deo*. *Opera*, EC. (1963), vol. 3.

———. *De diligendo Deo liber seu tractatus ad Haimericum S.R.E. Cardinalem et Cancellarium*. PL 182, cols. 973–1000.

———. *Epistolae*. PL 182, cols. 67–662. [*Letters*] *Life and Works of St. Bernard Abbot of Clairvaux*. Ed. Dom John Mabillon. Trans. and ed. Samuel J. Eales. Vol. 3. London: John Hodges, 1896.

———. *Five Books on Consideration, Advice to a Pope*. Trans. John D. Anderson and Elizabeth T. Kennan. Kalamazoo, MI: Cistercian Publications, 1976.

———. *De gradibus humilitatis et superbiae tractatus*. In *Opera* (1963), EC, vol. 3.

Also in *PL* 182, cols. 941–972. *The Steps of Humility*. Trans. George Bosworth Burch. Cambridge, MA: Harvard University Press, 1940; rprt. Notre Dame, IN: University of Notre Dame Press, 1963. *Treatises* II: *The Steps of Humility and Pride. On Loving God.* [*The Steps.* Intro. M. Basil Pennington, trans. M. Ambrose Conway. *On Loving.* Intro. and trans. Robert Walton.] CFS, vol. 13. Kalamazoo, MI: Cistercian Publications, 1973; rprt. 1980.

———. *Sancti Bernardi opera.* Ed. Jean Leclerq, C. H. Talbot, H. M. Rochais. Pref. Christina Mohrmann. Rome: Editiones Cistercienses, 1957+.

———. *Sermones super Cantica Canticorum.* In *Opera* (1957), vol. 1; (1958), vol. 2. *Cantica Canticorum: Eighty-six Sermons on the Song of Songs.* Trans. and ed. Samuel J. Eales. London: Elliott Stock, 1895.

[Bernardus Silvestris]. *Commentum Bernardi Silvestris super sex libros Eneidos Virgilii.* Ed. Guilelmus Riedel. Greifswald: Julius Abel, 1924.

———. *Commentum quod dicitur Bernardi Silvestris super sex libros Eneidos Virgilii. . . . : The Commentary on the First Six Books of the Aeneid of Vergil Commonly Attributed to Bernardus Silvestris.* Ed. Julian Ward Jones and Elizabeth Frances Jones. Lincoln: University of Nebraska Press, 1977. *Commentary on the First Six Books of Virgil's Aeneid.* Ed. and trans. E. G. Schreiber and T. E. Maresca. Lincoln: University of Nebraska Press, 1979.

———. *Bernardi Silvestris De mundi universitate libri duo, sive Megacosmus et Microcosmus.* Ed. Carl Sigmund Barach and Johann Wrobel. Innsbruck: Verlag der Wagner'schen Universitäts-Buchhandlung, 1876; rprt. Frankfurt: Minerva, 1964.

[*Il Bestiario moralizzato*]. Ed. Maria Romano. "Il 'bestiario moralizzato.'" In *Testi e interpretazioni: Studi del Seminario di Filologia Romanza dell'Università di Firenze.* Milano-Napoli: Riccardo Ricciardi, 1978. Pp. 72–888.

"Il bestiario toscano secondo la lezione dei codici di Parigi e di Roma." Ed. M. S. Garver and K. McKenzie in *Studi romanzi* 8 (1912). Rprt. Roma: Società Filologica Romana, 1912.

La Bible moralisée illustrée conservée à Oxford, Paris, et Londres. Société française de reproductions de manuscrits à peintures. Paris: Pour les membres de la Société, 1911–1927.

Bode, Georg Heinrich. *Scriptores rerum mythicarum latini tres.* Cellis, 1834.

Boethius. *The Theological Tractates, the Consolation of Philosophy.* Ed. and trans. H. F. Stewart and E. K. Rand. LCL. London: Heinemann, 1946.

Brunetto Latini. *Li Livres dou Tresor.* Ed. Francis J. Carmody. Berkeley and Los Angeles: University of California Press, 1948. *Il Tesoro di Brunetto Latini volgarizzato da Bono Giamboni.* Ed. P. Chabaille. Emendato da Luigi Gaiter. 4 vols. Collezione di Opere Inedite o Rare, 50–53. Bologna: Gaetano Romagnoli, 1878.

———. *Il Tesoretto.* In *Poeti del Duecento.* Ed. Gianfranco Contini. Vol. 2, pp. 285–393.

Bruni, Leonardo. See Solerti, Angelo, ed.

Buttimer, Charles Henry, ed. *Hugonis de Sancto Victore Didascalicon de studio le-*

gendi. A critical text. Studies in Medieval and Renaissance Latin, X. Washington, DC: Catholic University of America Press, 1939.

Chalcidius. *Timaeus a Calcidio translatus Commentarioque instructus*. Ed. J. H. Waszink in assoc. with P. J. Jensen. In vol. 4 of *Plato Latinus*. Gen. ed. Raymond Klibansky. London and Leyden: Warburg Institute and E. J. Brill, 1962.

Cicero, Marcus Tullius. [*De Officiis*]. *Cicero in Twenty-Eight Volumes, XXI: De Officiis*. Ed. and trans. Walter Miller. LCL. Cambridge: Harvard University Press; London: William Heinemann, 1913; rprt. 1968.

———. *De Senectute, De Amicitia, De Divinatione*. Ed. and trans. William Armistead Falconer. LCL. Cambridge: Harvard University Press; London: William Heinemann, 1923; rprt. 1946.

Le Consulte della Repubblica fiorentina dall'anno MCCLXXX al MCCXCVIII. Ed. Alessandro Gherardi. Firenze: Sansoni, vol. I, 1896; vol. II, 1898.

[Contini, Gianfranco, ed.]. *Poeti del Duecento*. 2 vols. Milano-Napoli: Riccardo Ricciardi, 1960.

[St. Cyprian]. *De Dominica Oratione*. In S. Thasci Caecili Cypriani. *Opera omnia*. Recensuit Guilelmus Hartel. CSEL. Vienna: C. Geroldi, 1868–1871. *The Lord's Prayer*. In *Treatises*. Trans. Roy J. Defferari. FC. New York: Fathers of the Church, Inc., 1985. Pp. 125–159.

———. *De montibus Sina et Sion*. In S. Thasci Caecili Cypriani *Opera omnia*. Recensuit Guilielmus Hartel [Wilhelm von Hartel]. CSEL. Vol. III, pars III, Vienna: C. Geroldi, 1871. [*Opera omnia* Vienna, 1868–1871.]

———. *Treatises*. Trans. Roy J. Defferari. FC. New York: Fathers of the Church, Inc., 1985.

Dante Alighieri. *De vulgari eloquentia*, ed. P. V. Mengaldo; *De Monarchia*, ed. B. Nardi; *Epistole*, ed. A. Frugoni and G. Brugnoli; *Egloge*, ed. E. Cecchini; *Questio*, ed. F. Mazzoni. In *Opere minori*. Vol. 2. Milano-Napoli: Riccardo Ricciardi, 1979.

———. *Il Convivio*. Ed. G. Busnelli and G. Vandelli, intro. Michele Barbi. 2nd ed. Antonio Enzo Quaglio. In *Opere di Dante*, vols. 4–5. Firenze: F. Le Monnier, 1964.

———. *Dantis Alagherii Epistolae: The Letters of Dante*. Ed. Paget Toynbee. 2nd ed. Colin Hardie. Oxford: Clarendon Press, 1966.

———. *Monarchia, Epistole Politiche*. Ed. Francesco Mazzoni. Torino: ERI, 1966.

——— *Vita Nuova*. Ed. Domenico De Robertis. In *Opere minori*. Vol. 1, pt. 1. Milano-Napoli: Riccardo Ricciardi, 1984.

[*Dictionary of Biblical Theology*] *Vocabulaire de théologie biblique*. Ed. Xavier Léon Dufour. Paris: Editions du Cerf, 1962; rev. 1968. Trans. as *Dictionary of Biblical Theology*. Trans. and ed. P. Joseph Cahill and E. M. Stewart. New York: Seabury Press, 1967; 2nd ed. 1973.

[DuCange]. *Glossarium mediae et infimae Latinitatis*. Conditum a Carolo du

Fresne Domino DuCange . . . cum supplementis integris D. P. Carpenterii . . . digessit G. A. L. Henschell . . . Editio Nova . . . Léopold Favre. Niort: L. Favre, 1883–1887.

[Festus the Grammarian]. *Sexti Pompei Festi De verborum significatu quae supersunt cum Pauli Epitome.* Ed. Wallace M. Lindsay. Leipzig: Teubner, 1913.

Garnier de Rochefort. *Allegoriae in universam Sacram Scripturam. PL* 112. [Attributed by Migne to Rabanus Maurus.]

Gioachino da Fiore. *Il Libro delle Figure.* Ed. L. Tondelli. Torino: SEI, 1940. 2 vols. 2nd ed. L. Tondelli, M. Reeves, B. Hirsch-Reich. Torino: SEI, 1953.

Gregory the Great, St. [*Homilies on the Gospel*] *Homiliarum in Evangelia libri duo. PL* 76, cols. 1075–1312.

———. [*Moralia*] *Moralium libri sive expositio in librum Job. PL* 75, cols. 509–1162; *PL* 76, cols. 9–782.

———. *Morals on the Book of Job.* LF. Trans. Members of the English Church. Oxford: John Henry Parker, 1844–1850.

Hennecke, Edgar. *New Testament Apocrypha.* Ed. Wilhelm Schneemelcher. Eng. trans. R. McL. Wilson. 2 vols. Philadelphia: Westminster Press, 1963–1965.

Horace. *Satires, Epistles and Ars Poetica.* Ed. and trans. H. Rushton Fairclough. LCL. Cambridge: Harvard University Press, rprt. 1966.

[Hugh of St. Cher] Hugonis de Sancto Charo. *In Libros Prophetarum Isaiae, Jeremiae et ejusdem Threnorum, Baruch.* Vol. 4. Venetiis: apud Nicolaum Pezzana, 1732.

[Hugh of St. Victor, attributed] Hugonis de Sancto Victore. *De bestiis. PL* 177, cols. 14–154.

[Hugh of St. Victor]. Hugonis de Sancto Victore. *De sacramentis. PL* 176, cols. 173–618.

———. *Didascalicon de studio legendi.* . . . Ed. Charles Henry Buttimer. Studies in Medieval and Renaissance Latin, X. Washington, DC: Catholic University of America Press, 1939. *The Didascalicon of Hugh of St. Victor: A Medieval Guide to the Arts.* Trans. Jerome Taylor. New York and London: Columbia University Press, 1961.

———. [*De Sacramentis*] *On the Sacraments of the Christian Faith.* Trans. Roy J. Deferrari. Cambridge: The Mediaeval Academy of America, 1951.

[Isidore of Seville, St.]. [*Etymologiae*] *Isidori Hispalensis episcopi. Etymologiarum sive originum libri XX.* Ed. W. M. Lindsay. 2 vols. Oxford: The Clarendon Press, 1911.

Jerome, St. [*Letters*]. Sancti Eusebii Hieronymi. *Epistulae.* Pars 1: *Epistulae I–LXX.* Recensuit Isidorus Hilberg. CSEL 54. Vienna-Leipzig: Tempsky and Freytag, 1910.

[Lactantius]. [*Divinae institutiones*] *Divinarum institutionum adversus gentes libri septem. PL* 6, cols. 111–1016.

Lactantius. *The Divine Institutes.* Trans. Mary Francis McDonald. FC 49. Washington, DC: Catholic University of America Press, 1964.

Leclerq, Jean, and Henri Roachais, eds. See St. Bernard of Clairvaux, *Opera.*

Léon-Dufour, ed. See *Dictionary of Biblical Theology*.

Lewis, Charlton T., and Charles Short, eds. *A Latin Dictionary*. Oxford: Clarendon Press, 1966.

Il libro della natura degli animali [Selections]. Ed. Cesare Segre. In Cesare Segre and Mario Marti, eds. *La prosa del Duecento*. Milano-Napoli: Riccardo Ricciardi, 1959. Pp. 297–310.

Livy. [*Ab Urbe condita: History*. Books I–II]. *Livy with an English Translation in fourteen volumes*. Vol. 1. Ed and trans. B. O. Foster. LCL. London: William Heinemann; Cambridge: Harvard University Press, 1919–1951.

Macrobius, Ambrosius Aurelius Theodosius. *Saturnalia: Apparatu critico instruxit, in Somnium Scipionis Commentarios* selecta varietate lectionis, ornavit Iacobus Willis. Biblioteca Scriptorum Graecorum et Romanorum Teubneriana. 2 vols. Leipzig: Teubner, 1963; 2nd ed. 1970.

Minucius Felix, Marcus. *Octavius*. Ed. Berhard Kytzler. Leipzig: Teubner, 1982.

———. *Octavius*. Trans. G. W. Clarke. ACW, vol. 39. New York: Newman Press, 1974.

Orosius, Paulus. *Historiarum Adversum Paganos Libri VII*. Ed. Karl Zangemeister. Leipzig: Teubner, 1889.

———. [*Against the Pagans*] *The Seven Books of History Against the Pagans*. Trans. Roy J. Deferrari. FC 50. Washington, DC: Catholic University of America Press, 1964.

Ovid. *Metamorphoses*. Ed. and trans. Frank Justus Miller. 2 vols. LCL. Cambridge: Harvard University Press; London: William Heinemann, 1916.

Paul the Deacon. See Festus the Grammarian.

Philo. *De opificio mundi* [*On the Creation*]. In *Philo* with Eng. trans. F. H. Colson and G. H. Whitaker. Vol. 1. LCL. Cambridge: Harvard University Press; London: William Heinemann, 1929; rprt. 1959.

Physiologus. Ed. P. T. Eden. See Theobaldus.

Physiologus. Trans. Michael J. Curley. Austin and London: University of Texas Press, 1979.

Pictor in carmine. Ed. M[ontagu] R[hodes] James. In *Archaeologia or Miscellaneous Tracts Relating to Antiquity* 94: 2nd Series 44 (1951), pp. 141–166.

[Pitra]. "De bestiis." Cap. IX in Jean-Baptiste Pitra, ed. *S. Melitonis Clavis. Analecta sacra spicilegio solemensi*. Vol. 3. Paris: Firmin Didot Frères, 1855.

[Plato]. *The Republic of Plato*. Trans. Francis Macdonald Cornford. Oxford: Clarendon Press, 1941; rprt. 1944.

[Plato]. *Timaeus a Calcidio translatus*. Ed. J. H. Waszink [with P. G. Jensen]. In Raymond Klibansky, ed. *Plato latinus*. London: Warburg Institute; Leiden: Brill, 1962. Vol. 4.

Pliny. *Natural History*. Ed. and trans. H. Rackham and W. H. S. Jones. LCL. London: William Heinemann; Cambridge: Harvard University Press, 1938–1956. [Esp. Liber VIII. Vol. 3:1–162.]

Poeti del Duecento. Ed. G. Contini. 2 vols. Milano-Napoli: Riccardo Ricciardi, 1960.

Rabanus Maurus. *De Universo*. PL 111, cols. 9–614.

Reallexikon für Antike und Christentum. Stuttgart: Hiersemann, 1950.

[Richard of St. Victor] Richard de St.-Victor. *De statu interioris hominis.* Ed. Jean Ribailler. *Archives d'histoire doctrinale et littéraire du Moyen Age,* 42ᵉ année (1967), pp. 7–128.

Richard of St. Victor. *Opera omnia. PL* 196, cols. 1–1366.

————. *The Twelve Patriarchs, The Mystical Ark, Book Three of the Trinity.* Trans. Grover A. Zinn. The Classics of Western Spirituality. New York: Paulist Press, 1979.

Sackur, E. See *Sibyllinische Texte.*

Servius. [*Commentary of the Aeneid*] *Servianorum in Vergilii Carmina Commentarium.* Editionis Harvardianae. Vol. 2 [*Aen.* I–II]. Ed. Edward Kennard Rand, et al. American Philological Association, Lancaster, Pennsylvania. Lancastriae Pennsylvaniorm e Typographio Lancastriano, 1946. Vol. 3 [*Aen.* III–V]. Ed. Arthur Frederick Stocker, et al. Special Publications of the American Philological Association, 1. Oxonii e Typographeo Universitatis, 1965. 2 vols.

————. *Servii Grammatici qui feruntur in Vergilii Carmina Commentarii.* Ed. Georg Thilo and Hermann Hagen. 3 vols. Leipzig: Teubner, 1881–1887.

The Sibylline Oracles. See *New Testament Apocrypha,* vol. 2, pp. 703–744.

Sibyllinische Texte und Forschungen: Pseudomethodius, Adso und die tiburtinische Sibylle. Ed. E. Sackur. Halle: S. M. Niemeyer, 1898; rprt. Torino: Bottega d'Erasmo, 1963.

Solerti, Angelo, ed. *Le vite di Dante, Petrarca e Boccaccio scritte fino al secolo decimosesto.* Storia Letteraria d'Italia, vol. 5. Milano: Francesco Vallardi, 1904.

Suetonius. *Vita Vergilii.* In *Suetonius* with an English trans. J. C. Rolfe. 2 vols. LCL. London: William Heinemann; New York: G. P. Putnam's Sons, 1920. Vol. 2, pp. 464–483.

Theobaldi. *Physiologus.* Ed. with critical apparatus, trans. and com. P. T. Eden. Leiden und Köln: E. J. Brill, 1972.

[Thomas of Cantimpré] Thomas Cantimpratensis. *Liber de natura rerum.* Ed. H. Boese. Teil 1: Text. Berlin-New York: Walter DeGruyter, 1973.

Tondelli, Leone, ed. See Gioachino da Fiore.

[Tyconius. *Regulae*] Tichonii Afri. *Liber de septem regulis. PL* 18, cols. 15–66.

[Vergilius Publius Maro]. *Virgil* with an English trans. H. Rushton Fairclough. 2 vols.: 1, *Eclogues, Georgics, Aeneid* I–VI; 2, *Aeneid* VII–XII, The Minor Poems. Rev. ed. LCL. Cambridge: Harvard University Press; London: William Heinemann, 1918; rprt. 1969.

Villani, Giovanni. *Cronica di Giovanni Villani.* 3 vols. Firenze: 1823. Rprt. Roma: Multigrafica Editrice, 1980.

[Vincent of Beauvais] Vincentii Bellovacensis. *Speculum naturale.* Strasbourg: Printer of the 1481 *Legenda Aurea,* ca. 1483. (In the University of Illinois Library, Urbana.)

Virgil. See Vergilius.

SECONDARY SOURCES

Authors are listed alphabetically; their works are listed chronologically.

Aglianò, Sebastiano. "fioco." *ED*, vol. 2 (1970): 892–893.
Albright, W. F. "The High Places in Ancient Palestine." *Supplements to Vetus Testamentum* 4 (1957): 242–258.
Alessio, Gian Carlo, and Claudia Villa. "Per *Inferno* I, 67–87." In *Vestigia: Studi in onore di Giuseppe Billanovich*. Roma: Storia e Letteratura, 1984. Pp. 1–21.
Alexander, Paul J. *The Oracle of Baalbek*. Washington, DC: Dumbarton Oaks Center for Byzantine Studies, 1967. [Study on early Sibylline texts.]
———. "Medieval Apocalypses as Historical Sources." *AHR* 73 (1968): 997–1018.
———. "Byzantium and the Migration of Literary Works and Motifs: The Legend of the Last World Emperor." *Medievalia et Humanistica* n. s. 2 (1971): 47–68.
Allen, D. C. *Mysteriously Meant*. Baltimore, MD: The Johns Hopkins University Press, 1970.
Allen, Judson Boyce. *The Ethical Poetic of the Later Middle Ages: A Decorum of Convenient Distinction*. Toronto: University of Toronto Press, 1982.
Alverny, Marie-Thérèse d'. "Notes sur Dante et la Sagesse." *REI* 11 (1965): 5–24.
Ammendola, A. "Il prologo della *Divina Commedia* e la sua profezia fondamentale." *Palaestra* 4 (1965): 287ff. [unconsulted.]
Anderson, William. *Dante the Maker*. London: Routledge and Kegan Paul, 1980; rprt. New York: Crossroad, 1982.
Angelitti, Filippo. "Sulla data del viaggio dantesco desunta dai dati cronologici e confermata dalle osservazioni astronomiche riportate nella *Commedia*." *Atti della Accademia Pontaniana del R. Osservatorio di Palermo*. 27. Serie 2ª, vol. 2, memoria 7 (1897), Napoli: Tipografia della R. Università, 1897.
Antognoni, Oreste. *Saggio di studj sopra la Commedia di Dante*. Livorno: R. Giusti, 1893.
Antonetti, Pierre. "Essai de lecture structurelle du chant I de l'Enfer." *SD* 49 (1972): 27–41.
Apollonio, Mario. *Dante, storia della Commedia*. Milano: F. Vallardi, 1951; 3rd ed. 1964, 2 vols.
Arezio, Luigi. "Il 'Veltro' e 'il Cinquecento diece e cinque' nel Poema dantesco." *GD* 32, n. s. 2 (1931): 3–58.
———. "Divergenze sul Veltro, su DXV e sulla datazione della *Divina Commedia*." *GD* 40 (1939): 87–140.
Arullani, Vittorio Amedeo. "Intorno al verso: 'Chi per lungo silenzio parea fioco.'" *GD* 2 (1895): 504–505.
Atti del Congresso Internazionale di Studi Danteschi. Ed. La Società Dantesca Italiana . . . (20–27 aprile 1965). Firenze: G. C. Sansoni, 1965.
Auerbach, Erich. *Dante als Dichter der irdischen Welt*. Berlin and Leipzig: Walter de Gruyter & Co., 1929. Trans. Ralph Manheim. *Dante, Poet of the Secular*

World. Chicago and London: University of Chicago Press, 1961; Ital. trans. *Dante, poeta del mondo terreno* in *Studi su Dante*. Milano: Feltrinelli, 1963a.

————. "Dante und Vergil." In *Das humanistisches Gymnasium* [Leipzig, Teubner] 42 (1931): 136–144; rprt. in *Gesammelte Aufsätze zur romanischen Philologie*. Bern und München: Francke Verlag, 1967; rprt. as "Dante e Virgilio." In *San Francesco, Dante, Vico*. Trans. Vittoria Ruberle. Bari: De Donato, 1970. Pp. 21–32.

————. *Mimesis: The Representation of Reality in Western Literature*. Trans. Willard Trask. Princeton: Princeton University Press, 1953; rprt. Garden City, NY: Doubleday, 1957.

————. *Studi su Dante*. Trans. Maria Luisa Da Pieri Bonino and Dante della Terza. Milano: Feltrinelli, 1963b.

————. *Literatursprache und Publikum in der lateinischen Spätantike und Mittelalter*. Bern: Francke Verlag, 1958; *Literary Language and Its Public in Late Latin Antiquity and in The Middle Ages*. Trans. Ralph Manheim. London: Routledge and Kegan Paul, 1965.

————. *San Francesco, Dante, Vico*. Bari: De Donato, 1970.

Austin, H. D. "Dante's Guides in the *Divina Commedia*." *The Romanic Review* 34 (1943): 71–74.

————. "Dante Notes: Notes on the 'Veltro' in Dante's Works." *The Romantic Review* 35 (1945): 257–265.

————. "Dante's 'Veltri.'" *Italica* 24 (1947): 14–19.

Bacchelli, R. "Da Dite a Malebolge: la tragedia delle porte chiuse e la farsa dei ponti rotti." *GSLI*, anno LXXI, vol. 131, fasc. 393 (1954): 1–32; rprt. in his *Saggi critici*. Milano: Mondadori, 1962. Pp. 845–878.

————. "'Per te poeta fui.'" *SD* 42 (1965): 5–28.

Baethgen, Friedrich. "Der Engelpapst." Vortrag gehalten am 15. Januar, 1933 in öffentlicher Sitzung der Königsberger gelehrten Gesellschaft von F. Baethgen. Halle (Saale): M. Niemeyer, 1933.

————. *Der Engelpapst: Idee und Erscheinung*. Leipzig: Koehler und Amelang, 1943.

Baglivi, Giuseppe, and Garrett McCutchan. "Dante, Christ and the Fallen Bridges." *Italica* 54 (1977): 250–262.

Balbo, Cesare. "Commento ai primi due canti dell'*Inferno*." In *Vita di Dante*. Scritta da C. Balbo con annotazioni di Emmanuele Rocco. Napoli: Presso Gabriele Rondinella, 1853. Pp. 401–419.

Ball, Robert. "Theological Semantics: Virgil's *pietas* and Dante's *pietà*." *SIR* 2 (Spring 1981): 59–79.

Ballerini, Carlo. "Il canto della paura." *L'Albero Lucugnano* [(Lecce) Rivista fondata da Girolamo Comi] 17–18 (1953): 34–49. Rprt. in *Studi sulla Divina Commedia*. Firenze: Olschki, 1955. Pp. 39–68. Pp. 34–38 rprt. as "La selva e il colle," in *La Divina Commedia nella critica*. Ed. A. Pagliaro. Messina-Firenze: Casa Editrice G. D'Anna, 1965. Vol. I, pp. 113–118.

Balthasar, Hans Urs von. *Herrlichkeit*, vol. 2. Eisiedeln: Johannes Verlag, 1962; *Dante*. Ital. trans. Giuseppe Magagna. Brescia: Edizioni Morcelliana, 1973.

Barbi, Michele. "Nuovi problemi della critica dantesca." *SD* 16 (1932): 37–67.

———. *Problemi di critica dantesca*. Prima serie (1893–1918). Firenze: Sansoni, 1934. Seconda serie (1920–1937). Firenze: Sansoni, 1941.

———. "Il gioachinismo francescano e il Veltro." *SD* 18 (1934): 209–211.

———. "Nuovi problemi della critica dantesca." *SD* 23 (1938): 5–77. [Esp. part V: "Veltro, Gioachinismo e fedeli d'amore: sbandamenti e aberrazioni," pp. 29–39.]

———. "L'Italia nell'ideale politico di Dante." *SD* 24 (1939): 5–37.

———. "L'ideale politico-religioso di Dante." In *Problemi fondamentali per un nuovo commento della Divina Commedia*. Firenze: G. C. Sansoni, 1955 [cover stamped 1956].

Barelli, Vincenzo. *L'Allegoria della Divina Commedia di Dante Alighieri*. Firenze: M. Cellini, 1864.

Barolini, Teodolinda. *Dante's Poets: Textuality and Truth in the Comedy*. Princeton: Princeton University Press, 1984.

Barone, Giuseppe. *Il dolore del Virgilio dantesco*. Torino: Loescher, 1899.

———. "L'arte d'istruire e d'educare nel Virgilio dantesco." *GD* 33 (1932): 189–200.

Barth, R. L. "*Inferno* I, II and XXVI: Dante as Poet and Wayfarer, Ulysses and the Reader." *Kentucky Review* 2, no. 2 (1981): 35–48.

Basile, Bruno. "Il 'Commentum' di Filippo Villani al canto I° della *Commedia*." *LI* 23 (1971): 197–224.

———. "viaggio." *ED* 5 (1976): 995–999.

———. "Il viaggio archetipo: note sul tema della peregrinatio in Dante." *Lett. classensi* 15 (1981): 9–26.

Bassermann, Alfred. *Orme di Dante in Italia*. Trans. Egidio Gorra. Bologna: Zanichelli, n. d. [Cited as *Orme*.]

———. "*Veltro*, Gross-Chan und Kaisersage." *Neue Heidelberger Jahrbücher* 11 (1901): 28–75.

———. "Veltro und Gross-Chan." *DDJ* 11 (1929): 173–182.

Battaglia, Salvatore. "Linguaggio reale e linguaggio figurato nella Divina Commedia." *Atti del 1° Congresso nazionale di studi danteschi: Caserta-Napoli*, 21–25 maggio 1961. Firenze: Olschki, 1962. Pp. 21–44. Rprt. *Filologia e letteratura*, 8 (1962), 1–26; *Esemplarità e antagonismo nel pensiero di Dante*. Napoli: Liguori, Parte 1ª, 1967. Pp. 51–82.

———. *Esemplarità e antagonismo nel pensiero di Dante*. Collana di Testi e Critica, 3. Napoli: Liguori, Parte 1ª, 1966; 2nd ed. 1967; rprt. 1975; Parte 2, 1974. Cited as *Esemplarità*.

———. "Il primo verso." *La Divina Commedia nella critica*. Ed. A. Pagliaro. Messina-Firenze: Casa Editrice G. D'Anna, 1965. Vol. I, pp. 105–112.

Benge, Wendy. "The *Divine Comedy*: Dante's Song of Exodus." In Robert M. Yule, ed. *From Dante to Solzhenitsyn: Essays on Christianity and Literature*. Wellington: Tertiary Christian Studies Program. Victoria University of Wellington, 1978. Pp. 9–33.

Benini, Rodolfo. *Dante tra gli splendori de' suoi enigmi risolti*. Roma: Attilio

Sampaolesi, 1919; repbd. Roma: Edizioni dell'Ateneo, 1952.

Berardinelli, Francesco. *Il concetto della Divina Commedia di Dante Alighieri.* Napoli: G. Rondinella, 1859.

Berg, William. *Early Virgil.* London: University of London, The Athlone Press, 1974.

Bernardo, Aldo. "The Three Beasts and Perspective in the *Divine Comedy.*" *PMLA* 78, no. 1 (1963): 15–24.

Bertana, Emilio. "Per l'interpretazione letterale del verso 'Chi per lungo silenzio parea fioco.'" *BSCI* 6, no. 3 (1 Nov. 1893); rprt. Modena: A. Namias, 1893, 11 pp.

Betti, Salvatore. *Postille alla Divina Commedia.* Città di Castello: Casa Editrice S. Lapi, 1865.

———. "Il Veltro allegorico di Dante." Chapter 12 in *Scritti danteschi in appendice alle postille del medesimo autore . . . raccolti da Giuseppe Cugnoni.* Città di Castello: Casa Editrice S. Lapi, 1893.

Bezzola, Reto R. "L'opera di Dante: sintesi dell'antichità e del medioevo." In *Atti del Congresso internazionale di Studi Danteschi.* Firenze: Sansoni, 1965. Vol. 1, pp. 379–395.

Bianchi, F. M. *Il Veltro: appunti per una interpretazione cateriniana di Dante.* Roma: Palombi, 1940.

Bickersteth, Geoffrey Langdale. *Dante's Virgil: A Poet's Poet.* Glasgow: Jackson and Son, 1951.

Bigongiari, D. *Essays on Dante and Medieval Culture. BAR* 71. Firenze: L. S. Olschki, 1964.

Biondolillo, Francesco. *Dante e il suo Poema.* Parte I: *L'Inferno.* Roma: Edizioni dell'Ateneo, 1948.

Bittanta, Ernesta. "La 'piaggia diserta' era proprio piana." *Convivium* 5 (1952): 732–735.

Blanc, Ludwig Gottfried. *Saggio di una interpretazione filologica di parecchi passi oscuri e controversi della Divina Commedia per L.G. Dr. Blanc.* Trans. O. Occioni. Trieste: C. Coen, 1865.

———. *Vocabolario Dantesco o Dizionario critico e ragionato della Divina Commedia di Dante Alighieri di L. G. Blanc.* Ital. trans. G. Carbone, 4ᵃ ed. Firenze: Barbèra, 1890 [German ed., 1852].

Bloom, Harold. *The Anxiety of Influence: A Theory of Poetry.* New York: Oxford University Press, 1973.

Bloomfield, Morton. "Joachim of Flora: A Critical Survey of his Canon, Teachings, Sources, Biography and Influence." *Traditio* 13 (1957): 249–311.

Boccaccio, Giovanni, and Leonardo Bruni Aretino. *The Earliest Lives of Dante.* Trans. James Robinson Smith (1901). Introd. Francesco Basetti-Sani. New York: Ungar, 1963.

Boehmer, Eduard. "Il veltro." *Jahrbuch der deutschen Dante-Gesellschaft* 2 (1869): 363–366.

Bolelli, Tristano. "Il 'dilettoso monte' del I canto dell'Inferno (v.77)." *Studi in Onore di Alberto Chiari.* Vol. 1. Brescia: Editrice Paideia, 1973. Pp. 165–168.

Bonfante, G. "Ancora le tre fiere." *Italica* 23 (1946): 69–72.

Bonfanti, Nicolina. *Fonti virgiliane dell'oltretomba dantesco.* Pt. I. Messina: T. di Francesco fu Giuseppe, 1918.

Borromeo, C. *Dante personificato nel Veltro.* Torino, 1901. [unconsulted.]

Bottagisio, Tito. *Il limbo dantesco: Studi filosofici e letterari.* Padova: Tipografia e libreria Editrice Antoniana, 1898.

Bowden, John Paul. *An Analysis of Pietro Alighieri's Commentary on the Divine Comedy.* New York: St. John's University, 1951.

Bowsky, William. "Florence and Henry of Luxemburg, King of the Romans: The Rebirth of Guelfism." *Speculum* 33 (1958): 177–203.

Bozzoli, Adriano. "Due paragrafi sul prologo della Divina Commedia." *Aevum italicum* 41, no. 5–6 (1967): 518–529.

Bronzini, Giovanni Battista. "Nel mezzo del cammin. . . ." *GSLI* 155, fasc. 490, anno XCV (1978): 161–177.

Brown, P. "Saint Augustine." *Trends in Medieval Political Thought,* ed. B. Smalley. Oxford: Blackwell, 1965.

Brugnoli, G. "Chi per lungo silenzio parea fioco." *Letterature comparate: problemi e metodo: Studi in onore di Ettore Paratore.* Vol. 3. Bologna: Patron, 1981. Pp. 1169–1182.

Bruni, Leonardo. See Angelo Solerti, ed., *Le vite di Dante, Petrarca e Boccaccio* [under "Primary Sources"].

Buck, August. "Gli studi sulla poetica e sulla retorica di Dante." In *Atti del Congresso Internazionale di Studi Danteschi.* Firenze: Sansoni, 1965. Vol. 1, pp. 249–278; partial rprt. in *CeS,* pp. 143–166; vol. rprt. as *Dante nella critica d'oggi,* ed. Umberto Bosco. Firenze: F. Le Monnier, 1965. Pp. 143–166.

Buonaiuti, Ernesto. *Dante come profeta.* 2nd ed., Modena: Guanda, 1936.

Buscaino Campo, Alberto. "Sul piè fermo." In his *Studi danteschi.* Pp. 7; 235–237.

———. *Studi danteschi.* Trapani: Tipografia Fratelli Messina, 1894.

———. *Studi di filologi italiana.* Palermo: Tipografia del Giornale di Sicilia, 1877.

Busnelli, Giovanni. *L'Etica Nicomachea e l'ordinamento morale dell'Inferno di Dante.* Bologna: Zanichelli, 1907.

———. *Il simbolo delle tre fiere dantesche: ricerche e studi intorno al Prologo della Commedia.* Roma: Civiltà Cattolica, 1909.

———. [Rev. of] "Lorenzo Filomusi Guelfi, *Nuovi studii. . . . Nuovissimi studii su Dante." BSDI* n. s. 20 (1913): 1–13.

———. "Dalla scuola di Virgilio alla scuola di Beatrice." In *Raccolta di Studi di Storia e critica letteraria dedicata a Francesco Flamini da' suoi discepoli.* Pisa: Tipografia Editrice del Cav. F. Mariotti, 1918. Pp. 65–92.

———. *Il Virgilio dantesco e il gran Veglio di Creta: indagine critica.* 2nd ed. Roma: Civiltà Cattolica, 1919.

———. "La colpa del 'non fare' degl'infedeli negativi." *SD* 23 (1938): 79–97.

Caligaris, Pietro. "Nota di esegesi dantesca." *LI* 2, no. 4 (1950): 241–243.

————. "Del Veltro e di altre questioni." *Lettere italiane* 3 (1951): 152–166.

————. *Saggio di interpretazioni dantesche.* Torino: SEI, 1967.

Callu, J.-P. "'Impius Aeneas'? Echos virgiliens du Bas-Empire." In *Présence de Virgile: Actes du Colloque des 9, 11, et 12 décembre 1976.* Paris: Société d'Edition "Les Belles Lettres," 1978. Pp. 161–174.

Cambon, Glauco. "Synaesthesia in the Divine Comedy." *Dante Studies* 88 (1970): 3–5.

Camilli, Amerindo. "La cronologia del viaggio dantesco." *SD* 29 (1950a): 61–84.

————. "Oscurità dantesche." *SD* 29 (1950b): 185–187.

Camus, Jules. "La 'lonza' de Dante et les 'léopards' de Pétrarque, de l'Arioste etc." *GSLI* 53 (1909): 1–40.

Canavesio, Sebastiano. *Il primo canto della Divina Commedia spiegato coll'Ypsilon di Pitagora.* Mondovì, n. p., 1875.

Capelli, L. M. "Per una nuova interpretazione dell'allegoria del primo canto." *GD* anno VI, n. s. 3 (1898): 353–375.

Carcopino, Jérôme. *Virgile et le mystère de la IVE Eclogue.* Paris: L'Artisan du Livre, 1930.

Carnevali, A. G. "Sulla prima terzina del poema dantesco." *Scienza e diletto*, anno V, no. 23 (Cerignola; 6 giugno, 1897). [unconsulted.]

Carroll, John S. *Exiles of Eternity: An Exposition of Dante's Inferno.* London, New York, Toronto: Holder and Stoughton, n. d. [but 1903].

Casanova, Alfonso. See Persico, Federico.

Casella, Giacinto. "Della forma allegorica e della principale allegoria della Divina Commedia" (1865). In *Opere edite e postume di Giacinto Casella.* Con prefazione del prof. Alessandro D'Ancona. Firenze: G. Barbèra, 1884. Vol. 2, pp. 369–396.

Casini, Tommaso. "Rime inedite dei secoli XIII e XIV." *Il Propugnatore* 15, parte 2 (1882): 331–349.

————. [Rev. of] "Francesco Cipolla. 'La lonza di Dante.' *Rassegna bibliografica della letteratura italiana*, 3 (1895), pp. 103–114." *BSDI* n. s. 2 (1895): 116–120.

————. *Canto I dell'Inferno*, letto da T.C. nella Sala di Dante in Or San Michele, il dì 17 maggio 1905. *Lect. fiorentina.* Firenze: G. C. Sansoni, 1905; rprt. as "Sulla soglia del tempio," in *Scritti danteschi*, 1913. Pp. 19–44.

————. *Scritti danteschi.* Città di Castello: Casa Editrice S. Lapi, 1913.

Cassata, Letterio. "Il lungo silenzio di Virgilio." *SD* 47 (1970): 15–41.

————. "morte." [esp "seconda morte."] *ED* 3 (1971): 1040–1041.

————. "Note sul testo del canto 1 dell'*Inferno.*" *Annali della Scuola Normale Superiore di Pisa: Classe di Lettere e Filosofia* 15, no. 1 (1985): 103–128.

Cassel, Paulus Stephanus. *Il Veltro der Retter und der Dichter in Dantes Hölle.* Berlin and Guben: Sallischer Verlag, 1890.

Cassell, Anthony K. "Failure, Pride and Conversion in *Inferno* I." *Dante Studies* 94 (1976): 1–24.

————. "Mostrando con le poppe il petto (*Purg.* 23, 102)." *Dante Studies* 96 (1978): 75–82.

————. *Dante's Fearful Art of Justice*. Toronto and London: University of Toronto Press, 1984.

Cento, Fernando. "Il Virgilio dantesco tipo ideale dell'Educatore." In *L'Umanesimo di Dante*. Ed. Giovannangiola Tarugi. Firenze: Olschki, 1967. Pp. 1–19.

Chase, Frederic Henry. *The Lord's Prayer in the Early Church*. Texts and Studies, vol. 1, no. 3. Cambridge: The University Press, 1891.

Chenu, Marie-Dominique. *La théologie au XIIe siècle*. Paris: J. Vrin, 1957.

Chevallier, R., ed. *Présence de Virgile: Actes du Colloque des 9, 11, et 12 décembre 1976*. Paris: Société d'Edition "Les Belles Lettres," 1978.

Chiampi, James Thomas. *Shadowy Prefaces: Conversion and Writing in the Divine Comedy*. Interprete, 24. Ravenna: A. Longo, 1981.

Chiarenza, Marguerite Mills. "The Imageless Vision and Dante's *Paradiso*." *Dante Studies* 90 (1972): 77–91.

————. "Boethian Themes in Dante's Reading of Virgil." *SIR* 3 (Spring 1983): 25–35.

Chiari, Alberto. *Il preludio dell'Inferno dantesco*. *Lect. Romana*. Torino: Società Editrice Internazionale, 1966. Rprt. *Convivium* n. s. 29, no. I (1961): 1–11.

Chiavacci Leonardi, Anna Maria. *"La guerra de la pietate": saggio per interpretazione dell'Inferno di Dante*. Napoli: Liguori, 1979.

————. "Dante e Virgilio: l'immagine europea dell'uomo." *Lett. Classensi* 2. Ravenna: A. Longo, 1983. Pp. 81–97.

Chimenz, Siro Amedeo. "Per il testo e la chiosa della *Divina Commedia*." *GSLI* anno LXXIII, vol. 133, fasc. 402 (1956): 161–188; esp. pp. 161–164.

Chiovenda, T. "Per Dante e pei suoi sottintesi." *Rivista Rosminiana di Filiosofia e Cultura* 35 (1941): 217–221.

Chistoni, Paride. *Sulla triplice partizione dei dannati nell'Inferno dantesco, commentato al c. XI dell'Inferno*. Potenza: Tipografia Lucana, 1901.

————. "La lonza dantesca." In *Miscellanea di studi critici edita in onore di Arturo Graf*. Bergamo: Istituto Italiano d'Arti Grafiche, 1903. Pp. 817–848.

————. *Il monogramma di Cristo e l'enigma dantesco del DXV*. Parma: Stab. Lito-Tipografico Luigi Battei, 1905a.

————. "Alcune nuove osservazioni intorno al Veltro dantesco." *GD* 13 (1905b): 194–198.

Cian, Vittorio. *Sulle orme del veltro: Studio dantesco*. Messina: G. Principato, 1897.

————. *Oltre l'enigma dantesco del veltro, con due appendici: Bibliografia e Florilegio profetico*. 2nd ed. Torino-Milano-Firenze: G. B. Paravia, 1945.

Cicchitto, L. "L'escatologia di Dante e il francescanismo." *Miscellanea Francescana* 47 (1947): 217–231.

Cioffari, Vincenzo. "Guido da Pisa's Basic Interpretation (A Translation of the First Two Cantos)." *Dante Studies* 93 (1975): 1–26.

Ciotti, Andrea. "Il concetto della 'figura' e la poetica della 'visione' nei commentatori trecenteschi della *Commedia*." *Convivium* n. s. 30, fasc. 3–4 (1962): 264–291; 399–415.

————. "Gli studi danteschi di R. Guardini." *Convivium* 34 (1966): 372–382.

Cipolla, Carlo. *Il trattato "De Monarchia" di Dante Alighieri e l'opuscolo "De potestate regia et paple" di Giovanni da Parigi.* Torino: Clausen, 1892.

————. "Dante a Verona," and "Cangrande I." In *Compendio della storia politica di Verona.* Verona: R. Cabianca, 1899 [cover dated 1900].

Cipolla, Francesco. "La lonza di Dante." *Rassegna bibliografica della letteratura italiana* anno III, no. 4 (aprile, 1895): 103–114.

Colacci, Mario. *L'Inferno di Dante Alighieri volto in prosa esplicativa con l'analisi critica degli episodi e dei personaggi di maggiore rilievo.* Napoli: Luigi Loffredo, 1947.

Comparetti, Domenico. *Virgilio nel Medio Evo.* 2 vols. Firenze: Seeber, 2nd ed. 1895; rprt. 1896; nuova ed. Giorgio Pasquali. Firenze: "La Nuova Italia" Editrice, 1937; *Vergil in the Middle Ages.* Trans. E. F. M. Benecke, intro. Robinson Ellis. London: Swan Sonnenschein; New York: Macmillan, 1895; rprt. Hamden, CT: Archon Books, 1966. [I have used the 1895 editions in Ital. and Eng.]

Consoli, Domenico. "Nota sul canto I dell'*Inferno*." *Nuova rivista di varia umanità* 1, no. 4 (1956): 30–35.

————. *Significato del Virgilio dantesco.* Firenze: F. Le Monnier, 1967.

————. "bene." *ED* 1 (1970): 569–572.

————. "colle." *ED* 2 (1970): 51–52.

————. "Virgilio." *ED* 4 (1976): 1034.

Contini, Gianfranco. "Dante come personaggio-poeta della *Commedia*." *Secoli vari ('300-'400-'500).* Libera Cattedra di Storia della Civiltà Fiorentina (Unione Fiorentina). Firenze: Sansoni, 1958. Pp. 23–48; partial rprt. in *Aggiornamenti di critica dantesca.* Ed. Silvio Pasquazi. Firenze: F. Le Monnier, 1972. Pp. 142–147.

————. *Un'idea di Dante.* Torino: G. Einaudi, 1976.

Cosmo, Umberto. "Le mistiche nozze di frate Francesco con madonna Povertà." *GD* 6 (1898): 49–82, 97–118.

————. *Guida a Dante.* Torino: F. de Silva, 1947; *A Handbook to Dante Studies.* Trans. David Moore. Oxford: Blackwell; New York: Barnes and Noble, 1950.

Costa, Dennis. "One Good Reception Deserves Another: The Epistle to Can Grande." *SIR* 5, no. 1 (1985): 5–17.

Courcelle, Pierre. "Les éxégèses chrétiennes de la quatrième Eglogue." *Revue des Etudes Anciennes* 60, no. 3–4 (1957): 294–319.

————. *Les "Confessions" de S. Augustin dans la tradition littéraire: Antécédents et postérité.* Paris: Etudes Augustiniennes, 1963.

Crema, E. "La simbologia del primer canto de 'la Divina Commedia.'" *Cultura Universitaria* [Caracas], 91 (1966): 1–16.

Crescimanno, Giuseppe. "Di quel umile Italia fia salute." *GD* 13 (1905): 81–91.

Cressey, J. "Suetonius as the Source of Dante: *Inferno* I, 62–63." *Liverpool Classical Monthly* 1, no. 3 (March 1976): 29.

Crivelli, E. "Questi non ciberà terra né peltro." *GD* annuario dantesco 1939, vol. 42 (1941): 71–78.

Crocco, Antonio. *Gioacchino da Fiore: La più singolare ed affascinante figura del Medioevo cristiano*. Napoli: Edizioni Empireo, 1960.

――――. *Simbologia gioachimita e simbologia dantesca: Nuove prospettive d'inter-pretazione della Divina Commedia*. Napoli: Edizioni Empireo, 1961; 5th ed. 1965.

Croce, Benedetto. *La poesia di Dante*. Bari: Laterza, 1920; rprt. 1952. [many rprts.]

Cuini, Carlo. *Qualche novità nella Divina Commedia: Il Veltro, "il gran rifiuto," ed altro*. Agugliano: Bagaloni, 1986.

Curtius, Ernst Robert. *European Literature and the Latin Middle Ages*. Trans. Willard R. Trask. New York: Pantheon Books for the Bollingen Foundation, 1953; rprt. New York: Harper and Row, 1963.

Daniélou, Jean. *Bible et Liturgie*. Paris: Editions du Cerf, 1951. *The Bible and the Liturgy*. Trans. Michael A. Mathis. Notre Dame, IN: Notre Dame University Press, 1956.

――――. *Sacramentum Futuri: Etudes sur les origines de la typologie biblique*. Paris: Beauchesne, 1950; *From Shadows to Reality: Studies in the Biblical Typol-ogy of the Fathers*. Trans. Dom Wulstan Hibberd. London: Burns and Oates, 1960.

Dante e Roma. Atti del convegno di studi: Roma, 8-9-10 aprile, 1965. A cura della "Casa di Dante"; sotto gli auspici del Comune di Roma, in colla-borazione con l'Istituto di Studi Romani. Comitato nazionale per le cele-brazioni sel VII centenario della nascita di Dante. Firenze: F. Le Monnier, 1965.

Davidsohn, Robert. "Il cinquecento dieci e cinque del *Purgatorio*." *BSDI* 9 (1902): 129–131.

――――. *Firenze ai tempi di Dante*. Ital. trans. Eugenio Duprè Theseider. Firenze: R. Bemorad, 1929.

――――. *Storia di Firenze*. Ital. trans. Giovanni Battista Klein. Rev. Roberto Pal-marocchi. 8 vols. Firenze: Sansoni, 1956–1968.

Davis, Charles Till. *Dante and the Idea of Rome*. Oxford: Clarendon Press, 1957.

――――. "Dante and Italian Nationalism." In *A Dante Symposium*, ed. William De Sua and G. Rizzo. Chapel Hill: University of North Carolina Press, 1965. Pp. 199–213.

――――. "Dante's Vision of History." *Dante Studies* 93 (1975): 143–160.

――――. "Veltro." *ED*, vol. 5 (1976): 908–912.

――――. "Poverty and Eschatology in the *Commedia*." *Yearbook of Italian Studies* 4 (1980): 59–86.

――――. "Rome and Babylon in Dante." *Rome in the Renaissance, the City and the Myth*. Ed. P. A. Ramsey. Binghamton, NY: CMERS, 1982. Pp. 19–40.

DeFlorio, F. "Risolto l'enigma del Veltro." *Corriere del Giorno* 1: 5 (1948).

De Leonardis, G. "La Roma di Dante." *GD* 3 (1896): 188–196.

――――. "Publio Virgilio Marone e Dante." *Rivista di filosofia e scienze affini* 5, no.2 (1903): 203–234.

Delhaye, Ph. "Le sens littéral et le sens allégorique du *microcosmus* de Geoffrey de Saint-Victor." *RTAM* 16 (1949): 155–160.

———. *Le microcosmus de Godefroy de Saint-Victor, étude théologique*. In *Mémoires et travaux publiés par les professeurs des Facultés catholiques de Lille*, fasc. 56. Lille: Facultés Catholiques; Gembloux: Editions J. Duculot, 1951.

Della Torre, Ruggiero. *Poeta-veltro*. 2 vols. Cividale: Tipografia Fulvio Giovanni, 1887–1890.

———. *Tra Feltro e Feltro: Nota Dantesca*. Cividale: Fulvio Giovanni, 1891.

———. *Sistema dell'arte allegorica nel Poema dantesco*. Cividale: Tipografia Fulvio Giovanni, 1892.

———. *Commento letterale al primo Canto della "Divina Commedia": ricostruzione logica dell'antefatto o proemio. La volontà. Lo Spazio e il tempo*. Torino: Carlo Clausen, 1898.

Della Volpe, Galvano. *Critica del gusto*. Milano: Feltrinelli, 1960.

Del Lungo, Isidoro. "Uguccione della Faggiuola e il Veltro dantesco." *Dino Compagni e la sua Cronica*. 2 vols. Firenze: Successori F. Le Monnier, 1873; rprt. 1879.

———. *Dal secolo e dal poema di Dante*. Bologna: Ditta Nicola Zanichelli, 1898.

———. *Canto I dell'Inferno letto da I. Del Lungo nella Sala di Dante in Roma, con appendice e facsimile concernenti la Lezione dei Versi 4–9. Lect. Romana*. Firenze: G.C. Sansoni, 1901.

———. *Dante: Prolusione alle tre cantiche e commento all' "Inferno."* Firenze: F. Le Monnier, 1921.

———. *Prolusione all' "Inferno" letta da I. Del Lungo in Roma, in Siena, in Padova, in Livorno, in Torino. Lect. Romana*. Firenze: G.C. Sansoni Editore, 1925.

Demaray, John G. *The Invention of Dante's Commedia*. New Haven and London: Yale University Press, 1974.

———. *Dante and the Book of the Cosmos*. Transactions of the American Philosophical Society, vol. 77, part 5. Philadelphia, PA: The American Philosophical Society, 1987.

Dempf, Alois. *Sacrum Imperium: Geschichte und Staatsphilosophie des Mittelalters und der Renaissance*. München-Berlin: Oldenbourg, 1929. Ital. trans. C. Antoni. Messina: Principato, 1933.

De Sanctis, G. B. [Rev. of] "Tommaso Ventura. 'Nuovi orizzonti. . . .'" *GD* anno XLIII, n. s. 13 (1943): 116–117.

Döllinger, Johann J. von. "Dante als Prophet." *Akademische Vorträge Nördlingen* 1 (1888): 78–117.

Doob, Penelope B. R. *Nebuchadnezzar's Children*. New Haven and London: Yale University Press, 1974.

D'Ovidio, Francesco. *Studii sulla Divina Commedia*. Milano-Palermo: Remo Sandron, 1901.

———. *Nuovi studii danteschi*. Milano: Ulrico Hoepli. 2 vols. *Il Purgatorio e il suo preludio*, 1906; *Ugolino, Pier della Vigna, i Simoniaci e discussioni varie*, 1907.

———. *Studii sulla Divina Commedia*, parte II, in *Opere di Francesco D'Ovidio*.

Caserta: Casa Editrice Moderna, 1931. [Rprt. of studies in *Studii* and *Nuovi Studii*.]

Dozon, Marthe. "Le thème de la louve et des loups dans la *Divine Comédie*: Echos d'un mythe étrusco-latin?" *REI* n. s. 15 (1969): 5–33.

Dragonetti, Roger. "Chi per lungo silenzio parea fioco." *SD* 38 (1961): 47–74.

———. "Le passage périlleux." *Convivium* n. s. 34 (1966), 1–4 [Omaggio a Dante]: 3–76.

Dunbar, Helen Flanders. *Symbolism in Medieval Thought and its Consummation in the Divine Comedy*. New Haven: Yale University Press, 1929.

Dupré-Theseider, Eugenio. *L'idea imperiale di Roma nella tradizione del medio evo*. Milano: Istituto per gli Studi di Politica Internazionale, 1942.

Elisei, R. "L'introduzione alle Epistole d'Orazio e l'introduzione alla *Divina Commedia*." *Il Mondo classico* n. s. 6 (1952): 9–21.

Ellspermann, Gerard L. *The Attitude of the Early Christian Writers Toward Pagan Literature and Learning*. Catholic University of America Patristic Studies, 82. Washington, DC: Catholic University of America Press, 1949.

Enciclopedia Dantesca. Dir. Umberto Bosco; ed. Giorgio Petrocchi. 5 vols. plus appendix. Roma: Istituto dell'Enciclopedia Italiana, 1970–1978.

Ercole, Francesco. *Il prologo del poema sacro*. Conferenza tenuta nella Sala della Società Siciliana per la Storia Patria, il 20 febbraio 1921. Palermo: A. Giannitrapani, 1921; rprt. in *Il pensiero politico di Dante*. 2 vols. Milano: Stabilimento Tipo-Litografico Terragni Vittorio, 1928. Vol. 2, pp. 314–322.

Erler, Adalbert. *Lupa, Lex und Reiterstandbild im mittelalterlichen Rom: Eine rechtsgeschichtliche Studie*. Sitzungsberichte der wissenschaftlichen Gesellschaft an der Johann Wolfgang von Goethe-Universität Frankfurt/Main 10, no. 4. Weisbaden: Franz Steiner Verlag, 1972.

Esposito, Enzo. "Dante traduttore di Virgilio." *L'Italia che scrive* 48 (1965): 335–336.

Falkenhausen, F[riedrich] F[reiherr] von. "Zur Veltro-Frage." *DDJ* 11 (1929): 157–172.

———. "Dante's Staatsidee." *DDJ* 18 (1937): 47–60.

Fallani, Giovanni. *Poesia e teologia nella Divina Commedia*. Milano: Carlo Marzorati, vol. 1, 1959; vol. 2, 1961.

———. "Virgilio e la 'pietas.'" In *Poesia e teologia nella Divina Commedia*. vol. 1, *L'Inferno*. Milano: Carlo Marzorati, 1959. Pp. 51–64.

Farnel, Stewart. *The Political Ideas of the Divine Comedy: An Introduction*. Lanham, MD: University Press of America, 1985.

Feist, A. "'Chi per lungo silenzio parea fioco.'" *Zeitschrift für romanische Philologie* 10 (1886): 567.

Fenaroli, G. "Il veltro allegorico della D.C." *Rassegna nazionale* 13 (ott. 1°, 1891).

Ferrante, Joan. *The Political Vision of the Divine Comedy*. Princeton: Princeton University Press, 1984.

Ferretti, Giovanni. "La matta bestialità." *Atti dell'Accademia degli Arcadi* 9–10 (1932); rprt. in his *Saggi danteschi* (1950): 77–112.

———. *I due tempi della composizione della Divina Commedia*. Bari: Laterza, 1935.

————. "Le tre fiere." In his *Saggi danteschi*. Firenze: F. Le Monnier, 1950. Pp. 27–42.

Fiammazzo, Antonio. "A proposito di due chiose dantesche [*Inf.*, I, 63] quelle di Bertana e Posocco." *BSCI* 1 (1893–1894), also publ. as an extract (Modena: A. Namias, 1894); rprt. in *Note dantesche sparse*. Savona: D. Bertolotto, 1913. Pp. 211–215.

————. "Il lungo silenzio di Virgilio (*Inf.*, I, 63)." *GD* 2 (1895): 36–41; rprt. in *Note dantesche sparse*, pp. 233–245, with expanded *Annotazione*, pp. 241–245.

————. "Virgilio veggente cristiano?" *GSLI* 102 (1933): 138–147.

Figurelli, Fernando. "Il canto I dell'*Inferno*." *Inferno: Letture degli anni 1973–76. Casa di Dante in Roma. Nuove Lett*. Roma: Bonacci, 1977. Pp. 9–34. Rprt. in his *Studi danteschi*. Napoli: Istituto Universitario Orientale, 1983. Pp. 97–118.

Filippi, F. *Il Veltro nel 1° Canto dell'Inferno di Dante*. Cecina: A. Carnieri, 1902.

Filipponi, Osvaldo. *Le profezie di Dante e del Vangelo eterno*. Padova: MEB, 1983.

Filomusi-Guelfi, Lorenzo. "L'Allegoria fondamentale del Poema di Dante." *GD* 17 (1909): 229–268; rprt. in *Nuovi studi su Dante*. Città di Castello: S. Lapi, 1911. Pp. 3–75.

————. *Studi su Dante*. Città di Castello: S. Lapi, 1908.

————. *Nuovi studi su Dante*. Città di Castello: S. Lapi, 1911.

————. "Intorno alle osservazioni di E. G. Parodi al commento Scartazzini-Vandelli." *NGD* 1, (1917): 60–85; esp. pp. 60–63 on *Inferno*.

Finzi, Giuseppe. *Saggi danteschi*. Torino: Loescher, 1888.

Fitzgerald, Robert. "The Style That Does Honor." *Kenyon Review* 14, no. 2 (1952): 278–285; rprt. in *Letterature moderne* 7, no. 4 (1957): 397–401.

Flamini, Francesco. "Il fine supremo e il triplice significato della *Commedia* di Dante." *GD* 9 (1901): 67–81.

————. "Un problema di ermeneutica dantesca: che bestia era la lonza?" *La Rassegna* 24 (1916a): 94–103.

————. *I significati reconditi della D.C.* pt. 2: *Il vero: l'allegoria*. Livorno: Raffaello Giusti, 1904; rev. and rprt. *Il significato e il fine della Divina Commedia*, pt. 2: *Il Vero: L'allegoria*. Livorno: Raffaello Giusti, 1916b.

Flanders Dunbar, H. See Dunbar, Helen Flanders.

Fletcher, Jefferson Butler. "The Crux of Dante's Comedy." *Essays in Memory of Barrett Wendell*. Cambridge: Harvard University Press, 1926. Pp. 61–92.

————. *Dante*. Intro. Mark Musa. Notre Dame, IN: University of Notre Dame Press, 1965.

Foberti, F. "Questioni dantesche e storia francescana (Veltro—Gioachinismo—Ubertino da Casale)." *Miscellanea francescana* 39 (1939): 153–171.

Fornaciari, Raffaello. *Studj su Dante editi ed inediti*. Milano: Enrico Trevisini, 1883; rprt. Prima Edizione Fiorentina: riveduta e accresciuta. Firenze: G. C. Sansoni, 1900.

Forti, Umberto. "Lume per la 'selva oscura.'" *L'Italia letteraria: Settimanale di Lettere, Scienze ed Arti* anno XI, no. 28 (1935): 1.

Foscolo, Ugo. *Discorso sul testo della Divina Commedia*. In *La Divina Commedia illustrata da Ugo Foscolo*, vol. 1. Londra: Pietro Rolandi, 1842; rprt. in *Opere*. Edizione Nazionale, vol. 10. Firenze: F. F. Le Monnier, 1953.

Foster, Kenelm. *The Two Dantes and Other Studies*. Berkeley and Los Angeles: University of California Press, 1977.

Fowlie, Wallace. *A Reading of Dante's Inferno*. Chicago: University of Chicago Press, 1981.

Franciosi, Giovanni. "Il veltro allegorico." *Discorsi detti nel R. Liceo Muratori*. Modena: n. p., 1870. Pp. 59–74.

———. *Scritti vari*. Firenze: Successori Le Monnier, 1878.

Frankel, Margherita. "Dante's Conception of the Ideology of the *Aeneid*." In *Proceedings of the Xth Congress of the International Comparative Literature Association/ Actes du Xe congrès de l'Association internationale de litérature comparée*. Ed. Anna Balakian, James J. Wilhelm, et al. New York: Garland Press, 1985.

Fransoni, Domingo. *Studi vari sulla Divina Commedia di Dante Alighieri, con prefazione di Enrico Fani*. Firenze: Tipografia della Pia Casa di Patronata, 1887.

Frascino, Salvatore. "Il preludio del poema dantesco." *Annuario del Liceo-Ginnasio "Carducci-Ricasoli" di Grosseto* (1954–57), pp. 5–37; partial rprt. as "Il preludio al poema" in *La Divina Commedia nella critica*, ed. A. Pagliaro. Messina-Firenze: D'Anna, 1965. Vol. 1, pp. 97–104.

Fraticelli, P. "Della prima e principale allegoria del Poema di Dante: Discorso di P. Fraticelli." In P. Costa-G. Borghi, ed., *La Divina Commedia*. Firenze: Fabris, 1840. Vol. 1, pp. i–xxviii. Rprt. in his own commentary (1852; rprt. 1873; Firenze: G. Barbèra, 1886 [1887]), pp. 23–39.

Freccero, John. "Dante's Firm Foot and the Journey Without a Guide." *Harvard Theological Review* 52 (1959): 245–281.

———. "Dante and the Neutral Angels." *Romanic Review* 51 (1960): 3–14.

———. "Dante's Pilgrim in a Gyre." *PMLA* 76 (1961a): 168–181.

———. "Adam's Stand." *Romance Notes* 2 (1961b): 115–118.

———. "The Sign of Satan." *MLN* 80 (1965a): 11–26.

———. "Infernal Inversion and Christian Conversion (*Inferno* XXXIV)." *Italica* 42 (1965b): 35–41.

———. "Dante's Prologue Scene." *Dante Studies* 84 (1966a): 1–25.

———. "The River of Death: *Inferno* II, 108." In S. Bernard Chandler and J. A. Molinaro, eds. *The World of Dante: Six Essays in Language and Thought*. Toronto: University of Toronto Press, 1966b. Pp. 25–42.

———. "Medusa: The Letter and the Spirit." *Yearbook of Italian Studies* 2 (1972): 1–18.

———. "Casella's Song, *Purgatorio* II, 112." *Dante Studies* 91 (1973): 73–80.

———. "Dante's Ulysses: From Epic to Novel." In *Concepts of the Hero in the Middle Ages and the Renaissance*. Papers of the Fourth and Fifth Annual Conferences of the Center for Medieval and Renaissance Studies, State University of New York at Binghamton. Ed. Norman T. Burns and Christopher J. Reagan. Albany: SUNY Press, 1975.

———. "Bestial Sign and the Bread of Angels (*Inferno* 32–33)." *Yale Italian Studies* 1 (1977): 53–66.

———. "Infernal Irony: The Gates of Hell." *MLN* 99, no. 4 (French Issue, Sept. 1984): 769–786.

———. "The Significance of *Terza Rima*." In Aldo S. Bernardo and Anthony L.

Pellegrini, eds. *Dante, Petrarch, Boccaccio: Studies in the Italian Trecento in Honor of Charles S. Singleton.* MRTS, XXII. Binghamton, NY: MRTS, 1983. Pp. 3–17.

———. *Dante: The Poetics of Conversion.* Ed. with intro. by Rachel Jacoff. Cambridge: Harvard University Press, 1986. [A collection of Freccero's previous articles.]

Fregni, S. *Sul Veltro allegorico di Dante.* Modena: G. Ferraguti, 1913.

Friedman, John Block. "Antichrist and the Iconography of Dante's Geryon." *Journal of the Warburg and Courtauld Institutes* 35 (1972): 108–122.

Frugoni, Arsenio. "Il giubileo di Bonifacio VIII." *Bullettino dell'Istituto Storico Italiano* 62 (1950): 1–121.

Funaiolo, Gino. "Dante e il mondo antico." In *Medioevo e Rinascimento in onore di Bruno Nardi.* Firenze: G. C. Sansoni, 1955. Vol. 1, pp. 323–338.

Gaiter, Luigi. "Postille al commento della D.C." *Il Propugnatore,* 16, no. 1 (1883): 270–273.

Galassi-Paluzzi, C. "Perché Dante scelse Virgilio a sua guida." *GD* 39, n. s. 9, annuario dantesco 1936 (1938): 285–326.

Galvani, Giovanni. *Postille ai primi X canti della Divina Commedia.* Modena: Vincenzi, 1828. *Alcune postille al 1° canto dell'Inferno.* Modena: Soliani, 1831. Rprt. in *Saggio di alcune postille alla Divina Commedia con una lettera di Celestino Cavedoni all'autore sopra un luogo del "Paradiso."* Ed. Giovanni Franciosi. CODIR, 9. Città di Castello: S. Lapi, 1894.

Gehl, Paul F. "Mystical Language Models in Monastic Educational Psychology." *The Journal of Medieval and Renaissance Studies* 14, no. 2 (Fall 1984): 219–243.

Gellrich, Jesse M. *The Idea of the Book in the Middle Ages: Language Theory, Mythology, and Fiction.* Ithaca and London: Cornell University Press, 1985.

Geninasca, J. "Note per un'analisi strutturale del primo canto della *Divina Commedia.*" *Problemi* 13 (1969): 572–577.

Gentile, Giovanni. "La profezia di Dante." In *Frammenti di estetica e letteratura.* Lanciano: R. Carabba, 1921. Pp. 253–296.

Getto, Giovanni. "Dante e Virgilio." *Il Veltro* 3 (ott. 1959): 11–20.

———. *Il canto 1 dell'Inferno. Lect. Scaligera* [letta in febb., 1960]. Firenze: F. Le Monnier, 1960; rprt. 1967; rprt. in *CeS* 4 (1965): 406–415, with title "Il canto introduttivo della *Divina Commedia*"; and whole volume rprt. under title *Dante nella critica d'oggi.* Ed. Umberto Bosco. Firenze: F. Le Monnier, 1965. Pp. 406–415. Article rprt. in *Aspetti della poesia di Dante.* Firenze: Sansoni, 1966. Pp. 1–16.

Giannantonio, Pompeo. *Dante e l'allegorismo.* Biblioteca dell'Archivum Romanicum 100. Firenze: Olschki, 1969.

———. *Canto I dell'Inferno. Lect. Neapolitana.* Napoli: Loffredo, 1980.

Giglio, Raffaele. "Il prologo della Divina Commedia." *Critica letteraria* anno I, no. 1 (1973): 131–160.

Gilson, Etienne. *The Christian Philosophy of Saint Augustine.* Trans. L. E. M. Lynch. New York: Random House, 1960.

——. *Dante and Philosophy*. Harper Torchbooks. New York, Evanston and London: Harper and Row, 1963.

Ginori Conti, P. See Conti, P. Ginori.

Girard, René. *Deceit, Desire and the Novel: Self and Other in Literary Structure*. Trans. Yvonne Freccero. Baltimore, MD: The Johns Hopkins University Press, 1965.

Girardi, Enzo Noè. "Virgilio nella poetica di Dante." *Dante e Roma*. Atti del convegno di studi: Roma 8-9-10 aprile, 1965. Firenze: F. Le Monnier, 1965. Pp. 237–241.

Giuliani, Giambattista. *Metodo di commentare la Commedia di Dante Allighieri*. Firenze: F. Le Monnier, 1861.

Glässer, Edgar. *Dantes "pietas" in der Wertwelt der Commedia*. Halle (Saale): Max Niemayer, 1943.

Gnoli, D. "Dante e Roma." *GD* 15 (1907): 154–157.

Goldstein, Harvey D. "Enea e Paolo: A Reading of the 26th Canto of Dante's *Inferno*." *Symposium* 19, no. 4 (1965): 316–327.

Goss, E. "Il primo canto della *Commedia*: chiave di volta di tutto il poema." In *Saggi letterari*. Torino: SEI, 1939. Pp. 77–100.

Goudet, Jacques. *La politique de Dante*. Lyon: Editions l'Hermès, 1981.

Gozzo, Corrado. *L'Enigma forte e quello del Veltro*. Milano: Società editrice libreria, 1921.

Grandgent, Charles Hall. "Lo bello stilo." In *Todd Memorial Volumes*. New York: Columbia University Press, 1930. Vol. I, pp. 171–184.

Graziadei, Vittorio. *Lo sdegno di Dante*. Palermo: Reber, 1904.

Grazzani, Virginio. *Esegesi del primo canto della Divina Commedia di Dante Alighieri dedotta dal "Convito."* Ed. V. Grazzani. Sondrio: Tip. Mevio Washington & C., 1921.

Green, William M. *'Initium omnis peccati superbia': Augustine on Pride as the First Sin*. University of California Publications in Classical Philology, 13. Berkeley and Los Angeles: University of California Press, 1949.

Grundmann, Herbert. *Studien über Joachim von Flora*. Leipzig: Teubner, 1927.

——. "Die Papstprophetien des Mittelalters." *Archiv für Kulturgeschichte* 19 (1928): 77–138.

——. "Dante und Joachim von Fiore zu *Paradiso* X–XII." *DDJ* 14 (1932): 210–256.

Guardini, Romano. *Der Engel in Dantes göttlicher Komödie*. 2nd ed. München: Kösel, 1951; and *Landschaft der Ewigkeit*. München: Kösel, 1958; both trans. in *Dante visionaire de l'éternité*. Trans. Jeanne Ancelet-Hustache. Paris: Editions du Seuil, 1962.

Guarnerio, P. E. "Ancora della Lonza di Dante." *Rassegna bibliografica della letteratura italiana* 3 (1895): 139–140, 203–204.

Guerri, Domenico. "Il piè fermo." *GD* 13 (1905): 177–189.

Guyler, Sam. "Virgil the Hypocrite—Almost: A Re-interpretion of *Inferno* XXIII." *Dante Studies* 90 (1972): 25–42.

Haller, Robert S., trans. and ed. *Literary Criticism of Dante Alighieri*. Lincoln: University of Nebraska Press, 1973.

Hardie, Colin Graham. "The Epistle to Can Grande Again." *DDJ* 38 (1960): 51–74.

———. "Beatrice's Chariot in Dante's Earthly Paradise." *DDJ* 39 (1961): 137–172.

———. "Cacciaguida's Prophecy in Paradiso 17." *Traditio* 19 (1963): 267–294.

———. "The 'Veltres' in the Chanson de Roland." *DDJ* 41–42 (1964): 158–172.

———. "The Mountain in *Inferno* 1 and 2, Mount Ida in Crete, and the Mountain of Purgatory." *DDJ* 46 (1970): 81–100.

Hardt, Manfred. *Die Zahl in der Divina Commedia*. Linguistica et Litteraria, 13. Frankfurt am Main: Athenäum, 1973.

Hauvette, Henri. "Les païens appelés par Dante au Paradis: pourquoi Virgile en est exclu." *Nouvelle Revue d'Italie* 18 (1921): 48–54.

Haywood, Richard M. "*Inferno* I, 106–108." *MLN* 74 (1959): 416–418.

Henry, Albert. "Trois types de composition dans l'*Inferno*." *Studi in onore di Angelo Monteverdi*. Modena: Società Tipografica Editrice Modenese, 1959. Vol. 1, pp. 323–332.

Herzman, Ronald B. "Cannibalism and Communion in *Inferno* XXXIII." *Dante Studies* 98 (1980): 53–78.

Hirsch-Reich, B. "Die Quelle der Trinitätskreise von Joachim von Fiore und Dante." *Sophia* 22 (1954): 170–178.

———. (1972). See under Reeves, Marjorie.

Holbrook, Richard Thayer. *Dante and the Animal Kingdom*. New York: Columbia University Press; London: Macmillan, 1902.

Holder-Egger, O. "Italienische Prophetien des 13. Jahrhunderts." *Neues Archiv* 15 (1889): 141–178; 30 (1904): 321–386; 33 (1907): 95–187.

Hollander, Robert. "Dante's Use of *Aeneid* I in *Inferno* I and II." *Comparative Literature* 20 (1968): 142–156.

———. *Allegory in Dante's "Commedia."* Princeton: Princeton University Press, 1969.

———. "Dante's Use of the Fiftieth Psalm (a note on *Purg.* XXX, 84)." *Dante Studies* 91 (1973): 145–150. Rprt. in his *Studies in Dante*, pp. 107–114.

———. *Studies in Dante*. Ravenna: A. Longo, 1980.

———. *Il Virgilio dantesco: Tragedia nella Commedia*. Firenze: Olschki, 1983.

———. "A Checklist of Commentators on the *Commedia* (1322–1982)." *Dante Studies* 101 (1983b): 181–192.

———. "Virgil and Dante as Mind-Readers: *Inferno* XXI and XXIII." *Medioevo Romanzo* 9, no. 1 (1984): 85–100.

———. "Dante's Pagan Past: Notes on *Inferno* XIV and XVIII." *SIR* 5 (Spring 1985a): 23–36.

———. "Ugolino's Supposed Cannabalism: A Bibliographical Note and Discussion." *Quaderni d'italianistica* 6, no. 1 (1985b): 64–81.

Holmes, George. *Dante*. Oxford-Toronto-Melbourne: Oxford University Press, 1980.

Howard, Donald R. *The Three Temptations: Medieval Man in Search of the World.* Princeton: Princeton University Press, 1966.

Huck, Johannes Chrysostomus. *Ubertin von Casale und dessen Ideenkreis: Ein Beitrag zum Zeitalter Dantes.* Freiburg im Breisgau: Herder, 1903.

————. *Joachim von Floris und joachistische Literatur: Ein Beitrag zur Geistesgeschichte des hohenstaufischen Zeitalters mit Benützung und teilweiser Veröffentlichung ungedruckter Joachimsschriften.* Freiburg im Breisgau: Herder, 1938.

Iannucci, A. A. "Beatrice in Limbo: A Metaphoric Harrowing of Hell." *Dante Studies* 95 (1979): 23–46.

James, M[ontagu] R[hodes], ed. "Pictor in carmine." *Archaeologia or Miscellaneous Tracts Relating to Antiquity* 94: 2nd Series 44 (1951): 141–166.

Jenaro-McClellan, L. *The Trecento Commentaries on the Divina Commedia and the Epistle to Cangrande.* Oxford: Clarendon Press, 1974.

Johnston, O. M. "Interpretation of the First Canto of Dante's *Divina Commedia*." *Philological Quarterly* 5, no. 1 (1926): 35–43.

Kampers, Franz. *Dantes Kaisertraum.* Breslau: G. P. Aderholz, 1908.

————. *Vom Werdegange der Abendländischen Kaisermystik.* Leipzig-Berlin: Teubner, 1924.

————. "Der Veltro und die Jenseitsfahrt." *DDJ* 11 (1929): 136–156.

Kaske, Robert E. "Dante's DXV and Veltro." *Traditio* 17 (1961): 185–254.

————. "Dante's Purgatorio XXXII and XXXIII: A Survey of Christian History." *University of Toronto Quarterly* 43 (1974): 193–214.

Katzenellenbogen, Adolf. *Allegories of the Virtues and Vices in Medieval Art from Early Christian Times to the Thirteenth Century.* London: The Warburg Institute, The University of London, 1939; rprt. New York: W. W. Norton, 1964.

Kay, Richard. "Dante's Razor and Gratian's D. XV." *Dante Studies* 99 (1979): 65–96.

————. "The *Mentalité* of Dante's *Monarchia*." *Res Publica Litterarum: Studies in the Classical Tradition* 9 (1986): 182–191.

Kearney, Milo F., and Mimosa S. Scraer. "A Better Interpretation of Dante's 'Cinquecento Diece e Cinque.'" *Italica* 59 (1982): 32–40.

Kirkpatrick, Robin. *Dante: The Divine Comedy.* Cambridge, London and New York: Cambridge University Press, 1987.

Knittel, Hermann. "Virgil bei Dante: Beobachtung zur Nachwirkung des sechsten Äneisbuches." Diss. Albert-Ludwigs-Universität zu Freiburg im Breisgau. Konstanz: Verlagsanstalt Merk, 1971.

Koenen, F. "Der Jagdhund und der Hirte." *DDJ* 18 (1936): 189.

Köppen, Klaus Peter. *Die Auslegung der Versuchungsgeschichte unter besonderer Berücksichtigung der Alten Kirche: Ein Beitrag zur Geschichte der Schriftauslegung.* Beiträge zur Geschichte der biblischen Exegese, 4. Tübingen: J. C. B. Mohr (Paul Siebeck), 1961.

Kraus, Clara. "Camilla." *ED* 1 (1970a): 774.

————. "Eurialo." *ED* 2 (1970b): 766.

————. "Niso." *ED* 4 (1973): 50.

————. "Turno." *ED* 5 (1976): 760.

Kraus, Franz Xaver. *Dante: Sein Leben und sein Werk, sein Verhältniss zur Kunst und Politik.* Berlin: Grote, 1897.

Kraus, Hans Joachim. *Worship in Israel.* Oxford: Blackwell, 1966. Pp. 134–178.

Lajolo, Gregorio. *Simboli e enigmi danteschi: esposizione ragionata delle allegorie più notevoli e controverse della Divina Commedia.* Vol. 1. Roma-Torino: Casa Editrice Nazionale Roux e Viarengo, 1906.

Lami, Giovanni. *Postille alla Commedia.* Firenze: Formigli, 1837.

Lansing, Richard H. *From Image to Idea: A Study of the Simile in Dante's Commedia.* Ravenna: A. Longo, 1977.

Lanza, Franco. "Roma e l'emblema della Lupa." *Dante e Roma.* Atti del Convegno di Studi danteschi: Roma 8–9–10 aprile 1965. Firenze: F. Le Monnier, 1965. Pp. 255–261.

Leclerq, H. "Oraison dominicale." In F. Cabrol and H. Leclerq, eds. *Dictionnaire d'Archéologie Chrétienne et de Liturgie.* 15 vols. (1907–1953). Vol. 12, part 2 (1936), cols. 2244–2255.

Lenkeith, Nancy. *Dante and the Legend of Rome: An Essay.* Diss. Medieval and Renaissance Studies, Supplement 2. London: The Warburg Institute, University of London, 1952.

Leo, Ulrich. "The Unfinished *Convivio* and Dante's Reading of the *Aeneid.*" *Medieval Studies* 13 (1951): 41–64.

Leonardo, Bruni. *Vita di Dante.* In Angelo Solerti, ed. *Le vite di Dante, Petrarca e Boccaccio scritte fino al secolo decimosesto.* Storia Letteraria d'Italia, vol. 5, pp. 97–107. Milano: Francesco Vallardi, 1904.

Levi, Attilio. "La lonza di Dante." *GSLI* 88 (1926): 190–194.

Levi, Giulio Augusto. "Volse i passi suoi per via non vera." *Convivium* n. s. 20, no. 4 (1952): 534–547.

Lexikon der christlichen Ikonographie. Ed. Kirschbaum, Engelbert. Freiburg im Breisgau: Herder, 1970. Esp. "Wolf." In vol. 4, pp. 536–539.

Leynardi, Luigi. "Canto primo." *Lect. Genovese: I canti I–XI dell'Inferno.* Firenze: Successori F. Le Monnier, 1904. Pp. 45–78.

Limentani, Uberto. *Dante's Comedy: Introductory Readings of Selected Cantos.* Cambridge, U. K., and New York: Cambridge University Press, 1985.

Locke, Frederick W. "Dante's Miraculous *Enneads.*" *Dante Studies* 85 (1967): 59–70.

Lubac, Henri de. *Exégèse mediévale: les quatre sens de l'Ecriture.* 4 vols. Paris: Aubier, 1959–1964.

MacVay, Anna P. "Dante's Strange Treatment of Vergil." *CJ* 43 (1948): 233–235.

McCulloch, Florence. *Medieval Latin and French Bestiaries.* University of North Carolina Studies in Romance Languages and Literatures 33. Chapel Hill: The University of North Carolina Press, 1960.

McKenzie, Kenneth. "The Problem of the 'lonza' with an Unpublished Text." *RR* 1, no. 1 (1901): 18–33.

————. "Virgil and Dante." In *The Tradition of Virgil: Three Papers on the History and Influence of the Poet.* Princeton: Princeton University Press, 1930.

———. "Three Notes on the *Divina Commedia* . . . 'Le tre fiere.'" *Italica* 23 (1946): 136–141, esp. pp. 137–139.

McWilliam, G. H. "Dante's Smooth Beast: A Commentary on the Opening Canto of the *Commedia*." *Hermathena* 113 (Summer 1972): 15–33.

Maddox, Sara Sturm. See Sturm-Maddox, Sara.

Maier, Bruno. "Le principali 'cruces' della *Divina Commedia* nella critica contemporanea." *CeS* 4 (1965): 271–284; vol. rprt. *Dante nella critica d'oggi*. Ed. Umberto Bosco. Firenze: F. Le Monnier, 1965.

Mâle, Emile. *Religious Art in France of the Thirteenth Century: A Study in Medieval Iconography and Its Sources of Inspiration*. Trans. Dora Nussey New York: E. P. Dutton, 1913; rprt. *The Gothic Image: Religious Art in France of the Thirteenth Century*. New York: Harper and Row, 1958.

Manacorda, G. *Da San Tommaso a Dante: Congetture e riscontri*. Bergamo: Istituto Italiano d'arti grafiche, 1901.

Mancusi-Ungaro, Donna. *Dante and the Empire*. New York: Peter Lang, 1987.

Mandonnet, Pierre. "Note de symbolique médiévale: *Domini Canes*." *Revue de Fribourg [Suisse]* 43 (1912): 568–574.

Manselli, Raoul. "Dante e l'Ecclesia Spiritualis." *Dante e Roma*. Firenze: F. Le Monnier, 1965. Pp. 115–135.

———. "Cangrande e il mondo ghibellino nell'Italia settentrionale alla venuta di Arrigo VII." In Vittore Branca and Giorgio Padoan, eds. *Dante e la cultura veneta: Atti del Convegno di Studi, Venezia, Padova, Verona, 30 marzo-5 aprile, 1966*. Firenze: Olschki, 1966. Pp. 39–50.

———. "Il Canto XX del Purgatorio." In *Nuove Letture dantesche* 4. Firenze: F. Le Monnier, 1970. Pp. 307–325.

Marchese, Vincenzo. "Del Papa angelico del medio evo, e il Veltro allegorico della *Divina Commedia*." In *Scritti vari. Opere del padre Vincenzo Marchese de' Predicatori*. Vol. 3. Firenze: F. Le Monnier, 1855. Pp. 291–316.

Marchetti, Giovanni. *Della prima e principale allegoria del poema di Dante*. Bologna: Gamberini e Parmeggiani, 1819.

Mariani, Andrea. "cammino." *ED* 1 (1970): 777–778.

Martini, P. A. *Dante francescano*. Arezzo: n. p. 1921. [unconsulted.]

Maruffi, G. "Il senso letterale del primo canto dell'*Inferno* e il verso 63°." *GD* 2 (1895): 394–396.

Marzot, Giulio. *Il linguaggio biblico nella Divina Commedia*. Saggi di varia umanità, 17, collana diretta da Francesco Flora. Pisa: Nistri-Lischi, 1956.

Masciandaro, Franco. "*Inferno* I–II: Il dramma della conversione e il tempo." *SD* 49 (1972): 1–26.

———. *La problematica del tempo nella Commedia*. Ravenna: A. Longo, 1976.

Massèra A. "Il sirventese romagnolo del 1277." *Archivio storico italiano* 72, no. 1 (1914): 1–17.

Masseron, Alexandre. *Les énigmes de la Divine Comédie*. Paris: Librairie de l'Art Catholique, 1922.

———. *Dante et Saint Bernard*. Paris: Editions Albin Michel, 1953.

Mastrobuono, A. C. *Essays on Dante's Philosophy of History*. Firenze: Olschki, 1979.

Matrod, H. "Le Veltro de Dante et son DXV: Khan e Can." *Etudes Franciscaines* [Tamine: Belgique] 31 (January 1914): 61–81.

Mazzamuto, Pietro. "Cinquecento, diece e cinque." *ED* 2 (1970): 10–14.

Mazzoleni, Achille. "Chi parea fioco: chiosa dantesca." *Atti dell'Accademia di Acireale* 5 (1893): 145–157.

Mazzoni, Francesco. [Rev. of] "André Pézard, 'Les Loups, Virgile et Dante.'" *SD* 36 (1959): 268–269.

———. "Pietro Alighieri interprete di Dante." *SD* 40 (1963): 279–360.

Mazzoni, Giacopo. *Discorso di Giacopo Mazzoni in difesa della "Commedia" del divino poeta Dante*. Ed. Mario Rossi. CODIR 51–52. Città di Castello: S. Lapi Tipografo-Editore, 1898.

Mazzoni, Guido. [Rev. of] "F. D'Ovidio, *Nuovi studi danteschi....*" *BSDI* 14 (1907): 241–255.

———. *Il Canto I dell'Inferno* letto da Guido Mazzoni nella "Casa di Dante." In Roma, l'8 febbraio, 1914. *Lect. Romana*. Firenze: G. C. Sansoni, 1918. Rprt. in *Almae luces malae cruces*.

———. "Il canto I dell'*Inferno*." And "Dante e Virgilio." In *Almae luces malae cruces*. Bologna: Nicola Zanichelli, 1941.

Mazzotta, Giuseppe. *Dante Poet of the Desert: History and Allegory in the Divine Comedy*. Princeton: Princeton University Press, 1979.

Medin, Antonio. "La Profezia del Veltro: Nota dantesca...." *Atti e Memorie della R. Accademia di scienze, lettere ed arti in Padova*. Anno CCXC [1888–1889], n. s. 5 (1889): 287–304.

Meier, Harri. "Zu *Inferno* I und *Purgatorio* I." *Romanische Forschungen* 54 (1940): 284–289.

Merejkowski, Demetrio. *Dante*. Ital. trans. Rinaldo Küfferle. Bologna: Nicola Zanichelli, 1938, rprt. 1940.

Mineo, Nicolò. *Profetismo e apocalittica in Dante: Strutture e temi profetico-apocalittici in Dante dalla Vita Nuova all Divina Commedia*. Università di Catania, Pubblicazioni della Facoltà di Lettere e Filosofia, 24. Edigraf, 1968.

Montanari, Fausto. "L'incontro con Virgilio." In *L'Esperienza poetica di Dante*. Firenze: F. Le Monnier, 1959. Pp. 117–133.

Montano, Rocco. *Storia della poesia di Dante*. Quaderni di critica e testi, 2. 2 vols. Napoli: Quaderni di Delta, 1962.

———. "Dante and Virgil." *Yale Review* 40 (1971): 550–561.

———, and Ugo Barra. *Comprendere Dante: Analisi storico-critica—Canti scelti e commentati. Presentazione unitaria della Divina Commedia*. Napoli: G. B. Vico Editrice, 1976.

Monti, Vincenzo. *Postille ai commenti del Lombardi e del Biagioli sulla Divina Commedia*. Ferrara: Domenico Taddei, 1879.

Moore, Edward. *Time References in the Divina Commedia and Their Bearing on the Assumed Date and Duration of the Vision*. London: David Nutt, 1887.

———. *Scripture and Classical Authors in Dante. Studies in Dante: First Series.* Oxford: Clarendon Press, 1896.

———. "The DXV Prophecy." In *Studies in Dante: Third Series: Miscellaneous Essays.* Oxford: Clarendon Press, 1903. Pp. 253–283.

Morawski, Kalikst. "Le mythe de l'Empereur chez Dante." *REI* 12 (1965): 280–301.

Murdoch, Brian O. *The Recapitulated Fall: A Comparative Study in Mediaeval Literature.* Amsterdamer Publikationen zur Sprache und Literatur. Amsterdam: Rodopi N. V., 1974.

Musa, Mark. *Advent at the Gates: Dante's Comedy.* Bloomington and London: Indiana University Press, 1974.

Musseter, Sally. "Dante's Three Beasts and the *Imago Trinitatis.*" *Dante Studies* 95 (1977): 39–52.

Nadiani, P[adre]. *Il "Veltro" della "Divina Commedia."* Extract from *La Verna* 9, no. 4–5 (1911); Arezzo: Cooperativa Tipografia, 1911; rprt. 1914.

Nardi, Bruno. "Il concetto dell'Impero nello svolgimento del pensiero dantesco." *GSLI* 78 (1921): 1–52. Rprt. in *Saggi di filosofia dantesca.* Pp. 239–306.

———. *Saggi di filosofia dantesca.* Milano-Genova-Roma-Napoli: Società Anonima Editrice Dante Alighieri; Albrighi, Segati & c., S. A. F. Perrella, 1930.

———. *Nel mondo di Dante.* Roma: Storia e letteratura, 1944. Esp. pp. 204–205.

———. *Dante e la cultura medievale: Nuovi saggi di filosofia dantesca.* Bari: G. Laterza, 1949.

———. "Il canto XI dell'*Inferno.*" *Nuova Lectura Dantis.* Dir. da Siro A Chimenz. Roma: Angelo Signorelli, 1950. Rprt. in *Letture dantesche.* Ed. Giovanni Getto. Firenze: Sansoni, 1962. Pp. 193–207.

———. *Dal Convivio alla Commedia (Sei saggi danteschi).* Istituto Storico Italiano per il Medio Evo, *Studi Storici.* Vols. 35–39. Roma: Nella Sede dell'Istituto, Palazzo Borromini, 1960a.

———. "Il punto sull'Epistola a Cangrande." *Lect. Scaligera.* Firenze: F. Le Monnier, 1960b.

———. "Il preludio alla Divina Commedia." In *Alighieri* 4, no. 1 (1963): 3–17; rprt. *Lect. Romana.* Torino: SEI, 1964.

———. "Tre momenti dell'incontro di Dante con Virgilio." *L'Alighieri* 6, no. 2 (1965): 42–53; rprt. in *Saggi e note di critica dantesca* (1966), pp. 220–237.

———. *Saggi e note di critica dantesca.* Milano-Napoli: Riccardo Ricciardi, 1966.

Nelson, Alan H. "The Temptations of Christ; or the Temptations of Satan." In Jerome Taylor and A. H. Nelson, eds. *Mediæval English Drama: Essays Critical and Contextual.* Patterns of Literary Criticism, 11. Chicago: University of Chicago Press, 1972. Pp. 218–229.

Neppi, M. A. "Virgilio etrusco e Virgilio dantesco." In *Dante,* 12 (1962), pp. 3–11. [unconsulted.]

Newman, Francis Xavier. "St. Augustine's Three Visions and the Structure of the *Comedy.*" *MLN* 82 (1967): 56–78.

Niccoli, Alessandro. "piede." *ED* 4 (1973a): 482–485.

———. "ritrovare." *ED* 4 (1973b): 994–995.

———. "silenzio." *ED* 5 (1976a): 248.

———. "trovare." *ED* 5 (1976b): 745–747.

Nicosia, Alfonso. *Attorno ad un verso di Dante*. Ragusa: Piccitto e Antoci, 1895, 24 pp.

Nicosia, P. *Dieci saggi sull'Inferno dantesco*. Messina-Firenze: D'Anna, 1969.

Nogami, S. "Dante e Virgilio." *Studi Italici* [Kyoto] 13 (1964): 1–6.

Oeschger, I. "Antikes und Mittelalterliches bei Dante." *Zeitschrift für romanische Philologie* 64 (1944), 1–87.

Ogle, Marbury B. "Peter Comestor, Methodius and the Saracens." *Speculum* 21 (1946): 318–324.

[Olschski, Leonardo] Olschki, Leonard. *The Myth of Felt*. Berkeley and Los Angeles: University of California Press, 1949.

———. "Tra feltro e feltro." *Nuova Antologia*, anno 87° (1952): 386–398; rprt. revised in *Dante poeta veltro*, as Appendice, pp. 94–117.

———. *Dante, 'Poeta Veltro.'* Firenze: Olschki, 1953.

Orr, Mary Acworth. *Dante and the Early Astronomers*. London and Edinburgh: Gall and Inglis, 1914; rprt. with intro. by Barbara Reynolds. London: Allan Wingate, 1936.

Ortalli, G. "Natura, storia e mitografia del lupo nel Medioevo." *La Cultura* 11 (1973): 257–311.

Ostlender, Heinrich. "Veltro und Fünfhundertzehn und fünf." *DDJ* 25 (1943): 175–185.

———. "Dantes Kaiser und sein Veltro." *DDJ* 26 (1946): 50–68.

Padoan, Giorgio. "Il Limbo dantesco." *LI* 21 (1969): 372.

———. *Il pio Enea, l'empio Ulisse: Tradizione e intendimento medievale in Dante*. Ravenna: A. Longo, 1977.

Pagliaro, Antonino. ". . . lo passo Che non lasciò già mai persona viva." In *Studi letterari: Miscellanea in onore di E. Santini*. Palermo: Manfredi, 1956a; and in *Nuovi saggi di critica semantica*. Messina-Firenze: D'Anna, 1956b. Pp. 247–264.

———. *Nuovi saggi di critica semantica*. Messina-Firenze: G. D'Anna, 1956b.

———. "Proemio e prologo della *Divina Commedia*" (19 febbraio 1966). *Lett. Classensi* 2. Ravenna: A. Longo, 1969. Pp. 113–150.

———. *Ulisse: Ricerche semantiche sulla Divina Commedia*. 2 vols. [continuous pagination.] Messina-Firenze: G. D'Anna 1961a; rprt. 1966, 1967.

———. "Di quell'umile Italia. . . ." *Dialoghi* 9, no. 2 (1961b): 125–135; rprt. as "L'umile Italia." In Antonino Pagliaro, ed. *La Divina Commedia nella critica*. Vol. 1, pp. 119–128. Rprt. *Ulisse*, pp. 45–56, 766 n. 16.

———. "'. . . chi per lungo silenzio parea fioco' *Inf.* I, 63." In *Altri saggi di critica semantica*. Messina-Firenze: G. D'Anna, 1961c. Pp. 265–284; and in *Saggi e ricerche in memoria di Ettore Li Gotti*. Palermo: Mori, 1962. Vol. 2, pp. 417–428.

———, ed. *La Divina Commedia nella critica: introduzione e saggi scelti ad uso delle scuole*. Vol. I: *Inferno*. Messina-Firenze: G. D'Anna, 1968.

Pagnini, Rossana Valenti. "*Lupus in fabula*: Trasformazioni narrative di un mito." *Bollettino di studi latini* 11 (1981): 3–22.

Palgen, Rudolf. "Die Virgilsage in der göttlichen Komödie." *DDJ* 14 (1932): 1–26.

———. *The Influence of Prophecy in the Later Middle Ages: A Study in Joachimism.* Oxford: Clarendon Press, 1969.

———. "Dante and the Prophetic View of History." In Cecil Grayson, ed. *The World of Dante.* Oxford: Clarendon Press, 1980. Pp. 44–60.

———, and Barbara Hirsch-Reich. *The Figurae of Joachim of Fiore.* Oxford-Warburg Series. Oxford: Clarendon Press, 1972.

Regis, Aurelio. "E sua nazion sarà tra feltro e feltro." *SD* 4 (1921): 85–97.

Renucci, Paul. "La 'lonza' dantesque est-elle un guépard?" *REI* 2 (1937): 372–374.

———. *Dante disciple et juge du monde gréco-latin.* Paris: Société d'Edition "Les Belles Lettres," 1954.

———. "Dante et les mythes du Millenium." *REI* n. s. 11 (1965a): 393–421.

———. "Dantismo esoterico nel secolo presente." *Atti del Congresso Internazionale di Studi danteschi.* Firenze: Sansoni, 1965b. Pp. 305–332.

Ribailler, J., ed. and intro. "Richard de Saint-Victor. *De statu interioris hominis.*" *Archives d'Histoire doctrinale et littéraire du Moyen Age* 42 (1967): 7–128.

Ricci, Corrado. "Roma nel pensiero di Dante." In *Cogliendo biada o loglio: scritti danteschi.* Firenze: F. Le Monnier, 1924. Pp. 35–61.

Richthofen, Erich von. *Veltro und Diana: Dantes mittelalterliche und antike Gleichnisse nebst einer Darstellung ihrer Ausdrucksformen.* Tübingen: Max Niemeyer Verlag, 1956.

———. "The Twins of Latona." In S. B. Chandler and J. A. Molinaro, eds. *The World of Dante.* Toronto: University of Toronto Press, 1966.

Robertson, D. W. *A Preface to Chaucer: Studies in Medieval Perspectives.* Princeton: Princeton University Press, 1962.

Rocca, Luigi. *Di alcuni commenti della Divina Commedia composti nei primi vent'anni dopo la morte di Dante.* Firenze: G. C. Sansoni, 1891.

Roedel, Reto. "Il proemio della Divina Commedia." *Svizzera italiana* 19, no. 139 (dicembre 1959): 1–12. Rprt. *Lectura Dantis: Letture e saggi.* Bellinzona: Banco di Roma per la Svizzera, Lugano; Istituto Grafico Gianni Casagrande, 1965. Pp. 26–40.

Ronchetti, Ferdinando. "Intorno a due versi dell' Inferno." *GD* 3 (1896): 335–345.

Ronconi, Alessandro. "Parole di Dante: per una semantica dei virgilianismi." *Lingua nostra* 11, no. 4 (1950): 81–85.

———. "Per Dante interprete dei poeti latini." *SD* 41 (1964): 5–44, esp. p. 31.

Ronzoni, Domenico. *Pagine sparse di studi danteschi.* Monza: Tip. Artigianelli Orfani dei Figli di Maria Immacolata, 1901.

Rosenberg, Nancy. "Petrarch's Limping: The Foot Unequal to the Eye." *MLN* 71 (1962): 99–105.

Rossi, Mario. *Gusto filologico e gusto poetico: Questioni di critica dantesca.* Biblioteca di Cultura Moderna. Bari: Laterza, 1942.

———. "Il canto proemiale del poema." In *Gusto filologico e gusto poetico.* Pp. 61–72.

———. "Il Virgilio allegorico e il Virgilio poetico." In *Gusto filologico e gusto poetico.* Pp. 112–128.

Palleschi, Filippo. *Il canto I dell'Inferno.* In *Lectura Dantis* 1905, Società Dante Alighieri Comitato di Cagliari. Cagliari: Montorsi, 1905. Pp. 6–51.

Palmieri, Ugo. "Della precessione degli equinozi in Dante e di una questione di metodo critico." *SD* 38 (1961): 131–141.

Paparelli, Gioacchino. "Virgilio e le anime del Limbo." *Questioni dantesche.* Napoli: Libreria Scientifica, 1967. Pp. 87–132.

Papini, Giovanni. *Dante vivo.* Firenze: Libreria Editrice Fiorentina, 1933; Eng. trans. Eleanor Hammond Broadus and Anna Benedetti, 1934. Rprt. Port Washington, NY and London: Kennikat Press, 1969.

Paratore, Ettore. "L'eredità classica in Dante." In *Dante e Roma.* Atti del Convegno di Studi. Firenze: F. Le Monnier, 1965. Pp. 3–50.

———. *Tradizione e Struttura in Dante.* Firenze: G. C. Sansoni Editore, 1968.

———. *Virgilio nell'età di Dante.* Roma: Casa di Dante, 1982.

Parodi, Ernesto Giacomo. "Sotto il titolo 'Ancora della lonza. . . .'" *BSDI* 3 (1895): 24–26.

———. "Note per un commento alla *Divina Commedia.*" *BSDI* 23 (1916): 1–67.

———. [Rev. of] "L. Filomusi Guelfi, 'Intorno alle osservazioni di E. G. Parodi. . . .'" *BSDI* 25 (1918): 97.

———. *Poesia e storia nella Divina Commedia.* Napoli: Società Anonima Editrice F. Perrella, 1920.

———. "L'Ideale politico di Dante." In *Dante e l'Italia nel VI Centenario della morte del poeta MCMXXI.* Roma: Fondazione Marco Basso, 1921. Pp. 75–134.

Parri, Walter, and Teresa Parri. *Anno del viaggio e giorno iniziale della Commedia.* Firenze: L. Olschki, 1956.

Pascoli, Giovanni. *Minerva oscura: Prolegomeni, La costruzione del poema di Dante.* Livorno: Tipografia di Raff. Giusti, 1898.

———. *Sotto il velame: Saggio di un'interpretazione generale del Poema sacro.* Messina: Vincenzo Muglia, 1900. Rprt. *Sotto il velame: Saggio di un'interpretazione generale del poema sacro.* 2ª ed. Bologna: Nicola Zanichelli, 1912.

———. "Virgilio in Dante." *Memorie della R. Accademia d. Scienze dell'Istituto di Bologna,* 22 giugno 1910. Rprt. *Conferenze e studi dantesche.*

———. *La mirabile visione: Abbozzo d'una Storia della Divina Commedia.* Messina: Muglia, 1902; 2nd ed. Bologna: Nicola Zanichelli, 1913.

———. "Il re pacifico"; "il Veltro." Chaps. 18 and 19 of *La mirabile visione: Abbozzo d'una Storia della Divina Commedia.* Pp. 226–239.

———. *Conferenze e studi danteschi.* Bologna: Nicola Zanichelli, 1915.

Pasquazi, Silvio. *All'eterno dal tempo.* Firenze: F. Le Monnier, 1966.

———. "Il prologo all'*Inferno* [*Inferno* II]." In *D'Egitto in Ierusalemme: Studi danteschi.* Biblioteca di Cultura, 311. Roma: Bulzoni, 1985.

Paton, Lucy Allen. *Les Prophecies de Merlin.* Ed. from MS. 593 in the Bibliothèque Municipale of Rennes. Published for the Modern Language Association of America. New York and London: D. C. Heath, 1926–1927. Vol. I introduction and text, 1926; vol. II studies on the contents, 1927.

Pauly-Wissowa, *Realencyclopädie der classischen Altertumswissenschaft, Suppl. XV.* München: Druckenmüller, 1978. s. v. "Wolf" cols. 960–967.

Peck, Russell A. "Number as Cosmic Language." In David L. Jeffery, ed. *By Things Seen*. Ottawa: University of Ottawa Press, 1979. Pp. 47–80.

Pedrazzoli, U. *Nove commenti alla "Divina Commedia": Quinta recreazione dantesca: Il Veltro celeste*. Roma: Casa Editrice Italiana, 1910.

Pépin, Jean. *Les deux approches du Christianisme*. Paris: Les Editions du Minuit, 1961.

Persico, Federigo. "Alfonso Casanova e la *Divina Commedia*." *Rivista Universale* [Genova], anno IX, 22, fasc. 153 (1875): 44–69; rprt. in *Due letti: Alfonso Casanova e la Divina Commedia*. Firenze: G. C. Sansoni, 1900. Pp. 28–64.

Peters, Edward M. "Pars, Parte: Dante and an Urban Contribution to Political Thought." In H. A. Miskimin, David Herlihy, and A. L. Udovitch, eds. *The Medieval City*. New Haven: Yale University Press, 1977.

Petrie, Jennifer. "Dante's Virgil: *Purgatorio XXX*." In David Nolan, ed. *Dante Soundings: Eight Literary and Historical Essays*. Dublin: Irish Academic Press, 1981. Pp. 130–145.

Petrocchi, Giorgio. *Il Canto I dell'Inferno. Nuove Lett*. Casa di Dante in Roma, anno 1965–1966. Firenze: F. Le Monnier, 1966a (rprt. 1968). Vol. I, pp. 1–16. "Il canto I dell'*Inferno*" (12 febbraio 1966). *Lett. Classensi* 2 (1966–1967). Ravenna: A. Longo, 1969. Pp. 151–170. Rprt. as "Il proemio del poema." In *Itinerari danteschi*. Biblioteca di critica e letteratura, 3. Bari: Adriatica Editrice, 1969a. Pp. 257–275. Rprt. as "*Inferno*—Canto I" in *Questioni di critica dantesca*. Napoli: Luigi Loffredo Editore, 1969b; 2ª ristampa 1970. Pp. 317–321.

———. *L'Inferno di Dante*. Milano: Biblioteca Universale Rizzoli, 1978.

Petrucci, Raphael. "Sur un passage obscur de la *Divine Comédie*: le 'Veltre.'" *Revue d'histoire littéraire de la France* 8 (1901): 460–461.

Pézard, André. "Donat, Virgile et Dante." Appendix IV in *Dante sous la pluie de feu*. Pp. 339–345.

———. *Dante sous la pluie de feu*. Etudes de Philosophie Médiévale, 40. Paris: J. Vrin, 1950.

———. "Les loups, Virgile et Dante." *REI* n. s. 4 (1957): 5–30.

———. "Ce qui gronde en l'éternel." *SD* 42 (1965): 205–233.

———. *Tant que vienne le veltre: Enfer I: 100–101*. Paris: Chez Tallone Editeur-imprimeur, 1978.

Pietrobono, Luigi. *Il poema sacro: Saggio d'una interpretazione generale della Divina Commedia. Inferno—Parte I e II*. Bologna: Nicola Zanichelli, 1915.

———. "Il prologo della Divina Commedia." *GD* 26, no. 4 (1923): 323–328; and 27, no. 2 (1924): 141–148. Rprt. in *Saggi danteschi*. Torino: SEI, 1954. Pp. 181–202.

———. *Il canto I dell'Inferno* presentato alla Casa di Dante a Roma il 15 febbraio 1925. *Lect. Romana*. Torino: S. E. I., 1925; rprt. 1959.

———. "Dante e Roma." *GD* 33 (1930): 1–24.

———. "Virgilio, l'impero e il al di là." In *Studi su Dante*. Pp. 76–108.

———. *Studi su Dante*. Milano: Hoepli, 1944.

———. "Il Veltro e la Lupa." *La Brigata degli Amici del Libro Italiano* (Napoli), 3, no. 4 (1958): 1–3. [Review of L. Olschki, *Dante, "Poeta Veltro."*]

Piromalli, Antonio. *Gioacchino da Fiore e Dante*. Ravenna: A. Longo, 1966.

Poletta, Giacomo. *Alcuni Studi su Dante Allighieri come appendice al Dizionario dantesco*. Vol. 8. Siena: Tipografia Editrice S. Bernardino, 1892.

———. "Le tre fiere." In *Alcuni studi su Dante Alighieri*. Pp. 67–84.

———. "Il Veltro." In *Alcuni studi su Dante Alighieri*. Pp. 85–120.

———. *La Santa Scrittura nelle opere e nel pensiero di Dante Alighieri*. Siena: Tipografia Pontificia S. Bernardino, 1909.

Porcelli, Bruno. "'Chi per lungo silenzio parea fioco' e il valore della parola nella *Commedia*." *Ausonia* 19, 5 (1964): 32–38.

———. *Studi sulla 'Divina Commedia.'* Bologna: Patron, 1970.

Porena, Manfredi. "Il Veltro." In *La Divina Commedia*, commentata da M. Porena. Vol. 1: *Inferno*. Bologna: Nicola Zanichelli, 1946–1948; rprt. 1951. Pp. 17–18.

———. "Una nuova chiosa alla profezia dantesca del Veltro liberatore." *Atti della Accademia Nazionale dei Lincei*: anno CCCL (1953), serie VIII, *Rendiconti: classe di scienza morali, storiche e folilogiche*, vol. 8, fasc. 5–6 (maggio-giugno 1953): 230–237.

Présence de Virgile: Actes du Colloque des 9, 11, 12 décembre 1976 (Paris E. N. S., Tours). Ed. R. Chevallier. Caesarodunum XIII bis, numéro spécial. Université de Tours, Institut d'Etudes Latines et Centre de Recherches A. Piganiol. Paris: Société d'Edition "Les Belles Lettres," 1978.

Previtera, Carmelo. "Il 'Messo di Dio' dantesco, il 'Cinquecento diece e cinque' svelato." *Atti della Reale Accademia Peloritana*, 38 (1936). Extract publ. Messina: Tipografia D'Amico, 1936.

Priest, Paul. *Dante's Incarnation of the Trinity*. Ravenna: A. Longo Editore, 1982.

Proto, Enrico. "Gerione (la corda—la sozza imagine di froda)." *GD* 7 (1900): 65–105.

———. "La lonza dantesca." *GD* 15 (1907): 1–16.

Pusateri, Pietro. *Dante e la critica nucleare dalla selva a Dite*. Messina-Firenze: G. D'Anna, 1961. Pp. 17–18.

Radke, Gerhard. "Die Deutung der 4. Ekloge Virgils durch Kaiser Konstantin." In R. Chevallier, ed. *Présence de Virgile*. Paris, 1978. Pp. 147–160.

Ragni, Eugenio. "selva." *ED* 5 (1976): 137–162.

Ragonese, Gaetano. "fiera": "le tre fiere." *ED* 2 (1970): 857–861.

Rahner, Hugo. "Flumina de ventre Christi: Die patristische Auslegung von Joh. 7: 37–38." *Biblica* 22 (1941): 367–403.

———. "The Christian Mystery and the Pagan Mysteries." In Joseph Campell, ed., and Olga Froebe Kapteyn, ed. and trans. *The Mysteries: Papers from the Eranos Yearbooks*. Bollingen Series 30, 2. New York: Pantheon Books, 1955.

Reade, William Henry Vincent. *The Moral System of Dante's Inferno*. Oxford University Press, 1909. Rprt. Port Washington, NY, and London: Kennikat Press, 1969.

———. "Dante's Vision of History." *Proceedings of the British Academy* 25 (1939): 187–215.

Reeves, Marjorie. "Joachimist Influences on the Idea of a Last World Emperor." *Traditio* 17 (1961): 323–370.

Russo, Francesco. "Rassegna gioachimito-dantesca." *Miscellanea Francescana* 38, fasc. 1–2 (1938): 65–83.

———. *Bibliografia Gioachimita*. Biblioteca di Bibliografia Italiana 28. Firenze: Leo S. Olschki, 1954. Esp. Parte IV, "Gioacchino e Dante." Pp. 137–148.

———. "Dante e Gioacchino da Fiore." *Dante e l'Italia meridionale Atti del II Congresso Nazionale di Studi Danteschi*. Firenze: Olschki, 1966. Pp. 217–230.

Russo, Vittorio. "'Timor,' 'audacia' e 'fortitudo' nel canto II dell'*Inferno*." *Filologia e Letteratura* 11 (1965): 391–408.

———. *Il romanzo teologico: sondaggi sulla "Commedia" di Dante*. Napoli: Liguori, 1984.

Ryan, Christopher J. "*Inferno* XXI: Virgil and Dante: A Study in Contrasts." *Italica* 59 (1982a): 16–31.

———. "Virgil's Wisdom in the *Divine Comedy*." *Medievalia et Humanitisca* 11 (1982b): 1–38.

Salsano, F. "paura." *ED* 4 (1973): 350–351.

Sampoli Simonelli, M. [Rev. of] "Leonardo Olschki. *Dante 'poeta veltro.'*" *SD* 32 (1954): 101–105.

Samuel, Irene. "The Veltro Once More: A Note on *Inferno* I, 101." *RR* 38 (1947): 13–15.

Sanesi, Ireneo. *Per l'interpretazione della Divina Commedia: Note*. Torino-Milano-Firenze: G. B. Paravia, 1902.

Sanguineti, Edoardo. "Dante, *Inferno* I–III." In *Tre studi danteschi*. Firenze: F. Le Monnier, 1961. Pp. 1–24.

Santi, Antonio. "Il Veltro dantesco: il Veltro è sinonimo di imperatore e di 'cinquecento diece e cinque' o 'DXV.'" *NGD* 2 (1918): 81–96; 3 (1919): 53–93.

Santoro, M. "Virgilio personaggio della *Divina Commedia*." *CeS* 4 (1965): 343–355; vol. rprt. as *Dante nella critica d'oggi*. Ed. Umberto Bosco. Firenze: F. Le Monnier, 1965.

Sapegno, Natalino. "Il canto III dell'*Inferno*." Lectura Dantis Scaligera. Firenze: F. Le Monnier, 1960.

Sarolli, Gian Roberto. "Dante 'scriba Dei.'" *Convivium* 31 (1963): 385–671; rprt. in *Prolegomena alla D.C.* Pp. 189–336.

———. *Prolegomena alla "Divina Commedia."* Biblioteca dell'Archivum Romanicum, Serie 1, vol. 112. Firenze: Olschki, 1971.

———. *Analitica della Divina Commedia, I: Struttura numerologica e poesia*. Bari: Adriatica, 1974.

Sayers, Dorothy Leigh. *Introductory Papers on Dante*. London: Methuen, 1954a.

———. "Dante's Virgil." In *Further Papers on Dante*. New York: Harper; London: Methuen, 1954b. Pp. 53–77.

Scaetta, Silvio. *Il Veltro*. Camerino: Borgarelli, 1893.

———. *La fama della Divina Commedia*. CODIR. Città di Castello: S. Lapi, 1896.

Scarano, Nicola. "Sul verso 'chi per lungo silenzio parea fioco.'" In *Saggi Danteschi* a cura di Isotta Scarano Napoli s.e. 1970, Nota letta alla R. Accademia di archeologia, lettere e belle arti, Napoli, 19 giugno 1894. Pp. 247–266, 269–280. [unconsulted.]

Scartazzini, G. A. *Dantologia: vita e opere di Dante Alighieri.* 2ª ed. Milano: Hoepli, 1894.

———. *Enciclopedia Dantesca: Dizionario critico e ragionato di quanto concerne la vita e le opere di Dante Alighieri.* 2 vols. Milano: Hoepli, 1896–1899; vol. 3, *Vocabolario-Concordanza delle opere latine e italiane di Dante Alighieri.* Cont. by A. Fiammazzo. Milano: Hoepli, 1905.

Scharl, E. *Recapitulatio mundi.* Freiburger Theologische Studien, 60. Freiburg im Breisgau: Herder, 1941.

Scherillo, Michele. *Alcuni capitoli della biografia di Dante.* Torino: Loescher, 1896. Esp. pp. 461–462.

Schiaffini, A. "Note sul colorito dialettale della *Divina Commedia.*" *SD* 13 (1928): 31–45.

Schiller, Gertrud. *Ikonographie der christlichen Kunst.* Vol. 1. Gütersloh: Gerd Mohn, 1966; *Iconography of Christian Art.* Vol. 1. Trans. Janet Seligman. Greenwich, CT: New York Graphic Society, 1971.

Schmidt, Gerhard. *Die Armenbibeln des XIV. Jahrhunderts.* Graz-Köln: Hermann Böhlaus Nachf., 1959.

Schmitt, Franciscus Salesius. "Dante und Anselm von Canterbury zum Prolog der *Divina Commedia.*" In *Medioevo e Rinascimento: Studi in Onore di Bruno Nardi.* Firenze: Sansoni, 1955. Vol. II, pp. 651–666.

Schneider, Friedrich. "Dante und Virgil." *DDJ* 36/37 (1958): 126–127.

Schoder R. V. "Vergil in the *Divine Comedy.*" *CJ* 44 (1949): 413–422.

Schrijvers, M. P.-H. "La valeur de la pitié chez Virgile (dans L'*Enéide*) et chez quelques-uns de ses interprètes." In R. Chevallier, ed. *Présence de Virgile.* Pp. 483–495.

Scolari, Antonio. "*Inferno* I, vv. 49–54." *SD* 54 (1982): 1–14.

Scolari, A. *Il Messia dantesco.* Bologna: N. Zanichelli, 1913.

Scolari, Filippo. *Note ad alcuni luoghi delli primi cinque canti della Divina Commedia.* Venezia: Picotti, 1819.

Scrocca, Alberto. "Le tre fiere." In *Saggi danteschi.* Napoli: Perrella, 1908. Pp. 1–50.

Seung, T. K. [See also Thomas K. Swing]. *Cultural Thematics: The Formation of the Faustian Ethos.* New Haven: Yale University Press, 1976.

Shoaf, Richard Allen. *Dante and the Currency of the Word: Money, Images and Reference in Late Medieval Poetry.* Norman, Oklahoma: Pilgrim Books, 1983.

Siebzehner-Vivanti, G. *Dizionario della Divina Commedia.* Ed. Michele Messina. Firenze: Olschki, 1954. Rprt. Milano: Feltrinelli, 1965.

Silverstein, H. Theodore. "Dante and Virgil the Mystic." *Harvard Studies and Notes in Philology and Literature* 14 (1932): 51–82.

Simone, Alberto. "Il canto I dell'*Inferno* dantesco." *Annuario del Liceo-Ginnasio "G. Carducci" di Viareggio* (1949–1959): 26–38; rprt. in *Saggi e letture critiche (da Dante ai contemporanei).* Pisa: U. Giardini, 1959. Pp. 7–22.

Singleton, Charles S. *An Essay on the Vita Nuova.* Cambridge: Harvard University Press, 1949.

———. *Dante Studies 1: Commedia, Elements of Structure.* Cambridge: Harvard

University Press, 1954. Rprt. as *Dante's Commedia: Elements of Structure.*
Baltimore, MD: The Johns Hopkins University Press, 1977.

———. "Virgil Recognizes Beatrice." *ARDS* 74 (1956): 29–38.

———. "The Irreducible Dove." *Comparative Literature* 9 (1957): 129–135.

———. *Dante Studies 2: Journey to Beatrice.* Cambridge: Harvard University Press, 1958. Rprt. as *Journey to Beatrice.* Baltimore, MD: The Johns Hopkins University Press, 1977.

———. "In Exitu Israel de Aegypto." *ARDS* 78 (1960): 1–24; rprt. in John Freccero, ed. *Dante: A Collection of Critical Essays.* Twentieth Century Views. Englewood Cliffs, NJ: Prentice-Hall, 1965.

———. "The Poet's Number at the Center." *MLN* 80 (1965a), 1–10.

———. "The Vistas in Retrospect." *Atti del Congresso Internazionale di Studi Danteschi . . . . 20–27 aprile 1965.* Vol. 1. Firenze: Sansoni, 1965b. Pp. 279–304. Rprt. in *MLN* 81 (1966): 55–80.

Sirago, Vito. "Dante e gli autori latini." *LI* 3 (1951): 99–134.

Small Stuart, G. P. "Vergil, Dante and Camilla." *CJ* 54 (1959): 295–301.

Solerti, Angelo. "Per la data della visione dantesca." *GD* 4, n. s. 3 (1898): 289–309.

———, ed. *Le vite di Dante, Petrarca e Boccaccio scritte fino al secolo decimosesto.* Storia Letteraria d'Italia, vol. 5. Milano: Francesco Vallardi, 1904.

Solmi, Arrigo. "Sulla traccia del Veltro." *Rivista d'Italia.* (marzo 1913). Rprt. as "L'Impero universale e l'allegoria del Veltro." In *Il pensiero politico di Dante: Studi storici.* Firenze: "La Voce," 1922. Pp. 82–105.

Spargo, John Webster. *Virgil the Necromancer.* Cambridge: Harvard University Press, 1934.

Spillenger, Paul W. "An Aspect of Vergil's Role in the *Commedia.*" *RN* 24, n. 1 (Fall 1983): 55–58.

Spitzer, Leo. "A Note on the Poetic and the Empirical 'I' in Medieval Authors." *Traditio* 4 (1946): 414–422.

Spoerri, Theophil. *Einführung in die Göttliche Komödie.* Zurich: R. Roemer, Speer-Verlag, 1946. Ital. trans. Marco Cerruti. *Introduzione alla Divina Commedia.* Milano: U. Mursia, 1966.

Spraycar, Rudy S. "Dante's 'lago del cor.'" *Dante Studies* 96 (1978): 1–20.

Staerk, W. "Anakephalaiosis." In *Realexikon für Antike und Christentum* 1 (1950): 411–414.

Stange, C. "Mi ritrovai per una selva oscura." *DDJ* 21 (1938): 164–172.

Steiner, Arpad. "St. Jerome and the First Terzina of the *Divine Comedy.*" *MLN* 52, no. 4 (1937): 259–260.

Stocchetti, Agostino. *Letture dantesche.* Milano: Edizioni Pro Cultura, 1962.

Sturm-Maddox, Sara. *Petrarch's Metamorphoses: Text and Subtext in the Rime Sparse.* Columbia, MO: University of Missouri Press, 1985.

Swing, Thomas K. [See also T. K. Seung]. *The Fragile Leaves of the Sibyl.* Westminster, MD: The Newman Press, 1962, rprt. 1965.

Tateo, Francesco. "inventio." *ED* 3 (1971): 489–490.

Thompson, David. "Dante's Ulysses and the Allegorical Journey." *Dante Studies* 85 (1967): 33–58.

———. *Dante's Epic Journeys*. Baltimore, MD: The Johns Hopkins University Press, 1974.

———, and Alan F. Nagel, eds. and trans. *The Three Crowns of Florence: Humanist Assessments of Dante, Petrarca and Boccaccio*. New York: Harper and Row, 1972.

Tobler, Adolf. *Dante und vier deutsche Kaiser*. Rede zur Gedächtnisfeier König Friedrich Wilhelms III, am 3. August 1891. Berlin: Buchdruckerei der Königl. Akademie der Wissenschaften (C. Vogt), 1891.

Todeschini, Giuseppe. "Del Veltro allegorico della *Divina Commedia* e del tempo in cui furono scritti i versi 101–105 del canto I. dell' *Inferno*. . . ." In his *Scritti su Dante*, a cura di Bartolomeo Bressan. 2 vols. Vicenza: Tipografia Burato, 1872. Vol.i, pp. 153–169.

Toffanin, Giuseppe. "Dante e Virgilio," "Ma quando fu . . ." and "Il limite di Virgilio." In *Perché l'umanesimo incomincia con Dante*. Bologna: Zanichelli Editore, 1967. Pp. 9–15, 17–25, 35–39.

Tommaseo, Niccolò. "Il veltro allegorico di Dante." *Antologia* [Vieusseux], (ott., 1831). [unconsulted.]

———. "Della seconda morte." "Dell'ultimo libro di C. Troya intorno al Veltro di Dante." In *Nuovi studi su Dante*. Torino: Collegio degli Artigianelli, 1865. Vol. 2, pp. 76–102, 271–277.

Tondelli, Leone. *Il Libro delle figure dell'abate Gioachino da Fiore*. Vol. 1: Introduzione e Commento. Le sue rivelazioni dantesche. Vol. 2: Tavole. Torino: SEI, 1940; rprt. vol. 1, ed. Leone Tondelli; vol. 2, ed. Leone Tondelli, M. Reeves, and B. Hirsch-Reich. 2nd ed. Torino: SEI, 1953.

———. "Nuove visuali sull'allegoria del Veltro." In *Da Gioachino a Dante. Nuovi Studii. Consensi e contrasti*. Torino: SEI, 1944. Pp. 107–121.

Töpfer, Bernhard. *Das kommende Reich des Friedens: Zur Entwicklung chiliastische Zukunfthoffnungen im Hochmittelalter*. Forschungen zur mittelalterlichen Geschichte, 2. Berlin: Akademie Verlag, 1964.

Torraca, Francesco. "Il Veltro dantesco e il DXV." *Rivista critica della letteratura italiana* anno 7, n. 6 (1892), cols. 183–186.

———. [Rev. of] "La Divina Commedia di Dante Alighieri con commento del prof. Giacomo Poletto: I, *L'Inferno*. . . . Roma: Tipografia Liturgica di San Giovanni, Desclée, Lefèbvre e C., 1894." *BSDI* n. s. 2, fasc. 9 (giugno 1895): 129–157.

———. *Di un commento nuovo alla Divina Commedia*. Biblioteca Storico-critica della letteratura dantesca, 7–8. Bologna: Nicola Zanichelli, 1899.

Torricelli, F. M. "Il Veltro." In *In omaggio a Dante*. Roma, 1865. [unconsulted.]

Townend, G. B. "Changing Views of Virgil's Greatness." *CJ* 56 (1960): 67–77.

Trenta, Giorgio. "Commento sui versi 82–87 dell'*Inferno*, primo canto." *GD* 2 (1895): 433–440.

Triolo, Alfred A. "'Matta Bestialità' in Dante's 'Inferno': Theory and Image." *Traditio* 24 (1968): 247–292.

Troya, Carlo. *Del veltro allegorico di Dante [1826] e altri saggi storici*. Ed. Costantino Panigada. Bari: Giuseppe Laterza e Figli, 1932.

Trucchi, E. "Il Virgilio dantesco." In *Studi su Dante*. Milano: Hoepli, 1940. Pp. 109–134.

Truffi, Riccardo. "La seconda morte." *GD* 2 (1895): 507–510.

[Ubaldini, Federigo]. Guido Vitaletti. "Le *Annotazioni* alla *Divina Commedia* di Federigo Ubaldini (1610–1657)." *GD* 26 (1923): 329–330.

Ungaretti, Giuseppe. "Commento al primo canto dell'*Inferno*." *Paragone* III, 36 (1952): 5–21; rprt. "Il c. I dell'Inferno." *Letture dantesche*. A cura di Giovanni Getto. Firenze: Sansoni, 1962; 3rd ed. 1964. Pp. 5–23.

Vaccalluzzo, Nunzio. *Dal lungo silenzio: studi danteschi*. Messina: Vincenzo Muglia, 1903.

Valeggia, Gildo. *Il I canto dell'Inferno dantesco*. Lanciano, 1900. [unconsulted.]

Valenti Pagnini, R. "'Lupus in fabula,' trasformazioni narrative di un mito." *Bollettino di studi latini* 11 (1981): 3–22.

Vallone, Aldo. "C. I *Inf.*, part. v. 63." In *Prime notarelle dantesche*. Quaderni di inediti e ricerche, vol. 2. Galatina: Mariano, 1947–1948. Pp. 18–20.

———. *Del Veltro dantesco*. Lect. Siciliana. Trapani: Edizioni Accademia di Studi "Cielo D'Alcamo." 1954; rprt. 1955.

———. "Ancora del Veltro e della preghiera di S. Bernardo in Dante." *Letterature moderne* (Bologna), 7, n. 6 (1957): 735–738; rprt. *La critica dantesca nel Settecento ed altri saggi danteschi*. Firenze: Olschki, 1961. Pp. 85–89.

———. "Interpretazione del Virgilio dantesco." *L'Alighieri* 10, no. 1 (1969): 14–40.

Vance, Eugene. "Augustine's *Confessions* and the Grammar of Selfhood." *Genre* 6 (1973): 18–22.

———. "Désir, rhétorique et texte—semances de différence: Brunet Latin chez Dante." *Poétique* 42 (avril, 1980): 137–155.

Vanossi, Luigi. "lupo e lupa." *ED* 3 (1971): 742–743.

Vaughan, P. H. *The Meaning of 'Bāma' in the Old Testament*. Society for Old Testament Study, 3. London: Cambridge University Press, 1974.

Vaux, R. de. *Ancient Israel: Its Life and Institutions*. New York: McGraw-Hill, 1961.

Ventura, Tommaso. *Nuovi orizzonti della Divina Commedia: La selva, il colle, il Veltro*. Roma: n. p., 1941. [unconsulted.]

———. *Il pensiero umanistico di Dante dalla Vita Nuova alla Divina Commedia*. Letture dantesche fatte alla Società Dante Alighieri di Roma. Collana di Cultura. Milano: Gastaldi, 1953.

Verdicchio, Massimo. "Il Veltro and Dante's Prologue to the Commedia." *Quaderni d'Italianistica* 5, 1 (1984): 18–38.

Vettori, Vittorio. "Il prologo dell'*Inferno*." In V. Vettori, ed. *Lectura Dantis Internazionale . . . Letture dell'Inferno*. Milano: Marzorati, 1963. Pp. 7–27.

Vinassa De Regny, Paolo. "Il primo verso della *Commedia*." *Atti della Accademia di Scienze, Lettere e arti di Palermo*, s. IV, Vol. 3, pt. 2, fasc. 3 (1942): 405–413.

Vincent, L. H. "La notion biblique du 'haut-lieu.'" *Revue Biblique* 40 (1948): 245–278; 438–445.

Viola, Italo. "Concezione simbolica e rappresentazione di Virgilio nella *Divina Commedia.*" *Istituto di Studi danteschi: Annali*, I. Serie 3: Scienze filologiche e letteratura, Milano: Università Cattolica del Sacro Cuore, Pubblicazioni, Contributi, 1967. Pp. 327–358.

Vitaletti, Guido. "Le *Annotazioni* alla *Divina Commedia* di Federigo Ubaldini (1610–1657)." *GD* 26 (1923): 329–330.

Vivier, Robert. "Ce que Virgile fut pour Dante: Genèse amoureuse de la *Divine Comédie.*" *Revue des Cours et Conférences*, 39ᵉ année (1ʳᵉ série), no. 2 (30 décembre 1937): 97–114. "Virgile, guide de voyage." No. 3 (15 janvier 1938): 250–260. "Virgile, guide littéraire de Dante." No. 5 (15 février 1938): 434–443.

Vossler, Karl. *Die Göttliche Komödie.* 2 vols. Heidelberg: Carl Winter, 1907–1910; *Medieval Culture: An Introduction to Dante and His Times.* Trans. William Cranston Lawton. 2 vols. New York: Harcourt, Brace and Company, 1929.

Warkentin, Germaine. "'Love's sweetest part, variety,' Petrarch and the Curious Frame of the Renaissance Sonnet Sequence." *Renaissance and Reformation* 11 (1975): 15 esp.

Wegele, Franz Xaver von. *Dante Alighieris Leben und Werke.* Jena: Gustav Fischer, 1879.

Whitfield, John H. *Dante and Virgil.* Oxford: Basil Blackwell, 1949.

———. "Dante e Virgilio." *Le Parole e le idee* 7 (1965): 3–16.

Whitman, Jon. "From the *Cosmographia* to the *Divine Comedy*: An Allegorical Dilemma." In Morton W. Bloomfield, ed. *Allegory, Myth and Symbol.* Harvard English Studies 9. Cambridge: Harvard University Press, 1981. Pp. 63–86.

Wieruszowski, Helene. "Der Reichsgedanke bei Dante." *DDJ* 14 (1932): 185–209.

Wigodsky, Michael. "'Nacqui sub Iulio': *Inferno*, I, 70." *Dante Studies* 93 (1975): 177–183.

Wilhelm, James J. *Il Miglior Fabbro: The Cult of the Difficult in Daniel, Dante, and Pound.* Orono, ME: National Poetry Foundation, 1982.

Wilkins, Ernest Hatch. "The Prologue of the *Divine Comedy.*" In *The Invention of the Sonnet and Other Studies in Italian Literature.* Roma: Ediz. di Storia e Letteratura, 1959.

Williams, Charles. *The Figure of Beatrice: A Study in Dante.* London: Faber and Faber, 1943. Rprt. New York: Farrar, Straus and Cudahy, 1961.

Wingell, Albert E. "The Forested Mountaintop in Augustine and Dante." *Dante Studies* 99 (1981): 9–48.

Witte, Karl. *Dante-Forschungen altes und neues.* Halle: G. Emil Barthel, 1869–1879; Heilbronn: Henninger, n. d.

Wlassics, Tibor. *Dante narratore: saggi sullo stile della Commedia.* Saggi di Lettere Italiane, 20. Firenze: Olschki, 1975.

———. "The *Villanello* (*Inferno* XXIV, 1–15)." *Lect. Virginiana* 1, 1 (1987): 61–72.

Woody, Kennerly M. "Dante and the Doctrine of the Great Conjunctions." *Dante Studies* 95 (1977): 119–134.

Zabughin, Vladimiro. "Quattro geroglifici danteschi." *GSLI*, suppl. 19–21 (1921): 521–544.

———. *Virgilio nel rinascimento italiano da Dante a Torquato Tasso.* 2 vols. Bologna: N. Zanichelli, 1921–1923.

Zingarelli, Niccolò. *Dante e Roma.* Roma: E. Loescher, 1895.

———. *La vita, i tempi e le opere di Dante Alighieri.* Milano: Vallardi, 1931.

Zolese, G. "Il primo canto dell'Inferno . . . interpretato." *Il Propugnatore* 19, no. 2 (1886): 3–31.

INDEX